Legacies of the 1964 Civil Rights Act

Race, Ethnicity, and Politics

Luis Ricardo Fraga and Paula D. McClain, Editors

Legacies of the 1964 Civil Rights Act

Edited by Bernard Grofman

University Press of Virginia • Charlottesville and London

The University Press of Virginia
© 2000 by the Rector and Visitors of the University of Virginia
All rights reserved
Printed in the United States of America
First published in 2000

Title page illustration: March on Washington, 1963 (Library of Congress)

Title page illustration: March on Washington, 1963 (Library of Congress)

LIBRARY OF CONGRESS CATALOGING-IN-PUBLICATION DATA
Legacies of the 1964 Civil Rights Act / edited by Bernard Grofman.
    p. cm. — (Race, ethnicity, and politics)
    Includes bibliographical references and index.
    ISBN 0-8139-1920-7 (cloth : alk. paper) — ISBN 0-8139-1921-5 (paper : alk. paper)
    1. Race discrimination—Law and legislation—United States—History. 2. Afro-Americans—Civil rights—History. 3. Race discrimination—United States. I. Grofman, Bernard. II. Series.
KF4757.L44 2000
342.73´0873—dc21

                                                          99-053299

Contents

Tables

Foreword

Paula D. McClain

The Civil Rights Act of 1964 is legislation that for many people, including myself, is difficult to discuss dispassionately. Although the essays in this volume provide a scholarly analysis of the importance of the Civil Rights Act of 1964, I relate several personal events in this foreword that serve to highlight the significance of the act for Americans of African descent. I also provide an integration of the importance of the civil rights movement into the policy agenda-setting literature.

I was born in 1950 in Kentucky but was raised in the Northeast and the West. During the summer we would take a one-month vacation, often to visit relatives on the East Coast when we lived in the West. Every year my parents would write away for the *Ebony Travel Guide*, published by *Ebony* magazine. For those unfamiliar with the publication, during segregation *Ebony* would publish an annual guide for blacks' use when traveling across the country. The guide told you where you could eat, where you could stay, where you could purchase gas, what cities you should not stop in, what cities or sections of cities were hospitable to blacks, and other relevant information. Thus, as you were moving across the country, from west to east on old Route 66 in our case, you would know what to do and what not to do.

I remember eating at the same restaurant in Gallup, New Mexico, and staying in the same hotel in Amarillo, Texas, on almost every cross-country trip. It still happened that we sometimes deviated slightly from our planned route, and either did not make or overshot our nightly destination. On those occasions when we found ourselves in an area that would not rent hotel rooms to blacks, we slept in the car on the side of the road.

In that situation, my father, who phenotypically looks white, was always the point person. He would get out of the car, go up to the restaurant or motel, and ask a simple, painful question: do you serve the public? There was no need for explanation; my father and the proprietor both understood what was being asked. Depending on the response, my mother, siblings, and I would either pile out of the car or continue on our journey.

My parents' position, like that of many blacks of that era, was to resist segregation wherever and whenever possible, and if that meant not eating in a segregated restaurant and going without food, or sleeping in the car, that was what they were going to do. And we did! This resistance by my parents and by many blacks in the United States then makes it difficult for me to analyze this period, this era in which blacks were denied basic protections by the Constitution and American society, dispassionately. For it was the Civil Rights Act of 1964, and the subsequent Voting Rights Act of 1965, that opened fissures in the barriers to equal opportunity and political participation for black Americans.

Public policy scholars have now put many of the events of the civil rights movement into a policy process theoretical perspective in order to assess the influence of various events on public policy formulation, in this case the Civil Rights Act of 1964.

The public policy process consists of four interrelated stages—agenda setting, formulation, implementation, and evaluation. The agenda-setting stage is where issues gain prominence and are raised to a level where some decision-making body decides they are important enough to address. It is at this first stage, the agenda-setting stage, that we can examine some of the events of the civil rights movement that are the focus of the Filvaroff and Wolfinger essay, the first chapter in this volume.

The early agenda-setting models developed in the 1970s in the early Cobb and Elder work (1972) not only focused on the manner in which policy issues were raised to the public and the governmental agendas, but identified the process of issue cycles in agenda setting. Regardless of the model of agenda setting, issues go through four phases—initiation, specification, expansion, and entrance (Cobb, Ross, and Ross 1976). Initiation is the articulation of the grievance; specification is the translation of the grievance into demands; expansion is the process of expanding the issue beyond whatever initially articulated the grievance; and entrance is the point at which the issue moves onto either the public agenda, where people be-

gin to talk about the issue, or the governmental agenda, where decision-makers begin to act on issues, or both.

The models of agenda setting are: (1) outside initiative, used by individuals who
are outside government, have no friends in government, have no access to government, but who, through social movements and mass demonstrations, are able to
get issues raised to the point where someone inside government considers them
important enough to handle; (2) mobilization, where items are placed on the policy agenda by individuals inside government or with close contacts to decision-
makers, but where in order to gain legitimacy the issue must be expanded to the
public; and (3) inside access, where individuals inside government or with access to
decision-makers place issues directly on the governmental agenda, but do not need
or want to expand the issue beyond the people necessary to exert pressure on the
decision-makers.

Ever since *Plessy v. Ferguson* (1896), there has been a continual stream of activity
by blacks to gain access to the political process to deal with issues of segregation.
What we now call the civil rights movement was in actuality a collection of local
initiatives aggregated under that rubric. We easily recall many local initiatives—
the bus boycotts in Baton Rouge (1953), Birmingham (1955), Tallahassee (1956),
New Orleans (1957). We also remember Freedom Summer (1964) and the Freedom
Rides (1961). Research on racial minority group input into the policy agenda-
setting process identifies the outside initiative model, although it was not so called
at the time, as the approach used by individuals in the civil rights movement. The
"turning point" in the movement, according to Andrew Young, was the push into
Birmingham in 1963. Birmingham was a key event in moving the issue of civil
rights onto the public, and eventually the governmental, agenda. Until Birmingham, the initiation and definition of the problem had occurred at the local level
through local mass activity.

Policy scholars argue that in order for an issue to move onto the public agenda,
and then onto the governmental agenda, it is necessary for the identification
group—those who initially raised the issue—to expand the issue to attentive
groups, those that can be mobilized quickly, and the general public (Cobb, Ross,
and Ross 1976, 128–29). Birmingham was, for the issue of civil rights and the eventual passage of the 1964 Civil Rights Act, that point where the issue was expanded
beyond the groups marching to those attentive groups in solidarity with the principles of the marchers and the general public at large.

Birmingham was the issue expansion point for several reasons. First, the movement changed strategies with the Birmingham demonstrations. Attempting to keep as many heads of households as possible out of jail, the decision was made to allow children to participate in the demonstrations. Masses of children voluntarily left school and demonstrated. Second, the movement leaders predicted that Bull Connor, police commissioner of Birmingham, would respond with force to the demonstrators, who now were school children.

Bull Connor met the children with fire hoses and attack dogs. The national networks finally decided that maybe there was something in this civil rights issue worthy of national coverage and dispatched news teams to Birmingham. So for the first time, through the national networks, the issue was expanded into the homes of the general American populace. Images of children being rolled over and over by these fire hoses and attacked by police dogs were beamed into millions of American homes. The issue of civil rights was thus expanded through the television media.

Coupled with other events, the Birmingham demonstrations also catapulted the issue through the entrance process onto the public agenda and finally onto the governmental agenda. Birmingham caused the nation to recognize black civil rights as an important policy issue deserving of governmental attention. In combination with other watershed events of 1963—the assassination of Medgar Evers, the March on Washington, the bombing of the 16th Street Baptist Church in Birmingham, and finally the assassination of President John F. Kennedy—Birmingham, the first in this series of events, pushed the issue of civil rights onto the policy agenda.

While this volume applauds the importance of the act, the present political climate makes clear the need to be ever diligent in the struggle for equal rights and protections. The challenges facing us today are monumental. Past opponents of racial equality and equal rights now cloak themselves in the tenets of the Civil Rights Act of 1964 and claim Martin Luther King as their patron saint. People should be judged by "the content of their character," not the "color of their skin." Policies that recognize people as members of a group, they argue (often disingenuously), are contrary to the teachings of Dr. King and the goals of the civil rights movement and the Civil Rights Act of 1964. U.S. society should be color-blind, and we should begin by repealing every statute and policy that appears to favor blacks and other persons of color (e.g., the California and Washington state Civil Rights Initiatives). External structural barriers to black social and political progress no longer exist. These are the ideas that have currency in the present political climate. Still, the rhetoric of a color-blind society is, often, a euphemism for the process of removing protections and rolling back gains made by black Americans and others.

Many forget the pain and suffering wrought by segregation and dismiss the continued salience of race in the American political fabric. Many who were born after 1960 have no memory of the pain and fault blacks for perpetuating group identity or pushing the notion of group membership. This perspective relieves the dominant society of any responsibility for continuing inequalities and discrimination by placing the responsibility on blacks themselves. The poignant autobiography of Gregory Howard Williams, dean of the law school at Ohio State University, reminds us of the extent to which race is a social and political construct that defines blacks as members of a group.

Life on the Color Line: The True Story of a White Boy Who Discovered He Was Black brings the reader face to face with the reality of how the identification of Williams as black, despite his "white" appearance, changed his life chances and the way society treated him. When people believed Williams was white, they deemed him bright, smart, and a future star. When they discovered that he was black, doors that were once open closed to him. He found himself judged and treated as a member of a group, a group that was discriminated against and limited in opportunities. As Williams so eloquently and painfully shows, the penalties for black group membership in the United States far outweigh any perceived or real benefits. His story, like those of millions of other black Americans, including myself, reinforces the importance of legal protections, like the Civil Rights Act of 1964, for blacks and other Americans of color.

Acknowledgments

Early drafts of many of the chapters in this volume were given at a 1994 conference that I organized commemorating the thirtieth anniversary of the Civil Rights Act of 1964. They have been revised and updated considerably for this volume. In addition, a number of pieces have been specifically commissioned for this volume.

The 1994 conference, held at the Federal Judicial Center, took place under the auspices of the FJC's Division in Judicial Education and was funded by the Joyce Foundation and the FJC. I am deeply indebted to the Federal Judicial Center and to the Joyce Foundation, without whose support the present volume would never have been possible. I would like to extend special thanks to Larry Hansen of the Joyce Foundation for his continuing encouragement when funding prospects for the conference appeared dim; to Dennis Hauptly, former director of the FJC Judicial Education Division, who initially authorized the FJC's sponsorship of the conference; to Robb Jones, subsequent director of the FJC Judicial Education Division; to Charles Arberg and Myrtle Berge of the FJC for their invaluable work in conference planning and logistics; and to Chandler Davidson, for the many lessons I learned from him during our nearly decade-long research collaboration. Our coedited volume (Grofman and Davidson, 1992) served as the model for this book. (Grofman and Davidson [1992] built on the proceedings of a 1990 conference commemorating the twenty-fifth anniversary of the Voting Rights Act of 1965, which was held at the Brookings Institution under the auspices of its program in Governmental Studies, directed by Thomas Mann, and was funded by the Rockefeller Foundation and the Brookings Institution.)

I am also very grateful for the continued encouragement and patience of the series editors Paula McClain and Luis Fraga and to Richard Holway at the University Press of Virginia. Valuable feedback on earlier versions of some of the essays in this volume was provided by a number of discussants at the 1994 conference, including Robert Belton, Bruce Cain, Richard Cohen, Leslie Goldstein, Paul Hancock, Shari-lynn Ifill, Gerald Jaynes, Pamela Karlan, Andrew Kull, Kevin Lang, Brian Lands-berg, Donald Nakanishi, Jack Peltason, and Marc Rosenblum, and by the eleven members of the federal bench who attended the conference. Last but not least, this volume would never have made it into print without the secretarial and biblio-graphic efforts of my past and present secretaries Dorothy Green and Clover Behrend and their student assistants Chau Tran, Grace Kang, Anna Datta, and Mi-nal Patel, or without the help of Cheryl Larsson, computer consultant at the UCI School of Social Sciences.

Introduction

The issue of race has been a bone in the throat of our country for centuries. In the 1960s, national leaders of both major political parties sought to come to grips with this issue once and for all through the enactment of major civil rights legislation. In conjunction with the Voting Rights Act of 1965, the Civil Rights Act of 1964 totally transformed the shape of American race relations.[1] Supporters of the Civil Rights Act of 1964 sought, at minimum, the elimination of segregation of the races in publicly supported schools, hospitals, public transportation, and other public spaces, and an end to open and blatant racial discrimination in employment practices. Judged in those terms, the act is a remarkable success story.[2] If ever any piece of legislation showed the power of the central government to change deeply entrenched patterns of behavior, it is the Civil Rights Act of 1964. Together, the Civil Rights Act of 1964 and the Voting Rights Act of 1965 broke once and for all the Jim Crow legacy of the post-Reconstruction South and largely ended the overt and legally sanctioned forms of discrimination against blacks that had been found throughout the nation.[3] In terms of the law, blacks were no longer second-class citizens.[4]

After the passage of the major civil rights legislation of the 1960s, race was largely off the national policy agenda. Civil rights policies in subsequent decades continued to be shaped by the earlier legislation, but with subtle changes in policy induced by judicial interpretation and modes of bureaucratic implementation taking place largely out of public purview and with little or no public debate. Now, as a result of a variety of factors—from concern over the violent crime rate among black teenagers and the seeming ineradicability of black poverty to the racial fissures revealed by opinion about the O. J. Simpson verdict and the protests of whites and others against practices of "race-norming" and racially targeted hiring—civil rights issues are once again a matter of major public debate. But the focus of that debate is now mostly about the negative side effects of affirmative action rather than about the need for positive measures to end discrimination.

Bookshelves are now laden with books about affirmative action and civil rights. Why another one? We believe this book is different in three ways. First, the volume includes representatives of a diverse set of views from a set of writers who generally reflect nondogmatic perspectives on civil rights—and the essays in it are not polemical in tone. Second, the essays are confined to neither purely normative nor purely legal debates about civil rights policies, although both of these areas are covered. Third, the volume is intended to be primarily retrospective and stocktaking, and a number of the essays are heavily fact-oriented.

The central aim of this volume is to provide a reference work on the Civil Rights Act of 1964 and its evolution over the past several decades.[5] Without denigrating the importance of the Civil Rights Act of 1964 for women, Hispanics, or other groups, the moral urgency of the act was triggered by revulsion against the American version of apartheid, and it is on the life chances of African Americans that the act has had its most striking impact. As a consequence of that fact, most of the essays in this volume focus on the act's implications for black Americans.

The contributors to this volume are a distinguished set of political scientists, historians, lawyers, statisticians, and sociologists, all of whom have written previously on civil rights issues. They have been asked to stand back from today's headlines, and the immediate controversies about civil rights they reflect, to provide historical and comparative perspective. We believe this book makes an important contribution to the national dialogue about race that President Clinton called for. Moreover, it is intended to make a contribution to scholarship that will not soon go out of date.

The book is organized into four parts. The first two cover the origins of the act and its historical evolution, the third part looks at the act's consequences in several different policy domains, and the fourth part looks ahead to the future of civil rights in the United States. Contributions in each part are divided into two categories: lengthy review essays and shorter notes and comments.

There is also a brief postscript by longtime observer of U.S. race relations and a specialist on comparative ethnic politics around the world, Robin Williams. Williams, who coedited with Gerald Jaynes the 1989 report of the National Academy of Sciences, *A Common Destiny: Blacks and American Society*, views civil rights policies in the United States in a comparative global perspective. Finally, there are appended to the volume two somewhat more technical essays on legal standards for statutory violations and statistical issues in measuring discrimination.

Paula McClain's foreword to this volume shows how the resistance to Jim Crow of the civil rights movement of the 1950s and 1960s forced civil rights legislation onto the national agenda. The central essay in part 1 of the volume, by David Filvaroff and Raymond Wolfinger, each of whom was "present at the creation," deals with the legislative history of the Civil Rights Act of 1964. The authors review the web of political forces and personal motives that led to the passage of the act. They observe that it had bipartisan (albeit primarily Republican) support in Congress under the aegis of Lyndon Johnson, the first president from the South elected during this century. Morgan Kousser's note in this section puts the Civil Rights Act of 1964 in historical perspective by comparing its features with the text of the key civil rights bills that were passed after the Civil War. Kousser argues that the success of the Civil Rights Act of 1964, as compared to the post-Reconstruction repudiation of its predecessors, was made possible by the heavily bipartisan consensus described by Filvaroff and Wolfinger. He suggests that the recent breakdown of that consensus bodes ill for future civil rights enforcement.

The lead essay in part 2, by Hugh Graham, deals with the evolving history of U.S. civil rights policy in the thirty-five years since the act's passage, in the context of the changing role of the federal government in regulating economic and political life. Graham elaborates the ways in which a civil rights model first applied to blacks was then extended to other groups. He also examines the ways in which civil rights policies changed from an early focus on eliminating direct forms of discrimination to a later concern for remedying the effects of past discrimination. His chapter is followed by a short essay by Stephen Wasby that looks at litigation and lobbying as complementary strategies for civil rights groups, and by some personal reflections by a leading civil rights attorney, Jack Greenberg, on the litigation strategies of the civil rights movement.

Part 3 deals with the three most important provisions of the act, Titles II, VI, and VII. The essays in it describe what we know about the consequences of the act for public accommodations, education, and employment. These essays remind us that, however bitter the current controversies, the United States is a very much different (and far better) society because of the passage of the Civil Rights Act of 1964. Even for someone who was already an adult when the act was passed, it is hard to believe that only a scant thirty-five years ago visible stigmata of discrimination such as segregated water fountains and back-of-the-bus seating could ever have been permitted, much less legally enforced.

Gary Orfield's essay argues that without the Civil Rights Act of 1964, the battle for ending *de jure* school desegregation would probably have been lost, and traces the time path of desegregation and resegregation in both the North and the South. Paul Burstein shows what happened to black employment after the passage of the act and helps elucidate the almost impossible task of attributing causation to changes in black employment in succeeding decades. Randall Kennedy's essay helps us explain why what at the time seemed the most controversial of the act's provisions—that requiring the desegregation of public accommodations such as hospitals—was implemented so immediately and with so little resistance.

The final part of the volume deals with the future of civil rights policy. To ground that discussion, we begin part 4 with a factual essay by Katherine Tate and Gloria J. Hampton examining white attitudes about race over the years since the passage of the Civil Rights Act of 1964. They find dramatic changes in many aspects of white public opinion dealing with race, with overtly racist views steadily diminishing.

The next three essays are the most normative in the volume. The first of these, by Luis Fraga and Jorge Ruiz-de-Velasco, emphasizes the relevance of the changing racial and ethnic composition of the United States. The authors suggest that the nature of discrimination against Hispanics may be distinct from the type of discrimination historically facing African Americans and may call for a different type of remedial approach. But most importantly, they argue for a view of "common citizenship" that recognizes individual achievements and respects group-based identities, but that places the greatest importance on shared ideals (as articulated in the Constitution) and common civic responsibilities.

Barbara Phillips Sullivan's brief note considers (and rejects) recent arguments for segregated facilities that have been based on notions of cultural autonomy.

The last essay in part 4 inventories the key arguments made against current civil rights policies. I argue there that most elements of that attack are either mistaken, overstated, or wrongly lump together as targets those practices used as needed remedies for demonstrated discrimination and those whose principal justification is a claimed need for diversity. I argue for a civil rights policy based on common decency and common sense, which recognizes that continued discrimination still exists and must be combated, but which also recognizes that most observed inequalities between white and black America are due to causes that the constitutional jurisprudence of civil rights is simply impotent to address. In particular, I argue that if we are serious about ending racial inequalities, the struggle must largely move from the courtroom to the (K–12) classroom.[6]

The appendixes to the volume consist of two essays on the role of social science and statistical analysis in the act's interpretation by the courts, with a focus on statistical issues in measuring employment discrimination. The first essay, by Joseph Kadane and Caroline Mitchell (statistician and trial attorney, respectively), reviews many of the major cases interpreting Title VII of the act and offers a detailed analysis of the nature of the conflicts between expert witnesses in these cases. The second essay, by Richard Lempert, extensively critiques the way in which courts have used statistics and offers some suggestions for how the use of statistics by courts might be improved.

The issues raised by these essays have become especially important in light of President Clinton's specific proposals to "mend, not end" governmental polices in the area of affirmative action, and in light of recent changes in civil rights case law such as the Supreme Court's 1995 decision in *Adarand*, which held that government set-aside programs for minorities could be legally justified only when there was a past record of discrimination and only when the remedy was narrowly tailored to correct the problem. It is impossible to understand the effects of the Civil Rights Act of 1964 and subsequent civil rights policies without coming to grips with what is to be taken as evidence of discrimination. Beginning in the 1970s, statistically significant disparities between minority and nonminority employment, promotion, or contract award levels, rather than direct evidence of overtly racist behavior or intent, have been the basis of most legal findings of discrimination. Moreover, even under President Clinton's "mend, not end" views of governmental affirmative action, statistical disparities remain the key to deciding when affirmative action programs such as minority set-asides are justified.[7]

Notes

1. The central aim of most supporters of the Voting Rights Act of 1965 was the elimination of formal barriers to full black suffrage. That aim was largely achieved by the early 1970s. A third major piece of legislation passed under Lyndon Johnson's presidency, the Immigration Reform Act of 1965, also had transformative consequences for race relations in the United States, but these were largely inadvertent. The act eroded the strong advantages European immigrants had as compared to those from other continents and made family reunification easier. However, the vast increase in the number of immigrants and the shift in the racial and ethnic composition of the United States caused by an inflow of immigrants from Mexico and Central America, and a lesser but still major flow from Asia, was in no way foreseen by the sponsors of that bill.

2. Of course, judged in broader terms, vis-à-vis its impact on the overall equality between whites and blacks in America, the act has been deemed by many a great disappointment (see, e.g., various essays in Lawrence and Matsuda 1997).

3. Although the civil rights and voting rights bills of the 1960s were once seen as applying largely or exclusively to the South, not long after its passage applications of each "moved North."

4. There are at least two other important legacies of the civil rights era in addition to the elimination of the most overt forms of racial discrimination: (1) the finishing blow to the Civil War political realignment, i.e., that in which southern whites were loyalist Democrats and blacks were loyalist Republicans (Huckfeldt and Kohfeld 1989; Carmines and Stimson 1989; Grofman and Handley 1998); and (2) the effective end of the states' rights doctrine as a significant force in either American political theory or American political life.

5. This volume parallels in structure and format my earlier coedited book dealing with the Voting Rights Act of 1965 and current controversies in voting rights (Grofman and Davidson 1992). The two volumes are complementary.

6. Even though African Americans now graduate high school at a rate close to that of whites, the mean reading and math skills of blacks in the twelfth grade lag behind those of whites from three to four grade levels, with the black-white gap wider still if we look at scientific problem solving (Thernstrom and Thernstrom 1997, 358). If we look at what proportion of African Americans possess the levels of basic language, math, and science skills realistically needed to cope with college-level course requirements, the picture looks even bleaker (see, e.g., Thernstrom and Thernstrom 1997, chapter 14).

7. For example, in a 1998 survey, the Department of Commerce looked for evidence of discrimination in the $190 billion federal marketplace by measuring levels of minority underrepresentation relative to the pool of potential contractors. They found that racial disparities differed considerably across different areas of procurement, with some procurement domains (at least in some regions of the country) showing no evidence of disparities. A White House spokesman summarized the implications of this study: "Measure discrimination. Turn off the programs where they no longer are needed—and keep them in place where there remains a disparity" (Christopher Edley, Jr., a Harvard University law professor who is an advisor to the White House on racial issues, quoted in Jonathan Peterson, "Clinton to Unveil New Job Preferences Policy," *Los Angeles Times,* 24 June 1998, p. A17). For present purposes, we would emphasize that in Professor Edley's remark "discrimination" and "disparity" are treated as essentially synonymous.

I

The Civil Rights Act of 1964 in Historical Perspective

1

The Origin and Enactment of the
Civil Rights Act of 1964

David B. Filvaroff and Raymond E. Wolfinger

The Civil Rights Act of 1964 was the greatest legislative achievement of the civil rights movement. Enacted amid extraordinary public attention, it is arguably the most important domestic legislation of the postwar era. Since the end of Reconstruction nearly a century earlier, Congress had failed to enact any but the most feeble legislation against racial discrimination. This sorry record notwithstanding, the 1964 act was broader and stronger than informed observers had expected at the outset or during most of the year it was before Congress.

There was precedent for the 1964 act in the laws enacted by many states and cities to prohibit discrimination in employment and/or public accommodations. These laws, however, were of mixed effect and confined to the North, where overt discrimination was thought to be a lesser and more easily remediable problem. At the federal level, advances had been limited largely to the judicial arena. The series of lawsuits initiated by the NAACP Legal Defense and Education Fund brought important victories declaring racial discrimination to be unconstitutional when engaged in by government. The fund's step-by-step strategy, culminating in 1954 in *Brown v. Board of Education,* succeeded in overturning the "separate but equal" doctrine and created a clear constitutional base for further legal claims. No less important, it put the issue of racial equality on the national agenda and renewed hope of progress toward a desegregated society.

But the *Brown* invalidation of legally mandated segregation in public schools engendered substantial and threatening opposition. Southern officials, including some state judges and even a few federal ones, worked to limit enforcement of *Brown* and denied that it was the "law of the land." Attempts were made to resurrect, as recognized law or as political rhetoric, the discredited nineteenth-century doctrine of interposition—the right of states to interpose their own sovereignty to vitiate federal authority within their borders.[1] And, most ominously, southern leaders organized "massive resistance" and promised that school desegregation would never occur.[2] Attempts to keep black students from entering schools under court orders to desegregate had brought on riots, beatings, and the intervention of federal troops.

Friends of the Supreme Court worried not only that its rulings would be frustrated, but that its very authority and legitimacy were in jeopardy. The justices nonetheless continued to expand the reach of the Constitution. By the early 1960s, the concept of state action had been broadened to bring some aspects of governmentally supported private discrimination within the ambit of the Fifth and Fourteenth Amendments. But given both the limits of existing constitutional doctrine and undiminished southern resistance to the Court's decisions, hope seemed slim of further advances through litigation.

At the same time, the federal executive branch was far from resolutely committed to ending discrimination. For example, it was only with great reluctance that President Eisenhower sent troops into Little Rock in 1957 to quell mobs blocking school desegregation ordered by a federal court. Attempts to enact civil rights bills in 1957 and 1960 resulted only in watered-down legislation of limited effect. Liberals in both houses of Congress often acted as if they did not expect significant legislation to pass. President Eisenhower "provided confused or minimum support, lukewarm at best. The civil rights forces themselves in the Senate were also confused and ineffectual. Only the southern Democrats looked like they knew what they were doing" (Stewart 1991, 30).

One sequel to the *Brown* decision was a partial revival of the black attraction to the Republican Party that had faded with the New Deal. Two out of five black votes in 1956 went to the Republican presidential ticket. The paratroopers dispersing segregationist rioters at bayonet point during Eisenhower's deployment of troops to Little Rock remained a memorable image. Both parties' platforms in 1960 had their strongest-ever civil rights planks. John F. Kennedy went a step further by promising that one of his first acts in the White House would be to ask a Democrat in each house of Congress to introduce the entire plank. He also assailed continued federal aid for the construction of segregated housing and declared that as president he would end the practice "with one stroke of the pen." A widely publicized telephone call when Martin Luther King was jailed in a small Georgia town helped Kennedy win 75% of the black vote.

Once in office, Kennedy initially did little on civil rights and proposed no legislation. (One of the congressmen he named in his campaign promise said that he had never expected to receive a presidential request to draft legislation once the election was over.) At the president's urging, however, some federal agencies took administrative steps against racial discrimination and his brother's Justice Department stepped up the pace of litigation. Nearly two years went by before Kennedy signed the order that ended federal funding for segregated housing. Kennedy's reluctance to keep his promise to propose legislation stemmed from his belief that the effort would be unsuccessful and would only provoke the hostility of southern committee chairmen whose cooperation was essential to the passage of higher priority measures.

In 1962 the administration gave lukewarm support to a bill providing that completion of the sixth grade would satisfy any state literacy test for voter registration, an idea suggested in the 1960 Republican platform. The House took no action on this measure and in the Senate two cloture petitions to stop a desultory filibuster both failed by twenty-one votes, garnering the support of just thirteen Republicans. Kennedy did send modest civil rights legislation to Congress early in 1963, but the prospects of passage were not great.

What changed to allow enactment of the monumental provisions of the Civil Rights Act of 1964?

The Birmingham Demonstrations and Their Consequences

The precipitating event was the confrontation in Birmingham, Alabama, in the spring of 1963 between the forces of Reverend Martin Luther King, Jr., and those of Eugene "Bull" Connor, the city's police commissioner. Repeated street demonstrations led by King's Southern Christian Leadership Conference (SCLC) seeking desegregation of Birmingham's lunch counters and other public accommodations, vividly portrayed not only the extent to which racial injustice permeated the city's social and legal structure but also the commitment to its maintenance, as evidenced by Connor's ready use of violence to put down any challenge. Pictures of peaceful marchers, many of them schoolchildren, being met with fire hoses and attack dogs were spread across front pages throughout the country and shown each evening on national television. The compelling images brought the reality of the South's racial caste system to popular awareness and posed a pressing legal and moral issue: whether the American ideal of equality and justice for all could be given practical meaning for southern blacks.

More particularly, Birmingham generated a new spirit and vigor in civil rights organizations which, individually and combined with allied interest groups in the Leadership Conference on Civil Rights, came to play an influential role in development and passage of the 1964 act. Labor, religious, and other groups joined traditional civil rights organizations in an intense lobbying campaign, both in Washington and at the grass roots level. Given the impact of Birmingham, these groups were able to convert a generally sympathetic public response into what Congress came to feel as widespread constituent demand for action.

These results were not accidental. Andrew Young, a key aide to King, explained that "We understood television at that time to be educational TV . . . to enlighten white Americans . . . to take an eleven percent Black population and find a way to get forty percent of the white population to add on and to create a majority" (Young 1991, 30). SCLC representatives met with the media to brief them on plans for the day. As demonstrations and violence spread, press and public demands for action grew.

Realizing that the stakes were rising, the president at first tried mediation, but a series of emissaries sent to Birmingham failed to resolve the situation. Early in May, the situation took a momentary turn for the better when black leaders and white businessmen reached agreement on some of the demonstrators' demands; restrooms, drinking fountains, and restaurants were to be desegregated by midsummer. King issued a victory statement and left town, but the respite lasted only one day. The next night one bomb exploded beneath the local motel room King had used and another at his brother's home in Birmingham. After Connor's fire hoses and attack dogs, this was too much for some local blacks who had never subscribed to King's Gandhian philosophy. That Saturday night, rock-throwing blacks made it clear that racial violence might not continue to be a one-way street. The civil rights crisis entered a new phase in which the administration dropped its reluctance to press for significant legislation.

Burke Marshall, the assistant attorney general in charge of the Civil Rights Division, returned from another trip to Alabama convinced that Birmingham was only the beginning: further demonstrations and potential disruptions would make federal legislation essential. He recommended a new law that would deal at least with segregation in public accommodations—restaurants, lunch counters, hotels, theaters, and the like. Marshall persuaded the attorney general and they carried the argument to the White House, where a heated dispute was in progress about how the president should respond to Birmingham and the broader crisis it symbolized.

The proponents of legislation emphasized both the strong moral base for action and the increasing public pressure for an affirmative response to the marchers' demands. There was, in addition, concern that the White House could not let the Republicans appear to take the lead on civil rights. Opponents of a major legislative initiative repeated the old argument that strong support for civil rights would not only alienate the president's southern support, both in and out of Congress, but would probably delay, if not defeat, key parts of his legislative program, most importantly his tax and farm bills.

The trumping argument was that without action to create new legal remedies, demonstrations would continue to spread throughout the South and into the North; the country would be torn by widespread civil disruption if not outright racial violence. The president and his party would be blamed. Such a climate would be as disastrous as an economic depression for Kennedy's prospects for re-election. In order to avoid widespread violence, the president had to make a serious attempt to deal with the demonstrators' grievances.

Birmingham thus had two important consequences. First, the graphic images of peaceful demonstrations being brutally suppressed heightened public receptivity to civil rights legislation. Second, the first signs of blacks' violent reaction to white violence strengthened the administration's growing belief that inaction would be harmful to the nation and electorally damaging in 1964. While the Justice Department was drafting a bill, the president told a national television audience that he would submit strong proposals to Congress to fulfil the long postponed promise of racial equality. That same night, Medgar Evers, the leader of the Mississippi NAACP, was shot dead on his doorstep.

Drafting the Bill

Deciding on the specific content of the bill involved a careful balance. An overly strong measure, on the one hand, would win the immediate praise of civil rights groups and liberals but would languish and die after a long struggle. Worse than sending no bill at all, it would reap all the resentments of success without any of the rewards. Moreover, it would do nothing to solve the underlying substantive problems. Too weak a bill, on the other hand, would signal the administration's lack of seriousness and do little to forestall future demonstrations.

In addition to desegregating public accommodations—the major focus of the Birmingham marches—legislation was needed to overcome the intimidation and discriminatory practices that prevented southern blacks from voting.[3] The experience of the Justice Department in litigating this issue one county at a time had shown that a more expansive approach was essential. The administration agreed with civil rights leaders that black access to the ballot was a prerequisite to broader change in the South.

Another provision in the bill would prohibit discrimination in any federally funded benefits and activities. The administration did not at first attach much substantive importance to this provision, which became Title VI. Members of Congress held a different view. Because of their pursuit of federal grants, congressional sources, especially southerners, expressed no doubts about the importance of Title VI. To the administration and the House leaders who insisted on its inclusion, the title's main virtue was the protection it would give against Powell amendments until, if necessary, it could be traded away during the anticipated legislative struggle.[4]

The administration's proposal on discrimination in employment would do no more than give congressional recognition to a presidential commission of unspecified power to deal with job discrimination by federal contractors and firms in programs financed by the federal government. In the previous dozen years, several broader fair employment bills had been introduced by liberal Democrats or Republicans. None had passed even one house of Congress and the administration believed that including a strong fair employment title might signal an intention to "demagogue the issue" rather than pursue feasible legislative goals.

Strategic Considerations

As the bill was being drafted, the White House pondered how to get it passed. Virtually no southern Democratic legislator would vote for any measure identified as a civil rights bill, yet without their southern contingent, the Democrats were a minority in both houses of Congress. The need for Republican support was obvious. But aside from a handful of liberals—who were also known to play politics with civil rights—the prospect of getting enough Republican votes was far from clear. The plain fact was that the Kennedys wanted a civil rights act to cool the racial climate and many Republicans did not see why they should bail out a Democratic president on the eve of his re-election campaign.

There were additional problems in the Senate, where a hard core of eighteen southern Democrats could be expected to use the traditional weapon of unlimited debate. The only counter to a filibuster was cloture, which required a two-thirds vote, a goal that had never been approached on a civil rights bill.[5] Civil rights supporters had come closest to success in 1946 and still fallen nine votes short. No cloture petition since 1950 had received even a simple majority of senators present and voting.

The 1957 and 1960 efforts to enact effective legislation had foundered in the face of real or threatened filibusters. Civil rights advocates had had to settle for weak measures worked out with southern opponents by Senate majority leader Lyndon Johnson. The failure of recent attempts to reduce the number of votes needed to impose cloture from two-thirds to three-fifths gave little hope of changing Senate rules.[6] Moreover, the Senate Judiciary Committee, to which any broad civil rights bill would have to be referred, was chaired by Mississippi segregationist James Eastland, who would do his best to keep the proposal from the Senate floor.

Beginning in the House offered two clear advantages. First and most important, only a simple majority was needed for passage. Second, the House Judiciary Committee was chaired by Brooklyn Democrat Emanuel Celler, a liberal administration loyalist who had been in Congress for forty years and had headed the committee for much of that time.

Civil rights supporters disagreed sharply over the strategy to be followed in the House. Experience suggested to many that the goal should be to seek the strongest possible bill at every stage of the legislative process. In 1957 and 1960, fairly strong House bills had been whittled down almost to nothing to secure passage in the Senate. Thus one apparent lesson of history was to begin with a very tough bill in the House Judiciary Committee in order to have some effective provisions left after necessary compromises were made later on. This approach had great appeal for civil rights groups, not only because they wanted everything they could get, but also because they had reason to doubt the administration's commitment. Going all out was also favored by many congressional liberals, mostly Democrats. Apart from tactical considerations, some were inclined to this position for ideological reasons, others perhaps as a result of constituent pressures.

This approach alarmed members who read 1957 and 1960 differently. Some worried that they would be taking a needless political risk if they voted for a strong bill only to see it weakened by compromises necessary to win Senate passage. Many Republicans doubted that the administration really wanted a meaningful law rather than a political issue. They wanted to avoid being put in a position in which Democrats would present them with legislation they considered onerous and then attack them for selling out the civil rights cause if they opposed it. Republicans were unsure not only about the president's real goals (which, of course, might change as the situation changed), but about the development of white opinion. Bailing out the Kennedy administration was one thing, but flouting a national majority on civil rights was another.

The Kennedys drew a different lesson from the history of the 1957 and 1960 bills and charted a course that diverged from the prescriptions of the civil rights lobby and many liberals in both parties. Recognizing the need for substantial Republican help even in the House, the administration aimed to develop strong but reasonable bipartisan provisions. Republican cooperation would be crucial to defeat the inevitable southern filibuster in the Senate. A bill that passed the House with substantial Republican support would incline Republican senators to vote for cloture without demanding emasculating amendments. If a bipartisan bill was to be worked out, the place to do it was the House Judiciary Committee. It could not be done on the House floor, where the disparate views of 435 members would come into full play.

Submitted on 19 June 1963, the administration's bill was referred to the House Judiciary Committee and thence to its Subcommittee No. 5, the only body to consider this bill that had a majority of northern Democrats.[7] Celler chaired both this subcommittee and the full committee. His Republican counterpart, William McCulloch, was the ranking minority member on both.

During the year the bill was before Congress, the Justice Department had primary executive branch responsibility for it as well as for civil rights generally. The lead negotiator, spokesman, and strategist was Deputy Attorney General Nicholas Katzenbach, seconded by Burke Marshall. The substance of what became the Civil Rights Act of 1964 was developed in a series of discussions between Katzenbach and McCulloch, whose critical role in achieving passage of the bill has gone almost wholly unrecognized. An unlikely major contributor to the dismantling of segregation, McCulloch came from Piqua, Ohio, and had represented a white small town and rural district since 1947. Respected by his party's mainstream, he had impeccable conservative credentials seemingly inconsistent with his promotion of legislation that expanded federal power at the expense of local authority and private property rights.

Although McCulloch shared the administration's view that legislation was both justified and necessary, he felt responsible to protect the interests of his party and his fellow Republicans as well. His committee position made him the point man on substance; Republican practice called for such issue specialists to stay in touch with the party leadership. On a matter as salient and explosive as civil rights, McCulloch would not operate independently of the House minority leader, Charles Halleck of Indiana. In 1959 Halleck had gained this post by deposing the incumbent, whom he attacked for being insufficiently partisan. Few events in Halleck's long career would justify charging him with this failing. Newspaper profiles often called him a "gut fighter."

In addition to Halleck, McCulloch probably consulted Everett Dirkson, the Senate GOP leader, not only to keep him informed but, more important, to lessen the likelihood that House Republicans would be left exposed if the bill they supported was seriously weakened in the Senate. Notwithstanding the need for such dual coordination, McCulloch had considerable leeway, which was fortunate for the civil rights cause. If McCulloch had been less sympathetic, he would have been more responsive to those Republicans who were willing to do something on civil rights, but not very much. He had played a constructive role in 1957 and 1960 and was open to improving the lot of southern blacks; but he was also skeptical of Democratic motives. He believed that his efforts in those earlier years were ill-repaid, that he and other Republicans who had joined in support of the House bills were then sold out by Senate Democrats.

House Republicans as a whole were sharply split on how to respond to the events in Birmingham and, more specifically, to Kennedy's proposals. Liberals (who earlier had attacked Kennedy for not acting vigorously on civil rights), favored strong legislation and feared that if their party held back it would be blamed for blocking House action. Even an appearance of reluctant support, much less overt opposition, they argued, would doom any hope of attracting more black voters to the GOP. On the other wing of the party were ultraconservatives who, out of prejudice or plain aversion to any expansion of the federal role, could be counted on to oppose almost any bill. This left the broad center of the party.

Republican strategists considered other questions: should they really give Kennedy a legislative victory that would benefit Democratic candidates in 1964? If the bill failed and racial violence spread, would they be blamed? Could they some-how defeat the bill without being blamed for it? Should they try to appeal to white southerners whose ancestral Democratic loyalties might evaporate if a Democratic president chose black interests over theirs? Republican House leaders, forced to confront the problem in advance of their Senate counterparts, had a lot to think about.

McCulloch and Katzenbach fairly quickly worked out a bill that deviated from the administration's draft chiefly by weakening the voting rights title. McCulloch evidently feared that removing barriers to black voting would disproportionately benefit the Democratic Party. These negotiations, faithful to the administration's bipartisan strategy, had the great disadvantage of ignoring northern Democrats on Subcommittee No. 5, which was busy holding public hearings. Skeptical of both Kennedy's bipartisan strategy and the strength of his commitment, egged on by interest groups that shared this skepticism, and resentful at being excluded, the subcommittee's liberal Democratic majority seized the initiative in spectacular fashion. One morning they produced a bill that took a far bolder approach than did most of the administration proposals and added, among other things, a fair employment practices provision to be enforced by an appointed commission. In complete control of the subcommittee, they then reported this bill to the full com-mittee.

McCulloch was furious. The majority party was up to its old tricks, trying once again to embarrass the Republicans. If the subcommittee bill reached the House floor, he told Katzenbach, it would be cut to pieces, nothing would be left, and he would not lift a finger to stop the debacle. Hearing protests that the administration was blameless, McCulloch replied that nevertheless it would have to take the lead in the full committee to cut back the bill. No Republican committee member would introduce an amendment to restore any or all of the bipartisan compromise. Nor would any Republican vote for such motions made by southerners. Republi-cans would back moderating amendments only from northern Democrats. They would not allow themselves to be portrayed as weak on civil rights.

These were tough terms. Northern Democrats had created the problem and few of them were likely to help solve it. But the White House was able to persuade one to sponsor the first of a series of modifying amendments. This was Roland V. Li-bonati, a product of Chicago's Democratic organization. Reputed to have ties to the underworld, Libonati had recently proposed an investigation of the Justice Depart-ment's prosecution of Teamsters Union president Jimmy Hoffa. With Libonati's amendment introduced in the full Judiciary Committee, a start was made on restoring bipartisanship.

Committee members, Republicans and northern Democrats alike, remained skittish. Libonati's amendment was not certain to pass. McCulloch asked that the attorney general appear before the full committee and, as McCulloch put it, "take responsibility for cutting the subcommittee bill back." The administration faced a hard choice. It could give up on bipartisanship, win the acclaim of civil rights groups by supporting the strong subcommittee bill, and—if that bill was shredded on the floor of the House—try to blame the Republicans. Or it could try to restore relations with McCulloch and continue working for a compromise measure that seemed to offer the only chance of passage. This strategy would provoke a confrontation with civil rights groups and their liberal supporters. The president decided that the attorney general would make it clear to the committee that moderating the subcommittee bill reflected administration policy. Several days of testimony by Robert Kennedy were, as expected, answered by widespread accusations that the administration was selling out the cause. Civil rights lobbyists stepped up their pressure to preserve the strong subcommittee bill.

When the committee reconvened to consider modifying the bill in accord with the attorney general's recommendations, Libonati dropped a bombshell by withdrawing his amendment.[8] After some parliamentary wrangling, a Republican opposed to the bill moved to report the strong subcommittee version. In the circumstances, this was an act of attempted sabotage. As the clerk called the roll, it seemed that everyone was voting yes: liberal Democrats, eager to see their handiwork moving toward the floor; Republicans, feeling betrayed, reluctant to be called bigots, or wishing to kill the bill without blame; and southerners, happy to send forth a bill they considered too strong for the House to swallow. The bill was headed for disaster. Before everyone had voted, however, bells rang, signifying that the House was in session, and a quick-witted administration supporter stopped the roll call with a point of order. Immediate catastrophe had been averted, but whether bipartisanship could be revived was doubtful.

Infuriated again, McCulloch saw yet another double cross; he could not believe that Libonati would take such a fateful step on his own initiative. Katzenbach once again asserted both the administration's innocence and its commitment to a bipartisan bill. McCulloch reluctantly agreed to try once more, but this time the Republicans would take no chances; their support would depend on guarantees that the committee Democrats would supply their full share of the votes necessary to report a compromise bill. That assurance, however, could not readily be given. The civil rights groups' attacks on the administration and their continued lobbying of northern Democrats had left the committee in disarray. The president's personal intervention was necessary to restore the situation and he now became directly engaged. In a series of sometimes heated meetings and phone calls he pressed both committee Democrats and House Republicans for commitments. Halleck was invited to the White House in an effort to seal the deal and guarantee the requisite number of Republican votes.

At the same time, it was necessary to renegotiate the bipartisan agreement on the substance of the bill. The subcommittee revolt and the fiasco in the full committee, coupled with the Leadership Conference's pressure, had altered the political terrain. The circle of negotiators widened to include other committee members whose demands pushed the boundaries of what was needed to build a majority. McCulloch and the administration had to give ground. The bill that they now agreed on was broader than the one fashioned by their previous compromise. Most important, it had gained a significant fair employment title, the liberals' biggest prize for accepting the bipartisan compromise.

After several postponements to restore the understandings shattered by Libonati's defection, the Judiciary Committee finally met again. In an atmosphere of sharp tension, a motion was made to substitute the latest compromise for the subcommittee bill and to report it. McCulloch and Celler each spoke for one minute and the roll was called. Northern Democrats and most Republicans joined to provide a healthy majority for what became, in almost every important respect, the Civil Rights Act of 1964. This crucial meeting came on the afternoon of 20 November 1963, two days before President Kennedy was assassinated.

Although McCulloch's role was pivotal, he could not have played it without Halleck's support throughout and, in the endgame, his active participation. Behind this seemingly steady collaboration was a continuing argument among mainstream Republicans about whether they should help solve a problem that could embarrass the president. Each derailment in the Judiciary Committee opened up the question once again. In each crisis, Republicans and Democrats alike were preoccupied with how credit and blame would be apportioned for whatever happened. The question was particularly difficult because the bill's fate was so uncertain. As several leading Republicans later explained it, their final calculation was simple: unable to discern the politically preferable position on the bill, they considered it better for their party to be as united as possible. Halleck's goal, then, was a compromise that could be supported by all Republicans except those who could not be expected to vote for civil rights under any circumstances. As the vote on final passage revealed, House Republicans were far more united than the Democrats, whose many southern members opposed the bill.

Halleck's search for party unity was not universally popular among Republicans. When he went to the floor after agreeing to the climactic compromise in November, he found at his desk a furled umbrella, the symbol of appeasement. Following the 1964 election, Halleck lost his leadership position to Gerald Ford. His action on the civil rights bill is believed to have contributed to his defeat.

The amendments offered in committee by liberals had been viewed by McCulloch and the administration as disruptive of the effort to develop a bipartisan bill and therefore as threatening to the passage of any effective legislation. Yet the pressure generated by the liberals and the Leadership Conference had expanded views of what might actually be done. The bill reported by the full committee went well beyond both the administration's original draft and what McCulloch had at first deemed acceptable to most Republican members. The most significant change was the addition of Title VII, with its broad prohibition of discrimination in employment. The version of Title VII in the final compromise was taken from a bill introduced previously by moderate and liberal Republicans. This sponsorship was an important consideration in GOP support for the committee bill and, it was hoped, would help with other Republicans on the floor. Other noteworthy changes included strengthening Title VI, which prohibited discrimination in federally funded programs, and authorizing the attorney general to initiate lawsuits vindicating civil rights.

On the Floor of the House

When the bill came to the House floor in February, debate was lengthy and vigorous. Specific provisions, and often the bill as a whole, were attacked by conservatives as excessive regulation that would disrupt the proper balance of power between federal and state governments. Southerners and some Republicans often described the bill as a "Kennedy power grab." On a number of such occasions, McCulloch would rise and, without rancor, express his view that the provision in question was responsible, reasonable, and necessary. Given his conservative credentials, this sort of brief statement generally sufficed to vitiate such ideological opposition. Southern members exaggerated the bill's scope and impact, thereby risking creation of legislative history that could strengthen its effect.[9] They particularly objected to Title VI, foreseeing this provision's potential breadth and force.

Southern efforts to defeat or weaken the bill on the floor extended beyond merely attacking its provisions. They sought to add to the bill in ways that would make it unpalatable to Republicans. A prime example of this approach was the amendment offered by the southern leader, "Judge" Howard W. Smith of Virginia, to add sex as a prohibited ground of discrimination in employment.[10] Most women representatives supported the "sex amendment." Although recognizing the reality of workplace discrimination against women, the bill's managers feared that the amendment would overload the bill and argued that the matter ought to be treated separately. They were defeated by a temporary revival of the familiar coalition of Republicans and southern Democrats, reinforced by some liberal Democrats. For the first time, "sex" was incorporated into the traditional litany of impermissible grounds of discrimination. Contrary, perhaps, to the belief of following generations, it had not always been so. It was only by virtue of a segregationist's attempt to work serious mischief that "race, color, religion, and national origin" grew to "race, color, religion, sex, and national origin."[11]

The sex amendment was the most important change the House made in the committee bill. There were several close calls on proposed amendments whose adoption would not only have weakened the bill but, perhaps, signaled an unraveling of the shaky bipartisan coalition. On 10 February 1964, after nine days of floor debate, an exceptionally long time for the House, the bill passed by a vote of 290 to 130. Seven southern Democrats voted yes and just thirty-four Republicans voted no.

The Senate

The overwhelming Republican vote was a valuable resource as the bill came to the Senate. Even so, speculation inside the beltway (as it would now be called), focused on which of the bill's major provisions would survive the Senate, historically the graveyard of civil rights legislation. With twenty of the sixty-seven Democrats sure to oppose cloture, exactly the same number of Republican votes was needed to end the inevitable southern filibuster.[12] At most, a dozen moderate to liberal Republicans might be recruited. Cloture could succeed only with the help of conservatives representing plains and mountain states with few nonwhites, active liberals, or union members.

The key to their support was Everett Dirksen of Illinois. Minority leader and ranking Republican on the Judiciary Committee, he combined in the Senate the roles played in the House by Halleck and McCulloch. Dirksen did not seem well cast as a civil rights champion. Known during his long career as a wily and conservative partisan, he had been reelected easily in 1962 with only a tiny share of black votes. He was said to have once ordered Clarence Mitchell, the NAACP's genial and widely respected Washington representative, out of his office. Having earlier endorsed a voluntary approach to desegregating public accommodations, Dirksen was thought therefore to be even less hospitable to Title VII, the more "difficult" provision. The proponents believed that Dirksen would decide the bill's fate, but they had no idea about his true intentions and no success in drawing him into early negotiations.

Civil rights lobbyists wanted to pressure Dirksen by denouncing his refusal to endorse the bill. The Senate floor manager, majority whip Hubert H. Humphrey of Minnesota, rejected this advice. Asked about Dirksen by reporters, Humphrey expressed his confidence that "when the time comes," Dirksen would demonstrate what a great American he was. As one observer put it, "Humphrey built a niche for Dirksen's bust and shone a spotlight on it." This tactic was designed to appeal to Dirksen's character and sense of drama. Secure in the knowledge that, if enacted, the bill would be judged a Democratic achievement, the administration was unconcerned about giving Dirksen his time on the stage.[13] And if Dirksen ultimately opposed the bill and it failed, his prominent role would make it easier to blame his party.

While Dirksen bided his time, the House bill came to the Senate and was "held on the table" instead of being referred to a committee. This procedure avoided Eastland's Judiciary Committee and set the stage for a motion to make the bill the pending business of the Senate. The southerners exercised their right of unlimited debate to keep this motion from coming to a vote and the filibuster was on. Led by Georgia's Richard B. Russell, a formidable power who had been a senator since 1933, the filibusterers, organized in three six-man teams, displayed the discipline and mastery of rules that had marked their previous victories.

A new day had dawned, however, for Senate civil rights supporters. For one thing, they had learned the rules and in the coming months matched their antagonists' command of parliamentary procedure. In addition, the House bill was generally recognized as setting the outer limits of the feasible. No serious demands were heard to strengthen it; no part of the coalition jeopardized its unity by demanding

improvements. Nor were there calls for concessions. With the tax and farm measures out of the way, President Johnson, who had strongly endorsed the civil rights
bill shortly after taking office, announced that Senate passage of an intact House
bill was his first priority. Washington analysis of Johnson's political situation concluded that, coming from the South, he had more to prove about racial issues than
had Kennedy and therefore needed to be seen taking a strong stand. The Justice
Department, still headed by Robert Kennedy, who maintained a low profile in the
months following his brother's death, had demonstrated during House floor consideration its commitment to the bill, mastery of the substantive issues (Marshall's
specialty), and political sensitivity (Katzenbach's department). This level of administration dedication and talent was a new departure for civil rights legislation.

The same was true of Senate floor leadership, in the hands of the two assistant
party leaders, Humphrey and his liberal Republican counterpart from California,
Thomas Kuchel. Every morning leading senators and their aides met with Katzenbach and Marshall. Staffs met again in the afternoon. Humphrey's office published
a daily "Bipartisan Civil Rights Newsletter" both to keep friendly senators informed and to provide material for their speeches and news releases. Two senators,
one from each party, led floor debate on each of the bill's major titles. As it had in
the House, the Justice Department supplied detailed briefing books, including
analyses of expected amendments. When serious debate began, it staffed an office
just off the floor with department lawyers available to help supporters.

Proceedings during the filibuster provided little of the drama seen in *Mr. Smith
Goes to Washington* and PBS specials. Speakers on both sides kept to the issues; no
one spun stories or shared down-home recipes. There were no cots in the cloak-
rooms because there were no round-the-clock sessions. The leadership concluded
that these practices had been essentially publicity stunts that would be counterpro-
ductive in 1964. The proponents' need for organization went beyond having well-
briefed speakers ready to take the floor. A southern senator could always halt the
proceedings merely by gaining recognition and saying, "Mr. President, I suggest
the absence of a quorum." This stopped everything until fifty-one senators showed
up. Because the southerners stayed away, it was up to the proponents to provide
the quorum; the alternative was public embarrassment. As media coverage and
public attention increased, some newspapers began to carry a front page box score
showing daily quorum performance. Failure to produce a quorum one Friday led to
a Saturday meeting for Democratic senators at which the normally taciturn majority leader, Mike Mansfield, shouted angrily at his colleagues.

For more than a month the filibuster was essentially a public relations duel. The proponents were waiting for Dirksen. It seems likely that he was lying low in order to take Johnson's measure and also to get the best possible reading of public opinion after the strong House Republican vote for the bill. The Republican presidential nomination campaign also may have affected his timing. Senator Barry Goldwater, the most likely nominee, was expected to vote against cloture and even against the bill itself. At least some of his Senate supporters, worried that these acts would harm his chances of being nominated, might have been tempted to vote the same way in order to give him some political cover. Prominent among these Goldwater backers were some of the same senators whose votes would be needed to end the filibuster. According to this line of thought, Dirksen wanted to delay the cloture vote until the nomination was settled.

The civil rights coalition concentrated on the dozen or so Republicans needed for cloture. Most of these members represented states where blacks were scarce and southern race relations largely a matter of indifference. Spontaneous constituent pressures were minimal, one way or the other. Because organized labor had only a modest presence in these areas, there was little leverage for the unions, usually a heavyweight element in the Leadership Conference on Civil Rights. The most appropriate advocates came from organized church groups, a relatively new element in the Leadership Conference. Religious delegations came to Washington to lobby their senators and hold prayer meetings on the Capitol grounds. Kuchel's office, informed of Republican senators' travel schedules, would arrange for local ministers, priests, and rabbis to encounter them on their home ground. The president and chairman of the National Council of Churches, a prominent industrialist and a Presbyterian church leader, called on the strategic senators, each time accompanied by local religious figures.

The Leadership Conference, the administration, and the Senate leadership were now on good terms. Satisfied with the House bill, the lobbyists had no thought of asking for more. And as long as the administration and Senate managers seemed to be standing fast on the House bill, there was no reason for disagreement. The NAACP's Mitchell and Joseph Rauh, a longtime Washington liberal and labor lawyer, attended Senate leadership meetings twice a week.

Eventually, Dirksen filed over one hundred amendments and indicated a willingness to talk. His amendments ranged from proposals to eviscerate each of the major titles to completely trivial changes. His intentions remained unclear. Was he serious about his more drastic amendments or were they designed to stake out a strong bargaining position, probe for weaknesses among the bill's Senate sponsors, or merely test the administration's resolve?

A series of meetings began that lasted for several weeks. Ostensibly they were between the minority and majority leaders, Dirksen and Mansfield. Actually there were multiple discussions, with widespread participation between the bill's supporters, including Justice Department officials on one side and Dirksen or his staff on the other. The proceedings took on the character of the usual committee markup that had been missing in the Senate: line-by-line reading, discussion, and negotiation.

It soon became clear that Dirksen wanted most of all to have his name on a bill that would be a monument to his role in achieving bipartisan collaboration. In the end, he demanded comparatively few significant alterations. Most of the differences between the House bill and what was labeled the Dirksen-Mansfield Compromise were largely cosmetic; even broad redrafting of major sections worked little, if any, substantive change.[14] Once he decided to cooperate, Dirksen apparently was concerned mainly with being able to point to the many marks he had left on the bill. Their limited impact notwithstanding, the number and seeming importance of the concessions he had won were enough to justify the support of his more conservative Republican colleagues.

On 10 June, the Senate imposed cloture by a vote of seventy-one to twenty-nine, four votes more than required.[15] The bill's supporters endured a few more anxious moments during the ensuing consideration of 104 amendments. Unacceptable amendments were voted down, but not always by comfortable margins, and some minor changes were accepted by the bipartisan floor leadership. Nine days later the bill passed, seventy-three to twenty-seven. Six Republicans voted no both on cloture and final passage, and each time Goldwater was one of them. On 2 July, with only six members voting differently than they had in February, the House accepted the Senate version. President Johnson signed the great bill into law later the same day.

In Retrospect

The 1964 Act is generally viewed as an accomplishment of the Johnson Presidency. And indeed it was: Johnson's strong endorsement of the bill shortly after Kennedy's assassination marked his determination to enact the measure his predecessor had negotiated to the House floor. The same was true of his unwavering commitment during the next seven months. Even marginally less forceful public support by the new president could have resulted in seriously weakening or even scuttling the legislation. Recognition of Johnson's importance, however, sometimes goes beyond acknowledgment of his legislative skills to the suggestion that if Kennedy had lived the bill would have died on Capitol Hill or passed without most of its major provisions.

There is, of course, no way to say with certainty what would have happened absent the assassination, whether the bill would have passed and, if so, in what form. But the assumption that Johnson's ascent to the presidency was a necessary condition for the bill's success is questionable. The Kennedy administration committed itself to securing a new law and the strategy for passage was fixed prior to the assassination. The key element was the bipartisan House bill, developed in cooperation with Representative McCulloch, an approach designed to lock in Republican support and set the stage for Senator Dirksen to be cast as saving the legislation from death by filibuster. Kennedy's skill and steadiness made this strategy work during the perilous passage through the House Judiciary Committee. In the crisis after the subcommittee revolt, Kennedy confronted groups comprising much of the Democratic Party's core constituency by sending his brother to support the latest bipartisan compromise. And in the decisive period following Libonati's defection, President Kennedy committed the full authority of his office and his own prestige to securing a bipartisan bill.

Kennedy's strategy was fulfilled, and the bill's content established, in the measure reported to the floor by the House Judiciary Committee on 20 November 1963. There was no change in strategy or implementation from that point forward; the Justice Department continued after the assassination to function as the administration's leader on the bill without a perceptible shift in role or in direction from the White House. In none of our interviews with congressional, White House, and Justice Department officials, as well as with civil rights lobbyists and opponents, was President Johnson described as personally playing an active role.[16] Events leading to passage followed as planned prior to 22 November, although few of those concerned expected quite such a complete success. We see no convincing reasons for thinking that the outcome would have been significantly different had Kennedy lived.

The 1964 Act, or something like it, was not inevitable, however. Other responses to Birmingham were possible; not the least probable would have been an emphasis on maintenance of public order and restoration of civic peace, rather than racial justice. Massive street demonstrations were new to recent national experience and many Americans would have responded affirmatively to a call for an end to the disruption in Birmingham and elsewhere. A respectable appeal to the need for restoration of order—deploring the brutality of Bull Connor's methods, acknowledging the marchers' grievances but decrying their methods and urging instead reliance on the courts—might have won the day. At the time, even some national leaders of the NAACP expressed disapproval of King's tactics, fearing that the marches would evoke a negative public response and adversely affect the overall struggle. Once the bill was introduced, the administration and congressional leaders worried that demonstrations in the North would jeopardize its chances. And, certainly, it was realistic to fear the consequences if even one major demonstration had turned violent.

The nation was fortunate that the seminal demonstrations in Birmingham were led by a student of Gandhi who was able to instill in his followers his own commitment to nonviolence. Even then, passage of the 1964 act was never certain and one hesitates to contemplate what might have happened had the legislative effort faltered or failed and leadership of the civil rights movement passed to others less clearly committed to peaceful methods. Even if viewed only as a change in rhetoric, the emerging black power movement generated serious unease among many white Americans whose reactions to black demands had been largely sympathetic.

The movement's success did not turn simply on good fortune or the absence of generalized violence. The demonstrations in Birmingham also reflected a sophisticated understanding of the task: "Our appeal and all of our efforts were to deradicalize our efforts and make them mainstream religious Americana . . . if we could use television and if we could work with the churches, if we could get key editorial writers to understand clearly what we were trying to do, that was the way to change America" (Young 1991, 32). Some of this same understanding helped inform the powerful and well-organized lobbying campaign conducted by the Leadership Conference on Civil Rights and its constituent members.

Civil rights forces organized the celebrated March on Washington in August 1963, while the bill was still before the House Judiciary Committee. Administration and congressional figures at first argued against the idea, warning that it could lead to disruption or violence and have a negative effect on Capitol Hill. But careful planning and the eventual cooperation of federal and District of Columbia officials contributed to making the march a triumph. More than two hundred thousand people from across the country, blacks and whites together, walked down the Mall to the Lincoln Memorial. The climax was King's "I have a dream" speech. Far from the unfortunate event that many feared, the march dramatized the broad base of support for the bill.

When the bill reached the Senate and attention focused on the pivotal vote for cloture, the Leadership Conference worked closely with its supporters who, under the smooth leadership of Humphrey and Kuchel, displayed unprecedented unity and sophistication.

The administration's consistency in pursuing Republican support, its refusal to seek momentary partisan advantage, and its commitment to obtaining effective legislation were essential ingredients of success. The determined and skillful efforts of Justice Department officials not only preserved the relationship with McCulloch during the recurring crises, but provided effective substantive support to congressional proponents in both houses, especially during the final negotiations with Dirksen.

Enactment was eased by the plain fact that the legislation was directed at the South and at discrimination against blacks. The bill was intended to remedy ills that were thought to be found largely in the old Confederacy and some border states. Its inclusive language notwithstanding, it was not generally perceived as applying elsewhere or as affecting other minorities. Moreover, many northern states already had public accommodations and fair employment laws, their own versions of Titles II and VII. Southern legislators were speaking the truth when they said— as if it were an accusation—that the bill was aimed only at their constituents. Despite both the reality of racial prejudice in the North and the 1964 act's ultimate national application, many members of Congress may have believed that it would have little if any practical impact on the lives of *their* constituents.

Finally, the act's passage was aided by the spirit of the times. The early 1960s were years of optimism and hope; there was a belief in possibilities and in a future that may seem dimmer today. Among the public and within government there was a conviction that things could be changed, that the nation's problems were manageable, that they could be dealt with if only we were smart enough, committed enough, and worked hard enough. Government programs and the law could make a difference. The decade witnessed, for example, the passage not only of the Civil Rights Acts of 1964, 1965, and 1968,[17] but also medicare and medicaid, the beginning of the War on Poverty in all its many aspects, and the enactment of the Elementary and Secondary Education Act of 1965.[18]

Although the Civil Rights Act of 1964 was a great success in substantive terms, neither party got what it wanted politically from supporting the bill. For the Democrats, the bill was motivated not only by the moral and political force of the cause but by the Kennedy administration's desire to ease racial violence and thereby remove a threat to the president's popularity when he ran for re-election. The bill did not, of course, cause the riots in northern cities in the late 1960s, but that racially based urban unrest was, along with Vietnam, a major reason for Humphrey's defeat in 1968 (Converse et al. 1969, 1085).

The Republican irony is more obvious. Republican majorities for civil rights were skillfully put together in both the House and Senate. But this all went for naught because one of the six Republican senators who voted no happened to be the most important one of all from the standpoint of the party's image: Barry Goldwater. Republican presidential candidates had won 40% of the black vote in 1956 and 25% in 1960. In 1964, for all the efforts of Dirksen, McCulloch, and Halleck, the Republican ticket got a mere 5% of the black vote and has not subsequently risen far above that level. What set American blacks' image of the Republican Party was not Halleck and McCulloch and Dirksen, but Goldwater.

These consequences for the parties are not the most important legacy of the Civil Rights Act of 1964. In addition to improving the lives of millions of blacks, the act reflected a sea change in American law and politics in the early 1960s. This transformation did not originate in Washington or in academia, nor did it come from liberal ideologues. It came from the people represented by Martin Luther King and others, anonymous marchers—black and white—who, like their leaders, risked and sometimes lost their lives in their quest for racial justice. The significance of the civil rights movement extends well beyond the changes worked by the 1964 act. It led to a major restructuring of Americans' sense of justice across broad reaches of national life. The movement was the stimulus, the precedent, and the model for achieving other major shifts in popular attitudes and in the law. The Civil Rights Act of 1964 was the model for extending legal protections to other disadvantaged groups. The successes of efforts on behalf of other minorities and causes, for women's rights, the rights of the disabled, gays, the elderly, and others are all based on the movement that found its most strategic expression in Birmingham.

Notes

David B. Filvaroff was a special assistant to the deputy attorney general in 1963–64. On leave from Stanford University in 1964, Raymond E. Wolfinger was an assistant to Senator Hubert H. Humphrey, the

Senate majority whip. After the bill's passage, Wolfinger conducted 164 interviews with most of the major participants. This chapter is based mainly on those interviews and the authors' observations. Other published accounts of the bill's passage include Loevy 1990, Mann 1996, and Whalen and Whalen 1985.

1. Demands to impeach Chief Justice Earl Warren, author of the unanimous *Brown* opinion, were frequent, most notably on billboards across the country. They were endorsed not only by opponents of the decision, but also by many conservatives who disliked other Court interpretations of the Constitution, especially those dealing with criminal justice.

2. The pace of southern school desegregation was glacial. In the fall of 1964, a full decade after *Brown*, just 2% of all black students in the South were attending school with whites (Jaynes and Williams 1989, 75).

3. Although the 1964 Civil Rights Act included modest provisions on voting, it was the Voting Rights Act of 1965 that responded most effectively to black disenfranchisement in the South.

4. Named after Representative Adam Clayton Powell (D-N.Y.), such an amendment to a liberal bill authorizing a federal program, e.g., aid to education, would prohibit any expenditure of that program's funds for segregated activities. Powell amendments invariably attracted the votes of many Republicans who, if the amendment passed, would then vote against the underlying bill. At the same time, moderate southerners who might vote for a measure without this prohibition could never do so once it was part of the bill. Powell amendments were also troublesome for liberal Democrats who did not give top priority to civil rights.

5. In addition to southerners, a few other senators who might have voted for civil rights legislation opposed cloture on principle. They considered unlimited debate a protection against majoritarian abuse, particularly for small states.

6. This change was finally made in 1975.

7. Judiciary subcommittees at that time were numbered rather than named in order to expand the full committee chairman's discretion in bill assignment. A decade would pass before the "Subcommittee Bill of Rights" established fixed subcommittee jurisdictions.

8. Various explanations were offered for Libonati's change of heart, but there was no mystery behind his next appearance in the news: an announcement that he would not be a candidate for reelection to his safe seat in 1964. His withdrawal was a result of the fury of Mayor Richard Daley, the unquestioned power among Chicago Democrats, at what he considered a personal betrayal. The mayor had gained Libonati's temporary cooperation at the request of the White House.

9. Southerners used the same rhetoric in Senate debate. In both houses, opponents argued that major parts of the bill were unconstitutional.

10. Even if all else failed and the bill were enacted, Judge Smith's amendment might lead to a host of complaints from women, thus reducing the attention that enforcement officials could give to cases involving blacks.

11. Taken by surprise when Title VII became part of a broadly supported bipartisan bill, Washington representatives of big business nevertheless were not too disturbed by the prospects of its passage. Most national corporations had adjusted to doing business in states with fair employment laws. But the sex amendment had few state counterparts and its addition to the House bill raised alarms at the National Association of Manufacturers (NAM). An NAM official explored with Senate Republican leader Dirksen the chances of defeating Judge Smith's handiwork in the Senate. Dirksen checked with his colleagues and reported that no Republican senator would introduce an amendment to strike "sex" from Title VII.

12. Two moderate southern Democrats were sure votes against cloture but did not participate in the filibuster.

13. Humphrey's anticipation of being rewarded with the vice presidential nomination possibly assuaged whatever discomfort he might have felt about Dirksen's potential starring role. Humphrey did become vice president and Dirksen was celebrated in some circles as the savior of the bill. The week af-

ter final passage, his picture appeared on the cover of *Time.* Dirksen's celebrity contrasts with the modest acclaim accorded McCulloch and Halleck, exemplifying the traditional difference between the "showhorse" Senate and "workhorse" House.

14. The label was somewhat misleading. This draft was primarily a product of detailed negotiations between Dirksen's Judiciary Committee minority staff and Justice Department officials. Introduced in the Senate as an amendment in the nature of a substitute to the House bill, it ultimately passed with little change.

15. Proponents believed that if his vote had been needed for cloture, Carl Hayden, an Arizona Democrat, would have provided it. Hayden was one of that dwindling band who, as a matter of principle, had never voted for cloture. He voted for the bill on final passage.

16. One exception might have been a concession on silver policy Johnson offered for what turned out to be the unneeded cloture vote of a Nevada senator.

17. Designed to end black disenfranchisement in the South, which it did fairly quickly, the 1965 act and its later amendments continue to affect electoral outcomes nationwide, most notably by influencing legislative apportionment. The 1968 act prohibited discrimination in housing.

18. This last measure, by providing billions of federal dollars to local public schools, made Title VI an important instrument to help end *de jure* school segregation.

2

What Light Does the Civil Rights Act of 1875 Shed on the Civil Rights Act of 1964?

J. Morgan Kousser

The 1964 Civil Rights Act was the first serious antiracist law to pass the U.S. Congress since a similar but much less comprehensive law was enacted eight-nine years earlier, during the First Reconstruction. What sort of struggle led to the proposal and adoption of the 1875 law, how has that law been viewed by historians, what effects did it have, and what parallels and differences were there between the 1875 and 1964 episodes? What can we learn about the Second Reconstruction by comparing it with the First? (See Kousser 1992 for a fuller discussion of the two eras, roughly 1865–95 and 1950–90.)

Much of the public's attention in 1964, especially in the South, focused on the public accommodations section, Title II of the act. Would segregation in hotels, motels, restaurants, and theaters, at public meetings, sports events, and governmental offices be swept away? What non-historians may not realize is how similar the provisions of the 1875 Civil Rights Act were to that section of the 1964 act. Thus, section 1 of the 1875 act stated, in pertinent part, "That all persons within the jurisdiction of the United States shall be entitled to the full and equal enjoyment of the accommodations, advantages, facilities, and privileges of inns, public conveyances on land or water, theatres, and other places of public amusement; subject only to the conditions and limitations established by law, and applicable alike to citizens of every race and color, regardless of any previous condition of servitude" (*U.S. Statutes at Large*, vol. 18, 335).

The relevant part of the 1964 act read: "All persons shall be entitled to the full and equal enjoyment of the goods, services, facilities, privileges, advantages, and accommodations of any place of public accommodation, as defined in this section, without discrimination or segregation on the ground of race, color, religion, or national origin" (Title II, Section 201 [a], Public Law 88-352 [2 July 1964]).[1]

In light of the similarities in language between the two acts, it is shocking how differently they have fared in history books.[2] The historiography of the 1964 act is almost wholly celebratory. The real question posed by Filvaroff and Wolfinger in the previous chapter is: who will share in the glory of the passage of the 1964 Civil Rights Act? In stark contrast, almost no one from 1875 to the present has asked that question about the 1875 Civil Rights Act. Indeed, much of the historiography of the First Reconstruction has been and still is very antagonistic. To oversimplify, the racist "Dunning School" of historians early in this century thought the First Reconstruction radical, antiracist, and therefore wrong, whereas many more recent historians, as strongly against racial inequality as the Dunningites were for it, believe the First Reconstruction too conservative and the Reconstructionists either too racist or too insincere, and therefore still wrong. (See Stampp 1965 and Foner 1988 for more balanced treatments.)

The 1875 act's condemnatory treatment by historians may have reached its climax in William Gillette's 1979 book, *Retreat from Reconstruction, 1869–1879*. Gillette's reading of the 1875 Civil Rights Act might be summed up in the questions: how can we destroy the illusion of idealism? How can we belittle its significance? He calls the act "an insignificant victory," "little more than the illusion of achievement, the most meaningless piece of postwar legislation" (271, 273). The only reason it passed, Gillette says, was that people expected that it "would never operate effectively." The summation of his chapter on the act, which is the longest recent treatment by a historian, could hardly be harsher:

The Republicans, then, had once again indulged in empty ritualism, the results of which were more often negative than constructive. The law thus represented the bankruptcy of legislative sentimentality and Reconstruction rhetoric, which demeaned noble ideals and undercut vital interests. For many disillusioned radicals the act was the expiring flash of a now obsolete philanthropy. For most other Republicans it was an unwelcome intrusion and an unnecessary initiative. Had great results followed, the cost would have been justified in some measure. But the statute had reaped the whirlwind of racist reaction and it served only to weaken the Republican party, to disappoint the blacks, and to further discredit the integrity of the law. It was the "deadest of dead letters." (Gillette 1979, 279)

In other words, in Gillette's view, the 1875 act was an insubstantial fraud that benefitted only reactionaries who used its shadow to frighten the gullible white masses. Are there any words or sentiments of disapprobation that the historian somehow neglected to include?

In fact, the reputation of the 1875 act among historians in the 1990s is probably worse than it was during the 1970s, because political history is so completely out of fashion today. A graduate student today who would choose the field of political history is considered Neanderthal, antediluvian. The cultural history of "texts"—and anything nonpolitical qualifies as a text—is the current fashion. Today, most young American historians would not even know of the existence of the 1875 act, and the few who did would almost surely be ignorant about the struggle that led to it and, indeed, to civil rights acts all over the country in the nineteenth century. For them as well as other audiences, let me recount a few not very well-known facts.

The hub of the nineteenth-century civil rights struggle was Boston. There, in 1842, the first well-documented movement for a civil rights law in a state legislature took place (Kousser 1988). After several incidents in which black passengers were excluded from "white" railroad cars, associates of the abolitionist William Lloyd Garrison agitated in the legislature to ban segregated railroad cars by law. The agitation failed to produce a statute only because the railroads in Massachusetts eventually all agreed to eliminate Jim Crow cars and to serve everyone equally.

The more lengthy and difficult campaign for school integration in the Bay State served through newspaper reports and pamphlets as a primer for racial reformers and their opponents throughout the North. Beginning in 1840 with a petition to the Boston School Committee, black and white Garrisonians pushed to abolish the "colored" schools of that city and to integrate children into schools common to all. When renewed and expanded petition drives in 1844, 1846, and 1849 failed, antislavery forces filed the famous case of *Roberts v. Boston* in 1849–50. Before the Massachusetts Supreme Judicial Court, the integrationists were represented by Robert Morris, perhaps the second African American to be admitted to practice law in the country, and Charles Sumner, the abolitionist Boston Brahmin who would be elected to the U.S. Senate in 1851. Sumner's eighty-page brief, which he arranged to have published by Benjamin Roberts, the black printer whose daughter was refused admittance into the white school, contained every argument that has been made in the twentieth century on school integration except those related to busing, which Sumner was not foresighted enough to anticipate. The abolitionists' defeat at the hands of Chief Justice Lemuel Shaw, who had extensive landholdings below the Mason-Dixon line, only increased the agitation, until in 1855 Massachusetts became the first state in the country to institute a school integration law. Interestingly, the

legislature that passed that law virtually unanimously was overwhelmingly dominated by the miscalled "Know-Nothings," who in Massachusetts, at least, were one
of the most liberal, antiracist, and egalitarian groups of the nineteenth century.

In 1865, Massachusetts became the first state to pass a public accommodations
law by banning racial discrimination in "any licensed inn, . . . public place of
amusement, public conveyance or public meeting." Nationally, once slavery
seemed on the road to ultimate extinction, Senator Charles Sumner began an assault on segregation that would end only with his death. In 1862 he was largely responsible for an amendment to the charter of the Washington, Alexandria, and
Georgetown Railroad, which prohibited Jim Crow cars. That action led to the first
U.S. Supreme Court case on integration, *Railroad Company v. Brown* (1873), in
which the majority on the Supreme Court, as liberals often do, decided the issue on
the narrowest possible grounds, in this instance that Sumner's amendment to the
railroad charter prohibited segregation. By following proper judicial practice, the
Court unintentionally allowed much more conservative courts to sidestep the
precedent when they considered the question of whether segregation violated common law or the Thirteenth or Fourteenth Amendment.

Sumner first introduced a national civil rights bill in 1867. It passed the Senate
in 1872, 1873, and 1874, and finally succeeded in the House in the lame-duck session
of 1875 after the Republicans lost 47% of their seats in the 1874 elections, bringing
the national phase of Reconstruction largely to an end.[3] In a compromise to obtain
the votes of a few marginal members, the Republicans, at the last moment, had to
delete from the bill provisions integrating churches and schools. Nonetheless, it
was quite a far-reaching and controversial law.

This was a bitterly fought and strictly partisan battle, which is one of the chief
differences between the civil rights movements of the nineteenth and twentieth
centuries. From 1867 through 1875, no Democrat in Congress ever voted for a version of Sumner's civil rights bill. In fact, throughout the whole nineteenth century,
no Democratic member of Congress ever voted for a civil rights or voting rights bill
(Kousser 1992, 150–51). In sharp contrast, bipartisan support was crucial to the
passage of the 1964 Civil Rights Act and the 1965 Voting Rights Act, as well as to the
renewals of the Voting Rights Act in 1970, 1975, and 1982. One reason that civil
rights progress was so fragile in the nineteenth century was that Republican proponents could rarely expect any assistance from even a small number of Democrats.
The issue marked the clearest line of partisan distinction, and Democrats resisted
every advance and repealed every pro-civil rights provision the first chance they

got. (To someone steeped in the facts of the nineteenth-century struggles, current Republican attacks on minority opportunities raise disturbing parallels.)

Another difference between the movements in the two centuries was that African American modes of action in the 1870s were much more traditional than were the sit-ins of the 1960s. To be sure, during the 1860s and '70s, there were a few boycotts of segregated streetcars. But mostly the newly freed and enfranchised slaves plunged into conventions, conferences, political canvassing, and legal cases—at least a hundred legal cases in the nineteenth century challenging racial discrimination in schools, for instance. Instead of a Selma march, blacks in the previous century wrote editorials in their own newspapers, ran for office, and framed antidiscrimination bills themselves.

There were three reasons for this rather surprising difference in the two eras. First, segregation was much less entrenched in the 1870s and race relations were much more fluid. We like to think of ourselves, of course, as living in the only enlightened era that has ever existed, but in many ways things were much worse in the 1950s and '60s—in particular, segregation had become so much more entrenched that it seemed nearly impossible to overthrow. To do so took drastic and extremely widespread action. Second, blacks were much better connected with the power structure in the 1870s than they were in the 1960s. They did not need thousands of sit-ins, because they could go right to their (mostly, but not all, white) Republican friends, and their Republican friends could pass whatever bills they wanted to because they had sufficient majorities in Congress before 1874. Third, the legislative structure was much more malleable; the rules were much simpler and more favorable to reform. Senate rules in the 1870s did not allow filibusters, and although the House permitted much more unlimited debate, it took only a small change in the House rules to cut off discussion and pass the Civil Rights Bill.

The comparative social and political rigidity of the two eras suggests a third broad contrast. Segregation was so much more ingrained and inflexible in the 1960s than in the 1870s that when the system began to give way, it shattered. Thus, the changes of the 1960s could become much more permanent because they replaced a much more well-defined structure, rather than the comparatively fluid pattern of race relations of the late nineteenth century. Likewise, after 1964, the filibuster no longer seemed so formidable a barrier to civil rights bills that they had to be abandoned or severely watered down. The climate in 1964 both made racial behavior change rapidly in the South and facilitated further governmentally sponsored change.

A fourth distinction between the two eras was that the 1875 law, which rested only on the equal protection clause of the Fourteenth Amendment, was ruled unconstitutional by the U.S. Supreme Court, while the 1964 act, which also referred to the commerce clause, passed the Court's muster (*The Civil Rights Cases* [1883]; *Heart of Atlanta Motel, Inc. v. U.S.* [1964]; *Katzenbach v. McClung* [1964]). Perhaps one explanation for the difference in historians' treatment of the two laws is that the 1875 act did not stay in effect long enough for its direct impact to be unmistakable. Historians celebrate victories that endure. But in a larger sense, the 1875 act both reflected and produced smaller victories, for nearly every state in the North and seven of the eleven ex-Confederate states passed similar laws, either as part of the agitation that led up to the national act, as a spin-off from that agitation, or as an attempt to rectify a wrong, at least at the state level, when the Supreme Court invalidated the national Civil Rights Act. In Ohio, for instance, where more school segregation cases were filed in the nineteenth century than in any other state, a comprehensive civil rights bill, which mandated racial integration in public accommodations and schools and lifted the previous ban on interracial marriages, passed in 1887, the end result of protests against the Supreme Court decision in *The Civil Rights Cases.*

A fifth contrast is that the two laws were passed at different points in the recurring cycles of attitudes about race and government. Both the First and Second Reconstructions witnessed rapid changes in white racial attitudes and behavior. But 1875, we are conventionally told, fell near the end of such a period of change, near the date that history books typically give for the end of the First Reconstruction (1877), while we know from survey research that a substantial liberalization of white racial attitudes continued long after 1964 (Schuman, Steeh, and Bobo 1985). In fact, however, northern white views and actions continued to alter in a liberal direction long after 1877, although southern white opinions generally did not (Kousser 1986; 1991). Conversely, most of the changes in white attitudes since 1964 have been confined to the South. Thus the contrast between the centuries may not be so stark as suggested, depending on the region on which one concentrates. A similar caution applies to comparisons between the two eras' degrees of governmental action. Both laws were passed in periods of activism, the Civil War and Reconstruction period being in many ways the greatest period of governmental accomplishment in America since 1787. Eighteen seventy-five came at the end of a period of national, but certainly not state level, energy. Nineteen sixty-four, by contrast, was the apogee of its period's activism, particularly at the national level. Both Reconstructions helped to bring about periods of reaction that reached their climax about thirty years after what might be called "High Reconstruction."[4] But that is the price we pay for these moments of liberal change that come so infrequently in American history.

The dissimilarities in the causes behind the moments of liberal opportunity in the two eras, a sixth contrast, affected their degree of radicalism and perhaps the permanence of their results. It is often some disastrous miscalculation by conservatives that produces the opportunity for change. The greatest miscalculation conservatives ever made in this country was the decision to secede in 1860, which led to quite terrible disasters for them as well as their opponents but also to the end of slavery and the passage of the Fourteenth and Fifteenth Amendments, which could probably not have passed at any other point in American history, including the present.[5] In 1964, by contrast, there was no such conservative debacle, nor was there a depression caused, in part, by the inaction of the proponents of laissez-faire economics, as in 1893 and 1932. At the time of the passage of the 1964 Civil Rights Act, the law could only be a response to a positive movement, the sit-ins and demonstrations in the South and not, as during the First Reconstruction, a response further propelled by conservative mistakes, mistakes that gave radicals, for a time, a free hand. As the previous chapter shows, liberals did not have a free hand in 1964 but had to win the support of moderates like William McCulloch and conservatives like Everett Dirksen. The Second Reconstruction was therefore less radical, relative to practices and beliefs of the time, than the First, but it was also probably more difficult to overthrow because it was based on a wider political consensus.

Although some of the consequences of both the 1875 and 1964 acts were unintended, I think Filvaroff and Wolfinger exaggerate when they say that no one in 1964 got what they wanted. In the 1870s, although the threat to pass the civil rights bill no doubt lost the Republicans some seats in 1874 and although courts killed the law after less than a decade, it did inspire similar state level laws, which were very seldom repealed, all over the North in the late nineteenth century. Every former abolitionist knew that the struggle for civil rights for African Americans was difficult and that every course, even passing a law that they favored, risked failure. In the more successful actions of the 1960s, it seems to me that the winners largely achieved their goals, while the losers accurately predicted what defeat would mean for them and the deeply racist society that they preferred to preserve. Pro-civil rights Democrats and northern Republicans got a remarkably effective bill. Within a year, African Americans could eat at most restaurants and stay at most motels anywhere in the country; public programs at hospitals and other facilities were pretty speedily desegregated; the fund cutoff provision eventually forced the dismantling of the formal structure of school segregation; and affirmative action greatly increased black employment in governmental and private sector jobs in a rapidly changing economy. Moreover, the Republican conservatives who were not concerned one way or another with civil rights eventually achieved their goal, a reaction against governmental activism on subjects that they cared more about. The Civil Rights Act of 1964 was not the only or even the most important law that encouraged that reaction, but it helped. Finally, southern Democratic conservatives lost dramatically. The meticulously segregated, thoroughly and openly discriminatory society and polity that they tried to protect withered, and after a generation the southern Democratic conservative largely vanished as well, gone with the wind of racial and partisan change.

As we enter a new world in which government, particularly the national government, seems to be withdrawing its protections against the vagaries of the free market and the prejudices of a society still firmly controlled by whites, it is appropriate to celebrate the accomplishments of bygone eras—and to see whether we can learn more about how society operates and what is politically feasible if we study not one but two parallel events together.

Notes

1. The differences in these sections of the two laws were chiefly in the greater specificity and detail in the more modern code and the explicit prohibition of segregation (a term not in wide use in 1875) in the 1964 law.

2. Of course, the 1875 act was much more limited than the 1964 act, having no provisions regarding employment, fund cutoffs, or voting. My comparison is meant to be limited to Title II of the 1964 act.

3. This was the third greatest percentage loss by a major political party in American history, exceeded only by Republican losses in the 1890 election (49%) and Democratic losses in the 1894 election (53%). By contrast, in 1994, Democrats lost 21% of their seats.

4. *Plessy v. Ferguson* was decided in 1896, thirty years after Congress passed the Fourteenth Amendment. Right-wing Republicans took over Congress in 1994, thirty years after the passage of the Civil Rights Act, medicare, and the War on Poverty. The phrase "High Reconstruction" is suggested by "High Renaissance."

5. President Andrew Johnson's calamitous 1866 campaign against the Radicals reinforced the slaveholders' earlier folly at precisely the right moment. For completely inept and unintended contributions to American liberty, he must rank with the greatest of American presidents.

II

The Evolution of U.S. Civil Rights Policies after 1964

3

The Civil Rights Act and the American Regulatory State

Hugh Davis Graham

In 1994 Americans commemorated the thirtieth anniversary of the Civil Rights Act in an atmosphere of gloom. The media in the 1990s have been filled with depressing reports about inner city violence and family breakdown, racial and ethnic isolation in schools and housing, campus turmoil over multiculturalism and political correctness and speech codes, the pathology of a heavily minority underclass. In 1994 the FBI issued its first annual report on hate crime statistics, as required by the Hate Crime Statistics Act of 1990, and found high levels of violent bigotry, black on white as well as white on black.[1] Polls showed both strong resentment among whites against minority preference policies and apprehension among minorities at rising complaints of civil rights favoritism (Hochschild 1995).

Why has the nation's extraordinary expansion of civil rights protections since 1964 left us with so little satisfaction? Our debates over the past two decades, polarized over the wisdom and effectiveness of race-conscious affirmative action policies, have grown repetitive and sterile. I want to broaden the focus of discussion by viewing the development of civil rights policy within the larger context of the evolving regulatory state. Since 1964 an elaborate network of federal regulation has been developed to enforce a growing list of civil rights protections. Yet it is striking how little attention has been devoted to civil rights policy and its implementation in the literature on federal regulation, deregulation, and regulatory reform.[2]

The vast literature on civil rights enforcement, dominated by lawyers and legal scholars, concentrates on litigation in federal courts over constitutional and statutory requirements in civil rights policy. The literature on federal regulation, dominated by economists and students of public administration, grew out of economic regulation involving the independent regulatory commissions established during the Progressive and New Deal periods. Although greatly expanded in the postwar years to address new complexities arising from the wave of social legislation of the 1960s and 1970s, the regulatory literature has generally avoided the field of civil rights regulation. This presents a puzzle, because Congress developed the "new" social regulation in response to a surge of social movements during the 1960s whose shared attributes gave the new form of regulation its name and distinguished it from the "old" economic regulation (Vogel 1981). Civil rights regulation shares many characteristics with the new social regulation. But the absence of civil rights topics in the regulatory literature hints at important differences.

The New Social Regulation

What were the shared attributes that linked civil rights reform and social regulation? One was a common origin in social movement mobilizations, first on behalf of African Americans, then on behalf of women, students, consumers, workers, the environment. Second, these grassroots movements sought protection from an array of social evils that included employment discrimination, a polluted environment, dangerous products and services, unsafe transportation and workplaces. Third, to provide this protection, Congress established an array of new regulatory agencies—the Equal Employment Opportunity Commission (1964), the National Transportation Safety Board (1966), the Environmental Protection Agency (1970), the Occupational Safety and Health Administration (1970), the Consumer Product Safety Commission (1972), and others. Additional enforcement subagencies were established by the executive branch, for example the Office for Civil Rights in HEW in 1965, the Office of Federal Contract Compliance in Labor in 1965, the Office of Minority Business Enterprise in Commerce in 1969.

These new agencies developed a model of social regulation that differed fundamentally from the older economic regulation. The latter emphasized independent, quasi-judicial boards and commissions, such as the Federal Trade Commission and the Civil Aeronautics Board. They responded to complaints (rate-fixing, anti-competitive practices, unfair labor practices) in adversarial proceedings, deciding cases with court-like decrees (complaint dismissal, rate approval, cease and desist orders, penalties and relief). Social regulation, on the other hand, was proactive, emphasizing future compliance to reduce risk and eliminate hazards rather than punishment for past misdeeds. The methods of social regulation, more legislative than adjudicatory, centered on notice-and-comment rule-making and emphasized scientific expertise for setting standards of compliance. The agencies of social and economic regulation also differed structurally. Economic regulation was generally organized vertically, with agencies presiding over specific industrial sectors (surface transportation, communications, securities, the airlines). Social regulation was organized horizontally, cutting across sector boundaries to clean the nation's air and water, eliminate employment discrimination, improve transportation safety, increase access for the handicapped, combat consumer fraud.

The dichotomies I have stressed are oversimplified. I will return to the comparison of economic and social regulation later, adding qualifications and stressing differences. Here I stress the common roots of the new social regulation in the insurgent politics of the 1960s and emphasize the need social regulators shared to enforce their rulings in a way that produced significant and measurable results quickly. Social regulation, unlike most economic regulation, was not sector specific—problems of air pollution, job discrimination, consumer fraud, or workplace safety were not peculiar to certain industries. Effective regulation would therefore require authority that cut across industrial boundaries and government jurisdictions. For federal agencies setting standards of compliance for air and water pollution or for industrial and consumer safety, the legitimacy of broad congressional authority over interstate commerce had been established by the New Deal. For federal agencies seeking to impose new nationwide controls, however, on the hiring and promotion practices of private firms or state and local governments, or on the educational policies of public and private schools and colleges, the authority of Washington was greatly narrowed by the traditions of federalism. For civil rights regulation, this was the decisive battleground of the 1960s.

The Watershed of the 1960s: Federal Aid and Title VI

When I attempt to reconstruct the postwar development of regulatory and civil rights policy, I am drawn to two great changes, one occurring in 1964, the other at the end of the decade, in the first years of the Nixon presidency. The first of these events is the enactment of Title VI of the 1964 Civil Rights Act. The second is the shift in enforcement strategy from traditional nondiscrimination policing, as exemplified by the antidiscrimination commissions in the northern industrial states and the original design of the EEOC, to minority preference requirements under the disparate impact standard adopted during 1969–71. Each of these two watershed events marks a rare moment of decisive change in our history. On either side of them, during the years 1945–64, and later during the 1970s, important changes were occurring in the nature of civil rights enforcement and the American regulatory state itself, but they were more gradual and cumulative and their meaning was heavily determined by the sea changes of 1964 and 1969–71.[3] After the 1980 election, the Reagan-Bush administrations mounted a counteroffensive that for the first time included civil rights regulation among the deregulatory targets. I will address the Reagan counterattack later in this essay.

From the perspective of the 1960s, the heart of the Civil Rights Act were Title II (desegregating stores, hotels, restaurants) and Title VII (banning job discrimination). From the perspective of the 1990s, it was Title VI, which barred discrimination in government-funded activities. The efficacy of Title VI as an instrument of federal regulation rested on the increasing financial dependence of state and local governments and the private industrial economy on federal grants and contracts. For the modern era this dependence began in 1946 with the Hill-Burton Hospital Survey and Construction Act, when Congress began to build an inventory of assistance programs to benefit local communities while requiring little from recipients in exchange. Between 1946 and 1963 the federal system experienced a fiscal revolution that increased the dollar amount of federal aid to state and local governments from $701 million to $4.8 billion.[4] Washington's financial assistance took the form mainly of categorical grants-in-aid to help cities and states build roads, airports, hospitals, water systems, and other facilities to support rapid metropolitan growth.

Because state sales taxes and local property taxes were inadequate to pay for needed support services, Congress tapped the growing pool of federal income tax revenue, voting frequently to add new aid programs while rarely needing to raise tax rates. Congress and the funding agencies attached few strings to the grant programs other than standard technical requirements. In the vernacular of the mission agencies, the metaphor of the popular grant-in-aid programs was "leave it on the stump and run." As James Sundquist (1969, 12) observed in a 1969 study of federalism, state and local governments were "subject to no federal discipline except through the granting or denial of federal aid"—a sanction that "is not very useful, because to deny the funds is in effect a veto of the national objective itself." The categorical grant programs were popular because they served local needs, were loosely administered by federal officials, and mutually served the political interests of Washington's triangular bargaining networks.

During the 1960s, the federal grant system expanded dramatically. In 1962 there were 160 categorical programs. In 1965 there were 330; by 1970 there were 530. Eighty percent of these were legislated after 1960—158 of them in 1965–1966 alone, the bonanza year of the eighty-ninth Congress and the Great Society. In the "categorical explosion" of 1964–1968, Congress poured money into the states and cities to aid education, rebuild urban areas and transportation networks, assist antipoverty programs, reduce water and air pollution. Federal aid outlays to state and local governments, $2.3 billion in 1951, grew to $7 billion in 1960 and to $23 billion by 1970 ($77.5 billion in 1990 dollars). As a percentage of domestic federal outlays, grants amounted to 16.4% in 1960 and 21.9% in 1970 (Reagan 1985). The proliferation of grants, when added to billions in annual contracts awarded by federal agencies for goods and services, especially during the years of the Vietnam War and the space race, meant that by 1970 federal assistance in the form of grants and contracts reached deeply into the recesses of 3,040 counties, 19,200 municipalities, 14,500 school districts, and 28,500 special districts. In the private sector, federal contracts funded the work of 250,000 businesses employing more than 20 million workers.

Accompanying this growth in the 1960s was a sharp increase in performance requirements for recipients of federal funds. The federal lunch had never been free, and the gradual attachment of additional strings to federal grants has a long secular history.[5] But most federal controls were project-specific rather than crosscutting. They were tailored by agency experts to fit the specific practical needs of projects in agricultural experiment and extension, water control, biomedical research, road and airport building, hospital construction. During the 1960s, however, the federal government made the most significant change in federal assistance programs and their control since the land grant program was created in 1862. The instrument of this change was Title VI.

In light of the extraordinary consequences of Title VI, the gravity of this change can be appreciated only in hindsight. Its magnitude was not discernible at the time because such consequences were not intended and were not expected (especially by their proponents). Indeed, for most participants in the debates of 1963–64, the subsequent applications of Title VI were scarcely imaginable. In emphasizing unintended consequences, it is important to recognize that the most important consequence of the Civil Rights Act was its intended consequence: the destruction of the racial caste system in the South. For this reason, most attention during the great debates of 1963–64 was riveted on Title II on public accommodations desegregation and Title VII on fair employment. I will concentrate here on two major *un*intended consequences of the great sleeper provision, Title VI: it provided the chief leverage for national enforcement after 1970 of a disparate impact standard in minority rights, and it created a model for comprehensive federal regulation through crosscutting requirements reaching far beyond the arena of race relations that dominated the events of 1964.

As proposed in President Kennedy's original, post-Birmingham civil rights bill of 1963, Title VI would deny funds to federally assisted programs that discriminated against individuals because of their race, religion, or national origin. This was the "universal Powell amendment," the provision floated in the summer of 1963 by the Kennedy White House. It found surprisingly wide and bipartisan support from non-southerners in Congress because it was explainable to constituents in practical terms (preventing tax dollars from strengthening segregation), and because it offered an escape from the perennial and often self-destructive Powell amendment.[6] Title VI's sole substantive prohibition provides: "No person in the United States shall, on the basis of race, color, or national origin, be excluded from participation in, be denied the benefits of, or be subjected to discrimination under, any program or activity receiving federal financial assistance" (Bureau of National Affairs 1964).

Title VI was debated in Congress and was attacked by southern conservatives, most notably by senators Sam Ervin of North Carolina and Richard Russell of Georgia, who deplored its vagueness in not defining the term "discrimination" (Russell called Title VI "the realization of a bureaucrat's prayers"). In the process of negotiations it was narrowed by various constraining amendments in the House and, in the Senate, by a "pinpoint" provision that confined its application to "the particular program or part thereof in which noncompliance has been found." But Title VI retained its simple purpose and its enormous potential power. Given the deep attachment of Congress to traditional patterns of federalism in domestic legislation, it is difficult to imagine congressional approval of such a mighty sword for the executive branch in any circumstance less explosive than the civil rights crisis of 1963–64. The target seemed self-evidently confined to the no longer tolerable world of Bull Connor.

In attacking segregated stores, hotels, and restaurants, Title II "tore old Dixie down" almost overnight. The Justice Department, working with Labor Department officials (especially the OFCC) and the EEOC, effectively used a combination of Title VI, President Johnson's Executive Order 11246, and Title VII to desegregate employment all over the South.[7] On the whole the Civil Rights Act worked quickly and efficiently (low costs, high benefits) in achieving its goal of destroying the Jim Crow caste system in the South. In our modern racial angst, this is too easily forgotten. In this, the "longest debate" in the history of Congress, I have seen no evidence that the supporters of the major titles of the Civil Rights Act, including Title VI, were insincere in believing that its use would be largely confined to punishing racial discrimination in the South (Orfield 1969, Whalen 1985). Nor is there any reason to believe that Senator Hubert Humphrey was insincere when he pledged to eat his hat if Title VII ever led to racial preferences in public policy.

The Enigma of Richard Nixon

The shift from the nondiscrimination or equal treatment standard of 1964 to the disparate impact or proportional results standard of the early 1970s is the second of the great sea changes in regulatory policy brought by the 1960s. It centers on the Philadelphia Plan, quietly developed during 1966–67 by federal agency officials alarmed by worsening racial riots in the cities. It would rapidly redistribute jobs to minorities by requiring contractors building federally assisted construction projects to show proportional minority representation in their workforce. The controversial plan, which appeared to violate the ban on racial ratios and quotas in the Civil Rights Act, was abandoned in 1968 under attacks by the construction industry, labor unions, the General Accounting Office, and conservatives in Congress.

Soon after Richard Nixon's inauguration in January 1969, the Philadelphia Plan was resurrected by Labor Secretary George P. Shultz in the early months of 1969 and escorted safely by the determined Nixon White House through a congressional counterattack led by an unusual coalition of southern Democrats, Republican conservatives, and organized labor. In *The Civil Rights Era*, I described this as a decisive turning point in the development of federal civil rights policy, one that was unlikely to have occurred in the absence of Richard Nixon's surprising defense of the minority hiring formulas developed by the OFCC. Paradoxically, a Republican president who nominated G. Harrold Carswell to the Supreme Court, denounced racial quotas, and seriously proposed a constitutional amendment against school busing nonetheless effectively institutionalized a system of minority employment preferences that rested on Title VI and on executive orders (including his own) directing its enforcement.

The causes for the national shift in rights enforcement policy during 1969–71 are complex. They include the urgency generated by the urban rioting of 1965–68, the skill of the civil rights coalition in lobbying legislators and agency officials and in staffing the new enforcement agencies, and the support provided by federal courts, especially in *Contractors Association* (1971) and above all in *Griggs* (1971). Within the Nixon administration they include the president's determination to split the labor–civil rights alliance, speed the growth of a conservative black middle class, associate "racial quotas" in the public mind with the liberal legacy of the Democratic Party, and appeal to working class resentment of court-ordered busing and "reverse discrimination" (Graham 1992, 150–69). These events helped produce a seismic shift in the American political landscape. It included the mass defection of southern and blue-collar whites from the New Deal coalition, the emergence of a Republican presidential majority and with it conservative trends in the executive and judicial branches, and a deep split in the civil rights coalition over the principle of constitutional color blindness (Edsall 1991). Despite Nixon's self-destruction at Watergate, his surprising initiatives in civil rights policy appear less puzzling in hindsight.

Federal Regulatory Expansion in the Nixon-Ford Years

Within a year of the passage of Title VI, Congress, in the Elementary and Secondary Education Act, authorized a billion dollar aid program to local school districts. Soon thereafter the newly established Office for Civil Rights in HEW began demonstrating the leverage provided by crosscutting regulations. In 1969 the OFCC, using the Philadelphia Plan, required sharp increases in minority employment in federally assisted construction projects. Then in 1970 the OFCC in Order No. 4 extended the model of proportional minority hiring to all government contracts.[8] The effectiveness of the Title VI model of crosscutting regulation in winning impressive gains in employment and education for racial and ethnic minorities was not lost on the leaders of other movements, most notably feminist groups, the physically handicapped, the elderly, and Hispanic activists. By 1975 advocacy groups representing all four constituencies had persuaded Congress to borrow the language of Title VI and apply it to their own regulatory needs (USACIR 1984, 70–91).

Feminist groups such as the National Organization for Women and the Women's Equity Action League, having persuaded Lyndon Johnson in 1967 to include sex discrimination in the executive order program enforcing Title VI, won similar inclusion of women from the OFCC in its Revised Order No. 4 in 1971. In 1972 Congress by voice vote passed Title IX, an amendment to the education statutes that barred federal financial assistance to any educational program or activity that practiced sex discrimination. The following year, 1973, Congress responded to similar pressures from disability rights organizations. In Section 504 of the Rehabilitation Act, Congress reshaped the familiar language of Title VI to read as follows: "No otherwise qualified handicapped individual in the United States shall, solely by reason of his handicap, be excluded from participation in, be denied the benefits of, or be subject to discrimination under, any program or activity receiving Federal financial assistance." In the Age Discrimination Act of 1975, Congress heeded the voice of the American Association of Retired Persons, once again borrowing the language of Title VI and filling in the modifier blank with "age" discrimination. Also in 1975, the OCR issued "Lau Guidelines" to school districts with large minority language populations, requiring bilingual/bicultural instruction in all basic school subjects (Stein 1986, 29–70).

These extensions of the Title VI device during the 1970s differed from the pioneering efforts of the 1960s in several respects. In each instance, a far-reaching expansion of crosscutting regulation occurred with little grassroots pressure from constituency movements, little attention in the media, and little congressional debate. Grassroots constituencies do not understand the arcane workings of federal regulation. Policy entrepreneurs in Congress, however, do. Working quietly with advocacy group lobbies, they extended Title VI's crosscutting formula to protect new groups, often "with virtually no discussion or debate about the similarities and differences in the forms of discrimination faced by different groups and the types of remedies that might prove most effective in dealing with them" (USACIR 1993, 9). Section 504 of the Rehabilitation Act, taken almost verbatim from Title VI and enacted without hearings, demonstrated an important difference between regulatory laws on behalf of civil rights constituencies (racial and ethnic minorities, women, the elderly, the handicapped), and legislation governing other forms of social regulation (consumer fraud, health and safety, environmental protection). In the detailed statutes governing EPA or OSHA, for example, Congress stipulated precise standards for agency enforcement. In the protected class extensions based on Title VI, by contrast, Congress delegated wide discretion to the enforcement agencies. In Section 504 of the Rehabilitation Act, for example, Congress surely did not mean what it appeared to say (that blind individuals could drive taxis so long as they were "otherwise qualified").[9] What Section 504 *did* require would be decided later, mainly by staff lawyers in the OCR and the OFCC, working in consultation with disability rights organizations. Their regulations, following the path of federal aid, would cover every school system in the country, most colleges and universities, 325,000 private businesses, and 23 million employees.

The Carter Administration: Enforcement Consolidation and Minority Contract Set-Asides

By the end of 1972, the federal government had moved civil rights regulation several large steps beyond the compact of 1964. *Griggs* had legitimized the disparate impact standard; the OFCC had survived the congressional attack on the Philadelphia Plan; Congress had extended Title VII coverage to state and local governments and educational institutions and given the EEOC authority to bring discrimination suits in federal courts. Tension remained, however, between the equal treatment model of 1964 and the equal results model associated with affirmative action. The EEOC pressed for proportional employment results by issuing guidelines on employment testing and employee selection, crosscutting standards that for most employers resembled the OFCC's rule making under Title VI and Executive Order 11246. Structurally, however, the EEOC remained a complaint processing agency. Mired in a court-like caseload of hearings, findings, conciliations, and litigation, the agency early accumulated a complaint backlog that often delayed action for years (Walton 1988).

The OFCC, on the other hand, designed as a rule-making rather than a reactive, complaint-driven agency, took more initiative. The OFCC defined standards of contract compliance, required contractors to report employment projections by protected class category, conducted inspections, and ultimately (although rarely) debarred contractors. Yet the OFCC shared contract compliance duties under Title VI and the executive order with eleven similar subagencies in a confusing sprawl of EEO machinery scattered throughout the executive departments. Employers complained during the 1970s about multiple coverage, conflicting requirements, growing burdens of record keeping and reporting, and vulnerability to both government sanctions and reverse discrimination lawsuits.

The election of Jimmy Carter in 1976 threw the weight of decision to proponents of more aggressive affirmative action, including the Leadership Conference and the Congressional Black Caucus. Carter, determined to streamline the federal government by reorganizing agency structures and functions, persuaded Congress in 1978 to approve a consolidation plan making the EEOC the preeminent civil rights enforcement agency in the federal government. In a separate executive order, Carter in 1979 consolidated the federal government's scattered contract compliance functions in the executive departments and renamed the already awkwardly named agency the Office of Federal Contract Compliance Programs (OFCCP). As a consequence, both the OFCCP and the EEOC experienced an extraordinary expansion in personnel. Between 1978 and 1980 the OFCCP expanded from 68 full-time staff members to 1,304, and the EEOC expanded from 267 to 3,433 (USCCR 1982, 14–54).

These changes in structure and authority were accompanied by far-reaching changes in regulatory strategy. Under the leadership of Eleanor Holmes Norton, appointed by Carter to chair the EEOC in 1977, the EEOC issued the Uniform Guidelines on Employee Selection Procedures, a set of rules grounded in disparate impact theory that sharply curtailed the use by employers of employee tests and other merit criteria. The threat of EEOC lawsuits based on "underutilization" of minorities, sweetened by the protection of an EEOC-approved affirmative action plan against "reverse discrimination" lawsuits by white males, "precipitated an enormous pressure on employers" (Blumrosen 1993, 167). American business leaders—faced with increasing EEOC complaint negotiations under Title VII, pressed by the strengthened OFCCP to adopt proportional minority hiring practices, denied under the EEOC's Uniform Guidelines the use of traditional employee tests without expensive and vulnerable validation procedures, and fearing liability from reverse discrimination suits like those filed by Allan Bakke and Brian Weber—shifted toward the proportional representation model for employing minorities and women as a necessary way of doing business.[10]

More important, in the long run, than Carter's consolidation of civil rights enforcement agencies was enactment in May 1977 of the Public Works Employment Act, which established the minority contract set-aside program. The set-aside provision was offered as an amendment on the floor of the House on 23 February 1977, by Rep. Parren J. Mitchell (D-Md.), chairman of the Congressional Black Caucus. It required that at least 10% of the $4 billion appropriation for public works contracts should go to minority business enterprises (MBEs). Mitchell's amendment stipulated that "minority group members are citizens of the United States who are Negroes, Spanish-speaking, Orientals, Indians, Eskimos, and Aleuts."[11] At the time, Mitchell's amendment attracted little notice. In retrospect, it was one of the most significant turning points in modern civil rights history. As Justice John Paul Stevens noted in his dissent in *Fullilove v. Klutznick* (1980), the Supreme Court's 6–3 ruling upholding the set-aside program, Congress "for the first time in the Nation's history has created a broad legislative classification for entitlement to benefits based solely on racial characteristics" (*Fullilove* 1980, 549).

Congress's creation of MBE set-asides in 1977 is significant in four ways. First, it was the handiwork not of presidential leadership but instead of policy entrepreneurs in the civil rights "sub-government." They included urban liberals in Congress (mostly Democrats), working with like-minded (mostly minority) officials in civil rights subagencies such as the OCR (HEW), the OFCC (Labor), and especially the OMBE (Commerce). Second, it was premised on a strong historical argument, documented by House subcommittee hearings and reports, that minorities faced formidable structural barriers to entry, even though government procurement had stressed nondiscrimination at least since 1961. Large established firms held great advantages over new entrants in the form of experience in bidding, bonding, sub-contracting, project performance, and reputation. Minorities were often excluded from lending or supplier networks and were unfamiliar with contracting agency protocols. In commercial enterprise generally in 1977, minorities accounted for 16% of the population, but comprised only 3% of the nation's 13 million businesses and generated less than 1% of gross business receipts.

Third, the extensive hearings on minority business problems avoided any discussion of the contract set-aside remedy. Sprung on the House floor, it was passed by both chambers with routine majorities and without any hearings at all. The sudden, low-profile launching of set-asides demonstrates the success of the civil rights coalition in redistributing jobs and contracts to minorities through the complex, obscure machinery of government regulation that few voters understood. During the 1970s, Congress heeded rising public resentment against direct federal intrusions, such as school busing and tax-funded abortion services, that directly affected community institutions (schools, universities, hospitals, clinics). But civil rights regulation, impinging indirectly on citizens and community institutions, was screened from public scrutiny.

Finally, the set-aside model, intended primarily to boost black and Hispanic businesses, proved irresistible to other civil rights constituencies. Following the Burger Court's green light in *Fullilove*, more than 280 American cities, counties, and states, including school and university systems, established MBE set-aside programs. By the 1980s most large American cities had either elected minority (mainly black) mayors or had city governments favoring MBE and often Women Business Enterprise set-aside programs. Similarly the Small Business Administration's 8(a) program, begun administratively in response to the urban riots of the late 1960s and given a statutory basis by Congress in 1978, became a magnet for immigrants seeking federally subsidized business loans and surety bonds. During the 1980s the SBA approved MBE eligibility for individuals on the basis of ancestry from virtually all of Asia and the Pacific islands (LaNoue and Sullivan 1994). These protected groups included not only Japanese and Chinese Americans but also Indonesians, Sri Lankans, Indians, Pakistanis—ethnic communities whose average family income and education in the United States considerably exceeded that of "white" families, and whose recent arrival contradicted the MBE justification as compensatory remedy for historic discrimination.

The Reagan Counteroffensive against Civil Rights Regulation

At the federal level, civil rights regulation, including the MBE set-aside programs, expanded even in the face of a deregulation movement that was pushed by the Carter administration and accelerated under President Reagan. Deregulation was fueled by a rising chorus of complaints from the business community and from state and local governments against excessive Washington control. By the early 1980s, the U.S. Advisory Commission on Intergovernmental Relations, established by Congress in 1959 to monitor the health of federalism, was describing the sprawling regulatory state as administratively fragmented, inflexible, inefficient, inconsistent, intrusive, ineffective, and unaccountable (USACIR 1984, 1993). The revolt against government regulation, spurred by the sluggish economy of the 1970s, made significant gains in the Carter administration with legislative deregulation in air and surface transportation. Deregulation concentrated initially on economic regulation, where agencies such as the Civil Aeronautics Board and the Interstate Commerce Commission protected established airlines and motor carriers in the classic tradition of regulatory capture (Derthick and Quirk 1985). Not surprisingly, the Reagan administration, riding a wave of antigovernment sentiment, broadened the attack on government regulation to include social regulators. The chief targets were environmental and consumer protection agencies whose rules burdened industry with heavy compliance costs, but Reagan conservatives also targeted civil rights regulation (Rabkin 1986).

As a presidential candidate, Ronald Reagan declared, "We must not allow the

noble concept of equal opportunity to be distorted into federal guidelines or quotas which require race, ethnicity, or sex—rather than ability and qualifications—to
be the principal factor in hiring or education" (McDowell 1989, 32). Once elected,
Reagan appointed conservatives to executive departments and the federal bench
and sought deregulation in voting rights law. At the end of his presidency Reagan's
record on civil rights was attacked in two books, one from the left and one from the
right. In *Civil Rights and the Reagan Administration,* Norman Amaker, a civil rights
lawyer and former NAACP staff member, described a reactionary effort to overturn
settled law and policy (Amaker 1988). In *Civil Rights under Reagan,* Robert Detlefsen, an academic political scientist, described an indecisive administration, weakened by internal disagreement in the face of a hostile liberal Congress and a liberal
federal judiciary (Detlefsen 1991). Both writers, however, agreed that Reagan had
largely failed.

Reagan was most successful, especially during his first term when Republicans
controlled the Senate, in appointing conservatives to the federal courts and to senior posts in the regulatory and mission agencies. The messy attempt to counter-
capture the nonregulatory Civil Rights Commission partially backfired, bringing
congressional intervention to blunt conservative ambitions. Reagan was more successful, however, in curbing civil rights regulation at the EEOC and, to a lesser extent, at the OFCCP. At the EEOC, chair Clarence Thomas, reversing Norton's enforcement strategy, shifted from class action litigation against large employers to
conciliation and lawsuits seeking make-whole relief for identified victims of discrimination. At the OFCCP, a similar shift of regulatory strategy doubled the rate
of compliance reviews but sharply reduced the number of back pay awards. In both
agencies the change in regulatory policy was accomplished not through formal notice and comment procedures but through internal policy directives (Belz 1991,
181–207; Blumrosen 1993, 267–74).

More significant, however, were three failed initiatives of the Reagan administration, two of them in Congress and one internal to the administration. First, during 1981–82, the civil rights coalition in Congress overwhelmed Reagan's attempt
to narrow the scope of Justice Department regulation under the Voting Rights Act.
As a result, the voting rights amendments of 1982 extended for twenty-five years
the Justice Department's pre-clearance authority, and declared in Section 2 that the
discriminatory effects of electoral arrangements violated the act irrespective of
their intent. Second, Congress overrode Reagan's veto of the Civil Rights Restoration Act of 1988, which reversed the Supreme Court's ruling in the *Grove City Col-*

lege decision of 1984 (Graham 1998). In that decision the Court held that agency regulations accompanying federal aid to public and private institutions applied only to the specific programs receiving the federal dollars (the college admissions office, a recipient of federal tuition aid), not to the entire institution. In both congressional defeats the Reagan administration faced a bipartisan coalition swollen by Republican defectors, especially in the Senate. Despite increasing conservatism among Republican leaders, party solidarity broke down on voting rights, where challenges to the Leadership Conference invited charges of racism (Graham 1993). And in the *Grove City College* case, Reagan's narrow view of regulatory jurisdiction unified the opposition of virtually all advocacy groups—racial and ethnic minorities, feminists, the physically and mentally disabled, the immigration bar.

Third, the campaign to revise Lyndon Johnson's affirmative action executive order of 1965, led by Assistant Attorney General for Civil Rights William Bradford Reynolds and supported by Attorney General Edwin Meese, died in a quiet collapse in 1986. Leading the cabinet-level opposition to any fundamental change in Executive Order 11246 was Labor Secretary William Brock, whose once lowly regarded department had risen in authority and esteem since 1965 largely on the strength of its status as the government's lead agency in contract compliance. Joining Brock in defending the affirmative action status quo within Reagan's cabinet were the Secretaries of State (George Shultz), Treasury (James Baker), Health and Human Services (Margaret Heckler), Transportation (Elizabeth Dole), and Housing and Urban Development (Samuel Pierce).[12] Their resistance reflected the reluctance of the nation's large employers to plunge into unknown waters (Seligman 1982). Strongly Republican and supporting deregulation elsewhere, big business preferred the known routines of underutilization analysis and minority hiring requirements to the unknown perils of reverse discrimination suits (Fisher 1985, Holmes 1991).

Moreover, the Republican administrations under Reagan and Bush were not consistent in their opposition to race-conscious affirmative action. First, like Nixon and Ford, Reagan and Bush courted African American and Hispanic middle-class constituencies by offering minority set-asides. During the 1980s, both Republican presidents expanded earmarked aid to historically black colleges and increased set-aside requirements in agency budgets to support minority businesses. Second, by the late 1980s Republican strategists had learned the partisan virtues of bipartisan support for strict voting rights enforcement. Republican-led Justice Departments pressed successfully for minority-majority districts whose increasingly bizarre configurations offered three partisan advantages: (1) they modestly increased the election of minority Democrats, (2) they rapidly increased the election of suburban white Republicans, and (3) they sharply reduced the ranks of white Democrats.[13] Finally, President George Bush, formerly chairman of Reagan's task force on regulatory relief, confirmed the permanence of the government's comprehensive regulatory regime in civil rights by signing into law the Americans with Disabilities Act in 1990 and the Civil Rights Act of 1991.

Civil Rights in the Bush Administration: The Americans with Disabilities Act and the Civil Rights Act of 1991

The legislative effort culminating in the Civil Rights Act of 1991, which featured Bush vetoing a "quota bill" in 1990 and Congress reversing a brace of Supreme Court decisions led by *Wards Cove*, received far more attention than did the Americans with Disabilities Act (ADA). Yet both statutes are civil rights laws. When considered together, they teach us more about our regulatory state than we learn from inspecting the 1991 act alone. First, not just the Democrats but both major parties have responded to the pressures of lobbying and electoral politics since the 1960s by supporting civil rights legislation to benefit well-organized constituencies. The ADA, affecting an estimated 43 million Americans, dealt with the largest minority in the country and, according to Edward Berkowitz (1994, 109), "the minority with the greatest propensity to vote Republican." Disability cuts across lines of race, sex, class, and party, and rehabilitation emphasizes Republican virtues—mainstreaming deserving individuals who sought self-improvement, turning them into taxpaying citizens. Although the ADA was a civil rights law, resting on the civil rights section of the Rehabilitation Act of 1973 (which in turn was a clone of Title VI of the mother law of 1964), the ADA appealed to conservative Republicans who otherwise thundered against government regulation.

Second, in passing both civil rights laws, Congress continued the tradition of concentrating on rights and benefits while paying little attention to costs. The ADA contains provisions requiring special employment accommodations, nondiscrimination against physically and mentally disabled workers and students, access to all public and private transportation, and removal of architectural barriers—provisions that carry large potential costs for private and government employers. Yet managers of the legislative hearings on the ADA, relying on assurances from President Bush and Attorney General Richard Thornburgh that the ADA would reduce social security payouts and increase tax revenues and consumer spending, decided not to introduce expert testimony on the cost-saving nature of the ADA. Similarly the Civil Rights Act of 1991, by making available for the first time jury trials and compensatory and punitive damages in cases of intentional sexual and disability discrimination (including the ill-defined area of sexual harassment), provided economic incentives for litigation with potentially vast consequences. By doing so the 1991 act, according to one commentator, "thereby fundamentally changes the legal model underlying federal employment discrimination laws. Whereas previously these laws focused on conciliation and the improvement of employer-employee relations, the Civil Rights Act of 1991 provides monetary remedies that have been traditionally associated with civil trials for tort damages" (Cathcart 1991, 9). Unfunded federal mandates, a staple of civil rights regulation, brought positive economic consequences to beneficiaries and employers alike during the 1960s and 1970s, when nondiscrimination destroyed barriers to the free flow of labor and talent. By the early 1990s the economic costs of civil rights regulation, never a topic of much interest to Congress, remained largely unexplored.

Third, in the Civil Rights Act of 1991 the political branches of government on the eve of a presidential election responded to lobbying from a formidable array of civil rights constituencies (racial and ethnic minorities, women, the disabled), by enacting a law grounded in contradictory interpretations of the statute's meaning. Unable to agree on substantial policy questions, such as a statutory definition of "business necessity," Congress accompanied the act with several conflicting memoranda of interpretation, authored by legislative leaders (Senators John Danforth, Robert Dole, Edward Kennedy, and Frank Murkowski and Representatives Donald Edwards and Henry Hyde), and published in the *Congressional Record*. One of these, Danforth's Interpretive Memorandum of 25 October 1991, is cited in Section 105(b) as having exclusive authority as a source of legislative history and congressional intent concerning the burden of proof in disparate impact cases. As one commentator observed, "This attempt within a statute to establish its own exclusive legislative history may be unprecedented in the United States Code."[14] Congress and the White House could not agree on a statutory meaning but could not resist passing the act anyway, while accompanying it with contradictory official explanations of what the new law meant. The federal courts would decide, by default.

Finally, the civil rights legacy of 1990–91, by intensely engaging a national network of Washington-centered policy elites while drawing little on grassroots support from the general public, reflected a widening gap between the policy preoccupations of Washington and a souring national mood. This alienation is profound and its causes extend far beyond disagreement over civil rights.[15] But unlike the 1960s, when the moral claims of protesting African Americans were unchallengeable, in the 1990s the American public was deeply divided in its passion over injustice.

The Tension between Effectiveness and Legitimacy

As the web of government regulation has thickened since the 1960s, its requirements have grown nettlesome to citizens in areas far removed from civil rights policy. Increasingly, government requires us to do this and not do that about auto emission testing, smoking, trash recycling, AIDS prevention, land use zoning, gun ownership, dog leashing, airport security. We are irritated by safety belt contraptions we must buckle, by aspirin containers we cannot open, by the need to strap our children into backseat harnesses and to buy and wear bicycle and motorcycle helmets. And we grumble about their necessity or wisdom or design. But we do not, as a rule, question the legitimacy of government responsibility for clean air and water or safe transportation and consumer products. My argument is that the standard-setting, rule-making model of social regulation that won acceptance during the 1960s and 1970s to reduce risk and harm from environmental, consumer, and safety hazards failed to win public acceptance when it was used to enforce civil rights policy.

Supporters of civil rights regulation under the disparate impact standard offer powerful arguments that the affirmative action regime developed since 1964 has been proactive, administratively flexible, effective when measured by economic outcomes, increasingly accepted by Congress, and preferred to unknown alternatives by employers. Critics counter that minority preference policies have become permanent regulation with a temporary rationale, exercised by captured agencies in the interest of selected clientele groups, with benefits accruing to advantaged parties, including millions of recent immigrants with no claims to past discrimination. There is enough truth on both sides of this accounting ledger to sustain indefinitely the crippling polarization over civil rights policy that grips our society. Since the beginning of the Nixon administration, the civil rights coalition has won most of the battles over establishing and defending a regulatory regime of affirmative action preferences. Unlike the nondiscrimination principles of 1964, however, and unlike social regulation to protect consumers and the environment, affirmative action regulation has been rejected by a majority of Americans as unfair.

In 1985, Democratic pollster Stanley Greenberg reported growing disaffection in Michigan among white working-class voters over minority job preferences. Subsequent national surveys by Gallup, ABC News–*Washington Post*, the University of Michigan's Institute for Social Research, and NBC News–*Wall Street Journal* showed growing resentment of affirmative action among whites of both sexes.[16] When a 1990 survey by the Times-Mirror Corporation asked a national sample of more than three thousand people whether they agreed that "we should make every possible effort to improve the position of blacks and other minorities, even if it means giving them preferential treatment," white men disagreed by a margin of 81 to 16%. White women, who comprise 40% of the U.S. voting population, and who have benefitted greatly from nondiscrimination policy since the 1960s and relatively little from gender preferences under affirmative action, shared the opinion of white men (Brown 1991). In *The Scar of Race,* Paul Sniderman and Thomas Piazza (1993), using experimental interview techniques to explore the dimensions of white racial prejudice, found that white attitudes toward blacks were diverse and pliable. Although white racial prejudice was still manifest in poll results, in housing patterns, and in school resegregation, Sniderman and Piazza found whites by increasing margins supporting not only policies banning deliberate discrimination based on race, but also government programs to provide income, services, and training to improve the economic and social circumstances of blacks. On issues of school busing for racial balance and affirmative action preferences, however, white Americans of both sexes are massively opposed.

Thus, as the regulatory state has extended its reach and increased its intrusiveness, it has met the stiffest resistance in the one area where the efficiency of modern social regulation has clashed with the core conviction of most Americans that individuals should not be harmed, especially by their government, on the basis of characteristics they were born with (Lipset 1992). There are many reasons for this growing resentment, including stiffening economic competition and the natural human tendency to blame others for our disappointments and shortcomings. But a major factor has been the demoralizing effect over a generation of a political process that pulls into protected-class status new groups with widely differing claims to preference. Since the immigration reforms of 1965, more than 20 million immigrants have come to the United States, three-quarters of them from Latin

America and Asia. By the historical logic of affirmative action, they qualify for remedies originally designed to compensate for centuries of African American slavery and segregation.

Public resentment of minority preference policies, contributing to Republican dominance of the presidency and the federal judiciary for a generation following Lyndon Johnson, produced no major policy reversals until 1989. In that year a slim conservative majority of Republican-appointed Supreme Court justices used the Warren Court's strict scrutiny standard under the Fourteenth Amendment's equal protection clause to sharply narrow state and local set-aside programs in *Richmond v. Croson*. The major benchmarks of resentment in the 1990s are familiar to recent memory: the Los Angeles rioting of 1992, with its worsening tension between blacks, Latinos, and Asians; the success of Proposition 187 and the Republican sweep of Congress in 1994; the Supreme Court's *Adarand* decision in 1995, reversing *Fullilove;* the attack on affirmative action by Governor Pete Wilson and the University of California Regents in 1995; passage of the California Civil Rights Initiative in 1996; and a similar anti–affirmative action initiative by Washington State voters in 1998. Much of this has fit our customary templates of ideology and party: the Republican Right attacking affirmative action, "progressive" Democrats defending it.

But not all. President Clinton as Democratic Party leader has remained consistently low-keyed and circumspect in defending affirmative action programs. More striking has been growing criticism of affirmative action from left of center. Since the publication of William Julius Wilson's *The Truly Disadvantaged* (1987), some liberals have complained that affirmative action programs chiefly benefit advantaged groups and are largely irrelevant to the underclass. Prominent defenders of affirmative action have objected to the way the proliferation of protected groups has increased the program's political vulnerability while diluting benefits originally intended for black Americans. Lawrence Fuchs, for example, who sat on the board of the Mexican American Legal Defense and Education Fund during the 1970s, has argued in the 1990s that affirmative action remedies should be limited to native-born black Americans with a unique history of slavery and segregation (Fuchs 1990, 453–57).[17]

In the 1990s, liberal critics have increasingly complained that minority preference policies and the politics of multiculturalism that have accompanied their spread have crippled the Left. "Identity politics" has fragmented the class-based New Deal coalition, argue writers such as Jonathan Rieder (1985), Jim Sleeper (1990), Thomas and Mary Edsall (1991), and E. J. Dionne, Jr. (1991). The prevailing climate has played into the hands of Republican elites whose policies have polarized the distribution of wealth and income in America to a degree not found in any other industrialized nation. *New Republic* editor Michael Lind, in *The Next American Nation* (1995), has called for replacing affirmative action with a color-blind, gender-neutral, class-conscious program of government enforced equality. Todd Gitlin, veteran of the New Left and the culture wars since the 1960s, blames multiculturalism's "obsession with group difference" for fracturing working-class solidarity and thwarting the emergence of a vital Left (Gitlin 1995, 230–31). It allowed the Right to seize the White House, Gitlin observed, while the Left seized the English department.

Our political system, in summary, is well designed to accelerate the additive, pluralist process of expanding constituencies for civil rights regulation, but badly designed to make it work. Government agencies enforcing affirmative action requirements tend to be captured by the constituencies that benefit from the programs. Programs adopted under a temporary rationale have become permanent. Over time, benefits have accrued more to the advantaged members of protected classes, less to the disadvantaged. As protected groups proliferate, policy rationales grow incoherent. In short, the American system of interest group liberalism is geared to ratchet up, but not down. Defenders of affirmative action who would protect it by confining benefits to African Americans threaten the coalition logic that made the system so powerful among elected political leaders. Even Republican leaders controlling Congress after the 1994 elections, including presidential candidate Bob Dole in 1996, were unwilling to campaign for civil rights deregulation. In the hostile stalemate that hardened during the 1990s, Americans looked to the judicial branch, as they so often have done in the past, to resolve deep disputes that defied resolution through the political process.

Notes

1. In 4,694 reported incidents motivated by racial bias, the hate crimes attributed to the 6,439 offenders were categorized as 46% anti-white, 34.7% anti-black, 8.5% anti-Hispanic, and 4.6% anti-Asian/Pacific Islander. See FBI 1994.

2. See, e.g., Reagan 1987, Eisner 1993. An exception is Wilson 1989, whose definition of regulation and its politics includes civil rights regulation.

3. I am indebted to Brian K. Landsberg, veteran Justice Department lawyer now at the McGeorge School of Law, for critical comments on this essay when it was originally presented at the thirty-year commemorative conference on the Civil Rights Act at the Federal Judicial Center in Washington on 11 November 1994.

4. In 1990 dollars, federal aid to state and local governments increased from $4.7 billion in 1946 to $20.5 billion in 1963. See USACIR 1978.

5. Prior to the New Deal, most federal grants supported agricultural experiment stations and extension, forestry management, vocational education, and rural highway building. Congress as early as 1892 limited working hours for laborers and mechanics employed on public work by the U.S. government and its contractors and subcontractors. In 1931 the Davis-Bacon Act rewarded organized labor by requiring federally assisted contractors to pay the "prevailing wage" in their area. Prior to the 1960s, however, most federal "strings" or controls accompanying grants programs, such as those governing hospital construction and airports and interstate highways, concerned technical requirements.

6. The Powell amendment, which would terminate federal funds to federally assisted programs practicing racial discrimination, was frequently proposed by Harlem congressman Adam Clayton Powell as an amendment to otherwise popular federal aid bills in the House. Customarily opposed by a coalition of southern Democrats and conservative Republicans in Congress, the Powell amendment often drew enough opposition to defeat the bill to which it was attached, yet voting against it in order to save the bill was difficult for representatives from urban districts and industrial states. See Graham 1990, 76–83.

7. Federal efforts to promote job desegregation in the South reach back to Roosevelt's wartime Fair Employment Practices Committee and achieved some success under the leadership of Vice President Lyndon Johnson during the Kennedy administration. See Graham 1990, 47–73.

8. The disparate impact model did not directly mandate minority proportionality in the workforce. Rather, statistical underrepresentation of protected groups (African Americans, Hispanics, Asians and Pacific Islanders, American Indians, etc.), created a *prima facie* case of discrimination and shifted to employers the burden of proving that restrictive job requirements (high school diplomas, employment test scores, technical training and skills, college or advanced degrees) were business necessities. The practical result by the late 1970s was "hiring by the numbers" for most blue-collar and service jobs but not in high-skilled and professional fields (engineering, computer software, university faculty, medicine, law).

9. On Section 504 see Berkowitz 1987.

10. For a critical view of this transformation, see Belz 1991, especially 111–33; for an approving view see Blumrosen 1993, especially 124–33, 161–81.

11. Section 103 (f) (2) of 91 Stat. 116, 42 U.S. 6705 (f); Rep. Mitchell quoted in 123 *Congressional Record*, Pt. 4, 23 February 1977, 5098.

12. See Seligman 1985, McDowell 1989. According to these sources, Meese was supported by the Secretaries of Education (William Bennett), Energy (John S. Herrington), Interior (Donald P. Hodel), and the Director of the OMB (James C. Miller III).

13. See, e.g., Pildes and Niemi 1993. For a differing view see Grofman 1995.

14. Cathcart 1991, 8. On the ADA see also Perritt 1992.

15. According to the University of Michigan's National Election Study data, in 1964 76% of Americans thought that "Washington can be trusted to do what is right" all or most of the time. In 1992 only 24% shared that view (Heatherington 1998).

16. According to Lipset (1992, 60), whites overestimate the extent of reverse discrimination; blacks on the other hand underestimate the extent of black economic progress—"due in part to the reluctance of black leaders to admit it."

17. Nathan Glazer, a leading critic of affirmative action since the 1970s, by the 1990s defended it for blacks and American Indians but not for Asian Americans and Hispanic Americans, (Glazer 1995).

4

Litigation and Lobbying as Complementary Strategies for Civil Rights

Stephen L. Wasby

The Civil Rights Act of 1964 was not only a landmark in terms of the substantive law it enacted; it also marked a major shift in the process by which civil rights policy was made. Litigation had been the primary means by which civil rights victories—including the end of the white primary (*Smith v. Allwright*, 1944), the end of judicial enforcement of racial restrictive covenants (*Shelley v. Kraemer*, 1948), and, most obviously, the invalidation of state-mandated school segregation (*Brown v. Board of Education*, 1954)—had been achieved. However, civil rights organizations had also lobbied the legislative and executive branches, most obviously in order to enact an antilynching statute, when the NAACP resorted to investigations, disclosures, conferences, publicity, negotiation with influential persons in government and business, lobbying, and litigation (Zangrando 1980, 17, 139). Even before the efforts to enact the 1964 law, lobbying efforts had led to the enactment of the Voting Rights Acts of 1957 and 1960. These successes, and particularly passage of the 1964 statute, meant that the focus on litigation now had to be adjusted. Civil rights advocates had used the courts almost exclusively to decide constitutional questions; now their focus shifted. Now they had to use the courts to defend legislative victories from challenge, and as a result they were engaged in debate over the meaning of statutory language.

Civil rights groups not only had to continue their legislative lobbying to protect judicial victories and to add to them; they also had to devote more attention to the executive branch, both to seek enforcement of the new laws and to assure that the regulations promulgated in connection with the statutes—for example, the HEW Desegregation Guidelines (see Orfield 1969; Radin 1977)—were consonant with what the groups thought they had achieved in the legislation itself. The need to lobby executive agencies can be seen in the creation of the Center for National Policy Review. Before the establishment of the CNPR, there had been no private advocacy organization with the capacity to deal with the regulations, cases, and issues arising from the passage of major civil rights statutes. The Center was therefore established to provide research, advocacy, and administrative skills for civil rights groups, including a program for the enforcement of civil rights laws through the lobbying of federal agencies.

That lobbying and litigation were not separate can be seen in the relationship between school desegregation cases and the HEW guidelines. Initially these guidelines provided that a school district under court order to desegregate was deemed in compliance with the guidelines even if the court order demanded less than the guidelines independently required; this led some previously resistant school districts to acquiesce in court orders (from nondemanding judges). The guidelines' requirements in turn became the basis for some desegregation orders that resulted from litigation, with some major school desegregation cases being brought because, to quote one participant, "administrative initiatives ran into a dead end." When the judges of the Fifth Circuit, in turn, demanded more than the guidelines then required, the judges' requirements became the basis for revision of the guidelines.

Civil rights policymaking has thus included both litigation and lobbying, but the relationship between the two has remained problematic and largely unexamined. The academic world has given insufficient attention to possible interrelations between litigation and lobbying, in part because the two are treated in different parts of the curriculum: interest group lobbying is discussed most often as part of the legislative or political process, while litigation is studied as part of the judicial process. To be sure, interest groups' *amicus curiae* activity has long been considered the judicial equivalent of legislative lobbying, but little has been done beyond drawing that parallel.

Controversy over the appropriateness of litigation to achieve civil rights, and particularly over whether it had been used without adequate consideration of alternative means of political mobilization, had been evident even during the formative years of the NAACP's legal efforts, long before the debates that took place in the aftermath of *Brown v. Board of Education*, when that ruling brought few results.

More recently it has been argued that although civil rights cases can lead to political mobilization, lawyers who bring these cases most often focus on mobilization *of* law, not on political mobilization *by* law (see Scheingold 1974). It has been suggested that there is need for a strategy in which litigation is conceptually and practically better integrated with nonjudicial political strategies for achieving social change (Kinoy 1983, 193), or, as Fraga and Ruiz-de-Velasco argue in chapter 10, that groups should pay less attention to a rights-based strategy focused on the courts and more to policy-based arguments in which greater attention is given to the legislature.

In the necessary examination of the relationship, or rather relationships, between litigation and lobbying, one certainly sees considerable parallels between the two; indeed, some say that litigation—particularly litigation for social change—is the same as other types of politics. A striking parallel is that interest groups bring similar criteria to bear in the process of selecting and emphasizing issues on which to work, whether it be for lobbying or for litigation. The key criteria for groups' selection of legislative lobbying targets are "the probability of success," whether and how the area selected "will contribute to the group's internal agenda," and whether a victory will have a "precedential or symbolic value" to the organization (Robyn 1987, 119)—criteria very much like those used by litigating interest groups. That the criteria are similar is reflected in parallel levels of interest and attention to particular topics. In civil rights, just as housing was the last area to receive congressional attention, housing litigation lagged far behind schools and jobs as a major area of civil rights litigation.

Another parallel may be seen in the fact that interest groups feel there are situations in both litigation and lobbying when their participation is required, even if they do not believe that participation is likely to produce substantive results. Sometimes major litigating interest groups—like the NAACP Legal Defense Fund—feel that they must participate as *amicus curiae* in Supreme Court cases because the Court expects them to do so and their absence would raise questions. Likewise, lobbying groups sometimes appear before legislative committees simply out of concern that their absence would be noticeable than their presence and might suggest a lack of commitment to the policy in question.

Also common to both lobbying and litigation is the importance of interorganizational cooperation between civil rights groups. Particularly important in lobbying is the Leadership Conference on Civil Rights, the umbrella lobbying organization of roughly 160 groups representing African Americans, Hispanics, women, senior citizens, the handicapped, religious groups, and labor unions, while in litigation, organizations cooperate in bringing cases and often file *amicus* briefs jointly. The litigators may even cooperate in lobbying efforts, as when the NAACP Legal Defense Fund, NAACP, Mexican American Legal Defense Fund (MALDEF), the Lawyers Committee for Civil Rights under Law, the National Center for Policy Review, and the American Civil Liberties Union (ACLU) participated in revising provisions of the Voting Rights Act when it was renewed in 1982.

Both lobbying and litigation, then, take place in civil rights policymaking, and some organizations engage in both. One must then ask, is the relationship planned or coincidental? Is strategic consideration given to the respective use of the two means of achieving policy goals? Certainly one can argue that the two approaches should be strategically coordinated rather than pursued on separate, if perhaps at times parallel, tracks. In this chapter, I look more closely at the situations and conditions in which one or the other has been used and then at linkages between the two, including their simultaneous and sequential use.

Conditions for Using Litigation or Lobbying

The standard justification for interest groups' litigating to achieve their goals is that, as the "discrete insular minorities" of Justice Stone's famous *Carolene Products* Footnote Four (1938), they are at an unfair disadvantage in the legislative arena. The courts are seen as able to protect the economically and politically weak and to redress harms they have suffered, so people litigate when they are temporarily or permanently disadvantaged in their ability to pursue their goals in the electoral process or within established political institutions or bureaucracies (Cortner 1968, 285).

One specific "political disadvantage" minorities faced in their struggle for civil rights was the long-standing control of congressional committee chairmanships by the southern wing of the Democratic Party, which prevented legislative action or even placing civil rights on the legislative agenda. Even the support of a sympathetic president like Harry Truman was relatively meaningless if it could not affect the distribution of legislative power. When the southern wing's control over Congress weakened, the role of the president became more important, particularly where the president and Congress could work together—as they did briefly but significantly in the field of civil rights in the mid-1960s. The passage of the Civil Rights Act of 1964 also illustrates that White House support is most effective when the executive not only is receptive to the goals being sought but understands the importance and intricacies of successful lobbying.

Here Lyndon Johnson's congressional experience was important in making him appreciate lobbying, so that he was comfortable with Clarence Mitchell and Roy Wilkins of the NAACP and Whitney Young of the Urban League; the alternative of mass demonstrations may also have made the position of these lobbyists more attractive (Ralph 1993). Ronald Reagan, by contrast, lacked legislative experience; combined with his personal hostility to civil rights, that made lobbying a less effective route. During the Reagan years, minorities were once again relegated to "relatively disadvantaged" status.

Unlike the 1950s, when Congress blocked civil rights initiatives while the Supreme Court remained favorable to them, in the 1980s a conservative president, reinforced by a conservative Supreme Court to which he had appointed several justices, was hostile to civil rights but Congress was willing to overrule the Court. It did so in the aptly named Civil Rights Restoration Act, in the 1982 revision of the Voting Rights Act, and, most notably, in the Civil Rights Act of 1991, in which no fewer than seven Supreme Court rulings were overturned (see Wasby 1993; Wasby 1995). In some of these legislative reformulations of earlier statutes, moreover, the new legislation was stronger than the original.

With the initiative on civil rights resting with Congress, lobbying senators and representatives should be an effective strategy. Just as political disadvantage in the "elected branches" may lead an organization to turn to the courts, so disaffection with results obtained in courts may lead them to turn to the other branches, as happened when unsatisfactory rulings in voting rights cases led to greater use of the administrative processes in Section 5 of the Voting Rights Act (Davidson 1994, 206–7). Even in instances when resistance has prevented implementation of favorable court decisions, litigating groups may sometimes turn to the legislative arena, and they may do so even when, as in the aftermath of *Brown*, they have little reason to hope for success (see Filvaroff and Wolfinger, chapter 1 of this volume).

Judges themselves further link lobbying and litigation when, in the course of rejecting policy arguments or rejecting legal arguments as policy-based or require statutory changes, they advise claimants to pursue their goals in Congress or state legislatures. Whether the typical response that "such changes are for the legislature, not the judiciary" amounts to self-abnegation or an open invitation to seek redress elsewhere is, in a sense, immaterial: the judge, the object of litigation, points the litigators toward lobbying the legislature.

The "political disadvantage" notion, while a potentially useful explanation for some litigation, does not sufficiently explain the participation of business associations or ideologically conservative public interest organizations (Epstein 1985) that have considerable strength in other political arenas (Olson 1990). However, it does explain why some interest groups, particularly those seeking civil rights goals, use the courts even when they do not necessarily expect to succeed there: they believe they will be *more* successful than in the legislature or executive branches. When the legislature and executive branches are inaccessible to groups, they have little choice but to litigate. For example, groups combating exclusionary zoning, like those in the Open Suburbs Movement (OSM), had to resort to litigation because they had little popular support and could not hope for results from the political process (Handler 1978, 132). In such circumstances, the courts may seem promising. Even groups that distrust the law go to court not so much because of "strong faith in state institutions but rather because, compared to other alternatives, litigation has some possibilities" (Milner 1992, 321).

In seeking support for civil rights, people can often do better in court than in the other branches of government. With respect to school desegregation, for example, federal appeals courts showed a greater, more persistent commitment to desegregating schools than did executive agencies, and their orders did more to abolish segregation than did school board or federal agency action (Halpern 1980, 36; see also Halpern 1995). More generally, at least starting with the Warren Court, courts have been "the most accessible . . . instrument of government for bringing about the changes in public policy sought by social protest movements" (Neier 1982, 9). Indeed, the Warren Court's civil rights record, including its easing of access to the courts for those wishing to challenge government action, increasingly led groups to turn to the courts, not as a last resort but as the first avenue for redress of their grievances. Indeed, litigation has become the principal, even, in some cases, the exclusive means of redress. When, however, the courts decide against them, especially when this becomes a pattern, interests must go to court, with defensive or responsive litigation, to fend off defeat. Such a response cannot be explained by the notion of political disadvantage, which explains interest groups' initiation of litigation.

Even for civil rights organizations at a disadvantage in other policymaking arenas, political disadvantage does not fully explain the use of litigation. The presence or absence of resources is also relevant; "in the judicial branch legal resources can sometimes offset political resources" (Olson 1990, 858). If an organization has salaried staff attorneys, even if they were originally hired for other purposes, the "start-up costs" of entering litigation are diminished. Staff lawyers' desire to demonstrate their worth is a reinforcing noneconomic pressure to litigate. Professional pride and the sense of being shoved aside by demonstrations and other civil rights activity in the 1960s help explain the NAACP Legal Defense Fund's involvement in a litigation campaign to eliminate the death penalty (Meltsner 1973, 36); likewise, the perception that litigation is like politics may diminish the lawyers' role as expert and eliminate their monopoly over certain issues, perhaps leading them to try harder to demonstrate that litigation is the most effective means to the desired end. When young lawyers with a positive inclination toward litigating join public interest law firms, formed specifically to litigate, that self-selection reinforces the organizations' orientation. And there is also the matter of momentum or inertia. After a group that began as an advocate for the disadvantaged becomes "mainline," the orientation towards litigation may continue, although such a change may also convert an exclusive emphasis on litigation into a dual focus on litigation and legislation.

Perhaps the most important factor explaining contemporary civil rights litigation, one that may bear out the notion of political disadvantage but is analytically separate, is ideology or mindset—not only with respect to policy goals but also in terms of the propriety of litigation itself. One such view of litigation that can foster its use is the "myth of rights"—the idea that rights exist and can be achieved through litigation. This idea, which tends to exaggerate the degree of change lawyers and litigation can accomplish, inclines people to litigate. Sometimes the "myth of rights" interferes with the allocation of resources to techniques of political mobilization that might more effectively achieve rights (see Scheingold 1974). Moreover, a rights-based strategy may result in court decisions that appear to achieve goals but ignore crucial issues that are not easily resolved through litigation. This is the argument of those who complain about overemphasis on "desegregation by the numbers" and who instead advocate greater emphasis on quality education in the ghetto. Not only may court decisions declaring rights not be implemented—a major complaint about the aftermath of *Brown v. Board of Education*—but attempts to secure rights may fail; a rights-based strategy did not save Japanese Americans from being relocated from their homes during World War II (Nakanishi 1994).

Ideology can also work against the use of litigation in achieving policy goals. While we tend to believe that civil rights lawyers are liberal ideologues, that is certainly not so, and conservative ideology can affect the use of litigation just as liberal ideology can. For example, conservative public interest law firms are constrained from litigation by the reluctance of many conservatives to use the courts for judicial activism, even if in aid of conservative goals (Epstein 1985, 144).

Lawyers' ideologies often influence the focus of their concerns—on client, group, or principle; their orientations toward law and toward clients; and their decisions to initiate litigation and to proceed with and appeal cases already initiated (Casper 1972, 74–75; Rathjen 1976; Kay 1980). However, lawyers entering litigation, even in the civil rights arena, do not invariably do so for ideological reasons but may treat litigation "as a practical necessity, not as an ideological opportunity" (Cover 1975, 160). Indeed, some prominent civil rights lawyers have not been social engineers but have been primarily pragmatic in their approach. Lawyers, even if they have an agenda they wish to achieve through appellate litigation, are obviously also aware of pragmatic considerations. The knowledge that bringing a case before a hostile judge might not only end in defeat but also produce a negative precedent tends to steer lawyers toward alternatives, as was the case with voting rights issues (see Davidson and Grofman 1994, 206–7).

Linkages between Litigation and Lobbying

There are many ways to combine litigation and lobbying. The two strategies may be used simultaneously; one may be used in one policy area while the other is used in another; or both may be brought to bear in the same policy area. They may also be pursued sequentially, with the sequence used reflecting changes in emphasis, or one strategy may be used to facilitate the other.

The use of litigation to assist legislative strategies requires strategic planning and is therefore infrequent, although it does happen, as when Common Cause litigated to increase publicity for its legislative agenda on campaign finance reform. Litigation may also be used, both for publicity and, through discovery, to obtain information for use at legislative hearings, as it was by those opposing army surveillance of civilians, although the outcome in *Laird v. Tatum* (1972) was unfavorable. Litigation has been used to produce political activity in the legislative arena on the issue of school desegregation. Since school board action usually results from political bargaining rather than from litigation, the filing of a lawsuit is "essentially another move in the political chess game" (Kirp 1978, 442). Litigation can also be "employed as a 'club' to compel concessions from non-supportive state officials and dominant social groups," even if no court victory results. Although it has been used in pay equity reform activities to obtain changes in private employers' pay scales, litigation was also used to achieve legislative reforms, most notably in the case of legislation benefitting public employees in the state of Washington (Mc-Cann 1994, 138, 154).

Lobbying can likewise be used in aid of litigation goals. The Supreme Court's own linkage of Fourteenth Amendment constitutional jurisprudence with congressional action provides one illustration—what Davidson (1994, 33, 396 n. 45) calls a "synergistic relation" between the two. At times, the Court has allowed Congress to set statutory requirements that go well beyond what it would have interpreted the Thirteenth, Fourteenth, and Fifteenth Amendments to require in the absence of congressional action. At other times, the Court's stance in constitutional rulings has affected—or infected, depending on one's perspective—its statutory interpretation. For example, the rule of *Washington v. Davis* (1976) that in employment discrimination cases intent to discriminate must be proved, was carried over into employment discrimination cases based on Title VII of the 1964 Civil Rights Act, particularly those dealing with seniority systems, and into the Court's interpretation of the Voting Rights Act, where the Court also imposed the same standard under both the Fifth Amendment and Section 2 of the statute.

Another way in which lobbying is a crucial aid to litigation can be seen in the way the Supreme Court relies on current signals from Congress to inform its judgment. Thus, in the years subsequent to a statute's passage, if Congress has taken actions favoring the goals of a statute it passed earlier, the justices are more likely to give that law an expansive reading; conversely, a restrained, narrow reading is more likely if the message from Congress has run counter to the statute's original goals. For example, the Court relied on "Congress's supportive stance during the 1970's" in upholding the Internal Revenue Service's interpretation of tax exemptions for private schools that discriminated on the basis of race in *Bob Jones University v. United States,* (1983) (Eskridge 1991, 401–2). The Court's willingness to accept as constitutional Congress's action to enforce the Fourteenth Amendment, even when that legislation went beyond what the Court would otherwise require, further underscores the need for lobbying instead of primary reliance on litigation.

Interest groups' attention to the Senate's confirmation of federal judges also demonstrates the need for lobbying as a reinforcement of litigation. Here interests attempt to affect the composition of the judiciary so as to produce a more favorable—or at least less hostile—reception for the cases in which they are engaged.

Such action, which dates at least from the NAACP's central involvement in defeating the Supreme Court nomination of Judge John Parker in 1930, was more visible in connection with the defeated Haynsworth and Carswell nominations forty years later (Grossman and Wasby 1971). The NAACP and other groups did not, however, systematically monitor and oppose judicial nominations until the late 1980s, when the Leadership Conference on Civil Rights played an important part in defeating the Supreme Court nomination of Judge Robert Bork. In this instance, and with nominations to the lower courts as well, we see a response to an administration inaccessible to civil rights groups and hostile to civil rights goals while there was a Democratic majority in the Senate (and thus on its Judiciary Committee).

The linkage between lobbying and litigation has affected nonjudicial nominations as well. A notable example is civil rights groups' success in defeating the nomination to deputy attorney general of William Bradford Reynolds, who, as assistant attorney general for civil rights, was the person most responsible for the Justice Department's civil rights litigation activity.

If civil rights groups can make the connection between litigation and lobbying, so can an executive wishing to help or hinder those groups. In an example of the former, during the Carter administration, the EEOC provided contracts to civil rights groups to train lawyers in Title VII law, while the Reagan administration attempted to thwart litigating interest groups by promulgating rules under which recipients of federal funds would have had to separate office space used in connection with lobbying from other facilities. In an effort to limit the groups' resources, the Reagan administration excluded public interest law firms from the federal employees' charitable fund campaign—an action upheld by the Supreme Court (*Cornelius v. NAACP Legal Defense Fund*, 1985).

Litigation and lobbying are related in a more fundamental way when statutes are written specifically so as to facilitate litigation. The 1964 Civil Rights Act, for example, gave the Department of Justice authority to file school desegregation cases (Orfield 1996), and statutes providing for damage awards in addition to injunctions may encourage litigants to seek redress of their grievances in court, just as provisions for attorneys' fees may facilitate their obtaining lawyers to bring their cases. Kagan argues that public interest law firms, in addition to their efforts to achieve favorable policy through the courts, "also lobbied hard and successfully, in legislatures . . . to make adversarial legalism the primary mode of accountability in the expanding regulatory-welfare state." That is, through legislation they created court-oriented mechanisms for enforcing and implementing the substantive policy of the statute. They did this, says Kagan, because of distrust of regulatory power, an antistatist stance one would not find in other western democracies (Kagan 1994, 35).

We see evidence of this process in statutes whose very terms allow individuals to bring suit to enforce the law, such as the "citizen suit" provision of environmental statutes. Given the reluctance of the Supreme Court to allow implied private causes of action when Congress has not itself spoken to the subject, such provisions are very important. Where courts are willing to infer certain matters from the legislative text, and particularly when judges turn to "legislative intent" to resolve statutory ambiguity, the importance of lobbying becomes clear. Here interest groups' use of the legislative record and committee reports to help write a "history" of legislative intent that can later be used to persuade judges is not only important but further illustrates the relationship between legislation and litigation. Interest group staff members may even work with legislators to fashion interpretive language to be included in committee reports and other documents accompanying the legislation itself (see Greenberg 1994, 476).

Litigating organizations' attention to fee-shifting statutes—those which, contrary to the prevailing American Rule that each side bears its own attorney fees, allow the prevailing side to recover attorney fees—further illustrates the close linkage between litigation and lobbying. This interest in attorney fees has not only forced litigating organizations to monitor attorney fee litigation in areas other than civil rights (such as the environment); it also makes it essential to keep an eye on changes in the federal rules, such as efforts to change Rule 68 of the Federal Rules of Civil Procedure to require payment of the other side's fees if a trial produced less than a settlement. Here there is a parallel between lobbying to protect a legislative victory (the rules are equivalent to a statute) and protecting their position from judges who interpret the rules adversely (see, e.g., *Marek v. Chesny,* 1985). The Reagan administration's efforts to limit fee amounts under the Equal Access to Justice Act, which led to the act's expiration for a short time before Congress renewed it, also show the litigation-lobbying connection. The subject of attorney fees illustrates, in addition, how a statute may both facilitate litigation and overcome Supreme Court decisions. The Civil Rights Attorneys Fees Act of 1976 certainly enables such litigation; the effort that led to its passage was largely a response to the Supreme Court's reaffirmation of the American Rule in the *Alyeska Pipeline* case (1975).

Both citizen suit and attorney fee provisions facilitate private enforcement of a statute. The 1964 Civil Rights Act shows that such enforcement can be crucial to the statute's success, even when litigators did not consciously seek a major place for private litigation in the statute itself. One of civil rights groups' complaints about Title VII, the employment discrimination provision, was that the government enforcement mechanism was weak. Efforts to strengthen that mechanism were unsuccessful, but civil rights groups were able to use that deficiency to their own advantage by stepping into the regulatory vacuum and mounting a well-planned litigation campaign. They were thus able to control the development of Title VII law, at least until the courts became more conservative in the mid-1970s.

Litigation intended to produce social change may occur simultaneously with other types of political activity, such as lobbying of legislators and executive branch officials and direct action. A good example is civil rights activity in Mississippi, where the presence of litigation correlated with mobilization of blacks into electoral politics (Stewart and Sheffield 1983, 15–16). The civil rights movement is most often associated with "direct action," but litigation was used consistently to assist mass demonstrations and other direct action. Sometimes it played a secondary rule, as when lawyers worked to release demonstrators from jail quickly; at other times, it was more central. In perhaps the best-known instance of direct action, the Montgomery bus boycott, "the legal system—more accurately federal law and federal judges—played a pivotal, indeed controlling, role in integrating Montgomery's buses" (Glennon 1991, 60).

The NAACP provides the longest simultaneous use of litigation and lobbying to advance the cause of civil rights. In attacking housing discrimination, for example, the organization "challenged suburban zoning in the courts, lobbied for open housing in Washington, and conducted educational efforts" (Danielson 1976, 115). The importance attached by the NAACP to both activities, and their simultaneous use, is evident in the equal respect accorded to Clarence Mitchell, the NAACP's long-time and highly regarded lobbyist, and Thurgood Marshall, its premier litigator, inside the organization as well as outside it.

Other groups have engaged in simultaneous lobbying and litigation. The Lawyers' Committee for Civil Rights Under Law, for example, often "uses a blend of several different techniques to approach an issue or attack a problem," engaging in "monitoring administrative agency actions, participating in agency proceedings, analyzing and drafting legislation, writing research reports, and keeping client groups informed about their legal rights and remedies" (Lawyers Committee 1965, 27–28). This illustrates that groups established with the intent of litigating have added lobbying activities, at least within the constraints imposed by the tax rules concerning lobbying by nonprofit organizations—though Greenberg has noted that lobbying "to ask Congress for what the courts wouldn't or couldn't do" has been facilitated by changes in the tax laws (Greenberg 1994, 474).

If individual groups engage simultaneously in lobbying and litigation, we find that coalitions of interest groups may also engage in the two simultaneously as they pursue different aspects of the civil rights agenda, some in court, some in the legislative arena. This can occur not only at the national level but in state policymaking arenas as well (see Rebell and Block 1982).

An important change is that, as interest groups have increasingly become full-service organizations, those that focused primarily on lobbying now engage in both lobbying *and* litigation. If we do not restrict ourselves to the best-known litigating units and to civil rights—where litigation has played a particularly important role—we find that most Washington, D.C., organizations give a low rank to litigation, at least in terms of the frequency with which they bring lawsuits (see Heinz et al. 1993). This, however, may be a result of comparative advantage: if some groups have become specialists in litigation, other interest groups are freed up to specialize in lobbying.

Organizations that engage simultaneously in litigation and lobbying do not generally use both in the same policy area. The NAACP's use of lobbying with respect to lynching and litigation with respect to voting discrimination and school segregation is typical of the general pattern. More recently, Native Americans have used legislative activity to deal with repatriation of sacred objects while using litigation, through the Native American Rights Fund, on matters such as taxation and tribal jurisdiction. At other times, however, as we see in major areas of civil rights, litigation and lobbying have been brought to bear on the same policy area. When civil rights organizations were lobbying Congress to overturn the Supreme Court's *City of Mobile* (1980) interpretation of Section 2 of the Voting Rights Act, they continued to litigate further cases under the act and, indeed, produced the more moderate ruling in *Rogers v. Lodge* (1982) before Congress revised the statute. This lobbying effort also illustrates the use of litigators as lobbyists, as major voting rights litigators Frank Parker and Armand Derfner became principal lobbyists, with the Lawyers Committee shifting Parker from its Mississippi office to Washington, D.C., where it set up a Voting Rights Project, while Derfner, usually operating from Charleston, S.C., was based at the Joint Center for Political Studies, the think tank focusing on blacks' political activities.

The Civil Rights Act of 1964 contained provisions best enforceable by private litigation—Title VII, for example—and some that were intended to be implemented by administrative enforcement, such as Title VI. Thus the law demanded that interest groups pay attention to both litigation and lobbying of the executive branch. When a statute designates administrative enforcement as the means by which the law's goals are to be achieved, litigation may still be involved—particularly if the agency charged with enforcement fails to carry out its duties for lack of will or absence of pressure from legislative oversight committees where lobbying could play a role. In the absence of effective agency action, interest groups can litigate to bring about enforcement. For such a strategy to be effective, however, the judiciary must be willing to find or imply a private cause of action, which it is often unwilling to do. And if it does not, or if it refuses to grant standing to those seeking enforcement of a statute, neither the administrative nor litigation routes will succeed (see Watson 1994, 130–31). Even when the Supreme Court does provide a cause of action or grant standing, the substantive law may be unavailing. Watson has suggested that difficulties in Title VI litigation stem from Congress's failure to provide a clear definition of prohibited discrimination. Thus, again, litigation requires lobbying—here, as a precursor—to ensure success.

Perhaps more common than simultaneous use of litigation and lobbying on a single issue is their sequential use, which can sometimes be a matter of changing emphasis. Although some organizations are established to engage primarily in one or the other, they may shift emphasis from litigation to lobbying, or vice versa, as circumstances require. At other times, the relationship between lobbying and litigation appears to be reciprocal: groups press for protection through statutes; the protection is forthcoming; groups then seek to implement, and perhaps to expand, that protection. One can see this dynamic at work in many areas of civil rights. Section 504 of the Rehabilitation Act provided some protection for the rights of the handicapped, whose organizations used that statute as a basis for litigation to assure their rights and then significantly expanded those rights legislatively through the enactment of the Americans with Disabilities Act (ADA).

Litigation experiences may stimulate legislative interest, as happened with desegregation in the aftermath *Brown v. Board of Education*, when the decision's promise was not satisfied (Filvaroff and Wolfinger, chapter 1 of this volume). In such situations, litigation nonetheless provides crucial background for legislation. Legislative action is particularly necessary to retrieve rights limited by the courts, as in the case of the Civil Rights Act of 1991 and earlier reversals of Supreme Court decisions, where an organization's commitment to achieve rights through litigation may lead to a corresponding commitment to legislation. When, as in the effort to rewrite Section 2 of the Voting Rights Act to overturn the *City of Mobile* decision, litigators develop expertise useful in the legislative arena, much legislative work is completed before the legislative campaign begins. The interaction between litigation and lobbying may be extended: legislation leads to litigation, with legislation then necessary to overturn negative judicial rulings, and further litigation becomes imperative to defend the "reversal statute" against a still hostile judiciary, as was the case with the Civil Rights Act of 1991 and the Supreme Court's subsequent non-retroactivity ruling.

The reverse—legislative lobbying leading to litigation—may also occur. Interest groups did not stop their activity with the passage of the Civil Rights Act of 1964 but continued in court (Burstein 1995; see also Burstein 1985). If legislative victories are to be preserved, groups must be prepared to go to court to see them sustained. This occurred with the Civil Rights Act's employment discrimination provision and the 1965 Voting Rights Act's provisions as well. Sometimes such litigation, instead of being proactive, is undertaken to fend off attacks on the statute or to combat opponents' efforts to obtain narrow interpretations of the statutory language. If legislation lacks adequate administrative implementation machinery, or if agencies charged with implementation are insufficiently assertive, litigation may be necessary to enforce the statute or even to force the responsible agency to act. The *Adams* litigation is a classic example: although they were ultimately put out of court for lack of standing, civil rights organizations representing blacks, women, and Hispanics sought to force action by the Office of Civil Rights to enforce Title VI of the Civil Rights Act of 1964, and did achieve some interim success.

When we talk about litigation in relation to lobbying, we usually think of lobbying of state legislatures or of Congress. But school boards and city councils are also legislative bodies, and activity directed at them also is lobbying. At the county, municipal, or school district level, litigation and other political activities often follow each other in clear sequences. Most obviously, litigation occurs after political activities appear to fail. At times, the turn from legislation to litigation is quick: the ink may not be dry on certain new statutes, such as those imposing conditions on obtaining abortions, before there is a rush to the courthouse for an injunction. At other times, for example in northern school cases, there was a lengthy sequence of bargaining, position taking, and rights claiming before African American complainants went to federal court (Kirp 1982, 58). This pattern has been described in greater detail as entailing the pressing of claims to school officials; school board appointment of an advisory study committee; release of the committee's report followed by the board's adoption of some of the recommendations; an election to recall school board members who supported desegregation; and election of a new board that revokes the earlier desegregation plan before adopting a more limited one. Only at that point does litigation begin (Combs 1984, 14–15).

Political activity may also follow litigation, when efforts are made to implement court victories in a community. Some school desegregation lawyers found that using litigation to circumvent the political process was a strength—but it was also a defect because, after going to court, the lawyers had to deal with those they had sued, the very people with the authority to put a judge's ruling into practice (Kirp 1978, 491). Once a defendant's liability for discrimination has been established, the most complex part of the case—crafting and agreeing on a remedy—is still ahead. Once consent decrees or judicial orders are obtained, monitoring is necessary to ensure proper implementation; this requires close attention to the political process. Indeed, treating litigation as separate from political efforts may hinder the implementation of judicial victories.

Strategy and Linkages

These parallels, linkages, and sequential and reciprocal uses of litigation and lobbying are important, but they are not always the result of conscious strategic planning within or among organizations. Lobbyists and litigators who join an organization already sharing its goals and then absorb even more of its ethos may engage in parallel activity even if they are not instructed to do so. We need to know whether lobbyists and litigators within an organization work together to develop an overall strategy with each assigned certain tasks, or whether their activities simply take shape over time. Do staff members engage in planning sessions, assigning different tasks? Or do lobbyists and litigators go their separate ways? Do lobbyists and litigators within an organization even communicate with each other on a regular basis?

The tendency is to accept a "rational actor" model and thus to assume that there is conscious planning and careful assignment of tasks, but what we know about civil rights litigation by interest groups suggests the opposite. While planned litigation campaigns do occur and can be successful, the pressure of events often helps determine the areas in which litigating organizations work, and they sometimes find themselves involved in cases that do not meet their criteria for case choice so that much of their work is responsive or reactive. Thus, in the days when Charles Hamilton Houston was the NAACP's general counsel, in spite of talk of strategic planning, the organization in fact would devote its resources to extinguishing brushfires (see Tushnet 1987). If this occurs in the realm of litigation alone, how much more likely it is to occur if an organization, or set of organizations, attempts to coordinate litigation efforts with lobbying activities.

Experience with abortion and the death penalty suggests the difficulty of developing coordinated strategies of litigation and lobbying. When defeat of the right to abortion seemed likely in the Supreme Court, especially after pro-choice forces suffered serious setbacks in the *Webster* decision (1989) and *Planned Parenthood v. Casey* (1992), there were calls for increased legislative efforts. But why were these setbacks necessary before the pro-choice organizations devoted serious attention to legislative lobbying? It would seem that litigation and legislative efforts should have been linked much earlier. However, this expectation fails to account for the natural forces of inertia or momentum. Litigation efforts, once begun, are difficult to halt, particularly with litigating lawyers committed to their mode of acting.

The campaign against capital punishment also illustrates that pursuing legislation as a last-ditch strategy may be no more successful than the litigation that prompted the legislative initiative. When opponents of the death penalty failed to persuade the Supreme Court that capital punishment discriminated against racial minorities, they said they would turn to Congress or state legislatures, but racial fairness provisions were still ultimately excluded from Congress's 1994 crime bill. And even with the Supreme Court's concession in *McClesky v. Kemp* (1987) that race affected the criminal justice process—a "powerful statement" that could serve as a basis for a legislative challenge to the death penalty—the claim that the matter would be pursued in state legislatures was ironic because the drive to abolish capital punishment had begun in the legislature and state legislative support for the death penalty had led opponents to litigate in the first place.

There are, however, instances in which civil rights groups, having lost in court, choose not to press for a different outcome in the legislature, including "many reasons endogenous to the political process" (Eskridge 1991, 363). An organization may accurately foresee legislative failure and decide not to "deplete valuable political capital or credibility" (Eskridge 1991, 363). This was the case in the aftermath of the Supreme Court's Title VII interpretation in *American Tobacco Co. v. Patterson* (1982) that a valid challenge to a seniority system required proof of intentional discrimination in adoption of the system. Here, civil rights groups did not seek an override, "probably because they did not have the votes for an override that benefited only African American workers and/or because they did not want to expend political capital to seek relief for an issue that pitted their interests against those of labor unions, which were often political allies in civil rights battles in Congress" (Eskridge 1991, 363).

Legislative lobbying and litigation ought to be considered together. Certainly those who study policymaking processes ought to treat them systematically as interdependent instead of as separate, independent processes. More important, those seeking to embed their preferences in the law need to consider using both, either in tandem or in sequence, as appropriate, to faciliate achieving their goals. Although organizational structures and maintenance needs may limit the extent to which litigation and lobbying can be joined in a coherent, strategically planned package, the ways each can assist the other should be given greater focus than has often been the case. The goal, after all, is to attain desired policy. Although the route taken—whether through the courts or the other branches of government— has implications for the practice of democracy, for those seeking desired policy outcomes, how litigation and legislation are ranked should not matter.

Note

Some of the ideas presented here are drawn from Wasby 1993 and Wasby 1995, which this chapter is intended to extend. The author also wishes to thank Bernie Grofman for stimulus and suggestions.

5

A Personal Reflection on Civil Rights Enforcement and the Civil Rights Agenda

Jack Greenberg

I became aware early on of the legitimate demands of other groups for recognition of their civil rights. The very first case I worked on as a law student was for the Japanese American Citizens League. Japanese Americans who had renounced their citizenship while in relocation centers sued to have it restored on the ground that it had been signed away under duress. I can also happily claim to be among the two or three founders of the Mexican American Legal Defense Fund. The situation of black Americans, however, is unique, persistent and of such long duration that it calls for special attention. I make this point because resistance to the aspirations of black people has not usually been stated in terms that blacks should be treated unequally but as a principle that denies the existence of discrimination. We find this denial in the Constitution, which perpetuated slavery, permitted the importation of slaves for years, and required the return of fugitive slaves who had escaped to the North, without ever referring to the fact that they were slaves or blacks. The Constitution refers only to a "person held to service or labor." At the same time, the Constitution designated slaves as part of the population of the South for the purpose of determining the apportionment of representatives in Congress. This, of course, gave the South more political power but indicated that each black was only three-fifths of a man—a formulation of denial or obfuscation that has persisted throughout the entire history of race in this country.

Plessy was a decision that nominally proclaimed equality and separation but, nevertheless, equality. Cases in which blacks were excluded from the Democratic

Party were rationalized as the prerogative of a private association to determine its membership. Enforcement of restrictive covenants that kept blacks out of certain neighborhoods and established residential apartheid was defended as mere enforcement of property rights. When I came to the Legal Defense Fund in 1949, cases against racial discrimination were rarely if ever defended on the ground that the behavior was justifiable but that the plaintiff had not exhausted his remedies, that the federal court should abstain while the state court decided matters, that the case should have been brought before a three-judge court if it had been brought before a one-judge court, or filed in a one-judge court if it had been heard by a three-judge court.

Only immediately after *Brown* was this discrimination for a time expressly racist. The most effective mode of discrimination and maintaining segregation after *Brown* became the pupil assignment laws. Every southern state passed one of these laws. They were racially neutral in their terms. They just put all sorts if impenetrable administrative obstacles in the way of obtaining a nonsegregated equation.

Then changes began occurring in the country. Blacks began moving in larger numbers from the South to the North. Whites in the North began moving to the suburbs and blacks began taking over the center cities. The possibility of integrating schools changed because most of the black population was moving to parts of the country where school desegregation doctrine, which required state law or some sort of state action, did not apply. In the early 1970s a Supreme Court decision changed that somewhat. School board rules or other kinds of official acts that had brought about segregation became amenable to redress in the courts. But during the long period when the North was immune from the equal protection clause, racial patterns became more deeply embedded. At the same time, enforcement began to shift from the private sphere to administrative agencies and the Department of Justice. That was good in the sense that it enlisted the massive federal bureaucracy to integrate and equalize schools. It was not so good, but inevitable and unavoidable, that once government came into the picture, issues became greatly politicized. The bureaucracy, in large part, did what the executive branch or the Congress might consider politically appropriate.

The Nixon administration tried to shut down school desegregation—the Supreme Court overruled it in *Alexander v. Holmes County Board of Education*. But civil rights lawyers didn't always succeed before the Supreme Court in situations of that sort. Moreover, the litigation, which was being brought by private lawyers, could not possibly cover the entire county. Litigation was becoming vastly more complex and expensive.

Then new groups inspired by the success of the NAACP Legal Defense Fund began to emerge, groups advocating the rights of women, Chicanos, Asians, Native Americans, the disabled, gays and lesbians, and so forth. Then came public interest groups not at all connected with racial, ethnic, or gender issues, but with environmental, consumer protection, health and safety issues.

Soon there prevailed a sort of public interest fatigue that helped to submerge the centrality of the issue of discrimination against blacks. The economic situation of minority groups also began to emerge more and more as a factor in keeping minorities in a disadvantaged position. At first the courts began to take little nibbles at this, but they quickly bowed out. I had a case in the Fifth Circuit, *Hawkins v. Town of Shaw*, which required equalization in black and white sections of town. But as the expensive implications of that case sank in and without even having heard the case, the Supreme Court overruled it in another case, *Washington v. Davis*. It held that we had not demonstrated intent to discriminate. *Hawkins v. Town of Shaw* went nowhere. There was no constitutional mandate to equalize unless we could prove intent, which was, of course, impossible.

In another case, *Dandridge v. Williams*, the Court put a cap on welfare benefits. *Rodriguez v. San Antonio Independent School District* held that education was not a fundamental right. Courts, at least the federal courts, could not require equalization of funding among school districts. That effort to equalize funding later succeeded in some state supreme courts, but again the link to the political process became clear. The Supreme Court of New Jersey, in *Abbott v. Burke*, held that the state had to equalize education, but nothing much happened. Then New Jersey had a governor, James Florio, who took that mandate seriously and raised taxes in part to equalize schools, with the result that the electorate ran him out of town. A new governor was elected who promised to reduce taxes, which would make it impossible or exceedingly difficult to equalize school funding. Some shift towards equalization has, however, been happening lately.

The civil rights revolution, as it has been successfully fought in the courts, has been an inspiration to oppressed people all over the world. Civil rights law has had many great successes but also some failures. The successes are the creation of a black middle class, which was nonexistent when all of this began. Gary Orfield and others have shown that a very small number of blacks graduated from high school before the victories of the civil rights movement. Now blacks graduate at the same rate as whites and the number of blacks in college is way up, though still not proportionally as high as the number of whites. When I went to Columbia College there were two blacks in my class—one American, one Haitian. Now 10% of the class is black. When I went to Columbia Law School, there were no American blacks in my class; now 10% of the law school is black. Columbia is not unique. It is typical of law schools and colleges. There are forty black congressmen, every major American city has or has at one time had a black mayor, blacks can be found in the cabinet and in the top ranks of other government agencies, both military and civilian.

But we have to temper these achievements with the reminder that even the successful black middle class remains victimized. I have a friend, a black law professor, who while shopping in Bloomingdale's was snatched by a security guard, handcuffed, dragged off into a back room, and accused of shoplifting. When he produced the receipt for the item he was accused of stealing, the store apologized and offered to take him and his wife out to dinner by way of recompense. When he declined, the store offered him $5,000, which he accepted. I told him he could have held out for $25,000, but he said he did not want the hassle. Not many months later, I read a story in the *New York Times* of a black federal judge from New Jersey to whom the same thing happened—also in Bloomingdale's.

Twenty-five percent of young black males are either in prison or on probation or parole. Five percent of young black males are victims of homicide, a fact that I find hard to imagine. That means one out of twenty. One wonders what can be done about it. One of the things that might offer hope to young blacks in the ghetto, those who are in single-family households ravaged by drugs and guns, is that other blacks from their neighborhoods have succeeded and moved into the middle class. They have succeeded, to a considerable extent, as a result of affirmative action. But affirmative action is under siege today. Nevertheless, in a generation or two, I think, those who have left are going to be more widely separated from those who remain in the ghetto. They are going to be marrying among themselves and marrying others who are not disadvantaged, and I wonder whether any influence at all is going to be able to affect those left behind. We need more of the fortunate majority to act on behalf of disadvantaged minorities.

III

Evaluating the Effects of the Civil Rights Act of 1964

6

The 1964 Civil Rights Act and American Education

Gary Orfield

The 1964 Civil Rights Act has probably had more impact on American education than any of the federal education laws of the twentieth century, yet it is rarely considered in discussions of education policy today and its critical role in building major civil rights responsibilities into the operations of American schools is rarely noted. This neglect may stem from the dramatic turn American politics took, after 1968, away from issues of race and toward a public debate that assumed that the problems of racial discrimination were either solved, unsolvable, or not very important. After the Reagan administration's 1983 *A Nation at Risk* report (National Commission on Excellence in Education 1983) turned attention to issues of standards, testing, and international competition and away from equity issues, very little attention was paid to civil rights enforcement policy.

The first great educational accomplishment of the 1964 law was a historic remaking of the schools of the South that was accomplished in just five years of active enforcement. The southern system of educational apartheid was declared unconstitutional by the Supreme Court in 1954, but the resistance of the South had been so intense that enforcement by private lawsuit could barely make a dent. Segregation remained virtually intact until the Civil Rights Act became law. Enforcement of the act broke the back of segregation in southern schools after many generations of legally imposed apartheid. When President Johnson signed the 1964 law, 98% of southern black students were still in all-black schools and almost 100% of white students were in virtually all-white schools (Sarratt 1966, 360–61).

Enforcement of the new law by the Johnson administration and the Warren

Court turned a region in which school segregation was almost total into the nation's most integrated within five years of the issuance of the first desegregation guidelines. The effect lasted for decades. The law's impact on racial practices in southern schools was far more powerful than that of the Civil War, Reconstruction, or any other political change in U.S. history. The law led to the rapid dismantling of one of the most fundamental and enduring features of American public education, the racial system in the schools of seventeen states. It turned what had always been the most backward region in local racial practices into an example for the rest of the nation (Orfield 1969).

The law transformed the role of the federal government with respect to discrimination, powerfully affected the desegregation of southern schools, brought federal education officials and the U.S. Justice Department into the center of making of civil rights policy, created the groundwork for a legal framework for dealing with Hispanic educational inequality, and set the model of federal civil rights enforcement in education. The model relied on regulations, litigation, and the cutting off of federal aid funds. When actively used, these procedures produced some of the largest changes in education in this century. (This model was later extended to the rights of girls and the handicapped through additional legislation, further transforming the schools.)

The 1964 Civil Rights Act was the most bitterly fought and most consequential legislative victory ever achieved by the civil rights movement. The more widely hailed Voting Rights Act shot through Congress in the space of weeks, but the 1964 law produced a deadlock that took more than a year to resolve and tied up the U.S. Senate in a massive filibuster by the South for thirteen weeks, as the nation set aside all other business to resolve questions pending since the Civil War and to engage the elected branches of government and the nation's bureaucracies seriously in the task of civil rights enforcement for the first time since Reconstruction ended in the 1870s (Whalen and Whalen 1985).

Background

The southern response to the *Brown* decision and to the demands of a great social movement for civil rights showed that the South would not change voluntarily; southern leaders committed huge resources to the preservation of segregation. Noncompliance with the law of the land was virtually universal in southern communities and endless legal battles were needed to initiate the slightest desegregation. The courts faced grave resistance to the transfer of even a handful of black children to white schools. As the issues expanded to include desegregation of public accommodations, the right to protest, voting rights, and job discrimination, it was clear that the courts were seriously inadequate to cope with the many problems of basic social restructuring in thousands of communities and school districts.

During the 1950s and early 1960s, civil rights organizations and their supporters developed a wide range of proposals for assisting the courts in the enforcement of *Brown*. The only one to be enacted before 1964 was the creation of the U.S. Civil Rights Commission in 1957 to conduct nonpartisan studies and hearings and make recommendations on civil rights. The commission's work showed the need for stronger enforcement (U.S. Commission on Civil Rights 1963).

Two important proposals received serious congressional attention but could not be enacted in the fifties—a proposal giving the attorney general power to enter civil rights litigation on behalf of the U.S. government, and a proposal cutting off federal aid funds from recipients who discriminated in defiance of constitutional requirements. The first idea, part of the Eisenhower civil rights bill, was eventually undermined by the president's lack of support and was defeated in 1957 after the president expressed skepticism about his administration's bill (Anderson 1964; Brownell 1993). Efforts by the Kennedy Justice Department to intervene in cases without such statutory authority were rebuffed by the courts (Sarratt 1966, 69–71).

The second proposal was a more radical one. After the *Brown* decision, the NAACP urged that federal aid to education be given only to systems complying with the constitutional requirements (Watson 1990, 298–300). The fear that such a requirement could be imposed had been one of the important southern arguments against federal aid to education ever since the Civil War. When black Congressman Adam Clayton Powell (D-N.Y.) implemented an NAACP proposal and proposed an amendment embodying this principle in the 1950s, even congressional liberals tended to oppose it because it made enactment of a significant aid program virtually impossible given the intensity of southern opposition. Several bills were hurt by the amendment and President Kennedy actually convinced Powell not to offer it in the early 1960s (Orfield 1969, 24–28).

Both proposals became parts of the omnibus civil rights bill that President Kennedy sent to Congress in the midst of a great surge of public concern created by Martin Luther King's Birmingham demonstrations. Kennedy proposed that federal agencies be authorized, but not required, to cut off aid to discriminatory local agencies (Parmet 1984, 264–73).

When the Civil Rights Act came out of Congress after Kennedy's assassination, it was stronger than the bill Kennedy had submitted because of the determination of supporters in the House of Representatives and the insistence of Lyndon Johnson on a comprehensive bill after President Kennedy's death. The law addressed educational discrimination from many directions:

1. It provided Justice Department authority to file civil rights litigation, giving the Civil Rights Division great influence in shaping the agenda of civil rights law and greatly increasing the resources available to initiate civil rights cases.

2. It established mandatory fund cutoffs, ending federal aid to discriminatory school districts through administrative processes (Title VI). This provision transformed the administrative agencies dispensing federal aid from passive bystanders to active enforcers of nondiscrimination requirements, putting them in a difficult relationship with their state and local clients.

3. It authorized research and monitoring, including a national study and report to Congress on school desegregation, a four-year extension of the Civil Rights Commission, and a broadening of the commission's functions (Titles IV and V).

4. It funded technical assistance and teacher training to ease the transition to desegregated schools (Title IV).

5. It supported community conciliation and help in dealing with racial tensions through establishment of Community Relations Service (Title X).

6. It prohibited job discrimination at the federal level (Title VII), which did not originally apply to teachers but would after the law was strengthened in 1972.

The law took a broad view of the problems of deep racial change, combining both administrative and judicial enforcement with the search for better understanding of the issues and practical help in dealing with the educational and community relations dimensions of a major change in local race relations. When all these tools were used together, the impact was enormous.

Though it was vigorously enforced for only a few years and staunchly attacked for many more as the civil rights reaction took sway in Washington, the influence of the 1964 law triggered deep and long-lasting transformations and extended far beyond the school desegregation issue the law was initially designed to address. It made the U.S. Justice Department a powerful force in initiating civil rights changes in education. It led to decades of battle over the desegregation and equalization of higher education in the South, a battle still underway. It provided the legal basis for the Supreme Court's 1974 *Lau v. Nichols* decision upholding federal requirements for bilingual education for non-English-speaking children. It provided the model for the creation of federal rights in American schools against sex discrimination and for the right to education by the handicapped. It provided the lever to force change in the desegregation of school faculties and for equity within schools in a good many districts. It led to the collection and publication of data on issues of race and national origin that had never been available in much of the United States, enabling communities to know what was happening and to demand change.

The Act and the Brown Decision

Though we celebrate the *Brown* decision as one of the greatest moments of American legal history, we usually ignore the fact that it failed to change the schools significantly until the 1964 law was enforced. American public life is dominated by lawyers, and lawyers devote much more time to the statement of principles than to analysis of actual change. Each year we celebrate the words of Chief Justice Earl Warren in *Brown* rather than the titles of the 1964 act. Yet, had the 1964 Civil Rights Act not been enacted and enforced in the South, the 1954 *Brown* decision might well have gone down in history as a well-meaning but failed effort to change a fundamental social practice in a democratic society.

Enactment of the law would have been inconceivable without the *Brown* decision and the civil rights movement it stimulated, but it was the operation of that law, not the courts, that made the southern schools the nation's most integrated within a few years. In fact, the Supreme Court did not create a set of principles actually capable of achieving desegregated schools until half a decade after the enactment and enforcement of the Civil Rights Act was transforming southern schools. (The Court would, however, become the dominant force in the drive for urban desegregation in the 1970s after the national administration changed directions.)

The law is a remarkable and sweeping document that has changed many phases of American education, reaching far beyond the question of desegregating classrooms. Its enforcement and nonenforcement have been very important political and legal issues throughout the past three decades. When there has been vigorous enforcement, there have been major, measurable changes. When the law has not been enforced or when authority granted by the law has been used by civil rights agencies to fight civil rights, the momentum of change has been slowed and even reversed.

The 1964 Civil Rights Act changed the balance of forces battling over civil rights

by throwing into the balance the legal, administrative, financial, and political resources of the federal government. It put the principles of the *Brown* decision into
the heart of statutory law and administrative regulations. Its language was so
broad and far-reaching that it was to give rise to major streams of policy development and legal change on issues that could scarcely be imagined at the time of its
enactment.

Although some of the consequences of the act were almost "constitutional" in
their reach and importance, the law was neither self-enforcing nor beyond amendment. A great deal of energy was to be invested in battles over legislative, appropriations, and regulatory changes intended to reverse or constrain efforts to enforce
provisions of the 1964 law. The first major attacks began only two years after President Johnson signed the act (Orfield 1975). Those battles had very important consequences.

Counterattack

The various tools included in the Civil Rights Act were considered radical by
many, even at the height of the civil rights movement. Using them to force racial
change produced great tension within the educational system, especially in the relationships between federal, state, and local agencies. After the 1960s the country
became extremely polarized by race, as election results over the next two decades
show clearly. When conservatives returned to power in the Nixon, Ford, Reagan,
and Bush administrations in a racially polarized nation, they promised to restore
local control and new directives went out from the White House.

Democratic candidates for president never received a majority of the white vote
from 1968 to 1996, while they typically received an incredible nine-tenths of the
African American vote. Enforcement of civil rights statutes was sharply curtailed
by administration appointees, and judges appointed to the federal courts were
chosen for their limited view of the role of the courts in enforcing social change.
The Nixon administration virtually stopped administrative enforcement of the
1964 Civil Rights Act within American schools, but the federal courts ordered its
resumption and struggled for fifteen years to enforce a succession of orders. Nixon
fired Leon Panetta, the official enforcing the school desegregation standards, and
denounced mandatory school desegregation; he privately often urged his chief of
staff, H. R. Haldeman, to stir up the busing issue for political purposes (Panetta
and Gall, 1971; Haldeman 1994, 126). During the mid-1970s, Congress adopted the

Eagleton-Biden amendment prohibiting administrative enforcement of busing as a remedy for school desegregation under the act, but no other legislative reductions in enforcement authority were enacted. During the Reagan administration, a much more conservative Supreme Court radically reduced the reach of the act in the *Grove City College* decision of 1984, making key parts of the law virtually unenforceable, much as the Supreme Court had done after Reconstruction. Congress, however, reinstated and perhaps even broadened its power in the Civil Rights Restoration Act, passed over presidential veto (Orfield 1995, 171–72).

The Act and the Conservative Reaction

Throughout the 1980s, the Justice Department and the Education Department's Office for Civil Rights were led by deeply committed conservatives opposed to many of the changes in the schools. Clarence Thomas, who later would become an intensely conservative Supreme Court justice, was President Reagan's appointee to head the Office for Civil Rights. Secretaries of Education, particularly in the Reagan administration, were deeply critical of a number of policies deriving from enforcement of the Civil Rights Act. William Bradford Reynolds, Reagan's assistant attorney general for civil rights, frequently used the power of the Justice Department to intervene in civil rights cases to oppose civil rights groups and argue for far more limited remedies (Amaker 1988). Nonetheless, much of the authority available to Education and Justice under the act remained intact during the Clinton administration, when leadership was turned over to officials previously connected with civil rights.

Before the Civil Rights Act, the federal government ever since the Civil War had implicitly accepted southern racial practices because of the vast power of the South and its allies in Congress. The seventeen states with apartheid laws had thirty-four votes in the Senate, more than enough to allow them to filibuster to death any civil rights proposals. One basic reason why the federal government was so late, compared to other advanced industrial nations, in formulating any national education policy, was the southern fear that federal power in education would lead to a challenge of the apartheid system, a fear that was greatly intensified after the *Brown* decision made mandated segregation unconstitutional.

The Civil Rights Act was designed to do exactly what the South had feared, engaging the administrative and financial power of the federal government, together with its educational expertise, in a social revolution. In hundreds of southern communities, school boards faced the choice between keeping their federal aid and complying with the law or defying the courts and federal school officials, losing their federal aid, and still facing the possibility of a law suit by Justice Department civil rights lawyers—who almost never lost. The law gave federal officials a degree of responsibility and a range of powers beyond the imagination of civil rights groups before the 1960s and the great demonstrations led by Martin Luther King, Jr. Since it was not self-enforcing, however, change depended on the willingness of the national administration to use its authority in spite of obvious political costs. (After the enactment of the major civil rights laws, the "solid" Democratic South ceased to exist and the Democratic nominee for president in 1968 carried only one southern state; Democratic candidates in the next three decades often carried a third or less of the southern white vote, as shown in table 6.1.)

The significance of the law was greatly enhanced by major developments in the year after its enactment. Lyndon Johnson's landslide election in 1964, with the Senate's most prominent civil rights supporter, Hubert Humphrey, becoming vice president, seemed to indicate that Republicans who had opposed the 1964 act had made a serious mistake. The election of the most liberal Congress since World War II made possible the enactment of a huge federal aid to education bill in 1965 that created unprecedented financial leverage over southern school districts and a powerful incentive for change (Fishel 1973; Jeffrey 1978). Southern leaders, whose civil rights filibuster had been beaten in the Senate for the first time since the Civil War and who faced a tidal wave of demands for civil rights laws, recognized that the status quo could not be maintained. The 1965 Voting Rights Act began to create a real constituency for civil rights, even in the South, through great expansion of the African American electorate. The necessary conditions for a social revolution were

Table 6.1 Percentage Voting Democratic, by Race, 1972–1996

Year	1972	1976	1980	1984	1988	1992	1996
Total No. Polled	36	50	41	40	45	43	49
Latinos	63	76	59	62	69	61	72
Asians						31	43
Blacks	82	83	85	90	86	83	84
White	31	47	36	35	40	39	43
White men	31	47	32	32	36	37	38
White women	31	46	39	38	43	41	48
Southern whites	23	47	35	28	32	34	36
Southern blacks	74	81	89	89	86	83	87

Sources: New York Times, 10 Nov. 1996, p. 28, reporting exit survey data from 1996 Voter News Service survey of 16,600 voters; 1992 Voter Research and Surveys; 1980–1988 surveys by New York Times and CBS News; 1972 and 1976 surveys by CBS News.

Table 6.2 Group's Percentage Democratic Vote Compared to National Total

Year	1972	1976	1980	1984	1988	1992	1996
Total No. Polled	36	50	41	40	45	43	49
Latinos	+27	+26	+18	+22	+24	+18	+23
Asians			−12	−6			
Blacks	+46	+33	+44	+50	+41	+40	+35
Whites	−5	−3	−5	−5	−5	−4	−6
White men	−5	−3	−9	−8	−9	−6	−11
White women	−5	−4	−2	−2	−2	−2	−1
Southern whites	−13	−3	−6	−12	−13	−9	−13
Southern blacks	+38	+31	+48	+49	+41	+40	+38
Highest income		−14	−15	−10	−13	−9	−11
Lowest income		+8	+8	+15	+17	+15	+10

Sources: *New York Times,* 10 Nov. 1996, p. 28, reporting exit survey data from 1996 Voter News Service survey of 16,600 voters; 1992 Voter Research and Surveys; 1980–1988 surveys by *New York Times* and CBS News; 1972 and 1976 surveys by CBS News.

in place, at least for a few years (Johnson 1971, 159–66; Fishel 1973; *Southern Education Report* September–October 1965).

The period of serious enforcement needed to produce large changes was surprisingly short. Desegregation enforcement became intense in 1965 and ended in some critical respects shortly after the 1968 election. After the 1966 midterm conservative revival in Congress and the race riots of the mid-1960s, public and congressional support for more civil rights enforcement rapidly declined, as civil rights went from the top to the bottom of the Gallup poll's ranking of important issues (Orfield 1988).

Nonetheless, a fundamental change in southern schools took place during that period, and it was built into the legal system and maintained through a period of conservative political domination from 1968 through the 1980s by the legal framework that grew out of the enforcement of the act and the Justice Department litigation begun in the Johnson era. Even fierce opposition by the Reagan and Bush administrations, which remade both the enforcement agencies and the federal courts, did not begin to significantly erode southern desegregation until the end of the 1980s, when conservative control of the courts was consolidated.

The Problems of Measurement

The Civil Rights Act has had powerful and sometimes very rapid effects not only on desegregation but on a number of other aspects of American education. In some cases the changes were so rapid and so directly related to policies created in enforcing the law that the effect is unambiguous. In others, a variety of simultaneous changes makes the relationships more difficult to analyze. Complete and reliable national and local data are available on some issues during some periods; in other cases much less complete statistics are on the record. As is often true of large and unexpected social changes, relatively little good social science field research is available on many of the changes, so it is necessary to rely heavily on those aspects that were measured and to discuss secondary effects on the basis of an understanding of processes derived from later research.

Many types of data that we now use routinely to measure racial situations and changes did not even exist before the 1964 Civil Rights Act. They are, in fact, products of the act. There was very little national, state, or local data on race and education before the Civil Rights Act. Few school districts reported racial composition of schools (or any other data) to state or federal governments. Limited data on segregation in the South were collected by a private association of southern journalists, the Race Relations Reporting Service (Sarratt 1966). It was not until 1967 that the government collected basic racial data on the country's schools; without such data it was impossible to enforce the provisions of the act. Without this information, we would not know what has happened in racial terms in our schools and colleges. Though the gathering of information was severely curtailed, particularly in the 1980s, this framework of racial information has survived and is the basis on which policy and analysis can be made.

The major changes directly related to policies developed and implemented under the 1964 Civil Rights Act include:

1. Southern and border state school desegregation;
2. Teacher desegregation;
3. Bilingual education;
4. College equalization and desegregation in the South;
5. Action against some types of in-school discrimination.

The direct effects are relatively simple to demonstrate by simple statistics, but there are also a number of indirect effects that are probably related to the Civil Rights Act. It will not be possible to discuss these complex questions here, but school desegregation plans, for instance, can have effects on changing the educational gap between white and minority students, on residential choice and the stability of integrated neighborhoods, on college careers of students, on adult attitudes toward students experiencing integrated schools, and so on (Hawley and Associates 1983). Much of the experience with educational choice and magnet schools grew directly out of the school desegregation enforcement process. College desegregation may also have a strong impact (Thomas et al. 1981). There are also very strong assertions and complex research findings on the impact of bilingual education, on the mis-assignment of minority students to classes for the handicapped, on unequal expulsion practices, and on other issues subject to regulation under the Civil Rights Act (Meier and Stewart 1991; Meier, Stewart, and England 1989; Arias and Casanova 1993). The bilingual requirements, which the Supreme Court upheld under Title VI in *Lau v. Nichols,* have also been the cause for the recruitment of Latino and Asian teachers in many communities.

In other words, there are many long-term economic and social consequences of educational policies that may ultimately derive from the implementation of the 1964 law. The experiences growing out of Title IV technical assistance for desegregation, and the Community Relations Service conflict resolution provisions, contributed to the policies on human relations training for staff and multiethnic curricula that became widespread in the nation under the 1972 Emergency School Aid Act, which produced evidence of significant educational and race relations benefits before it was repealed in 1981 in the first Reagan budget.

Future action under Title VI could well reach other major issues, such as the possibility of regulating grouping practices (tracking) with negative racial consequences. Discriminatory testing could be another subject for enforcement action. There are surely others that will come under scrutiny as problems in American society and its schools continue to evolve.

In a broader sense, the 1964 act's model of conditioning federal aid on compliance with civil rights influenced the development of other rights policies, especially those prohibiting discrimination against girls and the handicapped. In fact, the racial, gender, and disability groups all joined hands to defend the law in the 1980s when the Supreme Court moved to limit its reach. Certainly the enactment of the 1964 law reached very deeply into the operations of many thousands of schools in the United States, created new educational rights and opportunities for millions of students, and profoundly changed the nature of American education.

School Desegregation

A fundamental educational goal of the 1964 Civil Rights Act was the enforcement of constitutional requirements for desegregation. This was the educational issue that was discussed in the congressional debate and that dominated the administrative enforcement process until the Nixon administration. It was also the goal that provoked the most intense attacks. Most of the research on enforcement of the 1964 law deals with this issue.

When the civil rights bill went to Congress in 1963, the schools of the South were extremely segregated and the issue of school segregation outside the South had barely been explored. In the eleven states of the Old Confederacy, less than 1% of black students were in desegregated schools. The next year, as Congress debated the law, only 1.2% of blacks in the South were outside all-black schools, and most of this integration was in four states that had greater than 1% integration. Seven states had less than 1% integration. There were twenty-one black students in the entire state of Alabama in desegregated schools, nine students in South Carolina, and not a single student in Mississippi (U.S. Commission on Civil Rights 1964, 291). Desegregation was more significant but still limited in the six non-southern states and Washington, D.C., that had practiced *de jure* school segregation until 1954 (Delaware, Maryland, West Virginia, Kentucky, Missouri, and Oklahoma).

The Civil Rights Act was signed in July 1964. Change was already apparent in the fall of 1964 even though the federal officials had yet to issue regulations or gear up an active campaign of litigation. Schools opened with more than twice as many black students in white schools as there had been the year before. Part of this change may have been due to the momentum of judicial activity, building up as diehard resistance crumbled. In any case, desegregation doubled from its very small base (*Southern Education Report*, January–February 1966).

By 1965 there were guidelines specifying what all districts in the seventeen-state area had to do to continue receiving federal aid. Every school district was expected to meet a minimal requirement of opening all grade levels to voluntary "freedom of choice" transfers by black students to white schools within two years. Districts were expected to end racial gerrymandering of school attendance boundaries (Office of Education, 31 December 1964). The School Desegregation Guidelines issued in April 1965 went beyond many existing court orders in shortening the deadline for opening all grades to transfers, in emphasizing that results and not merely equitable procedures were important, and in regulating discrimination in

Table 6.3 Change in Black Segregation in the South, 1967–1991

Percentage of Students in Majority White Schools			
1954	.001	1976	37.6
1960	.1	1980	37.1
1964	2.3	1986	42.0
1967	13.9	1988	43.5
1968	23.4	1991	39.2
1970	33.1	1996	34.7
1972	36.4		

Sources: Southern Education Reporting Service in Reed Sarratt, *The Ordeal of Desegregation,* Harper & Row, 1966, p. 362; HEW Press Release, 27 May 1968; OCR data tapes; National Center for Educational Statistics, Common Core of Data statistics, 1991–92.

activities and busing (Office of Education, "General Statement of Policies," April 1965).

The first year of enforcement of the 1964 law showed that administrative agencies had been able to reach many more school districts and create much more desegregation in one year than had all the lawyers and federal courts of the previous decade. The *Brown* decision had been totally irrelevant in the great majority of southern districts because no one had ever filed a suit against them and there was virtually no voluntary compliance. (Border state districts, with their much smaller black populations and less rigid political and social traditions, had been far more likely to institute change without litigation.)

By 1965, after the School Desegregation Guidelines were issued and the federal government began to fund cutoff proceedings against some districts that refused to comply, virtually all southern districts began the desegregation process. The two years between George Wallace's 1963 stand in the schoolhouse door to defy federal officials desegregating the first school in Alabama and the fall of 1965 brought an end to the idea of preserving total racial separation in southern education. That fall, 6% of black southern students went to integrated schools. Although segregation remained the norm, the rate of change was accelerating both in the South and in the border states (Orfield 1969, 117).

By the fall of 1965, most southern school districts were in compliance with what the strictest federal courts were requiring of the small minority of school districts that had been under court order. In fact, a great many of the court orders required less than the new guidelines accomplished in what had been the nation's most resistant districts.

The most important contribution of the federal enforcement officials, however, was still to come. Even full compliance with the existing judicial standards often left segregation virtually untouched. Desegregation had been defined as requiring only a theoretical right for black students to transfer, not the breakup of the entire system of segregation. When the federal guidelines for 1966 were developed, HEW officials took on several very important policy issues that moved beyond existing judicial precedents.[1] What if desegregation required something more than merely permitting free transfers? What if community resistance, ingrained traditions, and families' fears of defying local practices meant that the system of segregation would remain virtually untouched under a choice system? The results of the first year of the desegregation guidelines showed that free choice was not likely to do much more than permit a tiny minority of black students to go to white schools, while the great majority would remain in totally segregated black institutions to which no white would ever voluntarily transfer.

The 1966 guidelines moved from procedural requirements to results, a fundamental change in school desegregation law. They changed the legal requirement from the creation of a transfer process to the requirement that the actual level of desegregation increase substantially each year. The focus changed from creating opportunities for individual students to seeing actual desegregation of both students and teachers as essential requirements and developing policies for integrated schools with integrated faculties. Until the issuance of the 1966 guidelines, the prevailing belief across the South was that the Constitution required nothing more than a good-faith opportunity to transfer to white schools. The new guidelines were promulgated in the face of serious debate among lawyers within the administration over the extent of HEW's authority to move ahead of the courts. The Johnson administration moved on faculty desegregation in spite of language in the 1964 Civil Rights Act that limited authority over employment issues and in spite of the fierce storm of political resistance from the South that erupted when the new standards became known. Districts were expected to double or triple their actual level of integration over the summer and to begin faculty integration in every school in districts where no black had ever taught any white child (Orfield 1969, 135–50, 274–85).

By the fall of 1964, desegregation had doubled. The next year it had nearly tripled. When schools opened in September 1966, more than 16% of the black students in the South were in integrated schools. Since the spring of 1964, the percentage of black students outside all-black schools in the South had increased by almost 1,400%. Most southern schools had begun faculty integration, something not actively pursued until very recently and something very rare in white schools in the North. The South was warned that more progress had to be made each year. Obviously, the process was pointing toward dismantling the entire southern system of segregated education (U.S. Commission on Civil Rights 1967, 164–65).

The Johnson administration, however, was in its last year and there was an increasingly bitter political battle over the law. A key to its lasting impact was the action of the federal courts in writing the new standards-based experience in enforcement of the 1964 Civil Rights Act into basic requirements for school desegregation remedies in the courts.

HEW and the Courts: Administrative Leadership and the Development of the Law

The 1964 Civil Rights Act was very important in the mid-1960s, in good measure because of the failure of the courts. Its enduring impact, ironically, came from its success in producing much tougher standards that the courts then embraced and continued to enforce as constitutional minimums after the political support for enforcement by the executive branch evaporated. It was apparent in 1964 that the courts, acting alone, had produced only slight and scattered exceptions to the prevailing pattern of total segregation and that they had not been able to devise an effective policy. The Civil Rights Act provided for judicial review of enforcement standards, but the courts had not even produced any reasonably clear statement of the ultimate goal in those districts where civil rights groups had been able litigate cases. Yet it was still up to the courts to define what the Constitution required and to decide whether or not HEW's standards were legal.

Administrative agencies often run afoul of the courts, particularly when they are actively pressing the boundaries of their regulatory authority in areas without clearly established rules. The potential problems were all the greater when working in areas of great sensitivity in which the courts had been making all the rules for a decade before the Civil Rights Act became law. Southern politicians and lawyers turned to the courts, accusing the Office for Civil Rights of violating the law and going beyond the proper judicial definitions of desegregation requirements. As it had since 1954, the South committed substantial political and legal resources to fighting enforcement of these standards, which were steadily moving far beyond the general understanding of school desegregation law in 1964.

Federal enforcement officials had decided that where a district was desegregating under a court order, that order, rather than the administrative standards, would apply. As the administrative standards became tougher, districts sought the sanctuary of sympathetic courts. During 1966, the many federal courts handed down a number of inconsistent opinions. "Some courts," the Civil Rights Commission reported, "issued decrees which substantially paralleled the requirements of the guidelines. Other courts entered orders imposing requirements which fell far short of the standards of the guidelines" (U.S. Commission on Civil Rights 1967, 202). Some decisions held that the free choice plan was adequate and that action on faculty integration could be delayed (U.S. Commission on Civil Rights 1967, 205). Even among the courts of appeals there were inconsistent standards, with two courts finding that free choice plans producing segregated neighborhood schools were sufficient (U.S. Commission on Civil Rights, 192–97, citing *Little Rock* and *Charlotte-Mecklenburg* cases).

The decision that would shape the law and eventually be recognized by the Supreme Court came in the crucial Fifth Circuit Court of Appeals. This court, with responsibility for desegregation in the most resistant states of the South, not only sustained the HEW regulations but adopted and enforced them as judicial standards across the Deep South. The HEW standards under the Civil Rights Act became constitutional standards and moved the courts toward the momentous conclusion that the *Brown* decision required uprooting the entire structure of southern education.

In his book on the Fifth Circuit and the desegregation crisis, Jack Bass recounted the pivotal 1966 decision in the *Jefferson Co.* decision, authored by Judge John Minor Wisdom. In *Jefferson,* Wisdom developed a model school desegregation order based on the guidelines. A school district's failure to comply with the guidelines resulted in loss of federal funds unless the district was under a federal court desegregation order. Many districts had sought "refuge in the federal courts."

By adopting the HEW guidelines as minimum standards . . . Wisdom's order ended the practice of school boards deliberately seeking a friendly district judge who would demand less than HEW.

The standard decree also created a means of control over recalcitrant district judges and for the first time established uniformity. . . .

The model decree included copies of HEW forms, letters to parents, and detailed criteria about faculty, facilities, and other administrative matters. The guidelines, Wisdom contended, "were carefully formulated by educational authorities," whereas judges lacked "sufficient competence—they are not educators or school administrators." . . . But he also noted, "To the members of this Court . . . it is evident that the HEW standards are strikingly similar to the standards the Supreme Court and this Court have established."

By legitimizing the HEW guidelines, Wisdom's order effectively locked in the expertise and experience of the executive branch under the 1964 Civil Rights Act as part of the enforcement process. "A national effort," Wisdom wrote, "bringing together Congress, the executive, and the judiciary may be able to make meaningful the right of Negro children to equal educational opportunities. *The courts acting alone have failed.*" (Bass 1981, 301–2)

The Fifth Circuit in the *Jefferson Co.* case adopted and extended the basic premise of the 1966 guidelines, that the only acceptable desegregation plan was one that actually produced desegregation. Any approach, such as freedom of choice, was acceptable only so long as it worked. The goal was not free transfers among black and white schools but the creation of a unified school district "in which there are no Negro schools and no white schools—just schools" (*U.S. v. Jefferson County* 380 F. 2d 385 [1967]).

In May 1968 a unanimous Supreme Court faced the same issue two months after HEW had issued a new set of guidelines calling for total desegregation by the fall of 1969. In its decision, the Supreme Court held that free choice plans could not be accepted unless they were rapidly eliminating desegregation in a district, something that very rarely happened. "The burden on a school board today is to come forward with a plan which promises realistically to work and promises realistically to work *now*" (*Green v. New Kent Co.* 391 U.S. 430). This decision was the basis on which the later requirements for urban desegregation were built.

It is not possible, of course, to say that the courts would not have moved toward much stronger standards without the 1964 Civil Rights Act. It is clear, however, that within four years of the enactment of the law and the entrance of HEW and the Department of Justice into the enforcement process, the legal requirements had changed beyond recognition. "All deliberate speed" was ended and a clear goal was announced for the first time. What had been a vague and gradual standard requiring no more than token integration of white schools over a number of years had become a requirement for immediate action moving toward prompt dissolution of the entire dual school system.

This account of events does not mean to imply that the development and implementation of policy was always smooth, coherent, and nonpolitical, either in the executive branch or in the courts. Civil rights groups bitterly criticized HEW for its gradualism and its earnest efforts to negotiate rather than cut funds off. The HEW decision to set the desegregation deadline for the South in September 1969 rather than complete the job before the 1968 election meant that the deadline arrived under a hostile Nixon administration rather than the more sympathetic Johnson administration.

The deadline held only after an extraordinary emergency Supreme Court decision in 1969, in which a unanimous and angry Court rejected the Nixon administration's efforts to delay desegregation in Mississippi, ruling that absolutely no further delays would be permitted (*Alexander v. Holmes* 369 U.S. 19 [1969]). HEW failed to devise workable desegregation policies for the North.

Nonetheless, in spite of all these weaknesses, the record was unprecedented for any U.S. administrative agency in dealing with a civil rights issue where there was intense resistance and high political costs. In only a few years, fundamental changes had taken place in southern education, and those changes depended largely on administrative enforcement of the 1964 law and on the development of standards that provided the framework for new understandings of constitutional mandates in the courts. The data show, in fact, that HEW tended to be more effective in the districts it supervised—most of which had been totally segregated in 1964—than were the courts in the districts under court order.

The South in the late sixties offered an opportunity to compare the effect of court-ordered desegregation in southern districts with the desegregation plans developed to comply with HEW regulations under the 1964 Civil Rights Act. A study of segregation levels in 1,362 southern school systems in 1968 and 1972 showed that those under the HEW plans were more desegregated than those under court orders. It also showed, however, that the differences were narrowing, perhaps reflecting the impact of court enforcement of the HEW standards (Giles 1975, 84–88).

A detailed comparative analysis of thirty-one districts in Georgia showed that the Civil Rights Act had been of decisive importance in the desegregation process, though judicial action was still needed:

Standing alone, the Court's early decisions did not produce great changes in school desegregation. . . . But in time the Court's actions were an important catalyst for very important policy innovations. Additionally, over the years, when Congress or the Executive branch has faltered on school desegregation, the courts have chastised and prodded them back toward the goal of racial equality. . . .

Court decisions and other laws frequently provoke political activities which facilitate achievement of policy goals (most frequently through stronger laws and/or more effective enforcement). (Rodgers and Bullock 1976, 124)

The Justice Department

HEW enforcement was, of course, only part of the attack on educational discrimination. Many in Congress had assumed that the dominant role would be played by the Justice Department, now clothed with authority to file and intervene in school desegregation litigation. Though the Justice role was less spectacular than that of HEW in the first years, federal lawyers were soon active in scores of school cases. This had several important effects. First, it made districts aware that they would probably be sued if they defied the HEW standards and that they would have to face the Justice Department in court. Second, it meant that trial judges would see not only representatives of black organizations in their courtrooms but lawyers for the U.S. government. Third, it meant that the adversary process in the major law-making cases in the appellate courts and the Supreme Court now had a powerful and influential new voice, one that was often decisive. The Justice Department rarely lost a civil rights case in that era.

The Justice Department had been participating in only one school case before 1964. In 1964 it became involved in two more. The next year its lawyers took on twenty-six more and in 1966, as the crucial showdown over desegregation standards unfolded, they entered seventy-three more cases. Less than three years after the law was enacted, the department was participating in 109 cases, including the key *Jefferson Co.* litigation (U.S. Commission on Civil Rights 1967, 65).

Litigation was not the center of activity during the Johnson administration but what was accomplished in the courts and the momentum of legal change that was created during that period were to prove decisive when a new administration decided to try to dismantle administrative enforcement of the 1964 law.

Politics and Enforcement of the 1964 Civil Rights Act

The statistics on racial change in the public schools showed a remarkable spurt in the late sixties. As table 6.1 indicates, there had been very little change in the South before the act and there would be very little in any part of the country after the Supreme Court's 1974 ruling against city-suburban desegregation, *Milliken v. Bradley* (418 U.S. 717). In fact, the nation would begin to regress in the late 1980s. Whether or not progress was made depended not just on the existence of the law but on the willingness to develop and enforce regulations addressing the causes of segregation. Throughout the last twenty years, this has been an important political question. It has, unfortunately, been one that has consistently been partisan, with Republican and Democratic administrations taking very different positions. Those positions have consequences. President Johnson's commitment to the Civil Rights Act sustained the enforcement process in the South in the face of bitter and intense political attacks, at great political cost to the Democratic Party. When the Republicans came to power, however, the process was almost immediately politicized and the principal sanction available to enforce the law, fund cutoffs, was renounced (Panetta and Gall 1971).

During both the 1964 and 1968 presidential elections, the Republicans followed a "southern strategy" in which they actively competed with Alabama Governor George Wallace, a strong advocate of continued segregation, for white southern support and opposed serious federal civil rights enforcement. The 1964 presidential nomination went to Barry Goldwater, who had joined the southern filibuster against the 1964 Civil Rights Act and was part of a small minority of Senate Republicans who voted against it. Goldwater had said that the bill was unconstitutional and that enforcement would "require . . . the creation of a police state." (Another rising politician who thought the bill was unconstitutional was Ronald Reagan.) The 1964 campaign began a long period of racial polarization over civil rights enforcement that produced a striking increase in white southern votes for the GOP and a virtual disappearance of what had been a very substantial black Republican vote (Phillips 1969, 225; Congressional Quarterly, *Congress and the Nation, 1945–1964,* 637). One summary of the Goldwater campaign noted, "Goldwater's campaign was marked by attacks upon the Supreme Court, by reminders that he had voted against the Civil Rights Act of 1964 because he believed sections of the bill were unconstitutional; and by promises that a Goldwater Presidency would . . . not tolerate civil disobedience and demonstrations of a kind associated . . . with the civil rights movement" (Polsby 1966, 88).

The first dramatic change in the administration of the Civil Rights Act came after the successful 1968 Nixon campaign. Running against Hubert Humphrey, who had managed the 1964 law in the Senate and considered it his greatest legislative achievement, Nixon hailed what he said had been a "needed revolution" in civil rights but insisted that no more laws were needed and that school desegregation enforcement policies had gone too far. He promised to enforce the 1964 act but to oppose requirements that went "beyond a mandate of Congress," such as busing (Nixon 1968, 98). Third-party candidate George Wallace carried the Deep South with bitter attacks on civil rights laws and promises to end school desegregation and other policies.

Nixon sharpened his attack on school desegregation law when he told southerners that no one was as "qualified . . . to make the decision as your local school board." He opposed any requirements that went beyond freedom of choice transfers. He said that the government must not use the threat of fund withholding to force "a local community to carry out what a *New York Times,* Federal administrator or bureaucrat may think is best . . ." (*Newsweek,* 19 August 1968; 13 September 1968). A major biographer of Governor Wallace reports that Nixon actually moved to the right of Wallace on school desegregation during the 1968 campaign (Lesher 1994, 402–3).

Within months of the Nixon election, HEW was under White House orders to end the use of the fund cutoff power; overt southern political intervention was changing the outcome of compliance investigations; the administration was transferring basic enforcement authority to the Justice Department; and Attorney General John Mitchell and the Justice Department Civil Rights Division were using their authority under the 1964 Civil Rights Act to argue in the Supreme Court for less desegregation (Panetta and Gall 1971; Murphy and Gulliver 1971; Dent 1978). The same basic approach was adopted by the Ford, Reagan, and Bush administrations.

The Nixon administration took office at a time when the great majority of southern districts were in compliance with HEW standards and had already met the requirements before the final 1969 deadline. Within weeks, HEW faced active White House political intervention and was granting exceptions to the deadlines. After a federal court in South Carolina asked the help of HEW experts in preparing desegregation plans, much in the spirit of the *Jefferson Co.* case, the plans were prepared for prompt desegregation, only to be overruled by administration officials who sent them to court with the original dates crossed out and a request for an additional year's delay. The new head of Justice's Civil Rights Division suggested that no "arbitrary deadline" was needed at all.

During the summer of 1969, both parts of the enforcement process were critically weakened. The HEW fund withholding procedure was abandoned in a policy announcement that also suspended the deadline and outlined problems that southern districts could use to justify delays. The next month the Secretary of HEW, Robert Finch, took the extraordinary step of writing to the Fifth Circuit Court of Appeals that the desegregation plans prepared by his department's own experts for Mississippi districts would cause "chaos, confusion and a catastrophic educational setback" and should be withdrawn. A few months later the head of the HEW civil rights office was fired by the White House, a move which led 1,800 HEW employees to sign a petition asking Secretary Finch to explain what the department's policies were. Needless to say, districts in many parts of the South withdrew previous commitments to desegregate (Panetta and Gall 1971; Murphy and Gulliver 1971; Dent 1978; Orfield 1978, 285–89).

Return to the Courts

The Nixon administration's changes in the administration of the Civil Rights Act posed fundamental questions to the courts. Should the new recommendations be treated as the earlier guidelines had been, with deference to executive expertise, or should the courts take notice of the political nature of the changes being imposed at the political level, over the strong objections of the department's own experts? Should the courts move back from the requirement of prompt desegregation toward the vague "all deliberate speed" standard followed for a decade after the *Brown* decision? Were the Nixon policy changes exercises of legitimate executive discretion or did they violate the plain requirements of the law?

Judicial Leadership

Decisive Supreme Court answers to these questions kept the momentum of desegregation alive in the South and maintained an important role for the 1964 Civil Rights Act in the desegregation process. Even as the advances in policy by the administrative agencies had strongly affected the courts during the Johnson administration, so now strong action by the courts to consolidate and then extend desegregation requirements, while at the same time holding the executive branch responsible for actually enforcing the 1964 act, defeated the Nixon policy and led to significant additional steps toward integrated schools in the early 1970s. For about a decade, in other words, the interaction between the executive branch and the courts generated by enforcement of the act continued to transform racial practices in southern education. In some other policy areas the impact would continue thirty years later.

The first clear Supreme Court defeat for the Nixon administration came in the fall of 1969 in a decision authored by Warren Burger, the conservative judge Nixon had appointed chief justice. The case came before the Supreme Court amid a well-publicized protest against the delay by nine-tenths of lawyers at the Justice Department's Civil Rights Division. The government's chief advocate, the solicitor general, refused to argue the case before the Supreme Court. The Court very rapidly handed down a brief unanimous decision, *Alexander v. Holmes,* categorically rejecting the administration's position and requiring immediate integration.

After a delay of some months, in which the Justice Department did nothing to enforce the Supreme Court directive in the cases on its docket, President Nixon announced a policy in March 1970 accepting the prompt completion of desegregation in the rural South but drawing the line at busing. Once this decision was made, the Justice Department announced that it would act against districts in the rural South that continued to resist, and resistance there rapidly declined (*Alexander v. Holmes* 396 U.S. 19; Nixon, 24 March 1970; Orfield 1978, 325–28). The administration even supported creation of a program of federal aid for some desegregation expenses, a program that evolved into the Emergency School Aid Act and had a very positive impact on the desegregation process, even though the aid could not be used for busing.

Though the issue of the rural South was now resolved, a much larger battle was taking shape in the courts over the question of segregation in the nation's urban schools, the great issue remaining in a society where a large majority of students lived in residentially segregated metropolitan areas. After the rural areas and the small towns of the southern and border states were desegregated, the great bulk of segregated education was in the cities and the worst problems were in the largest cities of the North. The legal struggle over the busing issue would find the Justice Department continuously in the midst of the contest and HEW buffeted by the conflicting pressures of law, politics, the White House, and the Congress.

Ever since the urban desegregation issue became serious in 1968, Justice Departments in Democratic administrations have supported busing when there has been no alternative way to achieve integration, but GOP administrations have strongly opposed efforts by the courts and have supported modifications of the Civil Rights Act, efforts to legislate limits on the powers of the courts, judicial appointment screening intended to reverse civil rights mandates, and a constitutional doctrine that defines desegregation as a temporary requirement rather than a long-term goal. Democratic administrations have opposed limits on the courts, defended urban desegregation requirements, filed a small number of urban cases, and made occasional efforts to use the administrative enforcement machinery to enforce Title VI.

The Justice Department filed its first urban cases late in the Johnson administration. It sued three districts, but only one case was resolved before the Nixon administration took over. In a 1968 campaign speech in Charlotte, N.C., candidate Nixon had promised to oppose busing. When his administration took office, the Justice Department became an active opponent of civil rights lawyers in the Charlotte litigation, which was to lead to the most important Supreme Court decision on urban desegregation. (Twenty-five years later, metropolitan Charlotte remained one of the nation's most desegregated regions [Orfield and Eaton 1996, chapter 7].) The Nixon Justice Department used its authority under the Civil Rights Act to resist busing and the president insisted that the desegregation assistance bill prohibit spending the money for busing even when the local school board wished to do so.

In the Charlotte case the Justice Department accused the federal district judge of "abuse of discretion" in his order. It took the position that there was nothing unconstitutional about segregated neighborhood schools. The Supreme Court, however, rejected the argument and decided that in cities with a history of *de jure* segregation, the Constitution required actual desegregation even if busing was the only way to do it. It sustained the district court order requiring that all schools in the large countywide school district approximately reflect the overall distribution of white and black students in the metropolitan area. School systems, said the Court, must actually be integrated no matter how "awkward" or "inconvenient" the method might be (*Swann v. Charlotte-Mecklenburg Board of Education* 402 U.S. 811 [1971]).

The Supreme Court ruling that southern cities must desegregate, by busing if necessary, meant that districts operating segregated neighborhood schools were violating the nondiscrimination requirement of the 1964 Civil Rights Act. Under the act, such discrimination required that the federal government withhold funds or initiate litigation if a plan for compliance was not adopted. For the first time, the federal government was obliged under the act to do something that directly conflicted with a basic political position of a president. Unlike the case on delaying desegregation in the rural South, however, the Supreme Court's decision in the Charlotte case did not lead to a presidential decision to comply.

Immediately after the decision, HEW officials complied with court requests to prepare large-scale busing plans for the metropolitan Nashville school district and for Austin, Texas. After fierce political attacks from southern politicians and from Alabama Governor George Wallace, the White House announced a policy of total opposition to busing (Orfield 1978, 332–33).

The president and the attorney general actively attacked the courts during the 1972 campaign and the administration went beyond nonenforcement and attempted to override the Supreme Court's urban desegregation requirement by simple legislation. The president's Equal Educational Opportunities bill not only forbade courts from sending children beyond the next closest school but also permitted reopening and reversing existing desegregation plans. This bill, which directly challenged basic parts of the Supreme Court's order, passed the House of Representatives and was blocked in the Senate only by a liberal filibuster. Needless to say, while it was before the Congress, no action was taken by the Justice Department to enforce urban desegregation requirements.

After President Nixon was reelected, the Justice Department enforced neither the Supreme Court ruling on southern urban desegregation nor the 1973 ruling in the *Denver* case, which extended busing to northern cities where there was a substantial history of intentional segregation. In late 1975, as the election campaign warmed up, new President Gerald Ford made busing a major issue. He assailed the court that had ordered the desegregation of Boston schools. He promised to send the Justice Department into battle, looking for a case to take to the Supreme Court to challenge the whole idea of urban desegregation. Ford sent another bill to Congress, the School Desegregation Standards and Assistance bill, that would have drastically limited both the scale and the duration of any busing policy, but it was blocked by congressional opponents (Orfield 1978, chapters 8 and 10).

In reality, the 1964 Civil Rights Act was simply not enforced in the cities, and the president ordered administrators not to cut off funds or sue to see that it was. The Justice Department was using the authority granted it by the Civil Rights Act to oppose civil rights groups.

Judicial Efforts to Require Enforcement of the Law

Once it became clear that the executive branch would not enforce the 1964 law, civil rights groups sued HEW for providing funds to school systems openly defying Supreme Court rulings. Thus began a remarkable period of judicial supervision of an extremely sensitive administrative agency. In rulings in 1972 and 1973, the federal district court and the court of appeals found that the executive branch had violated the law and ordered that enforcement resume. Judge John H. Pratt ruled that the administration had ignored the requirement to take action against hundreds of school districts operating in violation of principles defined by the Supreme Court. The court found that HEW had abandoned its fund cutoff sanction, though Title VI mandated action against recipients practicing illegal discrimination. When the government appealed the case, the court of appeals found that HEW was "actively engaged in supplying segregated institutions with federal funds contrary to the expressed purpose of Congress." HEW was ordered to set strict deadlines, an order to which it responded by speeding up the processing of cases rather than substantially changing their outcome. The more dramatic effect of this litigation came in the area of higher education desegregation, where the courts also found intentional nonenforcement, which will be discussed below (*Adams v. Richardson* 356 F. Supp. 92 [D.D.C. 1973]).

The Carter Administration and a Limited Revival

Jimmy Carter became president after a campaign in which he defeated the great anti-busing leader George Wallace in the South and promised to enforce civil rights law in spite of his personal opposition to busing. His choice for attorney general was Griffin Bell, who had been opposed to busing as a conservative judge on the Fifth Circuit. On the other hand, a number of people from civil rights backgrounds became administration officials, including the two key enforcers of the Civil Rights Act, the assistant attorney general for civil rights and the director of HEW's Office for Civil Rights.

After a slow start, the Carter administration attempted to revive the fund cutoff enforcement. Cutoff action was initiated in Kansas City, where the federal government had had evidence of constitutional violations for years. Once it became clear, however, that any reasonable remedy in the city would have to include substantial busing, Congress passed an amendment stripping from the executive branch the power to compel busing to avoid the loss of federal aid. Ironically, the only major limiting amendment adopted by Congress to the 1964 law was the Eagleton-Biden Amendment, pushed by two liberal Democrats, Thomas Eagleton of Missouri and Joseph Biden of Delaware, when Kansas City and Wilmington faced major desegregation plans.

The Justice Department filed a few school cases during the Carter administration and changed the position of the government very substantially in some of the old cases on the Justice docket. Some of the filings represented important new initiatives. The government filed its first city-suburban desegregation case in Houston and its first combined school-housing case in Yonkers, N.Y. During a period when it appeared that the Supreme Court was actively considering a serious curtailment of urban desegregation requirements, the department defended city-suburban desegregation in Wilmington, resisted efforts to scale back integration in Omaha and elsewhere, and played a very important role before the Supreme Court in the 1979 *Dayton* and *Columbus* cases, successfully defending the principle of citywide desegregation in the North.

When the department began to move more actively in this field late in the Carter administration, Congress reacted, passing legislation in 1980 forbidding the Justice Department to bring cases requiring busing as a remedy. President Carter vetoed this legislation as unconstitutional, and his veto was sustained. Although these approaches might have produced breakthroughs had Carter been granted a second term, the Carter Justice Department generally defended existing legal requirements rather than breaking new ground or making significant strides in enforcement. And the Eagleton-Biden amendment seriously weakened Title VI.

In contrast to the Carter administration's modest efforts, the Reagan administration launched a determined governmental attack on urban school desegregation standards. Attorney General William French Smith and Civil Rights Division Director W. Bradford Reynolds repeatedly attacked the courts, said that busing was harmful and unnecessary, urged the courts to cut back requirements, and supported local school districts wishing to return to neighborhood schools. The Reagan administration also succeeded in eliminating the major desegregation aid program and in changing federal education programs to reduce federal leverage.

The Reagan Justice Department invited school districts to attempt to reverse existing desegregation orders and sometimes intervened even in cases where the local school board had made no such request. It unsuccessfully urged the Supreme Court to authorize tax exemptions for segregated private schools and colleges. It opposed the Seattle desegregation plan, attacking the one major city in the United States that had fully desegregated without a court order. It negotiated a desegregation plan in Chicago that left 80% of black children in virtually all-black schools, dropped the Houston desegregation case, and settled other cases for voluntary remedies of the sort that had failed elsewhere. In addition, the Justice Department took the position that Congress had the power to drastically limit the power of the courts and that the courts should reflect "the groundswell of conservatism evidenced by the 1980 election" (Citizens Commission on Civil Rights 1982, 61–62).

The changes produced intense conflict within the Justice Department Civil Rights Division and repeated protests and resignations by civil rights lawyers. One attorney, for example, wrote to the attorney general complaining that Civil Rights Division Director W. Bradford Reynolds had bitterly fought the request of civil rights lawyers representing the black community to participate in the Charleston, S.C., case. He reportedly told his staff to make "those bastards . . . jump through every hoop" to get into the case (*Washington Post* 22 October 1983, p. A3). Another attorney resigned with a statement charging that the Justice Department was treating minorities as "the new enemy" in school cases (*Education Week* 26 October 1983). There were numerous other protests by professional staff members.

Under the Reagan administration the authority of the Civil Rights Act was used energetically to reverse school desegregation. Under new leadership, federal civil rights agencies became active opponents of the civil rights groups that had fought to have the laws enacted. W. Bradford Reynolds and Clarence Thomas, who ran the OCR, were among the nation's most prominent critics of systemic remedies for school segregation violations.

The Impact on Segregation

Statistics from the South and individual southern states show the powerful impact during this period of active enforcement of civil rights law in the southern and border states. The impact of desegregation policies reached its high point for black students in the early 1980s. Since that time, there has been no additional progress but in fact some regression. During this period the population of Hispanics in the nation's schools has increased extremely rapidly and their segregation has become significantly more severe than that of black students as their *barrios* have grown and there has been no desegregation policy.

The data show that the most dramatic changes in segregation levels for any region since passage of the 1964 law occurred in the South between 1964 and 1970. This large change was the only one that had a substantial impact on the national pattern of desegregation over a brief period. In the South, black students in majority white schools went from 2% in 1964 to a peak of 44% in 1986 before beginning to reverse direction in the late 1980s. The major breakthrough was directly related to the 1964 Civil Rights Act.

The last major initiative for desegregation during the twentieth century came with the urban court orders in large cities or metropolitan areas of various regions. Hundreds of new desegregation plans requiring busing were rapidly implemented in the South after the 1971 Supreme Court decision in the *Charlotte* case. Following the *Denver* decision in 1973, orders were handed down each year in a few big cities, since minority students were concentrated in fewer districts in most states outside the South and a major effort was required to prove the history of discrimination in each northern city. There were few such orders in the Northeast and that region became the nation's most segregated. The decisions by the presidents and Congress not to enforce the act in the urban North, and the Supreme Court's 1974 decision protecting the suburbs from desegregation, help explain the failure to achieve more progress.

There never was any significant attempt to desegregate Latino children, except in a handful of districts. As their numbers grew, their segregation steadily increased. The Supreme Court did not recognize the right of Latino children to desegregated schools until 1973, after the Nixon dismantling of the enforcement apparatus was complete. The Nixon administration substituted the goal of bilingual education for that of desegregation (Orfield 1978, chapter 9). The Hispanic pattern shows a steady gradual increase of segregation in all portions of the country with substantial Hispanic populations, except Colorado (probably a result of the *Denver* court order). The increase in segregation of Hispanics was strongest in the Midwest and the West. In the Midwest, the typical Hispanic student was in a school that was almost two-thirds white in 1970 but about half white in 1980. In the West, the number fell from 53% white to 40% white and the percentage of Hispanic students attending predominantly minority schools rose from 55% in 1968 to 74% by 1991. By 1991, Latino students in California were more segregated than were black students in Alabama and Mississippi (Orfield 1983, 12–15; Orfield 1993, 9–14).

Quite possibly, without the federal push for desegregation of black students and the litigation following the busing decisions, the general pattern of growing segregation for Hispanic students would have been similar for blacks. The substantial increase in the number of predominantly minority central city school systems and the outward expansion of ghettos during the period were forces working in that direction.

Whatever the precise nature of the impact of the enforcement process, the statistics clearly show large changes during the periods when the law was seriously enforced either administratively or by the courts. There was also a powerful two-way relationship between the administrative agencies and courts. In more liberal periods, it brought a rapid ratcheting up of requirements; in periods of political retreat it tended to delay and sometimes to stop the attempted reversals of civil rights policy. The transformation of southern education was clearly a deep and long-lasting impact of the Civil Rights Act.

The impact of desegregation mandates was very deep and long-lasting. Not only did black desegregation tend to remain at its highest level from the early 1970s to 1988, but there was also substantial evidence showing growing public support for desegregation during this period (Gallup Poll, *USA Today* 12 May 1994, p. A8). It was not until the appointees of Presidents Reagan and Bush transformed the Supreme Court that the country began to move clearly in the opposite direction for black students (Orfield and Eaton 1996).

Bilingual Education

Although school desegregation was the most visible consequence of the act, it also provided the legal basis for forcing school districts across the country to provide educational services for children who did not speak English. This effort, which became very important to the nation's rapidly growing Hispanic and Asian populations, was created by federal civil rights officials.

Even as the Nixon administration was shutting down HEW enforcement of school desegregation, it was expanding efforts to deal with the language issue. In 1970, HEW announced that it would enforce the little-noticed provisions forbidding discrimination on the grounds of "national origin." Wherever Hispanic students were not performing on a par with Anglos, HEW pressed for implementation of a bilingual education program. This meant that virtually every district with a significant Hispanic enrollment was told to implement a new and often unpopular method of teaching, often requiring new and specially trained staff, or face the loss of its federal aid funds (Pottinger 1970).

The Supreme Court recognized and upheld HEW's authority to regulate in this area in its 1974 decision, *Lau v. Nichols* 414 U.S. 563 (1974). The Court responded to a case about the lack of intelligible instruction for Chinese-speaking children in San Francisco with an order deriving the right to educational aid for linguistic minorities not from the Constitution but from the 1964 act. This decision recognized the authority of federal civil rights officials. In 1975 federal officials distributed a document known as the "Lau Remedies," which spelled out the standards school districts were supposed to meet in bilingual programs and was to be the dominant enforcement tool for the remainder of the decade. The regulations led to bilingual programs in districts across the country, a large demand for teachers trained in the technique, state laws and policies supporting the goal, and a change in the educational experience of millions of children. It was a very dramatic reflection of the extent of the power granted by the Civil Rights Act (U.S. Commission on Civil Rights 1974).

The policies were not, however, immune to the kind of ideological change that affected desegregation policy under the Civil Rights Act. Early in the Reagan administration, a draft Carter administration regulation formally imposing specific bilingual requirements was rescinded. Federal aid for bilingual education was cut sharply and districts were encouraged to request permission to follow different educational models (Orfield 1986, 13–18; *Washington Post* 28 February 1986). By the end of the Reagan administration, however, the first Latino secretary of education, Lauro Cavasos, was in office and the attack on bilingual education greatly diminished.

It was the authority created by the 1964 Civil Rights Act that enabled the government to establish bilingual education as a normal educational practice for linguistic minority students, and those requirements created programs and constituencies that lasted through very tough challenges in the 1980s. In the most important state for limited English students, however, California prohibited bilingual education in a state referendum in 1998 and the Clinton administration did not try to block it with Title VII.

The 1964 Civil Rights Act applied to colleges receiving federal aid just as it did to public schools, though the distinctive nature of colleges, curricula, and college enrollment decisions all created special problems in devising policies. Since 1954 the operation of college systems with *de jure* segregation had been clearly illegal. In fact, it had been a series of earlier decisions on college segregation and inequality that had led to the *Brown* case. Nineteen states had established racially defined colleges and universities. Relatively little attention was given to higher education, however, during the great battles over public school systems. The impetus for a serious enforcement effort finally came when a federal court found HEW guilty of nonenforcement of the 1964 law in the 1973 *Adams* case and set deadlines for the development of statewide college desegregation plans. The problem was, of course, most acute in the South.

As late as 1964 there were still five southern states where at least 97% of black students were attending black colleges. More than three-fourths of the black collegians were in segregated institutions in all of the southern states. Part of the separation, of course, was caused by the important role of black private colleges operating in those states, but the public campuses, including recently established institutions, were very highly segregated. Black enrollment in black public colleges grew rapidly, rising from 38,000 to 85,000, a 126% increase, between 1953 and 1968 (Weinberg 1977, 281). By 1991, by contrast, a study of twelve states with a history of *de jure* segregation in higher education showed that less than a third of the average state's black collegians attended historically black campuses (Southern Education Foundation 1995, 30).

Although little attention was paid to the segregation of higher education in the early years of enforcement of the Civil Rights Act, interest increased after a Tennessee federal court decision ordering the preparation of a state plan for desegregation of public colleges. During 1969 and 1970, HEW notified seven southern states and Oklahoma, Maryland, and Pennsylvania that their public higher education systems were illegally segregated and that they must prepare a state plan for desegregation. Federal courts were also involved in several states, including Alabama. After the initial HEW findings produced strong political criticism and institutional resistance, HEW did not actively pursue the issue until ordered to do so by a federal court (Weinberg, 314–22).

Federal District Judge John Pratt ruled in 1973 that HEW had failed to meet its obligation to enforce the Civil Rights Act in the higher education systems of ten states, and he set deadlines for submission of new state desegregation plans or for the initiation of fund cutoff proceedings (*Adams v. Richardson* 356 F. Supp. 92 [D.D.C. 1973]). After HEW sent specific requirements to the states in 1973 and 1974, it approved plans for eight of the ten states and asked the Justice Department to sue Louisiana and Mississippi, where no adequate plan was forthcoming. In early 1977, Judge Pratt found the plans inadequate in six of the states and ordered HEW to develop stronger standards and obtain new plans by the fall of 1977 (Fairfax 1978, 36).

The 1977 order led to another round of difficult and highly controversial negotiations, particularly in North Carolina, where the university strongly resisted the desegregation requirements. A critical issue was the problem of desegregating black campuses. If the white schools merely increased their black enrollment and the black colleges lost blacks without gaining whites, the inequality among the schools would only increase. Since the administration did not wish to follow the example of a federal district judge in Nashville who ordered the merger of two state universities—one black and one white—the alternative was to upgrade and assign very desirable special programs to the previously black institutions exclusively. The idea was to weaken the negative image of those schools and create a strong incentive for whites to overcome their stereotypes and begin to desegregate the campuses. The Carter administration issued standards that also called for achieving equal access to college for black and white high school graduates within five years (43 C.F.R. 6658–64, February 1978). It also initiated fund cutoff proceedings against one of the South's most important universities, the University of North Carolina (Dentler, Baltzell, and Sullivan 1983).

During the period of enforcement, there were significant changes. Between the 1975–1976 and 1980–1981 academic years, the percentage of southern black graduates receiving B.A. degrees from predominantly white institutions climbed from 32.1% to 41.2% and the number receiving degrees at these institutions grew by almost a third, much more rapidly than the growth in black degrees in white colleges outside the South (Trent 1984, 298–99). There are many other signs of the impact of civil rights requirements. By 1976, for example, black students in community colleges in the South were less segregated than in any other region, though all the other regions had a lower percentage of black students (Thomas, McPartland, and Gottfredson 1981, 339–40).

When the Reagan administration took office, it quickly abandoned the approach of the 1978 requirements and did not enforce the plans intended to implement them. It settled cases in Louisiana and North Carolina for far less. The policy retreat in the University of North Carolina case was sufficiently clear that the Justice Department attorneys handling the case refused to sign the settlement that ended the most important case of the previous administration. (*Congressional Record* 4 August 1981, E3981). The plans required neither the transfer of desirable programs to black campuses nor the merger of black and white programs or campuses doing the same thing in close proximity to one another. Desegregation was not required and the emphasis was on plans providing temporary funds to improve the black campuses (Justice Department Press Release 26 August 1981).

The NAACP Legal Defense Fund responded to the Reagan policies by suing for contempt of court. In March of 1983, in yet another decision on administrative defiance, the district court rejected the Reagan policies and required submission of plans showing substantial actual progress (*Washington Post* 24 May 1983). For fifteen years there was a series of efforts by the courts, sometimes with support of federal administrative officials, to obtain desegregation of higher education. There have been many problems and repeated judicial findings that enforcement has been inadequate.

The limitations of a long-term strategy of using the courts to force reluctant administrations to enforce the 1964 law became apparent, however, in the mid-1980s. President Reagan's secretary of education, William Bennett, broke decisively with the idea of requiring southern colleges and universities to produce actual progress in desegregation and educational opportunity for black students. Bennett announced that states would be certified for full compliance with the law, regardless of results, so long as they had taken the specific steps outlined in their plans, such as upgrading the facilities in the historically black institutions. If even fewer of the state's black students were going to college and the flagship state campus had become even more heavily white, it would make no difference under Bennett's plan. The Education Department ruled that states where black access to college was shrinking were in full compliance with the law.

The federal courts had kept pressure on for enforcement since 1973, but they gave up in 1988. The courts had always been unwilling to decide policy, preferring to force progress with deadlines and procedural requirements for completion of various enforcement steps. After fifteen years of judicial enforcement of Title VI, the U.S. Court of Appeals for the District of Columbia circuit (widely considered the most important appeals court in the nation) decided to end the *Adams* case in an extraordinary ruling that held that the courts should have never heard the case in the first place. The court of appeals, home to judges Clarence Thomas and Robert Bork, among others, had been transformed by a succession of conservative appointments by the Nixon and Reagan administrations. The court restored the agency to conservative administration control. During the period of the *Adams* case, the courts had been transformed, in some areas of civil rights policy, from the most liberal to the most conservative of the three branches of government.

More twists and turns in higher education civil rights policy, however, were still to come. Just when it was least expected, the Supreme Court handed down a decision that the state governments bore more responsibility than the Reagan administration theory would allow, creating the possibility of more extensive civil rights regulation. At this point, after four decades of silence, the Supreme Court entered the field with a major decision in the 1992 *U.S. v. Fordice* case, which overturned lower court rulings that Mississippi need achieve no measurable desegregation and ruled that state higher education systems were responsible for seriously pursuing the end of segregation (112 S.Ct. 273). At a very late date, then, the Supreme Court mandated a positive obligation on the part of state higher education officials to achieve desegregation. The decision, however, offered no special protection for the preservation and expansion of historically black campuses. A great deal depended on how the lower federal courts interpreted this decision.

Shortly thereafter, Clinton succeeded Reagan as president and appointed more liberal administrators to the key civil rights enforcement offices—Deval Patrick as assistant attorney general for civil rights and Norma Cantu as assistant secretary for civil rights in the education department. Both indicated a strong concern for the preservation of black campuses in the design of new state plans ("Notice of Application of Supreme Court Decision," 59 C.F.R. 4271–72, 31 January 1994). The struggles over shaping the state plans in Alabama and Mississippi were still underway at the end of President Clinton's first term.

A great many problems remained to be resolved in civil rights enforcement in higher education. It is undeniable, however, that there has been a very significant change, especially in the South, where civil rights enforcement was concentrated from the beginning.

Data and Research

Civil rights achievements are so much an accepted part of policy discussion, news coverage, and research today that it is easy to forget that it was virtually impossible to make an accurate description of racial conditions in America until the government, responding to the 1964 Civil Rights Act, collected racial data from schools and colleges across the United States. Many institutions, including big city school districts, either had not collected or had refused to release racial data before the act required them to do so. Few states collected or published such data. For this reason it is impossible to make precise statements about national patterns of school segregation before the late 1960s, about Hispanic education until the 1970s, about racial conditions at many colleges, and so on.

Accurate data are absolutely essential to understanding racial discrimination, for operating a serious civil rights enforcement program, and for mobilization and policy debate. Collection and publication of data made it possible to understand racial trends in U.S. education, to describe our successes and failures, to target enforcement priorities, and, in many cases, for minority groups and their advocates to create and justify new policy demands. Had the 1964 law not been enacted, the country would be moving into a period of massive demographic change with much less adequate information.

The Civil Rights Act also stimulated basic research on segregation and desegregation. It extended and strengthened the Civil Rights Commission and commissioned the first national study of school desegregation, the 1966 report *Equality of Educational Opportunity* (often known as the Coleman Report). That report triggered decades of research on the relationship between race, class, and schooling. During the next two decades, the Civil Rights Commission produced many extremely important and influential studies documenting the desegregation process, developing understanding of neglected issues like Mexican American education, and strongly influencing the development of the law. The courts frequently relied on these study findings as they began to insist on plans that actually worked. During the same period, the federal government carried out studies of desegregation, particularly in influential research under the Emergency School Aid Act and in research commissioned by the National Institute of Education.[2] Much of what we know about race relations in American schools and colleges came out of these efforts, which to a considerable degree grew out of requirements of the 1964 law.

Training and Desegregation Assistance Centers

Relatively little attention has been paid to a final provision of the 1964 law. Title IV called for technical assistance grants to school districts for planning desegregation and training teachers and staff about to undertake this major change. It also provided for the creation of university-based centers to advise school systems. These provisions were implemented with varying success. At their best, the university centers made an extremely positive contribution to school leaders and staff attempting to cope with difficult and unprecedented changes. These centers and the experts they produced sometimes became invaluable resources for the courts and administrative agencies attempting to enforce the law and devise workable remedies.

Title IV was always a small program, but it was the precursor for a much larger one, the Emergency School Aid Act, which made substantial grants for desegregation-related educational programs in school districts and funded many of the most interesting educational experiments in the country, particularly in the large cities. Very important research about race relations in the schools came out of the research component of this program. After the desegregation program the largest federal education program, ended during the Reagan administration, Title IV again became the only source of federal assistance, one that was expected to respond to many more forms of discrimination with greatly diminished resources.

The Civil Rights Act also established a federal agency to deal with racial tension, the Justice Department's Community Relations Service. The CRS brought federal expertise to bear on racial crises, some of which grew out of mobilized opposition to civil rights enforcement and court orders. It was invaluable in some of the most serious school desegregation crises and offered very helpful advice to the leadership of many communities faced with major social change.

In addition, the act influenced American education through the Treasury Department's decision to end the tax subsidies provided by tax exempt status to private educational institutions that openly practiced racial discrimination. Tax exemptions are extremely valuable for any private nonprofit institution and represent a considerable sacrifice of revenue for the government. The Treasury Department relied on the broad antidiscrimination mandate of the 1964 Civil Rights Act as legal authority for ending these exemptions. When the Supreme Court affirmed the policy and rejected the Reagan administration's efforts to restore the tax exemptions, it cited the 1964 law: "Congress, in Titles IV and VI of the Civil Rights Act of 1964 clearly expressed its agreement that racial discrimination in education violates a fundamental public policy. Other sections of that Act, and numerous enactments since then, testify to the public policy against racial discrimination" *(Bob Jones University v. U.S)*.

Perhaps nothing more fundamental can be said about the 1964 law than that it did create, for the only time in U.S. history, a clear public policy against discrimination in all institutions and activities supported by federal funds or federal tax subsidies. This was a basic redefinition of the core responsibilities of government and the large nonprofit tax exempt sector, which includes most of private education. It had immense consequences.

The Reagan Administration's Assault on the Act

From its earliest days, the 1964 Civil Rights Act has been a subject of controversy. Different administrations have responded to its broad commands in very different ways. The distinguishing feature of the Reagan and Bush administrations was their root-and-branch attacks on virtually all components of the act affecting segregation and discrimination in American education. Not only did the administration deny responsibility for enforcement; it also drew frequently on the authority provided by the act to oppose such remedies and even to advocate the dismantling of desegregation in cities where it had been ordered by a court to correct a proven history of discrimination. The Reagan administration succeeded in terminating the major desegregation aid program and recommended zero appropriations for Title IV technical assistance efforts. It went to the Supreme Court to try to restore tax exempt status to discriminatory private institutions. Like the Nixon administration, it was found to be in violation of the 1964 law for not enforcing the college desegregation requirements. It weakened the bilingual education requirements that rested on Civil Rights Act authority. President Reagan successfully broke the tradition of an independent nonpartisan Civil Rights Commission and converted the agency to a partisan body packed with opponents of current school desegregation policies and faculty desegregation practices. By the mid-1980s, the authority provided by the 1964 law and the institutions created or expanded by that law were being used against policies advocated by minority groups and in favor of policies that would prevent further progress or even increase racial inequality in American education.

The Reagan administration policy reversals were limited, to some extent, by the federal courts and Congress. The courts struck down the tax exemption policy, rejected administration positions in the Seattle, Nashville, and a number of other school desegregation cases, ordered the Education Department to resume enforcing college desegregation, and placed other limits on the administration. The Supreme Court itself, however, sharply limited the reach of Title VI in the *Grove City College* decision, a sign of the increasing success of Reagan's judicial appointment policies in remaking the courts. During the 1980s, however, Congress reasserted sweeping coverage of the 1964 law when it enacted the Civil Rights Restoration Act (Orfield 1995).

During the three decades after the enactment of the 1964 law, opponents of the law never simultaneously controlled the Supreme Court, the White House, and the Congress. For thirty years, until the 1994 election, the House of Representatives was always under Democratic control. Solid conservative control of the Supreme Court was not assured until the appointment of Justice Clarence Thomas by President Bush. Conservative control of the Congress, won in the 1994 and 1996 elections, was checked by the Clinton presidency. This balance of forces enabled many of the revolutionary changes integral to the 1964 law, and other laws modeled on Title VI, to be built into the structure of American education.

The Significance of the 1964 Civil Rights Act

The 1964 Civil Rights Act is the most important civil rights measure ever enacted by Congress. It commits the executive branch of the federal government to act against discrimination and provides a broad array of powers and techniques to carry out that responsibility. Although its reach extends far beyond education, few measures in American history have ever had so profound an effect on our schools.

The law provided vast power to accomplish its ends. Its capacity to address even seemingly intractable problems is apparent when one examines the record of the few years in which it was actively enforced in the South. In a few years' time, the principal bastion of segregated education in the United States became the most integrated region, and the legal requirements were transformed from gradual token integration to total desegregation without further delay. Even when the law was enforced over the objection of executive branch officials, the Civil Rights Act could have a large impact. The *Adams* decisions, for example, have had considerable impact on higher education in the South and on desegregation in some smaller school districts.

The law's effects have extended far beyond those discussed in the many weeks of debate in Congress in 1964. The act has become the foundation, for example, for the development of civil rights policies against discrimination toward Hispanics in public schools, policies that included the requirements that made bilingual education part of American schooling.

The central problem with enforcement of the law has been political resistance at the state and local levels and unwillingness in the four GOP Administrations since 1964 to employ the ultimate sanctions under the law. Political pressures prevented the development and enforcement of policies for desegregation of schools in the nation's great cities, particularly those outside the South, even after the Supreme Court established the legal obligations of northern districts with a history of discrimination. When the Carter administration showed signs of addressing this issue, Congress took enforcement power for urban desegregation away from the Department of Education in the only major weakening amendment to the 1964 law. It is no accident that these cities are now the center of segregated education in the United States. It is not the case that civil rights enforcement would have made no impact on these extremely difficult problems. In fact, civil rights agencies were not allowed to try. The courts, acting alone and often faced with executive branch opposition, have had little more success than the courts of the South before the 1964

Civil Rights Act. By the early 1990s, the Supreme Court had come under control of a conservative majority and was actually pressing for the end of desegregation orders (Orfield and Eaton, 1996).

The Civil Rights Act makes serious civil rights enforcement possible in American education, but it only works effectively when the executive branch is committed to full implementation and when this standard is supported by the courts. Unfortunately, since 1986 the enforcement process has been under severe political attack and during twenty of those years the White House has been occupied by some of the attackers. All too often the power created by the Civil Rights Act, particularly the power of the Justice Department's civil rights division, has been used against civil rights litigation and in ways that protect discrimination. Although the act was preserved by the ideological stalemate between the branches of government, a rededication to enforcement of the law is needed if the act is to retain a central role in American education.

Our experience under the Civil Rights Act shows that the law created the tools needed to force policies to change discriminatory schools and colleges in the past. The power of the law has been largely preserved and even extended in some respects. Since the 1960s, however, we have not had national leadership willing to commit substantial political power to the enforcement of this law. Nevertheless, many of the changes forced by the law have lasted and become basic parts of American education. When the nation experiences future waves of reform emphasizing expansion of opportunity and racial equity in American education, actions taken under the 1964 law are likely to shape an important part of the national response.

Notes

1. Before the creation of the U.S. Department of Education in 1980, education issues were under the jurisdiction of the Department of Health, Education, and Welfare (HEW), whose name was changed to Health and Human Services after an independent Education Department was created.

2. The Emergency School Aid Act was a federal desegregation aid bill enacted in 1972 and repealed in 1981.

7

The Impact of EEO Law
A Social Movement Perspective

Paul Burstein

A reader of the social scientific literature on the impact of equal employment opportunity (EEO) law—including Title VII of the Civil Rights Act of 1964, other laws, and executive orders—could easily reach two contradictory conclusions: that EEO law has done little good, or that it has done a great deal of harm.[1] Economists contend that EEO law has done little to reduce employment discrimination—even its strongest supporters see little impact since the mid-1970s—while many writers claim that it has led to widespread reverse discrimination, attacks on the merit principle, and a decline in American productivity.[2]

In this chapter, I argue that both of these conclusions are wrong and that EEO law has done more good and less harm than is often claimed. Positive consequences have been underestimated because the economists responsible for them pay little attention to the social, political, and cultural contexts in which EEO law is implemented. And negative consequences are overestimated because opponents of affirmative action search far more assiduously for negative consequences than for positive ones. To reach sounder conclusions about the impact of EEO law, I argue, we should adopt what I call the "social movement" approach, in which EEO law is viewed as just one aspect of a broad, long-term movement against discrimination. EEO law was the product of a decades-long struggle to influence the American people and the three branches of government, and its enforcement has both affected and been affected by that continuing struggle. Only by placing EEO law in its broader context can we hope to gauge its consequences.

Three Approaches to Assessing the Impact of EEO Law

There have been two main approaches to assessing the impact of EEO law: the neoclassical/econometric approach, which, I argue, underestimates the impact of EEO law; and the worst-case approach, which overestimates its negative consequences. I propose the adoption of a third, "social movement," approach, which addresses significant flaws in the first two.

The Neoclassical/Econometric Approach

The most rigorous analyses of the consequences of EEO law are those conducted by social scientists (almost all of them economists) using large data sets and sophisticated statistical techniques (see, e.g., the reviews in Smith and Welch 1989; Donohue and Heckman 1991; Gunderson 1989). Sometimes they conclude that EEO law has had no significant effect on labor market discrimination; sometimes they find a small or temporary effect; they never seem to find a large or lasting effect. Their work leads them almost inexorably to conclude that EEO law does little good.

Why might they reach this conclusion? There are three likely possibilities. The most obvious is that EEO law really has little impact. According to mainstream economic theory, the impact of EEO law (and other labor laws) on labor market outcomes will necessarily be much smaller than the impact of productivity. Indeed, EEO law is intended to get employers to pay more attention to productivity, and less to race, sex, national origin, and religion, when they evaluate workers. Economists thus frequently argue that the impact of EEO law on labor market outcomes will be marginal at best, and some believe that its cost in reduced efficiency and administrative expenditures is sure to outweigh its benefits (see, e.g., Epstein 1992; Posner 1987; Smith and Welch 1989).

Or EEO law may appear to do little good because those who study it may be focusing most on the group that benefits least and less on groups that benefit more. Title VII prohibits discrimination on the basis of race, color, religion, sex, and national origin, but most studies of the impact of EEO law focus only on black men. There are a number of reasons for doing so—the centrality of black-white relations to American history, the focus on the plight of black men in the congressional debate on Title VII, and the availability of vast amounts of data on racial differences, for example—but if discrimination against black men is more pervasive and resistant to change than discrimination against other groups, EEO law might be less effective against it. The focus on black men may lead social scientists to underestimate both the total impact of EEO law and its impact on particular groups.

Finally, economists may underestimate the impact of EEO law because of how their theories influence their research. Because economists assume that labor market outcomes will be almost entirely the product of basic economic forces, they have done relatively little theorizing about how other factors, including politics and law, might influence labor market outcomes. As a result, when economists want to estimate the impact of EEO law, they typically just add a variable or two, purportedly measures of enforcement effort, to their standard economic models. Tacking unproven measures onto highly developed models is almost bound to produce exactly the result the economists find—that the new variables have little impact (for a comparable argument, see Donohue and Heckman 1991, 1604). Thus, economists' conclusion that EEO law has little impact might be accurate—or it might be the result of their focus on black men and their neglect of noneconomic forces.

The Worst-Case Approach

The econometric approach is nearly always used to estimate the positive effects of EEO law—that is, how much it has reduced discrimination against minorities and women. Possible negative consequences of EEO law—especially reverse discrimination, attacks on the merit principle, and declining productivity—are generally approached in a different way. Adopting what may be called the worst-case approach, those concerned about harm caused by EEO law seek out anecdotes purportedly showing flagrant injustices perpetrated in the name of EEO or affirmative action, including judicial decisions imposing quotas, bureaucratic decisions undermining the merit principle or requiring excessive paperwork, and demands for statistical parity in employment made by blacks or women (mostly the former). A reading of such work leads almost inexorably to the conclusion that EEO enforcement does vast harm (see, e.g., Glazer 1978; Hatch 1980; Belz 1991; Nieli 1991, among many other works).

Maybe this is in fact the case, but one cannot legitimately reach that conclusion on the basis of the worst-case approach, for two reasons, one quite obvious and the other less so. The obvious reason is that for a conclusion about the impact of EEO law to be convincing, evidence of harm must be weighed against evidence of benefits. A diligent search for foolish or harmful judicial decisions, bureaucratic regulations, and employer policies is bound to be successful after thirty-five years of nationwide experience with EEO law. But without systematically weighing the foolish and harmful against the sensible and beneficial, the conclusions reached through the worst-case approach are dubious at best. Whatever the flaws of the neoclassical/econometric approach, its adherents appreciate the importance of analyzing the full range of labor market outcomes; those who rely on the best-case/worst-case approach do not.

The second reason to be dubious about the worst-case approach is that its conclusions are inconsistent with much of what we know about economics and politics. For EEO law to be as harmful as proponents of the worst-case approach claim, vast numbers of employers would have to engage in economically irrational practices—rewarding unqualified workers and adopting burdensome, inefficient procedures, for example—over long periods of time, without either their or better-qualified workers' being able to get the government to change its policies. Such a scenario is extremely implausible. For one thing, according to mainstream economic theory, employers and workers would evade regulations requiring inefficient procedures. In addition, all theories of democratic politics argue that government is highly responsive to demands from business, and there is considerable evidence that it responds to public opinion as well (Posner 1987; Lindblom 1977; Stimson, MacKuen, and Erikson 1995).[3]

Thus, while econometric work on EEO enforcement typically concludes that it has had little impact, the worst-case/best-case approach almost inevitably leads to the opposite conclusion—by focusing on the most egregious examples of EEO enforcement gone too far and ignoring the moderating forces of economic rationality and democratic politics. Is there a better way?

A Social Movement Approach

Title VII was the product of a vast, long-term social movement against discrimination, a movement seeking equal treatment not only in employment, but in education, public accommodation, government programs, politics, and other areas as well. Adherents of the movement used a wide variety of means to achieve their goals, not only legislation but also education, persuasion, electoral politics, marches and demonstrations, litigation, and whatever other means they could devise—all the tactics of democratic politics. And their activities did not end with the passage of Title VII and other civil rights laws. Civil rights groups, women's organizations, and others concerned about EEO have assisted potential litigants, sought to influence how judges and administrative agencies interpret the law, pressured businesses and unions to adopt strong EEO policies, demanded that the Equal Employment Opportunity Commission and other agencies enforce the law aggressively, and worked for the passage of amendments to strengthen the law. Their strategies have, in turn, changed over time in response to the reactions—and sometimes the resistance—of Congress, the courts and administrative agencies, employers, the general public, and groups opposed to affirmative action and other aspects of the struggle for EEO (see, e.g., Belton 1990, 1993; Blumrosen 1993; Burstein 1985, 1991a, 1991b, 1993; Wasby 1993; Wood 1990). The passage of Title VII might best be viewed as a "critical moment" in the struggle against employment discrimination—the moment at which the goal of EEO was enacted into law and the law began its role as an important focus (though not the only focus) of continuing struggle.

It is difficult to see how any satisfactory attempt to analyze the impact of EEO law could ignore the antidiscrimination movement, but that is precisely the key flaw in both the neoclassical/econometric and worst-case approaches to EEO. Econometric work incorporates none of the factors just described, beyond a measure or two of enforcement effort—most often, federal expenditures on EEO enforcement. Adherents of the worst-case approach sometimes describe the demands of civil rights and women's organizations, and changes in legal doctrine or administrative decisions, but they do so without reference to the broader political process or any systematic attempt to track the relevant factors over time.

Not only is it plausible that the broad context of enactment and enforcement would influence the impact of EEO law; there is a growing body of evidence that it actually does. Public opinion on employment discrimination strongly influenced congressional action on EEO, and it continues to influence enforcement and labor market outcomes. Social movement organizations play a role in the litigation of many EEO cases; their involvement is associated with higher rates of victory for minorities and women, and such victories, in turn, affect labor market outcomes. New ideas about discrimination have influenced administrative agencies and the courts, whose actions have affected how employers and unions treat minorities and women. Careful, detailed historical analysis of the movement for EEO has convinced even some prominent economists—usually very reluctant to attribute importance to noneconomic factors—that labor market outcomes are affected by the whole package of civil rights laws, the federal enforcement effort, the activities of the civil rights and women's movements, and, for women, cultural expectations about gender roles and the household division of labor.[4]

To take account of the context of enactment and enforcement, I propose a social movement approach to studying EEO law. This means that both the enactment of EEO law and its specific content must be seen as the result of a number of forces, including public opinion, protest activity, lobbying, electoral politics, media coverage, and political leadership (Burstein 1985). Enforcement depends on the funding of enforcement agencies, the development of legal doctrine and administrative expertise, involvement in the enforcement process by those favoring strong action and those opposing it, the broader policy context, electoral politics, and other factors (Blumrosen 1993; Burstein 1985, 1991a; Burstein and Edwards 1994; Donohue and Heckman 1991). Estimating the consequences of EEO law requires that variables describing the broader context be taken into account, so that the enforcement process can be understood and each factor having an impact is given its due. And estimating the consequences of EEO law also requires consideration of its impact on legal, social, organizational, cultural, and political outcomes as well as on changes in labor markets.

The social movement approach is too new to have led to the development of comprehensive models of EEO impact. Here I provide examples of what can be learned by taking a broader-than-usual view of the consequences of EEO laws, focusing on:

—the impact of EEO law on the organizations it regulates, describing what the law prohibits (employment discrimination), what it sometimes requires (affirmative action), and the organizations' response;

—some political and social consequences of EEO law, including its impact on the civil rights and women's movements, and on gender roles;

—the impact of EEO on the labor market outcomes of minorities, women, and white men; and

—some possible implications of EEO law for American politics.

Two caveats are in order. The first was best stated by Judge Richard Posner (1987, excerpted in Burstein 1994, 151): "Disentangling the effects of Title VII from all the other things that have been going on since 1964 and that bear on the wages and employment of blacks seems well-nigh impossible. Even disentangling the effects of all government programs to combat racial discrimination from the effect of other developments is extraordinarily difficult." In much of what follows, I make no attempt to distinguish the impact of Title VII from that of other EEO laws and executive orders because of the difficulty of doing so.

Second, at this stage the search for evidence and its subsequent analysis cannot be limited to what fits conventional econometric models. As Donohue and Heckman write (1991, 1604), the evidence supporting the conclusions reached below "is more like that assembled by Sherlock Holmes rather than that routinely published in Econometrica."

What Are Regulated Organizations to Do?

Defining "Discrimination": What Is Prohibited?

Title VII prohibits employment discrimination on the basis of race, color, religion, sex, or national origin. But it does not spell out what discrimination is. It prohibits the failure "to hire" based on these categories (42 U.S.C. 2000e, sec. 702[a]), but then adds that it shall be an "unlawful employment practice . . . otherwise to discriminate," without spelling out what that means.

Why might a statute prohibiting employment discrimination fail to define its central concept, employment discrimination itself? Some scholars and politicians argue that there was no need for Congress to define "discrimination" in detail, because the definition is so obvious. It means that "motivated by a worker's race [or color, religion, sex, or national origin], an employer treats the worker less favorably than a worker or another race would have been treated" (Gold 1985, 431), and it prohibits being "color-conscious" rather than "color-blind" (Glazer in Nieli 1991, 5; see also Belz 1991, 9, 15–16; U.S. Department of Justice 1987, 1).

"Obviousness" does not seem a satisfactory explanation for congressional vagueness, however. Those who write statutes know very well that what seems obvious before a statute is drafted often becomes the subject of much contention when the exact wording is at issue, and of even more dispute when it is being interpreted by the courts. Edelman points out that Title VII defines "employer" and "person" in great detail, even though their definitions might also seem obvious (1992, 1536).

Probably the best explanation for congressional vagueness is that a comprehensive definition of employment discrimination useful for legal purposes did not exist in 1964, when Title VII was adopted. Social scientific definitions available at the time had not been used to distinguish discriminatory employment practices from nondiscriminatory ones, and there had been too few decisions by courts in states with their own EEO laws to provide a detailed legal definition (Blumrosen 1993, 107–10; Burstein 1990). As a result, Congress stated its intention to prohibit employment discrimination as best it could, and, as economist Barbara Bergmann has written, "left to the courts to define what behavior is discriminatory and what is not" (1986, 150; cf. Edelman 1992, 1536).

No law can predictably influence behavior—in this case, employment discrimination—unless the behavior itself is clearly defined, so the task left to the courts was a major one. Indeed, according to Alfred Blumrosen, first chief of the office of conciliations of the EEOC and now a law professor at Rutgers University, what was left to the courts was "the fundamental legal question under Title VII: how is discrimination defined?" (1972, 66).

Thus, one of the most important consequences of Title VII was to require that what it prohibited be precisely defined. And by implicitly delegating so much power to the courts, Congress virtually ensured that the process of defining discrimination would be dynamic, lengthy, and contentious, occurring as plaintiffs and defendants argued for definitions that would serve their interests in particular cases.

The process has indeed been contentious. Many groups and individuals have tried to influence the definition—writing treatises, representing or assisting litigants, filing briefs as *amicus curiae*, lobbying Congress, and appealing through the mass media. The impact of their efforts? No one in 1964 could possibly have imagined the issues that would arise in defining discrimination, or how they would be resolved. Hundreds, perhaps thousands, of decisions have focused on defining which kinds of actions are discriminatory and which are not.

Collectively the decisions have been both consequence and cause of continuously changing theories about discrimination, and some have been so controversial that they brought the definitional issues back to Congress. In what is often described as the most important and controversial decision in EEO law, for example, the Supreme Court decided in *Griggs v. Duke Power Co.* (401 U.S. 424, 1971) that practices having a disparate (or "adverse") impact on minorities or women could be considered discriminatory, even if those adopting them had intended no harm, unless the employer could demonstrate that the practices really helped distinguish good employees from poor ones (Schlei and Grossman 1983, chapter 1).

The *Griggs* decision led to significant changes in how employers evaluate workers (see Edelman 1992) and to intense protest by employers, legal scholars, and politicians who wanted to define discrimination more narrowly (see, e.g., Gold 1985; U.S. Department of Justice 1987). The Supreme Court responded to the protests in 1989, effectively reversing significant aspects of *Griggs* in *Wards Cove v.*

Atonio (490 U.S. 642, 1989); the Court's action prompted Congress, in turn, to reenact much of the *Griggs* definition into law in the Civil Rights Act of 1991.

Similarly, when the Court interpreted Title VII as saying that differential treatment on the basis of pregnancy did not constitute sex discrimination (*General Electric v. Gilbert*, 429 U.S. 125, 1976), Congress responded to the widespread protest that ensued by enacting the Pregnancy Discrimination Act of 1978, which explicitly defined such treatment as discriminatory. Controversies over employers' accommodation of employees' religious differences have prompted involvement by the EEOC and Congress as well as the courts (Beckley and Burstein 1991), as have other issues.

Some of those involved in the struggle over EEO have been pleased by the outcomes of these disputes over definitions, while others have been horrified.[5] But all agree that the disputes have potentially important consequences. Both those who consider the definition "obvious" and those who favor a definition continually being refined agree that legal acceptance of the "obvious" would slow the advance of minorities and women, while acceptance of the alternative view would hasten it.[6] The competing points of view are strongly held and have very different implications for the struggle over equal opportunity; because each has been adopted by important political groups as well as by scholars, the controversy over how discrimination should be defined will play a role in legislative and legal disputes over EEO for years to come.[7]

Defining "Affirmative Action": What Is Required?

What are covered organizations to do if they wish to obey Title VII and other EEO laws and regulations? Obviously, they are not to discriminate. At times, however, their obligation goes further: they are to engage in "affirmative action."

The term "affirmative action" first made its appearance in federal EEO law in Title VII, which is as vague about affirmative action as it is about discrimination. Section 706[g] states that if a court finds that an employer, labor union, or employment agency has engaged in unlawful discrimination, the court "may enjoin the respondent from engaging in such unlawful practice, and order such affirmative action as may be appropriate, which may include, but is not limited to, reinstatement or hiring of employees . . . or any other equitable relief as the court deems appropriate." Executive Orders 11246 and 11375 are somewhat more specific, albeit only with regard to the federal contractors whose activities they regulate; they require employers to take "affirmative action" to recruit, hire, and promote minorities and women whenever those groups had been "underutilized" in the employer's workforce relative to their "availability" in the labor market, regardless of whether the employer had been shown to have discriminated (see Schlei and Grossman 1983, chapter 25 and appendix).

When Title VII and the executive orders went into effect, no one had much of an idea what "affirmative action" was to be. The term as used in the Civil Rights Act appears to have been borrowed rather casually from the National Labor Relations Act, and there was little history of interpretation to clarify what it meant. Indeed, the term is arguably more problematic than "discrimination," because there was no "obvious," seemingly intuitive definition to draw on.

As with discrimination, the definition of "affirmative action" has been (and continues to be) worked out in the courts, enforcement agencies, and, much less often, Congress; but debates over what it means have proven even more intense than those about discrimination. Most Americans oppose discrimination, and some favor a bit of special help for groups which have been the victims of discrimination, but most oppose anything they see as preferential treatment for minorities.[8] Because affirmative action involves doing things for protected groups, it inevitably provokes accusations that the action being taken—whatever it might be, and whether it is in response to proven acts of discrimination or not—involves preferential treatment; and because Americans oppose preferential treatment, it is with regard to affirmative action that EEO law is most vulnerable to attack. Affirmative action has become a lightning rod, attracting more organized attacks than any other aspect of EEO enforcement (see, e.g., Glazer 1978; Belz 1991; Nieli 1991). The political implications of these attacks will be considered below.

The Organizational Response

The goal of the EEO laws was to reduce labor market discrimination; the means were to be changes in the behavior of those creating and implementing employment and referral policies for employers, labor unions, and employment agencies.

How did the regulated organizations respond to this mandate for change? Some discriminatory practices were so clearly prohibited, and their violation was so obvious, that they were abandoned relatively widely and quickly; for example, explicit "whites only" clauses were removed from union constitutions and bylaws, many explicitly racist hiring policies were eliminated, and requests to employment agencies stopped specifying "white only" or "Christian" (see Blumrosen 1993, chapter 5). And Title VII also provided many employers with an excuse to end discriminatory practices that had proven costly—preventing them from hiring workers on the basis of merit—but had been reluctantly maintained because of social and economic pressure from the employers' communities (Heckman and Payner 1989).

Nevertheless, the response of many organizations was minimal, for several reasons. What the law required was often unclear (for example, "discrimination" was not defined in detail). State EEO laws, adopted by most states outside the South by 1964, had never been strongly enforced, so employers could easily conclude that they had little to fear. Traditional attitudes seemingly made it difficult for many organizations to understand what might be required of them; one infamous example of this incomprehension was newspapers' struggle to maintain separate sections of want ads for men and women in the face of a prohibition of sex discrimination (Blumrosen 1993, chapter 10). There are many organizational forces that resist all change, including those imposed by outside agencies (Baron 1992). And of course many employers and white workers were simply hostile to the advancement of minorities and women.

Little by little, however, it became clear that the EEO laws would be interpreted broadly and enforced seriously. Although the EEOC had significant organizational and political problems from the start, its guidelines most often took a broad view of what constituted discrimination and what was required of the organizations covered by Title VII.[9] Many of the cases brought to court in the years right after Title VII went into effect were class action suits in which the plaintiffs were aided by civil rights and other organizations; they urged the courts to take a broad view of Title VII and other civil rights laws, and the courts obliged, frequently finding for the plaintiffs and interpreting the statutes liberally (Blumrosen 1984; Burstein 1991a; Burstein and Edwards 1994). Information about developments in EEO law was widely and rapidly disseminated—the *Wall Street Journal* published more than 350 articles about specific firms involved in EEO disputes between 1964 and 1986 (Hersch 1991), and major publishers created EEO newsletters soon after Title VII went into effect. In addition, a rapidly growing "EEO industry" of lawyers, consultants, and human resources specialists was utilized by large numbers of employers and unions to help them decide how to conform to the law and avoid the risks of lawsuits.

How have employers and unions responded to the development of EEO law and its enforcement? Unfortunately, we know little about their response. Until recently most economists and sociologists interested in labor markets treated organizations as "black boxes," paying little attention to how they responded internally to changes in their environments (Baron 1992). This neglect is partly the result of difficulties involved in gaining access to large samples of organizations and systematically studying their operations. As a result, the information we have about organizational responses to EEO is based on relatively small samples of organizations, often not random samples.[10]

We can be reasonably certain, nevertheless, that a high proportion of covered organizations eventually responded to EEO law. Some adopted employment tests or quotas and then abandoned them when the courts decided to discourage their use. Many eventually adopted the procedurally oriented policies favored by the courts and federal agencies, particularly formal antidiscrimination policies and rules for hiring and promotion (Edelman 1992; Dobbin, Sutton, Meyer, and Scott 1993). Lots of articles in personnel and business management journals argued that the procedures combined efficiency with equity—by formalizing and rationalizing their employment practices, employers would improve their allocation of labor and simultaneously reduce discrimination. Many employers created new offices for dealing with EEO and affirmative action as well.

Dobbin et al. (1993) argue that the changes in employment practices were the result of a complex set of interactions among the civil rights and women's movements, the government, and employers. In their view, pressures from the civil rights and women's movements affected both the adoption of EEO legislation and some employers' inclination to act against discrimination; the specific practices employers adopted, however, were chosen through a process involving bargaining and litigation as the parties involved tried to figure out what to do.

There is some debate about whether these organizational changes were intended to be effective or were merely window dressing intended to impress potential plaintiffs, enforcement agencies, and the courts. We do know that many of the changes have become thoroughly entrenched. They are most often implemented through personnel departments, meaning that they may become integrated with other personnel practices more fully than if implementation were done through special EEO offices only. The new practices have come to be seen by many organizations, particularly government and nonprofit agencies, as valuable because they are "up-to-date" (Dobbin et al. 1993, 421). And they have come to be seen as standard operating procedures, so much so that when the Reagan administration tried to eliminate "goals and timetables" from Executive Order 11246, it was resisted not only by civil rights groups but by big business as well (Detlefson 1993; Fisher 1985; "Rethinking Weber" 1989).

EEO law has led many organizations to alter their employment practices. Unfortunately, we have not begun to trace systematically exactly how the changed practices affect labor market outcomes for minorities and women.

Some Political and Social Consequences of EEO Law
The Civil Rights and Women's Movements

Enactment of a strong federal EEO law was one of the highest priorities of the civil rights movement. Civil rights groups influenced the content of the bill that became Title VII and continue to influence its implementation. Title VII, in turn, has become an important part of the environment in which the struggle against discrimination is being pursued. Having been influenced by the civil rights movement, Title VII has come to influence it in turn, and to affect the newly revitalized women's movement as well.

Title VII gave litigation-oriented civil rights organizations an additional weapon in their struggle against discrimination (Burstein 1991a). Before 1964, proponents of a federal EEO law almost unanimously wanted its enforcement provisions to be similar to those of the National Labor Relations Act and some state EEO laws, concentrating enforcement powers in an administrative agency similar to the National Labor Relations Board. This approach was rejected during the debate on Title VII; in what was widely seen as a defeat for longtime proponents of EEO legislation, Title VII required those who believed they had been discriminated against to go to court if conciliation failed.

In retrospect, the failure to win administrative enforcement may have been a blessing in disguise for the civil rights and women's movements. State EEO enforcement had been extremely weak, partly because complainants had so little say in the process; state agencies often closed cases they considered satisfactorily resolved without consulting the complainants. Despite the cumbersome and costly judicial process, the decision to make the courts central to EEO enforcement gave plaintiffs and their advocates a more central role in the enforcement process than they would have had otherwise. Civil rights litigators could use their skills to pursue EEO through the courts.

For a while they were successful. The federal courts (particularly the appellate courts) were very responsive to plaintiffs, deciding in their favor in a high proportion of cases (far more than would normally be expected when members of relatively powerless groups sue their employers), and adopting an expansive view of what constituted discrimination and what kinds of evidence could be used to demonstrate its occurrence. Such pro-plaintiff judicial decisions seem to have played a crucial role in blacks' economic advance in the first dozen or so years after Title VII went into effect. Established civil rights organizations responded to their success in court by putting additional resources into the mobilization of law, and their example encouraged the development of comparable strategies by other groups (Burstein 1991a; Burstein and Edwards 1994; Blumrosen 1984).

Title VII had an especially dramatic impact on the women's movement. The movement had been "in the doldrums" since World War II (Rupp and Taylor 1987), but in the early 1960s it showed some signs of a rebirth. The Equal Pay Act, requiring equal pay for men and women doing the same jobs, was adopted in 1963; cultural and economic forces were creating an environment favorable to the renaissance of the movement; and the President's Council on the Status of Women (PCSW), encouraged by President Kennedy, served as a locus for the study of "women's issues" and aided the development of comparable state agencies and the coordination of their activities (see, e.g., Freeman 1975; Harrison 1988; Rosenfeld and Ward 1991).

The enactment of Title VII crystallized the nascent changes in the political environment. Ironically, as many have reported, it was women's weakness in the enforcement process that stimulated the growth of the women's movement. Many women who cheered the prohibition of sex discrimination in Title VII were extremely disappointed to discover that most EEOC commissioners did not take sex discrimination seriously; the commissioners saw their primary task as attacking discrimination against black men. In response, some women who had been brought together through the PCSW, along with others interested in its activities, formed the National Organization for Women in 1966; one of their major goals was to see that the ban on sex discrimination was enforced. It would be an exaggeration to say that Title VII was responsible for the rise of the contemporary women's movement, but it was an important catalyst.

After both civil rights and women's movement organizations began using Title VII to attack employment discrimination, the relationship between EEO enforcement and politics became a dynamic one. Some Title VII and other cases provided opportunities to develop important new ideas about discrimination. Those accepted by the courts became part of the legal environment employers and unions had to deal with and, often, part of public debate about discrimination as well. When the courts rejected plaintiffs' arguments, civil rights and women's organizations sometimes got Congress to overrule the judicial decisions—as it overruled *General Electric v. Gilbert* with the Pregnancy Discrimination Act of 1978 and important parts of *Wards Cove v. Atonio* and several other Supreme Court decisions with the Civil Rights Act of 1991, for example (Blumrosen 1993, 284–86). In this way, the access to the courts provided by Title VII stimulated thinking by proponents of EEO; judicial decisions affected the civil rights and women's movements by encouraging further litigation when plaintiffs were victorious and a turn to Congress when they were not; and, perhaps, movement activity declined when neither the courts nor Congress seemed receptive to further claims.

Gender Roles

Declines in labor market discrimination against blacks (whether the result of EEO law or other causes) have had the consequences predicted by EEO proponents in the 1950s and 1960s: blacks have won higher incomes, access to a greater variety of jobs, and such other benefits of upward mobility as suburban homes, greater political influence, and so on.

The consequences of the fight against sex discrimination could not have been predicted so readily. Women were less unified than blacks; those who wanted policy change disagreed about both goals and how to reach them, and many women did not see women as a group as having any shared policy interests at all (Harrison 1988). Women were not as well organized as blacks to pursue policy change; and very few people took their demands as seriously as blacks'.

As it turned out, Title VII provided the opportunity to challenge many attitudes and institutional practices that defined traditional gender roles and kept women and men in them; and many of the challenges met intense resistance, leading to broad and deep conflicts over gender roles that continue to this day. Proponents of change have found that many women as well as men are profoundly committed to traditional gender roles (Fleming 1988) and will struggle to maintain them. They have also discovered that gender roles seem so "natural" to most people that attempts to challenge them meet more with incomprehension than with organized resistance. Examples include the initial, seemingly baffled response to demands for gender-neutral want ads and the continuing power of assumptions that women are found in few nontraditional jobs because they simply and naturally lack interest in them (Schultz 1990).

Nevertheless, Title VII has been used successfully to attack state paternalism in the labor market (overturning protective labor laws, for example), employers' beliefs that pregnancy is incompatible with labor force participation, and many assumptions about women's alleged inability to do many kinds of work (see, e.g., Goldstein 1989). Title VII has also stimulated new ways of thinking about how men and women are to relate to each other in the workplace and about the relationship between work and family. It is difficult to imagine that the concept of "sexual harassment" would have developed as it did, or that Congress would have enacted the Family and Medical Leave Act, without the prior adoption of Title VII (see MacKinnon 1979; Burstein, Bricher, and Einwohner 1995).

The many changes in gender roles during the last thirty-five years cannot be attributed to any single cause (see Epstein 1988), but given the importance of Title VII to the contemporary women's movement and its usefulness for challenging gender discrimination and stereotyping, it must be given some credit as a force for change. It remains for future work to specify its impact.

EEO Law and Labor Market Outcomes

It is hardly a matter of chance that Title VII prohibits discrimination on the basis of race, color, religion, sex, and national origin. Racial, religious, and national-origin minorities had suffered greatly from labor market discrimination, as had women; all had pushed for federal EEO legislation—blacks, Jews, Hispanics, and other minorities since the 1940s, women more recently—and all had hopes that it would help them (Burstein 1985). Thus any attempt to estimate the impact of Title VII, if it is to be true to its history, the desires of the groups supporting it, and the intent of those who voted for it, must consider its effect on discrimination against all the protected minority groups and women. In addition, because Title VII prohibits discrimination against white men as well as minorities and women—and allegations of such discrimination have provoked tremendous protest—it is necessary to consider its impact on them as well.

Before attempting to gauge the impact of EEO law, it is necessary to note two factors that place especially important limitations on our ability to do so. Very little information is available about trends in discrimination against some groups covered by Title VII; we cannot assess the impact of EEO law on discrimination without information on discrimination being available in the first place. In addition, because we lack satisfactory models of how EEO law interacts with social, political, and organizational factors, it is often extremely difficult to distinguish the effects of EEO law from the effects of these other factors.

Race and Color

Labor market discrimination against black men has been studied far more extensively than has discrimination against any other group, and two conclusions about it are clear. Historically its impact on their earnings was huge, and its impact has declined markedly in recent decades.[11] Estimates vary, but black men may have earned as little as 60% as much as equally productive whites up through the late 1950s or early 1960s (much less in the South than elsewhere), with much if not all of the difference due to discrimination. By the mid-1970s, however, black men's earnings had risen to perhaps 85–90% of those of equally productive white men. By 1979–1980, their earnings may have risen even a bit higher, with estimates ranging as high as 94%, and by the late 1980s, young black men may have reached virtual parity with whites if differences in verbal and mathematical skills are taken into account.[12]

Much less is known about labor market discrimination against black women, but a good argument can be made that the trend is even more striking. As of the late 1940s (which is as far back as most studies go), black women earned far less than black men, white men, and white women, and there is no doubt that they experienced intense and pervasive discrimination. By 1980, however, their earnings essentially equaled white women's, leading Farley and Allen to conclude (1987, 340) that they "no longer suffer from racial discrimination in wage rates." (They do still suffer from sex discrimination, however; see the review in Burstein and Edwards 1994.)

How much of the decline in discrimination has been due to EEO law? As noted above, we would expect econometric analyses to conclude that EEO law has had little impact, and that is indeed their most common conclusion. Smith and Welch (1989) argue, for example, that EEO enforcement has had no long-term impact on black men's wages. They claim that it produced what they call a "wage bubble" for a few years just after Title VII went into effect, dramatically increasing black men's earnings relative to those of white men; but the bubble soon burst, and their wages went back to what might have been expected on the basis of their productivity and whatever discrimination they continued to face. Other scholars find EEO law to have had an effect, but a very modest one; even Smith and Welch's most visible opponents, Donohue and Heckman (1991), say that although EEO law significantly and permanently raised black men's earnings in the decade after passage, it has had no impact since the mid-1970s.[13]

How can these conclusions be reconciled with the fact that discrimination against blacks seems to have declined so greatly? We cannot be sure at this point, but probably in two ways suggested by a social movement approach. First, econometric studies take a very narrow view of how EEO law might affect labor market outcomes, typically focusing only on enforcement expenditures or reviews of hiring by federal contractors. Taking into account other aspects of enforcement—the courts' adoption of broad definitions of discrimination, receptiveness to class action suits, and willingness to impose substantial penalties on discriminators (including affirmative action), the aggressive strategies pursued by the EEOC in its early years, its impact on formal personnel procedures, etc.—would surely lead to higher estimates of its impact.[14]

Second, much of the decline in labor market discrimination may be the result of the broader struggle against discrimination, of which EEO enforcement is only a part; for example, the activities of black, Jewish, and other groups over the last hundred years may have reduced prejudice; the reduction in prejudice may have led to a drop in discrimination and paved the way for civil rights legislation; the moral force of the law may have led to further declines in prejudice; and attacks on discrimination across a broad front, in education, public accommodations, and other areas as well as employment, may have led to the reinforcement of changes in each area by changes in the others. Trying to assess the impact of the legal struggle against discrimination by focusing on particular aspects of the enforcement process seems unduly restrictive in this context (see Burstein 1985; Donohue and Heckman 1991; and Heckman and Payner 1989 for brief reviews of these arguments). This argument is somewhat speculative, but without the adoption of a social movement perspective, it is not likely to be pursued.

What about other racial minorities? Asians and American Indians have suffered grievously from labor market discrimination, but it has been the subject of so little quantitative work that changes in its impact cannot be estimated statistically. Without knowing how the impact of labor market discrimination has changed, we obviously cannot gauge how much it has been affected by EEO law.

Religion

It is difficult to get many people, even those active in the civil rights community, to take religious discrimination seriously. Compared to other forms of discrimination, it seems utterly inconsequential. But if it were inconsequential, that would be noteworthy indeed. Religious conflict, including labor market discrimination on the basis of religion, has a long history around the world, and a glance at almost any daily newspaper shows that there is no reason to think it declines automatically with the passage of time. In the United States, hostility toward Roman Catholics, Jews, Mormons, and other groups has been pervasive, intense, and longstanding.[15] Yet almost nothing has been heard about religious discrimination in employment since Title VII was adopted. What happened? Did religious discrimination disappear of its own accord at the moment Title VII was adopted?

Religious discrimination has surely declined greatly in the United States over the last century or more. This does not mean it has disappeared completely, but its current economic impact on groups large enough to appear in surveys in significant numbers seems minimal (cf. Cain 1986, 766). About 2.4% of complaints to the EEOC under Title VII are based on claims of religious discrimination, with a slightly smaller proportion of EEO cases reaching the federal courts (with Jews, Seventh Day Adventists, and other Christian sabbatarians being the largest groups of plaintiffs; see Beckley and Burstein 1991). As with racial minorities other than blacks, we lack the data needed for measuring trends in discrimination against religious minorities, so it is therefore impossible to gauge the impact of EEO law on religious discrimination.

Nevertheless, a good argument can be made that the struggle for EEO law, if not the law itself, reduced religious discrimination. One plausible interpretation of the struggle against religious discrimination is that it mostly succeeded—Title VII is one of its successes and a decline in religious discrimination another. Jews and other groups had been fighting religious discrimination long before the adoption of Title VII. Before EEO laws seemed constitutionally permissible, they used a variety of means—negotiations with employers, educational efforts in the schools and elsewhere, etc.—and once such statutes seemed likely to pass, they shifted some resources to winning passage. As a result of these efforts, the workings of the market, and forces no one really understands, religious discrimination declined so much that the adoption of Title VII essentially ratified changes in attitudes and employment practices that had already taken place. By the time Title VII passed, it may have been largely unnecessary for the economic betterment of religious minorities; but it should be viewed as an important symbol of the decline in discrimination that had already taken place in American society.

Sex

Social scientists, like much of the public, were long oblivious to what is now thought of as sex discrimination.[16] In addition, many believed—some still do—that women earn less than men because of their devotion to home and family rather than discrimination. As a result, less is known about trends in sex discrimination than about race discrimination, and the impact of EEO law on women is studied less than is its impact on black men.[17]

The definitive work on gender discrimination in the labor market is Claudia Goldin's *Understanding the Gender Gap* (1990). In opposition to the conventional view among economists that economic progress necessarily leads to a decline in discrimination, she argues that wage discrimination against women probably rose substantially during the first half of this century, as women moved from manufacturing to office work and their new employers adopted discriminatory policies (Goldin 1990, chapter 4). There was little change from the 1950s through the 1970s and probably something of a decline during the 1980s. During the period when gender discrimination was most pervasive, women, arguably, were rewarded less than were black men for their productivity (see Cain 1986, especially 759–60).

How has EEO law affected women's labor market outcomes? Econometric studies reach conclusions similar to their conclusions about black men: some show a significant impact, some show little or no impact, none shows a tremendous impact. But some evidence suggests that the impact of EEO law on women—both black and white—may be greater for women than for black men.[18] This finding, particularly if it is confirmed by further research, has significant implications for estimates of the impact of EEO law. Our conclusions about its impact are based largely on studies of black men. If discrimination against women—a large group—has been reduced by EEO law more than has discrimination against black men—a relatively small group—then the previous focus on a group that is relatively small and helped relatively little may have led us to greatly underestimate the total impact of EEO law.

National Origin

Like religious minorities, national-origin minorities long suffered from employment discrimination, beginning proverbially with "No Irish Need Apply" in the mid-nineteenth century. Such discrimination was probably especially intense when national origin was combined with membership in a minority religion (particularly Roman Catholicism) or race (as with discrimination against Asians; see, e.g., Lieberson 1980; Takaki 1993).

Discrimination against many national-origin groups (including Americans of Irish Catholic, Italian, and Polish background), has declined so much that these groups do at least as well as the longest-established groups from northwestern Europe (Neidert and Farley 1985; Cain 1986). Among national-origin groups, Hispanics seem to suffer most from discrimination, though there is some dispute about whether they suffer more from discrimination or from poor English-language skills and other factors associated with recent arrival to the United States (compare Neidert and Farley 1985 to Cain 1986, 762–66).

National origin is the basis of about 10 to 12% of charges to the EEOC and a slightly lower percentage of federal appellate level EEO cases (Burstein 1991a). The majority of cases is brought by Hispanics, but substantial numbers are brought by whites of southern and eastern European origin, leading to accusations that discrimination against such whites is unjustifiably ignored by lawyers and social scientists (Munafo 1979).

So far as I know, no study has ever attempted to estimate the impact of EEO enforcement on economic outcomes for national-origin minorities. With the increasing importance of Hispanics in the United States, as well as of groups from Asia that may be viewed in either racial ("Asian") or national origin terms (Chinese, Japanese, Korean, etc.), surely such studies should be done.

White Men

No examination of labor market discrimination would be complete without considering its impact on white, nonminority men. Traditionally, many white men were the beneficiaries of labor market discrimination; by discriminating against women and minorities, white men could guarantee themselves the best jobs with the best pay.[19] During the last couple of decades, however, many white men have come to see themselves as the victims of discrimination; they claim that overzealous EEO enforcement has forced employers to give preferential treatment to minorities and women, making white men the victims of "reverse discrimination." Much of the white public thinks that blacks are frequently given special consideration and hired before whites; many social scientists and elite journalists agree with Christopher Jencks's statement that at some point "the federal emphasis [in EEO enforcement] switched from eliminating overt discrimination to increasing the number of black workers regardless of their apparent qualifications or past performance."[20]

Yet there is much less quantitative evidence for reverse discrimination than for race and sex discrimination. Reverse discrimination does appear to have benefitted blacks in academia (Sowell 1976); there is some experimental evidence that it occurs elsewhere (Turner et al. 1991); and plaintiffs in some reverse discrimination cases have shown that it has occurred in specific employment settings (Burstein 1991b; Merida 1995). But no study has ever shown that the impact of reverse discrimination on the labor force as a whole is anywhere near as great as the impact of discrimination against minorities and women—by showing, for example, that minorities or women are more highly rewarded, on the average, than equally productive white, nonminority men.[21]

Nor has anyone found, thus far, solid evidence that affirmative action or reverse discrimination has harmed the economy as a whole. The most systematic attempt to determine whether affirmative action leads to reverse discrimination is Jonathan Leonard's, and his conclusions are a model of caution:

Has this [affirmative action] pressure led to reduced discrimination, or has it gone beyond and induced reverse discrimination against white males? The evidence is least conclusive on this question. Direct tests of the impact of affirmative action on productivity find no significant evidence of a productivity decline, which implies a lack of substantial reverse discrimination. However, since the productivity estimates are not measured with great precision, strong policy conclusions based on this particular result should be resisted. The available evidence is not yet strong enough to be compelling on either side of this issue. (1990, 61–62)

American Politics and the Antidiscrimination Movement

It is very difficult to trace the impact of a particular law, or even a whole set of laws and regulations, on labor market outcomes; but it is even more difficult to assess their impact on the political system. Labor market outcomes are specific and relatively easy to measure, and the theories that try to explain them are relatively rigorous by social science standards. Political outcomes are often broader in scope and difficult to measure, and theories of political change are more problematic.

Nevertheless, it is essential to try to describe the impact of EEO law, and the struggle for equality more generally, on American politics, because there is every reason to think that the impact is both long-lasting and profound. Here I will just touch on the effects of the struggle for race and gender equality on American party politics, political organization, and ideology.

Race has long been central to American politics. Often it has been the most intensely felt issue on the public agenda and at other times it has been kept off the agenda because politicians well understood its power to disrupt established political alliances (see Riker 1982, chapter 9; Carmines and Stimson 1989).

Race was kept off the national agenda from the end of Reconstruction until the 1950s, for the most part. But the New Deal paved the way for its return.[22] The New Deal coalition contained groups that shared an interest in ending the Depression but were fundamentally incompatible in other ways: southern whites committed to the continued subjugation of blacks and northern blacks who, unlike those in the South, had access to the ballot box. The coalition was initially kept together by the exigencies of the Depression and then World War II, along with President Roosevelt's continuing success in distancing himself from the issue of race; but its fault line was eventually discovered by the Republicans.

The Republicans, of course, had a strong interest in breaking up the New Deal coalition—it had ended their control of the federal government and made them the minority party. For a long time it was not clear that race was the issue that would enable them to do so; civil rights was neither an especially important issue nor a partisan one. The dramatic growth of the civil rights movement in the 1950s and 1960s made the issue important, and with the 1964 Goldwater candidacy Republicans began to find a way to exploit it. They developed a doctrine of "racial conservatism" that opposed federal intervention in racial issues while supporting the principle of equal opportunity. With this stance they were able to make race a partisan issue and convince much of the public that there was a link between liberalism on racial issues and the kind of "big government" that has seldom been popular in the United States. Their strategy aided the rise of the Republican Party in the South, increased its strength elsewhere, improved Republican chances in presidential campaigns, and kept race in a central place on the public agenda.

Of course it was not Title VII that produced this transformation; indeed, the Goldwater campaign occurred before Title VII went into effect in July 1965. But the issue of employment discrimination was central to the civil rights movement. Demands for change in employment and education provoked more resistance than any others, and antagonism toward what is characterized by conservatives as preferential treatment for blacks has been a crucial resource for conservative candidates and for the Republican Party in their quest for office (see, e.g., Lipset 1992). Indeed, it is plausible—though not proven—that the impact of EEO laws declined in the 1980s because Republican administrations did not enforce them as strongly as Democrats might have (Burstein and Edwards 1994; Wood 1990).

Gender has become a political issue as well, and the fight against gender discrimination in the labor market has had consequences well beyond the matter ostensibly at hand. The principle of equal treatment, regardless of gender, has won such widespread acceptance that politicians are very reluctant to attack it directly. But this does not mean that there has been no political response to women's drive for EEO. A number of scholars have argued convincingly that much of the public debate about abortion and family policy is really about whether women are to be treated as autonomous individuals capable of competing on equal terms with men or are to be defined primarily in terms of their roles as wives and mothers (Luker 1984; Cohen and Katzenstein 1988). The legal and ideological developments stimulated by Title VII and the women's movement challenge traditional roles in fundamental ways and have provoked a countermovement that has managed to bring what its adherents see as traditional values to the center of political debate.

Conclusions

What are the consequences of Title VII? If one took into account only what has been quite conclusively shown in neoclassical/econometric analyses, the answer would have to be "not much." According to such studies, EEO law may have raised black men's earnings, though not a great deal; some part of that total increase could then be attributed to Title VII. EEO law has improved women's earnings relative to men's, probably by more than it increased black men's relative to white men's but, again, not by a great deal.

If one adopted the worst-case approach, in contrast, the answer would have to be that Title VII has caused considerable harm in the form of attacks on the merit system, quotas for hiring and promotion, and reverse discrimination.

I have argued, however, that neoclassical/econometric work underestimates the impact of Title VII, and EEO law more generally, in three ways, and that worst-case analyses exaggerate the harm EEO law causes. Neoclassical/econometric work underestimates the impact of EEO law, first, because those gauging its impact devote the greatest share of their attention to a relatively small group—black men; pay less attention to a much larger group arguably more strongly affected—women; and pay no attention at all to some groups protected by the law—racial minorities other than blacks, and religious and national-origin minorities. Focusing on one group, they fail to estimate the total impact of EEO law on all protected groups. Second, the statistical work fails to consider how EEO law (and struggles over how it should be enforced) have affected how discrimination is defined and how organizations have changed their personnel procedures. And third, such work has ignored the effects of Title VII beyond the labor market—on the civil rights and women's movements, gender roles, and American politics. The worst-case approach exaggerates the harm caused by EEO law because it fails to weigh evidence of harm against evidence of benefit and ignores political and economic theory.

A social movement approach to EEO—an approach that sees the adoption and enforcement of EEO law as part of a broad social and political process, involving many groups, influencing and being influenced by the law—leads to different conclusions and further questions. From this perspective, the impact of EEO law on labor market outcomes seems larger, as we add up the total impact on all protected groups and observe that the impact on some groups has not even been assessed. The struggle over EEO has led to changes in how discrimination is defined and in organizational practices. It stimulated the growth of the contemporary women's movement and influenced the strategy and tactics of the civil rights and women's movements. It has led to changes in gender roles, to claims of reverse discrimination, and to counterattacks by those who claim that enforcement has gone "too far." And it has, arguably, played a role in profound changes in American politics.

Unfortunately, I have not been able to provide a rigorous accounting of these effects. Because attempts to move beyond the neoclassical/econometric and worst-case approaches is just beginning, we do not have well-developed models for describing and explaining the effects of EEO law or the data needed to investigate them. But I hope that the examples provided here make the case that the effort required to do so would be most worthwhile.

Notes

1. Title VII (as amended; 42 U.S.C. §2000e et seq.) is the broadest and most important equal employment opportunity law, but a number of other federal laws prohibit at least some forms of employment discrimination: the Equal Pay Act of 1963 (29 U.S.C. §206[d]); the Civil Rights Acts of 1866 and

1871 (42 U.S.C. §1981 and §1983); the Railway Labor Act of 1926 (45 U.S.C. §151–88); the Labor Management Relations Act of 1947 (29 U.S.C. §151 et seq.). Also important are the U.S. Constitution and Executive Orders 11246 and 11375. See Schlei and Grossman 1983. All these are treated together in this essay under the rubric "EEO law," for reasons to be described below.

2. Work on the impact of EEO law on discrimination is best summarized in the exchange between Smith and Welch (1989), who contend that it has had virtually no lasting effect, and Donohue and Heckman (1991), who argue that it had substantial impact through the mid-1970s but not since. Allegations of harm are found in Glazer 1978; Belz 1991; Epstein 1992; and in many of the chapters in Nieli 1991. A note on terminology: the legal term "employment discrimination" and the economists' term "labor market discrimination" will be treated as equivalent in this essay.

3. An instance of worst-case proponents ignoring theories of democratic politics is provided by Nathan Glazer. In 1978, he expressed surprise at the slowing of what had earlier seemed to him an "apparently inexorable" trend toward distributing jobs on the basis of race (1978, x). It did not occur to him that his own work might have influenced the debate or that the government might have responded to opponents of the trend. For an argument similar to mine, see O'Neill and O'Neill 1992, 103.

4. On the impact of public opinion and other noneconomic factors on labor market outcomes, see Burstein 1985; on social movement organizations and litigation, see Burstein 1991a and Burstein and Edwards 1994; for a broad approach to enforcement, see Blumrosen 1993. The economists Donohue and Heckman (1991) and Goldin (1990) reach their conclusions reluctantly because they find their work moving them away from conventional modes of economic analysis. Donohue and Heckman go so far as to say that their new approach "violates . . . canons of current professional standards" in economics (1604); see also Goldin, 217; Burstein 1992.

5. For systematic analyses of disputes over the definition of discrimination, see Blumrosen 1993; Burstein 1990; Ralston 1990; cf. Gamson and Modigliani 1987. One especially influential document in the struggle is MacKinnon 1979.

6. The economists Ashenfelter and Oaxaca (1987, 322) argue, for example, that without the adverse impact doctrine enunciated in *Griggs*, it would be easy for employers to evade the law: "It is not hard to see that the appearance of disparate treatment [that is most often thought of as the "obvious" definition of discrimination] is easy for an employer to eliminate without making any change in behavior at all. . . . To most economists the insistence on finding 'smoking gun' evidence of discriminatory actions, intent, or motivation seems quite irrelevant to determining whether labor market discrimination exists" (cf. Posner 1987, 517–18).

7. The long controversy over how discrimination is to be defined has been ignored by most social scientists, who ignore the legal definition and continue to utilize definitions virtually identical to those extant in 1964. Empirical work on discrimination is not harmed as much as it might be by this because social scientists generally try to measure the consequences of discrimination, not the prevalence of discrimination itself (see Burstein 1990).

8. For a summary of recent public opinion polls on preferential treatment, special programs for blacks, and reverse discrimination, see Lipset 1992. Responses on these issues are very sensitive to question wording, but is quite clear that large majorities of Americans oppose both discrimination and reverse discrimination. A fair proportion seem to favor giving some special help to blacks, but not much; see also Kluegel and Bobo 1993.

9. Because the EEOC had no enforcement powers, it could not issue regulations, only "guidelines." On the history and impact of the EEOC, see Blumrosen 1993.

10. Thus conclusions about organizational responses to EEO law have to be especially cautious. The EEOC collects data from large numbers of firms about how women and members of minority groups are distributed among different kinds of jobs, but the data provide no information about the organizational processes that produce the distributions.

11. Earnings (or related measures, such as hourly wages) are the labor market outcomes focused on here. Some legal scholars and social scientists contend that occupation is at least as good a measure of

labor market outcomes, and that it has the advantage of reflecting potential as well as current earning capacity (see the review in Blumrosen 1993, chapter 18). In addition, EEO enforcement focuses more on access to jobs (within occupations) than on earnings, so arguably it would make sense to focus on occupational attainment when trying to estimate the impact of EEO law. Unfortunately, occupation and occupational differences between groups are more difficult to conceptualize and measure than earnings; as a result, there are very few studies that consider the impact of EEO law on occupational change. The trends in occupational change seem to be generally similar to those for earnings, but we can say very little about how much of the change can be attributed to EEO law and how much to other factors, compared to what we can say about changes in earnings. See Blumrosen 1993; Carlson 1992.

12. Particular estimates of the impact of discrimination are necessarily approximate, but so many researchers have found discrimination to have declined that there can be no doubt about the trend; see Cain 1986; Jencks et al. 1979, 210; Featherman and Hauser 1978, chapter 6; Bound and Freeman 1989; Ehrenberg and Smith 1991, 534; Smith 1993. On the impact of verbal and mathematical skills on racial differences in earnings and estimates of discrimination, see O'Neill 1990, especially 41, table 5, part B; Farkas et al. 1994, especially table 7; and Ferguson 1995; cf. Smith 1993, 82).

13. O'Neill and O'Neill conclude their review of work on EEO enforcement by writing that federal contractors increased the employment of black men in response to affirmative action requirements but that, on the whole, the employment effects, "although statistically significant, are not large enough to have produced any noticeable impact on the average relative earnings of black men" (1992, 96).

14. Similarly, the apparent slowing of black men's progress in recent years could be explained by the weakening of aspects of enforcement ignored in econometric studies, as well as by other factors; see Burstein and Edwards 1994; Ferguson 1995.

15. As part of the campaign for EEO legislation, Jewish groups provided congressional committees with evidence of widespread employment discrimination against Jews well into the 1950s; see Lieberson 1980; Burstein 1985.

16. Social scientists often prefer the term "gender discrimination," but because Title VII refers to "sex," I will sometimes use the latter term.

17. Also, gender discrimination may be more difficult to analyze than race discrimination because doing so requires taking the relationship between work and family into account; see Goldin 1990 on these issues. Judges as well as economists often assume that women lack interest in jobs traditionally dominated by men (Schultz 1990).

18. See Burstein 1985, chapter 6, and Gunderson 1989. Similar results in Great Britain add credibility to this conclusion; compare Zabalza and Tzannatos 1985 to Brown and Gay 1985. Leonard 1989 argues that affirmative action specifically has had less impact on women than on blacks, however.

19. Many economists argue that white men's beliefs were mistaken; by interfering with market processes that match individuals to the jobs for which they are best qualified, discrimination reduces the efficiency of the economy as a whole and thus, in the end, harms everyone (see, e.g., Epstein 1992; Posner 1987). Often, however, groups seek short-term gains from discrimination for themselves, unaware of the prospect of long-run losses for all.

20. Jencks 1985, 731; see also Epstein 1992, 391, and the review in Burstein 1991b; on the white public's attitudes, see Jacobson 1985 and Lipset 1992, 69; cf. Kluegel and Smith 1986.

21. For reviews, see Burstein 1991b; 1992. This is obviously not to say that reverse discrimination is not a serious matter where it occurs, or that white men are wrong to be concerned. I am only pointing out that there is no evidence that its impact is anywhere near as large as the impact of discrimination against minorities and women.

22. This discussion draws heavily on Carmines and Stimson 1989. For example, no member of Congress, not even the most conservative, has introduced a bill to weaken or repeal EEO laws against sex discrimination or any bill intended to get women out of the labor force and back into the home (Burstein, Bricher, and Einwohner 1995).

8

The Struggle for Racial Equality in Public Accommodations

Randall Kennedy

This chapter explains the circumstances that prompted the enactment of Title II of the Civil Rights Act of 1964, which prohibits racial discrimination in public accommodations. It argues that Title II has been a striking success and suggests explanations for the provision's effectiveness that highlight both the remarkable ways in which the Civil Rights Act changed American life for the better and the frustrating reality that the most complete reforms are those that have done the least to challenge the obstacles that continue to impede African Americans in the late twentieth century.

Title II of the Civil Rights Act was a response to one of the most courageous and inspiring aspects of the civil rights movement: the demand that blacks be accorded the same treatment as whites in places of public accommodation—restaurants, lodgings, places of entertainment, and the like.[1]

Protests against unequal treatment often took the form of "sit-ins" in which blacks would occupy places reserved for whites only.[2] Responses to these protests varied. Sometimes proprietors of targeted establishments would ignore the protesters, refuse to serve them, and wait for them to give up in sheer exhaustion or to be driven out by white supremacists. More frequently, proprietors or other disapproving observers would call police, who typically arrested the protesters under local laws for trespassing or disorderly conduct or violation of a state segregation statute. Much distress was inflicted by local officials in this way on the protesters. But if the protesters were lucky enough to be represented by such attorneys as

Thurgood Marshall, Matthew Perry, Jack Greenberg, or Robert Carter, they stood a good chance of having their convictions reversed on federal statutory or constitutional grounds.

In the early 1960s, the Supreme Court showed notable solicitude toward nonviolent, well-disciplined civil rights protesters and crafted for them a broad legal umbrella.[3] Protesters arrested for sitting in at bus station lunch counters, for example, had their convictions voided on the grounds that the federal Interstate Commerce Act prohibited racial discrimination in interstate travel.[4] Protesters arrested for breach of the peace often had their convictions reversed on the grounds that there was no evidence of their having actually created a disturbance.[5] In still other cases, the Court voided trespass convictions on the grounds that the face lines traversed by protesters were imposed not by the owners of the establishments in question but rather by local ordinances; while federal constitutional law permitted private owners of public accommodations to engage in racial segregation or exclusion, federal constitutional law in the aftermath of *Brown v. Board of Education* prohibited states or the federal government from engaging in invidious racial discrimination.[6]

In spite of this judicial solicitude, the protesters failed to extract from the Supreme Court what they most wanted: a ruling that racial discrimination in places of public accommodation violated the federal Constitution.[7] They persuaded three Justices—Earl Warren, William O. Douglas, and Arthur J. Goldberg—to adopt this position.[8] But the majority held fast to the well-established proposition (which is still "good law") that the federal Constitution prohibits only state action that discriminates invidiously on the basis on race and that policies imposed by owners or managers of private corporations alone do not count as state action within the meaning of the Fourteenth Amendment.

In the absence of a constitutional prohibition against racial discrimination by private businesses, protesters had few sources of relief. They could seek to change the minds of business owners or managers through boycotts. But this was a tactic of limited scope; a victory at one establishment was unlikely to affect the policies of many others. They could seek to enact state statutes outlawing invidious racial discrimination in places of public accommodation. But this was a futile gesture throughout the South because southern state governments were tightly controlled by white supremacists openly hostile to the civil rights movement. The other potential sources of relief were the legislative and executive branches of the federal government. It was to them that civil rights leaders principally appealed. As Martin Luther King, Jr., declared in his famous "I have a dream" speech of 28 August 1963, during the epochal March on Washington:

We've come to our Nation's Capital to cash a check. When the architects of our republic wrote the magnificent words of the Constitution and the Declaration of Independence, they were signing a promissory note to which every American was to fall heir. . . . This note was a promise that all men, yes, black men as well as white men, should be guaranteed the inalienable rights of life, liberty, and the pursuit of happiness. . . . It is obvious today that America has defaulted on this promissory note insofar as her citizens of color are concerned. . . . We can never be satisfied as long as our bodies, heavy with the fatigue of travel, cannot gain lodging in the motels of the highways and the hotels of the cities. . . . We can never be satisfied as long as our children are stripped of their selfhood and robbed of their dignity by signs stating: "For Whites Only."[9]

Moved by this plea and in the hope of impressing the large audience to which it appealed, politicians proposed federal legislation outlawing racial discrimination in places of public accommodation.[10] This proposal was highly controversial. Some opposed it because of their commitment to an old-fashioned white supremacy. Others opposed it because they feared that such legislation would prompt federal overreaching and unduly impinge on the prerogatives of local governments and private entrepreneurs. Others expressed qualms about the constitutionality of the proposed legislation.

After the longest congressional debate in American history, the Civil Rights Bill of 1964 was passed into law. Title II of that bill provided that "All persons shall be entitled to the full and equal enjoyment of the goods, services, facilities, privileges, advantages, and accommodations of any place of public accommodation . . . without discrimination or segregation on the ground of race, color, religion, or national origin." The Senate report that explained Title II declared that its primary purpose was to address "the deprivation of personal dignity that surely accompanies denials of equal access to public establishments. Discrimination is not simply dollars and cents, hamburgers and movies; it is the humiliation, the frustration, and embarrassment that a person must surely feel when he is told that he is unacceptable as a member of the public because of his race or color."[11]

The legality of Title II was challenged immediately by the owner of the Heart of Atlanta motel, who charged, among other things, that Congress had no authority under the federal Constitution to prohibit racial discrimination in places of public accommodation.[12] He had a point. After all, in 1883, in *The Civil Rights Cases*, the Supreme Court had invalidated a provision of the federal Civil Rights Act of 1875 that had also attempted to outlaw racial discrimination in places of public accommodation.[13] In the Court's view, Congress had disregarded a fundamental tenant of federalism by seeking to regulate private conduct directly, without regard to whether the state had prompted, encouraged, or discouraged the conduct at issue. "It is State action of a particular character that is prohibited" by the Fourteenth Amendment, Justice Joseph P. Bradley observed, writing for the Court. "Individual invasion of individual rights is not the subject matter of the Amendment," which was the constitutional provision relied upon as authority by Congress.[14] Despite a strong dissent by Justice John Marshall Harlan, the ruling in *The Civil Rights Cases* remained largely intact when the Court considered the constitutionality of Title II. By 1964, the Court had enlarged the conception of what constituted state action. But it continued to recognize a distinction between state action and private action; while the former was subject to federal jurisdiction pursuant to the Fourteenth Amendment, the latter lay outside the reach of that amendment.

In deference to the authority of *The Civil Rights Cases*, the Kennedy and Johnson administrations insisted that Title II be presented as legislation based principally on the commerce clause of the Constitution. In so doing, the allies of the legislation in the executive branch sought to sidestep *The Civil Rights Cases* and capitalize on the capacious readings that the Supreme Court had given to the interstate commerce clause ever since the New Deal. While some observers complained that this strategy amounted to a superficial evasion that devalued the human rights championed by Title II, the fact is that in *Heart of Atlanta Motel v. United States*, the Supreme Court upheld the public accommodations provision on the basis of the commerce clause.

Although Title II was probably the most talked about section of the Civil Rights Act, the section about which emotions ran highest, the section over which the most blood had been spilled, it quickly faded in significance. It became, to paraphrase Hugh Davis Graham, a welcome casualty of success.[15] As James W. Button (1989, 183) put it, Title II "clearly broadened and deepened the federal commitment to ending segregation in public accommodations. Compliance with the law in the South was relatively prompt and extensive, although acceptance in rural, Old South areas tended to be 'minimal and grudging.'"

The relative success of Title II is reflected to a large extent in the comparative simplicity, uniformity, and continuity of the case law built upon it. There arose no effective, concerted campaign of resistance like that which opposed the desegregation of public schooling, thereby prompting the courts and the Congress to create new devices and doctrines for its enforcement. Moreover, the legal issues that did arise were dramatically less complex than those which surrounded, and continue to vex, Title VII of the Civil Rights Act, the provision that outlawed racial discrimination in many areas of the employment market. While Title VII has been amended on several occasions, Title II has never been amended. While the case law of Title VII—consider, for example, the creation of the disparate impact model of discrimination—provides sufficient grist for a large treatise or a discrete law school course,[16] the case law of Title II is barely mentioned even in comprehensive treatments of modern civil rights developments.[17]

The most important themes of Title II jurisprudence are rather clear and easy to recite. On the one hand, interpretation of the law's substantive provisions has been liberal. Hence, courts have applied Title II so that it reaches practically any lodging place or restaurant regardless of the tenuousness of the claim that a given establishment is really engaged in interstate commerce. On the other hand, exceptions to Title II have been interpreted narrowly; private clubs, for instance, are excepted from coverage. Courts have applied the private club exception with rigorous strictness, permitting only associations that are "truly private"[18] to escape Title II's anti-discrimination mandate.[19]

This is not to say that the law of Title II is wholly devoid of problems, complexities, and frustrations. It is interesting to note that Title II fails to prohibit gender discrimination. It is disturbing to learn that "a great many establishments are not covered, including retail stores, many establishments offering services (professional and other), private hospitals, and proprietary schools."[20] It is morbidly fascinating to observe the fight that took place in the Seventh Circuit Court of Appeals over whether the Boy Scouts of America constitute a place of public accommodation—a divided court ruled that the scouts are outside Title II's purview.[21]

Decided cases, moreover, offer only a partial history of any statute; the costs of litigation almost always ensure under-enforcement of statutory norms. For every successful multimillion-dollar judgment or settlement reported in newspapers[22] there are scores of racist incidents in which people of color, because of their race, are either refused service altogether or given service that is inferior to that given to white customers.[23]

Still, the overall evaluation of Title II clearly points toward striking success. Gone are the conditions that prompted Roy Wilkins of the NAACP to declare in anguish that while Congress debated whether to enact Title II, "Negro Americans throughout our country will be bruised in nearly every waking hour by differential treatment in, or exclusion from, public accommodations of every description.

From the time they leave their homes in the morning, en route to school or work, to shopping, or to visiting, until they return home at night, humiliation stalks them."[24]

A trip by car between Washington, D.C., and Columbia, S.C., is radically different today than it was thirty-five years ago. Gone is the fear that one might feel the need to use a toilet outside those few areas in which gas station attendants permitted "colored" to use the facilities. Gone are signs distinguishing between restrooms for "Negro Women" and "White Ladies." Gone is the sense that the southbound highways out of the District of Columbia constituted a vast no-man's-land to be traveled only after careful planning and still at one's peril. Gone are the overt, assertive banners of Jim Crow pigmentocracy.

There have been other changes, as well. The reformist spirit of Title II has reached farther than its text. I noted above that Title II is, in certain ways, surprisingly narrow in its definition of public accommodations. This law has changed social expectations so thoroughly, however, that many people assume that it covers more than the language of its provisions actually states. Thus, while the letter of the law is surely under-enforced in some settings, in other settings the ethos of the law has helped to change hearts and minds and conduct in a fashion beyond what many sit-in protesters could ever have imagined.

What accounts for the clear-cut effectiveness of Title II in relation to the more ambiguous records of other provisions of the act, such as Title VII? The principal explanation is that Title II attacked a simpler and more vulnerable target than did other provisions. Racial discrimination in places of public accommodation was, for the most part, a peculiar feature of southern folkways. It was therefore a largely regional problem, unlike the national problem of racial discrimination in employment. Racial discrimination in places of public accommodation was a simple matter of naked racism or acquiescence to naked racism. Employers, by contrast, who equate race with preferred or undesirable traits, experiences, or skills rationalize their decisions as a matter of "good business" rather than racism, an argument that is not always easy to refute, given real differences between whites and blacks in average levels of education and other background resources.[25] The attack on racial discrimination in public accommodations did not entail the redistribution of valuable opportunities, as the campaign against discrimination in employment did. Unlike desegregation of the workplace, where people's jobs could be involved, the integration of public accommodations did not require much sacrifice on the part of most whites. Indeed, Title II freed white entrepreneurs in the South to sell their goods and services to a wider desegregated clientele without fear of retaliation by white bigots; the Civil Rights Act gave them cover to do what market forces would have prompted them to do anyway, absent the emotional factor of racial prejudice. And while southern white supremacists of the old school felt keenly the loss of their symbolic racial privileges, many other white Americans viewed such sensibilities as primitive, disreputable, and unworthy of deference.

Bayard Rustin understood this as far back as 1965. Speaking on behalf of the civil rights movement, he observed that

in desegregating public accommodations, we affected institutions which are relatively peripheral both to the American socioeconomic order and to the fundamental conditions of life of the Negro people. In a highly industrialized, 20th century civilization, we hit Jim Crow precisely where it was most anachronistic, dispensable, and vulnerable—in hotels, lunch counters, terminals, libraries, swimming pools, and the like. For in these forms, Jim Crow does impede the flow of commerce in the broadest sense: it is a nuisance in a society on the move (and on the make).[26]

Rustin was careful not to minimize the movement's victories, noting that "the decade spanned by the 1954 Supreme Court decision on school desegregation and the Civil Rights Act of 1964 will undoubtedly be recorded as the period in which the legal foundations of racism in America were destroyed."[27] He was also careful to avoid "making light of the human sacrifices involved in the direct action tactics (sit-ins, freedom rides, and the rest) that were so instrumental to this achievement."[28] But with all due respect for the sacrifice and accomplishment, Rustin also insisted on a sober, realistic view of what had been won and what remained to be done. Such realism is needed now more than ever as, looking back, we celebrate the Civil Rights Act of 1964 and, looking forward, we consider new challenges in our quest for social justice.

Notes

1. "Public accommodations" is a vague term, the definition of which has varied over time. See Singer 1996, 1283. Title II defines a place of public accommodation as:

"(1) any inn, hotel, motel or other establishment which provides lodging to transient guests, other than an establishment located within a building a building [sic] which contains not more than five rooms for rent or hire and which is actually occupied by the proprietor of such establishment as his residence; (2) any restaurant, cafeteria, lunchroom, lunch counter, soda fountain, or other facility principally engaged in selling food for consumption on the premises, including, but not limited to, any such facility located on the premises of any retail establishment; or any gasoline station; (3) any motion picture house, theater, concert hall, sports arena, stadium or other place of exhibition or entertainment; and (4) any establishment (A) (i) which is physically located within the premises of any establishment otherwise covered by this subsection, or (ii) within the premises of which is physically located any such covered establishment, and (B) which holds itself out as serving patrons of such covered establishment."

Other statutes offer broader definitions of covered public accommodations (see Lerman 1978).

2. See, e.g., Chafe 1981; Wolff 1990; Zinn 1964; Pollitt 1960, 315.

3. See Kalven, Jr., 1965; Greenberg 1968, 1520; Marshall 1965, 785.

4. See *Boynton v. Virginia,* 363 U.S. 454 (1960).

5. See *Garner v. Louisiana,* 368 U.S. 715 (1961).

6. 347 U.S. 483 (1954). See also *Bolling v. Sharpe,* 347 U.S. 497 (1954); *Gayle v. Browder,* 352, U.S. 903 (1956).

7. See Paulsen 1964, 137, analyzing the Supreme Court's avoidance of what was then "one of this nation's most troublesome constitutional questions: To what extent does the Fourteenth Amendment forbid the states to support private choice, when under the Constitution that choice could not be made by the state itself?"

8. See *Bell v. Maryland,* 378 U.S. 226 (1963).

9. See Meier, et al. 1971, 347–49.

10. See generally Graham 1990; Whalen 1985.

11. See U.S. Code Congressional and Administrative News, 2, 99th Congress, Second Session, 1964 (Senate Report) at 2370.

12. See Kurland and Casper 1975, 283.

13. 109 U.S. 3 (1883).

14. In *The Civil Rights Cases,* the Court rejected the claim that the Thirteenth Amendment armed Congress with the authority to outlaw private racial discrimination in places of public accommodation. The Court expressly left open the question of whether the commerce clause could provide the proper authority to Congress for such a statute.

15. See Graham 1990, 5.

16. See, e.g., Schlei and Grossman 1983.

17. See., e.g., Eisenberg 1991, 630–35.

18. Lerman 1978, 224.

19. A private club defense has never prevailed before the Supreme Court. There are, however, some lower court decisions upholding private club defenses. See, e.g., *Golden v. Biscayne Bay Yacht Club,* 530 F.2d 16 (CA 5), cert denied, 429 U.S. 872 (1976); *Cornelius v. Benevolent Protective Order of the Elks,* 382 F. Supp. 1182 (D. Ct. 1974).

20. Lerman 1978, 222.

21. See *Walsh v. Boy Scouts of America,* 993 F.2d 1267 (CA 7 1993).

22. See, e.g., Hawkins 1993, 98, detailing charges that the Denny's fast-food chain has engaged in racial discrimination against black customers and describing an ensuing settlement with the Department of Justice.

23. See Feagin and Sikes 1994, 37–56.

24. Quoted in U.S. Code Congressional and Administrative News, 2, 99th Congress, Second Session, 1964 (Senate Report).

25. See Strauss 1991, 1619–57; Sunstein 1991, 751–74.

26. Quoted in Meier, Rudwick, and Broderick 1971, 445.

27. Quoted in Meier, Rudwick, and Broderick 1971, 444–45.

28. Quoted in Meier, Rudwick, and Broderick 1971, 445.

IV

The Future of Civil Rights

9

Changing Hearts and Minds
Racial Attitudes and Civil Rights

Katherine Tate and Gloria J. Hampton

There has got to be the sentiment, the goodwill, the good sense of a whole citizenry that enforces law. In other words, you have got to win the hearts and minds of men to the logic and the decency of a situation before you're finally going to get real compliance. Law alone, as we found out in the Prohibition experiment, does not cure some of the things it's set out to cure.

—President Dwight D. Eisenhower, responding to *Brown v. Board of Education*

I do not insist that the taxi drivers who will not stop unless I am dressed as they prefer . . . are racists in the same sense that members of the Ku Klux Klan are racists. People are more complicated than that, and I have little doubt that some of the same people who will not open the doors of their jewelry stores when I am in my blue jeans will send large contributions to the Southern Poverty Law Center to do the good work of keeping the Klan at bay. For doing so, I charge them with neither insincerity nor hypocrisy "simply with normal human complexity."

—Stephen L. Carter, Professor of Law at Yale University

President Dwight D. Eisenhower's famous declaration that white Americans would never comply with civil rights laws that violated their core beliefs and feelings about race greatly underestimated the public's ability to change, the power of law, and his authority as president in effecting such change. Although change then seemed improbable, given the pervasiveness of Jim Crow in the South and white opinion about blacks, in less than a generation civil rights legislation ultimately won broad public support. However, while an overwhelming majority of whites came to favor the idea that blacks should have equal opportunities for jobs and education, most rejected and continue to reject federal efforts aimed at reducing the scale of racial inequality and racial segregation in society. Public opinion researchers have offered strikingly different explanations for why, when the majority of whites no longer seek to deny equal rights to blacks, most remain implacably opposed to government steps to reduce racial inequality. Research on racial attitudes, in fact, has become heatedly controversial. Some scholars argue that white opposition to programs that might bring about real racial change reflects to a large extent the tenacious strength of white racism. Others strongly object to this claim, arguing that racial issues have become more complicated, and should not be read as indicators of white intolerance or insincerity.

Researchers in this field have often made a distinction between attitudes about abstract principles of racial equality and policies designed to implement such principles. For example, Schuman, Steeh, and Bobo define implementation questions as those that deal with "approval or disapproval of steps the government might take to combat discrimination or segregation or to reduce racial inequalities in income or status" (1985, 86). This dichotomy misleadingly implies that governmental efforts or policies were not originally part of the push for civil rights but came afterwards, belatedly, as the problem of urban poverty began to receive greater attention and moved to the center stage of national politics.[1] However, in light of the scale of southern resistance to *Brown*, civil rights activists and legislators recognized from the beginning that federal intervention would necessarily be a part of the new civil rights legislation. The 1964 Civil Rights Act not only outlawed discrimination in housing, education, employment, and public accommodations but also authorized the Justice Department to initiate class action suits. This itself was a compromise; civil rights supporters had originally sought a larger enforcement role for the federal government by empowering the Equal Employment Opportunity Commission, not the Justice Department, to file antidiscrimination suits. As historian Hugh Davis Graham notes, the opponents of the civil rights bill, principally Senator Dirksen, much preferred that enforcement authority be given to the Justice Department since it "posed a smaller threat of potential harassment to employers than a new mission agency like the EEOC" (1990, 146).

The principles-implementation framework glosses over important differences between racial policies and their trends as well. Much has been made of the fact that most whites now support the principle of racial equality, while they remain near unanimous in their opposition to busing and affirmative action. But many whites also remain averse to the federal government's enforcement of equal opportunity in employment, to its enforcement of integration in public schools, and to the principle of open housing. To understand where whites stand on civil rights, opinions on broad policy issues must be evaluated separately.

In this chapter, we examine trends in the racial attitudes of white and black Americans. Which groups today remain the most supportive of, or the most hostile to, civil rights enforcement and government programs that aid blacks? The second part of the chapter focuses on the debate over how to explain white opposition to racial policies that favor the economic advancement of African Americans. Although a wealth of research has been devoted to this issue, no consensus view has yet emerged, nor is one likely to emerge in the near future. At minimum, there appears to be agreement that racial and civil rights attitudes are complex. They are also a consistent reflection of the political times and of political leadership.

Trends in Whites' Racial Attitudes

In their comprehensive review of trend data on white racial attitudes, Schuman, Steeh, and Bobo (1985) found that:

1. There has been a "strong and steady" movement of white attitudes favoring the general principle of equal treatment and equal opportunity. By 1966, nearly 90% of whites said that blacks should have "as good a chance" as whites to get any kind of job. By 1982, 90% said that white and black children should go to the same schools.

2. Less support exists for the principle of integration. White attitudes on integration, they write, represent the "one jarring note" in the generally consistent movement toward white acceptance of equal opportunities for blacks (1985, 86). Most whites, when asked if they favor integration, segregation, or "something in-between" preferred "something in-between." By 1977, about 60% wanted a compromise between integration and segregation, while 35% favored "integration." This 95% support for "integration," but mostly for "something in-between," represents about a 10% increase from 1964, when the question was first posed.

3. Younger whites continue to express far more liberal attitudes than older whites toward equal opportunity in jobs and education and toward integration. The traditional North-South division in attitudes on race principles has steadily eroded. Although the dramatic shift in support for civil rights principles first occurred in the North, over time white southern attitudes have steadily become more

liberal. The attitudes of northerners and southerners have converged as northern support has hit a ceiling of near-unanimous support. The effect of education has remained constant, with better-educated whites much more supportive of the general principle of racial equality than less educated whites.

4. Although white attitudes have become progressively more liberal on the general principle of racial equality, there has been little movement in the attitudes of whites against government intervention to ensure equal opportunity or integration. Fewer than 40% of whites felt in 1964 or 1974 that the federal government should see to it that blacks receive fair treatment in jobs. Moreover, the level of white support for government assistance to blacks and other minorities has declined. Fewer than 20% supported government programs to improve the economic and social position of minorities and blacks either in 1970 or today. Similarly, on the question whether the federal government should intervene to see to it that black children go to the same schools as whites, decreasing percentages of whites felt that the government should get involved. While 44% of whites in 1964 favored government intervention in schools, only 25% did so in 1978, a decline of 19%. White support for busing and open housing laws, in contrast, has increased moderately over time. However, even as late as 1983, less than half of the whites interviewed favored open housing law, and only one- fifth supported busing. The only federal intervention policy that the white majority supports unreservedly is in the area of public accommodations.

5. Younger whites are more supportive than older whites of federal efforts to improve the economic and education opportunities and status of blacks. Regional and educational differences also exist, with whites being most supportive in the North and among the college-educated.

6. To update these findings, we examined white racial attitudes over a twenty-year period from 1972 to 1992 on six issues: (a) integration, (b) open housing laws, (c) federal intervention in employment, (d) federal intervention in schools, (e) federal assistance to blacks and minorities, and (f) busing. The data are shown in table 9.1. (The question wording of these six items is shown in a note at the end of this chapter.)

Progressive trends continue in the two general principle areas where white support has been weakest: integration and equal opportunity for blacks in housing. Opposition to segregation has increased by 17% from the period of 1972–1976 to 1989–1992, and now well over two-thirds of whites reject the notion that whites "have a right" to keep their neighborhoods segregated. Support for open housing

Table 9.1 Liberal Trends in Whites' Racial Attitudes

	Percentage Giving Liberal Answer				
	1972–76	1977–78	1983–88	1989–92	Change, 1972–92
Whites have right to keep segregated neighborhoods (GSS)	60.2	64.9	74.3	77.8	+18
Favor open-housing law (GSS)	34.5	38.4	48.4	55.8	+21
Federal job intervention (ANES)	37	—	29.8	33.3	–3.7
Federal school intervention (ANES)	30.9	27	37	27.4	–3.5
Government aid for blacks (ANES)	28.6	22.1	24.5	19.3	–9
Favor busing (GSS)	14.0	15.1	23.1	29.7	+16

Sources: Data are from the General Social Surveys (GSS) and the American National Election Studies (ANES). Question wording appears at the end of chapter 9.

Note: "No interest" and "don't know" responses were included in the distributions from which these percentages are calculated. Dashes indicate that the question was not included in the survey for those years.

laws increased more dramatically during this same period. At the start of the 1990s, a majority of whites (56%) expressed support for open housing laws.

Similarly, little or negative movement was found in the implementation area where Schuman and his colleagues originally reported no or negative change. White support continues to decline for government assistance to blacks and minorities, government enforcement of fairness for blacks in employment, and school integration. Minority and black aid attracts the least support among whites, anywhere from 15 to 20%, while only about one-third of whites are willing to support government efforts to ensure that blacks have equal opportunities in employment. Fewer whites than ever before want to see the federal government involved in integrating public schools, about 27%. Paradoxically, white support for busing has nearly doubled, with the largest increase occurring in the late 1980s and early 1990s. Most whites remain opposed to busing as a means to achieve racial balance in public schools, but whereas 14% favored busing during the early 1970s, about 30% support busing today.

Which groups are the most supportive of civil rights principles and policies? To present the data in a way that permits the broadest interpretations, tables 9.2 through 9.7 show the six racial policy questions broken down by the respondent's gender, age group, level of educational attainment, place of residence, region, ideology, and party identification. The percentages shown are for those giving the liberal answer to the question.

Among whites, there were virtually no differences by gender in attitude on racial policies. Although research has found that women tend to be somewhat more liberal on welfare policy and defense spending issues than men (Shapiro and Mahajan 1986), on matters of race, white women were no more liberal than white men. Young whites remain still far more liberal than their older counterparts on racial issues (see also Steeh and Schuman 1992). Those over the age of fifty held the most conservative views on whites' right to maintain residential segregation and on open housing. Yet younger groups, the thirty-five to fifty-nine-year-olds, resem-

Table 9.2 White Opinion on "Whites Have Right to Segregated Neighborhoods," by Social and Political Groups

| | Percentage Giving Liberal Answer | | | | |
	1972–76	1977–78	1983–88	1989–92	Change, 1972–92
Male	61.5	66.1	75	78.7	+17
Female	59.1	64	73.7	77.1	+18
N	2,581	3,854	4,502	2,418	
18–24	74.5	75.7	84.1	85.3	+11
25–34	70	73.1	83.1	84.9	+15
35–49	59.6	67.2	79.7	84.1	+24.5
50–64	52.9	57.9	66.9	68	+15.1
65+	46	51.8	57.2	65.7	+20
N	2,567	3,842	4,449	2,407	
< High school	47	49.9	56.1	61.2	+14
High school graduate	63.5	68.2	76.7	78.7	+15
College graduate	80.5	82.6	82.6	89.7	+9
N	2,567	3,842	4,495	2,407	
Urban	65	69	76.8	79.2	+14
Rural/small town	50.8	57.1	68.1	74.6	+24
N	2,581	3,842	4,495	2,407	
Non-South	64.8	70.1	76.8	79.2	+14
South	78.6	53.3	68.1	74.6	+24
N	2,581	3,854	4,502	2,418	
Liberal	72.5	72.4	78.9	83	+10.5
Moderate	58	62.7	3.3	77.3	+19
Conservative	56.4	63.5	73.3	75.6	+19
N	1,261	3,724	4,354	2,332	
Democrat	54.7	60.8	71.4	78.2	+23.5
Independent	68.1	70	78	77.5	+9
Republican	58.8	63.3	73.2	77.6	+19
N	2,519	3,821	4,440	2,389	

Sources: Data are from the General Social Surveys (GSS) and the American National Election Studies (ANES). Question wording appears at the end of chapter 9.

Note: "No interest" and "don't know" responses were included in the distributions from which these percentages are calculated. Dashes indicate that the question was not included in the survey for those years.

Table 9.3 White Opinion on "Oppose Open-Housing Law," by Social and Political Groups

	Percentage Giving Liberal Answer				
	1972–76	1977–78	1983–88	1989–92	Change, 1972–92
Male	32.8	36.4	46.7	54.8	+22
Female	35.9	39.9	49.8	56.6	+21
N	3,922	2,622	5,860	2,804	
18–24	52	53.2	61.6	72.7	+21
25–34	44.8	52.5	60.8	64.7	+20
35–49	32.2	36.6	52.3	62.1	+30
50–64	25.3	26.4	36.5	46.6	+21
65+	21.5	24.8	31	36.1	+15
N	3,909	2,610	5,839	2,802	
< High school	27.3	30	41.5	41.1	+14
High school graduate	36	39.6	48	58.4	+22
College graduate	44.8	48	58.4	60.7	+16
N	3,909	2,616	5,851	2,797	
Urban	38.3	43.0	51.4	59.3	+21
Rural/small town	26.9	29.5	41	47.3	+20
N	3,922	2,622	5,860	2,804	
Non-South	39.1	43.5	51.9	59.2	+20
South	24.1	27.2	40.8	48.2	+24
N	3,922	2,622	5,860	2,804	
Liberal	47.4	50.9	58.4	65.2	+17
Moderate	33.4	37.2	48.2	54.8	+21
Conservative	26.7	31.6	43.8	50.7	+24
N	2,505	2,526	5,005	2,719	
Democrat	34.7	39.4	50.4	54.8	+20
Independent	38.8	43	50.7	61.2	+22
Republican	27.4	30.2	43.3	52.5	+25
N	3,848	2,600	5,790	2,765	

Sources: Data are from the General Social Surveys (GSS) and the American National Election Studies (ANES). Question wording appears at the end of chapter 9.

Note: "No interest" and "don't know" responses were included in the distributions from which these percentages are calculated. Dashes indicate that the question was not included in the survey for those years.

bled those in the sixty-plus age group in their anti-busing views, while those under age thirty-five held the most liberal views. In fact, the increase in support for busing among whites is mostly due to the liberal attitudes found among young whites. Younger whites were also less likely than older whites to object to government enforcement of racial fairness in hiring for blacks. And although more supportive of government intervention in school desegregation, their support has dropped over the twenty-year period, as has support among older whites. Support for minority

Table 9.4 White Opinion on Busing, by Social and Political Groups

| | Percentage Giving Liberal Answer | | | |
	1972–76	1977–78	1983–88	1989–92	Change, 1972–92
Male	13.1	14.2	21.2	29	+16
Female	14.8	15.8	24.5	30.2	+15
N	5,128	3,878	4,631	2,706	
18–24	23.1	23.1	38.5	46.3	+23
25–34	15.8	17.7	29.3	37	+21
35–49	11.6	13.8	19.2	25.3	+14
50–64	10.7	9.7	16	23.8	+13
65+	12.1	15.2	19.2	25	+13
N	5,115	3,869	4,628	2,695	
< High school	14.9	17.4	27.4	32.3	+17
High school graduate	11.9	13.1	20.5	27.7	+16
College graduate	19.4	18.3	25.2	33.2	+14
N	5,114	3,869	4,628	2,695	
Urban	14	15.8	23	29	+15
Rural/small town	13.9	13.9	23.3	31.3	+17
N	5,128	3,878	4,631	2,706	
Non-South	15.5	16.9	24.1	32.4	+17
South	10.5	11	20.7	23.8	+13
N	5,128	3,878	4,631	2,706	
Liberal	20.9	21.9	31.6	40.5	+20
Moderate	13.4	14	24.4	28	+15
Conservative	8.9	10.5	15.8	23.1	+19
N	3,652	3,712	3,854	2,611	
Democrat	16.5	16.8	26.5	33.5	+17
Independent	14.1	15.6	24.8	31.3	+17.2
Republican	9.2	11.8	17.3	24.6	+15
N	4,986	3,839	4,583	2,685	

Sources: Data are from the General Social Surveys (GSS) and the American National Election Studies (ANES). Question wording appears at the end of chapter 9.

   Note: "No interest" and "don't know" responses were included in the distributions from which these percentages are calculated. Dashes indicate that the question was not included in the survey for those years.

assistance, which has declined among whites since the 1970s, has fallen especially among the young, by about fourteen percentage points. This drop contrasts with that among those sixty and older, whose support for minority assistance declined by only six percentage points. Thus, while young whites remain the most consistently liberal group among whites on most racial issues, this may no longer be the case with respect to government programs to provide economic assistance to blacks and other minorities (see also Dowden and Robinson 1993).

As with youth, education is ordinarily linked to liberal racial attitudes. However, white college graduates were, in fact, the most liberal of the three educational groups on only four of the six policy issues. College graduates were no more in favor of busing or government intervention in schools than were high school dropouts. Notably, college graduates have become less liberal over time at a faster rate than have the other education groups on four of the six racial issues. Their support for government intervention in schools fell by eight percentage points over

Table 9.5 White Opinion on Government Intervention in Schools, by Social and Political Groups

	Percentage Giving Liberal Answer				
	1972–76	1977–78	1983–88	1989–92	Change, 1972–92
Male	31.2	26.0	31.0	33.1	+2
Female	30.7	27.9	29.6	30	–1
N	4,927	2,279	1,085	2,702	
18–24	39.6	36.3	40.3	35.4	–4
25–34	33.2	27.9	32.7	28.1	–5
35–49	28	24.5	30.6	26.8	–1
50–64	27.8	22.7	22.6	22.6	–5
65+	28.9	26.5	27.3	27.6	–1
N	4,891	2,269	1,083	2,696	
< High school	31.9	29.3	27.1	27.6	–4
High school graduate	28.1	24.8	28.5	26	–2
College graduate	38.9	31.8	38.2	30.6	–8
N	4,913	2,271	1,073	2,643	
Urban	32.2	28.7	34	32.9	+1
Rural/small town	29	23.7	22.3	27.1	–2
N	4,927	2,279	1,085	2,702	
Non-South	31.9	26	25.6	32	+0
South	28.9	28.9	21.7	30.3	+1
N	4,927	2,279	898	2,702	
Liberal	51	37.2	45.7	36.9	–14
Moderate	27.9	26.1	26.4	29.7	–2
Conservative	23.4	21.3	25.6	22.4	+1
N	3,041	1,661	814	2,331	
Democrat	35	32.5	34.8	34.8	0
Independent	30.3	26	29.3	25.9	+4
Republican	25.4	19.3	24.0	22.4	+3
N	4,844	2,207	1,055	2,559	

Sources: Data are from the General Social Surveys (GSS) and the American National Election Studies (ANES). Question wording appears at the end of chapter 9.
     Note: "No interest" and "don't know" responses were included in the distributions from which these percentages are calculated. Dashes indicate that the question was not included in the survey for those years.

Table 9.6 White Opinion on Government Intervention in Jobs, by
Social and Political Groups

	Percentage Giving Liberal Answer			
	1972–76	1977–78	1983–88	1989–92	Change, 1972–92
Male	39.5		34.2	34.9	–4.6
Female	35		26.2	31.9	–3.1
N	2,382		2,391	1,873	
18–24	47.4		31.1	39.6	–7.8
25–34	37.2		32.1	33.3	–3.9
35–49	34.6		35.6	37.3	2.7
50–64	35		27.1	32.9	–2.1
65+	33.8		19.6	22.9	–10.9
N	2,367		2,381	1,873	
< High school	34.4		17	25.6	–8.8
High school graduate	34.8		26.9	30.6	4.2
College graduate	52.3		48.4	45.4	–20.1
N	2,379		2,362	1,873	
Urban	38		33	35.2	–2.8
Rural/small town	35.7		22.7	27.4	–8.3
N	2,382		2,391	1,873	
Non-South	38.7		31.5	34.2	–4.5
South	33.1		26	31.4	–1.7
N	2,382		2,391	1,873	
Liberal	59.7		46.6	48.2	–11.5
Moderate	33.5		26.8	27.7	–5.8
Conservative	33.7		30.7	26.1	–7.6
N	1,406		1,092	1,760	
Democrat	37.2		31.6	39.6	–2.4
Independent	40.5		30.5	34.3	–6.2
Republican	32		28.4	27	–5
N	2,343		2,347	1,745	

Sources: Data are from the General Social Surveys (GSS) and the American National Election Studies (ANES). Question wording appears at the end of chapter 9.

Note: "No interest" and "don't know" responses were included in the distributions from which these percentages are calculated. Dashes indicate that the question was not included in the survey for those years.

the twenty-year period, compared to only two percentage points among high
school graduates. While support increased among high school graduates and
dropouts for government intervention in creating minority job opportunities, it
decreased among college graduates by three percentage points. Support for minority
aid in 1989–1992 among white college graduates also fell at a slightly higher rate
than the rate among high school graduates.

Table 9.7 White Opinion on Government Assistance to Blacks and Minorities, by Social and Political Groups

	Percentage Giving Liberal Answer				
	1972–76	1977–78	1983–88	1989–92	Change, 1972–92
Male	28.4	20.8	23.7	17.8	–8
Female	28.8	23.2	25.1	20.7	–8
N	6,030	5,088	6,391	3,563	
18–24	41.8	27.4	30.2	28.2	–14
25–34	32.6	24.4	26.2	19.2	–13
35–49	28	20.6	25	19.3	–9
50–64	23	20.2	22.8	16.9	–6
65+	22.4	18.8	19.1	16.5	–6
N	5,984	5,075	6,354	3,563	
< High school	24.8	22.3	23.7	18.1	–7
High school graduate	27.9	19.5	22.5	16.4	–11.5
College graduate	40.4	30.5	32.1	27.8	–13
N	6,003	5,076	6,321	3,503	
Urban	32.8	25.5	26.9	21.3	–11.5
Rural/small town	22.4	15.8	19.8	13.6	–9
N	6,030	5,088	6,391	3,563	
Non-South	29.8	26.0	23.7	20.7	–9
South	26.4	22.6	23	16.2	–10.2
N	6,030	5,088	2,008	3,563	
Liberal	55.2	41.6	42.1	32.6	–23
Moderate	28.9	18.5	22.8	16.9	–12
Conservative	18.3	15.4	17.8	12.8	–6
N	4,192	3,449	4,578	3,503	
Democrat	33.8	28.7	31.9	27.3	–6.5
Independent	29	21.1	23.4	18.6	–10
Republican	20.2	12.1	16.3	12.3	–8
N	5,924	4,954	6,252	3,403	

Sources: Data are from the General Social Surveys (GSS) and the American National Election Studies (ANES). Question wording appears at the end of chapter 9.

Note: "No interest" and "don't know" responses were included in the distributions from which these percentages are calculated. Dashes indicate that the question was not included in the survey for those years.

Examining differences and trends among whites living in urban areas as opposed to rural areas, or those in the North versus those in the South, one finds that past differences have narrowed slightly, especially in attitudes toward integration and open housing. This is in part because the attitudes of whites in the South have liberalized at a faster rate than have those of white northerners. This is also in part because differences between northerners and southerners on issues such as busing, minority aid, and government intervention to ensure equal educational and job opportunities for blacks have never been that great. The same is true for rural and urban whites.

Self-identified liberals hold consistently more liberal opinions on the six racial policy issues than do self-identified conservatives. What is most noteworthy, however, is that, as with college graduates, liberal support for government assistance to blacks and minorities has fallen considerably, from 55% in 1972–1976 to 33% in 1989–1992. Liberal support for government intervention in schools has dropped as well, by 14%, while among conservatives and moderates, support has remained relatively constant. In the early 1970s, Democrats were more likely than Republicans to express the view that whites had a right to maintain segregated communities. By the 1990s, however, Democrats had become as liberal as Republicans on this matter. Though they now match Democrats in their support for fair housing, white Republicans are significantly less liberal on the four remaining racial policy items, and especially on the issue of minority assistance.

These trends among the various groups in support for the principle of integration and open housing, government enforcement of equal opportunity for blacks, and busing and federal aid to blacks and minorities indicate that the gap between principle and policy has gotten wider. This is not only because whites are increasingly hostile to government programs that assist blacks, but also because they are less likely today to support *government enforcement* of civil rights, except in the area of public accommodations. Traditionally racially conservative groups, such as southerners and older Americans (but still under sixty-five), express more liberal views on integration and open housing. However, traditionally racially liberal whites—college graduates and self-identified liberals—have become less liberal in their attitudes toward government enforcement of equal opportunity for blacks and, especially, toward government spending to improve the economic and social position of blacks and other minority groups.

Trends in Blacks' Racial Attitudes

Very little research has focused on the racial attitudes of black Americans. In early surveys, blacks respondents were not asked their opinions on civil rights issues, presumably because researchers thought that they already knew the answers (Schuman, Steeh, and Bobo 1985). Furthermore, because no more than one hun-

Table 9.8 Liberal Trends in Blacks' Racial Attitudes

	Percentage Giving Liberal Answer			
	1972–76	1977–78	1983–88	1989–92	Change, 1972–92
Whites have right to keep segregated neighborhoods (GSS)	—	88.9	88.5	91	+2.1
Favor open-housing law (GSS)	—	70.7	78.8	81.4	+10.7
Federal job intervention (ANES)	84.1	—	72	71	–13.1
Federal school intervention (ANES)	68.9	57.4	59.5	58.2	–10.7
Government aid for blacks (ANES)	67.8	48.2	44.9	43.1	–24.7
Favor busing (GSS)	54.6	53.3	58.3	60.4	+5.8

Sources: Data are from the General Social Surveys (GSS) and the American National Election Studies (ANES). Question wording appears at the end of chapter 9.

Note: "No interest" and "don't know" responses were included in the distributions from which these percentages are calculated. Dashes indicate that the question was not included in the survey for those years.

dred to two hundred blacks generally fell into such surveys, in-depth analysis of blacks' racial attitudes was not possible.

As table 9.8 shows, the vast majority of blacks (over 70%) favors school integration, fair housing, and federal enforcement of equal employment opportunities. Blacks, therefore, in stark contrast to whites, believe not only in the twin principles of integration and equal opportunity but also that the government should be involved in the protection and expansion of these rights. Only in the matter of busing to achieve racial balance in schools were blacks somewhat divided, with roughly 40% today opposed to it. Since the late 1970s, however, some blacks have begun to back away from the position that the federal government should be directly involved in ensuring that blacks have equal opportunities in employment and racial balance in schools. Black support for federal intervention in jobs and schools has declined by over 10% over the twenty-year period. But the most dramatic drop, of 25%, has occurred over the matter of whether the government should help improve the economic and social positions of blacks and minorities. Today, more blacks oppose government aid to blacks and other minority groups than support it.

These new reservations about the role of the federal government in the area of civil rights are expressed almost evenly among all black subgroups. Table 9.9 displays black opinion on government aid for blacks and minorities by a number of social demographic and political groups. In general, as expected, self-identified black liberals and Democrats are more supportive of the concept of minority aid than are self-identified black conservatives and Republicans. Black women and the

Table 9.9 Black Opinion on Government Assistance to Blacks and Minorities, by Social and Political Groups

	Percentage Giving Liberal Answer				
	1972–76	1977–78	1983–88	1989–92	Change, 1972–92
Male	70.3	47.8	41.1	40.1	–30.2
Female	66.5	48.4	47	45	–21.5
N	574	542	829	571	
18–24	75	45.2	48.8	49.2	–25.8
25–34	67.1	48.5	38.4	42.9	–24.2
35–49	70.4	47.9	49.5	44.6	–25.8
50–64	67.9	50.4	47.8	40	–27.9
65+	59.6	48.5	38.8	38.9	–20.7
N	563	541	823	570	
< High school	65.1	44.4	40.7	43.7	–21.4
High school graduate	70.3	50	47.3	41	–29.3
College graduate	74.4	60	43.9	48.6	–25.8
N	572	541	829	564	
Urban	68.4	50.6	46.7	43.3	25.1
Rural/small town	66.3	39.3	40.1	42.3	–23.5
N	574	542	829	571	
Non-South	69.9	54.5	51.9	43.5	–26.4
South	66.4	43	40	42.9	–23.5
N	574	542	829	571	
Liberal	78.9	63	50.6	53.4	–25.5
Moderate	69.8	54.3	46.6	47.2	–22.6
Conservative	54.3	38.7	43.4	29.3	–25
N	322	256	480	327	
Democrat	70.9	51.2	48.1	44.3	–26.6
Independent	64.9	43	38.9	42.9	–22
Republican	46.7	31.8	44.7	34.6	–12.1
N	574	523	810	553	

Sources: Data are from the General Social Surveys (GSS) and the American National Election Studies (ANES). Question wording appears at the end of chapter 9.

Note: "No interest" and "don't know" responses were included in the distributions from which these percentages are calculated. Dashes indicate that the question was not included in the survey for those years.

young also gave more liberal responses to this question. However, with the exception of black Republicans (whose support for minority aid was lower than that of black Democrats and independents), among every subgroup, black support has declined by twenty percentage points or more. That every group has registered a drop in support for minority aid points to a period effect. Blacks have become less supportive of federal intervention during what has amounted to a successful conservative backlash against racial programs and policies. The political climate and its impact on racial attitudes in America is a topic to which we shall return in the concluding remarks of this chapter.

Explanations for Whites' Racial Attitudes

That white Americans exhibit racially egalitarian attitudes and yet remain hostile to government remedies for racial discrimination, inequality, and segregation has generated a number of conflicting explanations. Broadly, two lines of argument have emerged. Those on one side of the debate argue that racial prejudice remains the fundamental factor behind white opposition to racial policies such as busing and affirmative action. White racism has not disappeared; education has merely given more white Americans the ability to appear more racially tolerant than they really are (Jackman and Muha 1984). In fact, according to this view, racial intolerance, combined with fundamental American values about the work ethic and individualism, explains negative white attitudes toward government efforts to eradicate racial inequality (Sears 1988; Kinder 1986; Kinder and Sears 1981; McConahay 1986; McConahay and Hough 1976). Using their defense of traditional values as a cover for their resentment and fear of blacks, whites strongly object to policies that would change the racial status quo.

Those on the other side of the debate account for white opposition to racial policies differently, focusing on factors other than racial prejudice, and not only because they provide a more flattering portrayal of white Americans. This position offers a more nuanced and complex portrayal of white attitudes, because racial intolerance is conceptualized as only one part of the many motivations of whites who reject policies intended to benefit blacks. This group views ideology and moral values and beliefs as the major factors underlying white opposition to racial implementation policies. Politically conservative whites, for example, object to such policies because of their dislike of "big government" (Sniderman, Brody, and Kuklinski 1984; Sniderman et al. 1991; Margolis and Hague 1981; Kuklinski and Parent 1981). In addition, these scholars point to the "natural contradiction" between the white majority's commitment to individual rights and freedoms and its preference for a limited government and support for new government programs that would favor blacks (Carmines and Merriman 1993; Sniderman and Hagen 1985). Programs designed to promote racial equality conflict with the very values, including color blindness, that most whites now espouse.

Along these lines, other scholars have sought to link whites' racial attitudes to their beliefs about the causes of racial inequality and stratification. Several scholars have shown that whites will not support programs that assist blacks if they believe that the system is fair and that blacks themselves are not working hard enough to get ahead (Kluegel and Smith 1986, 1983; Sniderman and Hagen 1985). While civil rights organizations have asserted that blacks are denied equal opportunities to get ahead, most white Americans express full faith in the abundance of opportunity in American society. Their faith contrasts sharply with that of blacks (Kluegel and Smith 1986, 67–68; see also Kluegel and Bobo 1993; Sigelman and Welch 1991). In the 1990 general social survey, 72% of blacks but only 37% of whites thought that racial discrimination was a main factor in the unequal outcomes for blacks in jobs, income, and housing. Given that most whites believe that blacks currently have equal opportunities and that the economic system works well, most oppose programs that demand equality of outcomes.

Whites are more willing to support preferential treatment programs for women than for blacks (Kluegel and Smith 1986; Sniderman and Piazza 1993). One reason for this is that the public expresses far fewer negative attitudes about women than about blacks (Kluegel and Smith 1986, 243), indicating once again that whites' hostility toward blacks cannot be dismissed as a motive for their opposition to racial policies. Another reason for this difference is that while most whites feel that blacks have equality of opportunity, the same is not true of their views of women as a class (Kluegel and Smith 1986). However, that whites see flaws at all in America's opportunity structure suggests that other motivations beyond "blind faith" in the system may fuel their opposition to racial policies. Some scholars have argued that whites oppose racial equalization policies because of their collective stake in preservation of the racial status quo (Bobo 1983; Jackman and Muha 1984).

Whites are conceptualized as a self-interested group, and those in Lawrence Bobo's study most hostile to governmental programs were also those most unhappy with the "push for civil rights" and the swift pace of racial change. Like ideological or stratification beliefs, racial prejudice cannot adequately explain why a large majority of whites opposes policies like busing. Whites, in other words, need not fear or hate blacks in order to reject their demands for greater economic equality or integration. Nor do individual interests necessarily play a role; whites do not have to be personally threatened by the prospect of integration in their schools or racial quotas in their workplace to object to them. Instead, as Lawrence Bobo writes, "people can form an opinion about an ongoing and controversial issue like busing simply by thinking in terms of the interests of 'myself and people like me'" (1983,

1208). In the 1990 general social survey, about 70% of whites thought it "very" or "somewhat" likely that a white job applicant would be passed over for an "equally or less qualified" black applicant. It would seem that along with values and ideological conservatism, whites' perception of their collective interest may help to explain their opposition to government efforts to assist blacks.

New research on racial politics and voting has continued to identify factors other than the racial attitudes of whites in white rejection of black political candidates and white defection from the Democratic party (see Glaser 1994; Giles and Evans 1986; Huckfeldt and Kohfeld 1989; Fossett and Kiecolt 1989; Giles and Hertz 1994; Giles and Buckner 1993). It is not that racial prejudice is dismissed as irrelevant in these new studies, but the racial behavior of whites is conceptualized as more situationally based than attitudinally based. Although contrary to mainstream work on political attitudes, the recognition that behavior is a function of the social context as much as of individual predispositions in attitude is consistent with some of the new work in social psychology.

Finally, the notion that racial prejudice remains central to white racial attitudes has been further undermined by revisionist work on how opinions are formed. Attitudes are less and less viewed as fixed predispositions formed early in one's childhood. While the issue of race often seems to provoke entrenched and stubborn views, longstanding racial attitudes have in fact changed as whites have become more tolerant racially. In survey-based thought experiment, Sniderman and Piazza show that white attitudes on issues of race are pliable (1993, chapter 6). People can be "talked out" of their original position, regardless of what that position is. Elite discourse is part of the process of developing and changing an opinion (Zaller 1992). One way that the political elite shapes opinion is through the framing of new issues. Issue frames provide the "story line that provides meaning to an unfolding set of events. . . . The frame suggests what the controversy is about, the essence of the issue" (Gamson and Modigliani 1987, 143; see also Kinder and Sanders 1990). In their study of framing effects on affirmative action, however, Kinder and Sanders (1990) found that whites opposed affirmative action policies regardless of how they were framed. Neither question they tested was framed in a way that suggested affirmative action was a necessary remedy for past discrimination, as proponents of affirmative action often present it. Instead, one suggested that affirmative action was "reverse discrimination" and the other implied that affirmative action gave blacks an "unfair advantage." Both frames were expected to increase white opposition to affirmative action, but the researchers found that different motivations lay behind that opposition, depending on how the question was framed. Determining how elite debates frame racial policy issues and drive public opinion appears to be the most promising new area for research.

It would be a mistake to conclude that as researchers have steadily moved the focus away from racial prejudice in their examination of white racial attitudes, a great consensus has emerged that racial prejudice is no longer a relevant part of whites' racial attitudes. Assertions that racism no longer dominates the attitudes of whites on racial issues are still very much contested; even those scholars cited above who have chosen to de-emphasize racial prejudice in their work have stressed the research showing that racial prejudice persists. Many whites are still willing to describe blacks in quite unfavorable, negative terms. In the 1990 general social survey, for example, 47% of the white respondents thought that blacks were "lazy" as opposed to "hard working," and 54% said blacks were prone to violence. Another 31% felt that blacks were unintelligent, and 59% said that blacks were more likely to "live off welfare" than be "self-supporting." Southern and non-southern whites did not differ as much as one might expect; negative stereotypes about blacks are pervasive. Moreover, roughly 20% of blacks themselves rated blacks negatively as a group on these four dimensions. On the question of violence, more than 40% of black respondents labeled blacks, as a group, prone to violence. Overall, it is clear that racial stereotypes about blacks still exist. Thus, there is no denying that racial prejudice accounts for at least some part of whites' racial attitudes. But exactly how much remains in dispute, and the question is unlikely to be satisfactorily resolved given the diversity of research methods and data and, most importantly, how our conceptualization of the problem continues to evolve and change.

One of the more radical theoretical shifts involves a change in the meaning of racial prejudice (see Sniderman, Tetlock, and Carmines 1993 for a similar discussion). Once considered an archaic, irrational need to make scapegoats of others, research has consistently supported another view, that racial bias is ubiquitous, forming naturally in a person's mind through social group interactions (Rothbart and John 1993). Nor do social psychologists roundly condemn such stereotypes as irrational and without purpose; instead they are viewed as a necessary part of the normal process of making everyday decisions and snap judgments (Nisbett and Ross 1980). While minority groups can be victimized by them, stereotypes still serve a legitimate and necessary role in society.

The new definition of prejudice as an instinctive and widespread phenomenon can be interpreted in two ways. On the one hand, the very ubiquitousness of racial stereotypes undermines their relevance in the study of white racial attitudes. Because stereotypes are so widespread, whites' opposition to racial policies must depend more heavily on other factors, such as whites' beliefs about the causes of racial inequality, their ideologies, and their perceptions of collective interests. The eradication of racial stereotypes, even if it were possible, would not necessarily get more whites to support government efforts to assist blacks. On the other hand, the ubiquitous nature of racial stereotypes reveals the depth of racial prejudice in society today. Jim Sidaneous and Felicia Pratto (1993) argue that all societies across time have been hierarchically organized, and that stereotypes as well as other myths help give highly stratified multiracial and multiethnic societies their stability. Black inferiority is one of the many fictions that helps society to legitimize racial inequality and maintain the status quo. Such fictions enable whites to reject government efforts to eradicate racial inequality. If anything, we have come full circle again, with a new set of researchers—although still representing the minority—arguing that racism remains the fundamental force behind white racial attitudes.

Conclusions and Implications

Researchers have spent considerable time wrestling with the question of whether white Americans in their hearts and minds now accept the basic principle of racial equality, or whether they feel ill will and aversion toward blacks. Even after their exhaustive study of American racial attitudes, Schuman, Steeh, and Bobo can accept neither portrayal of white Americans as genuinely progressive or persistently racist, writing that "what has occurred is a mixture of progress and resistance, certainty and ambivalence, striking movement and mere surface change" (1988, 212). Increasingly, however, racial prejudice is defined as a problem less of the heart than of the mind. And while the human heart remains unfathomable, many social scientists have labeled the mind, to paraphrase Stephen Carter, author of *Affirmative Action Baby*, "complex." To social scientists, complexity means that whites' racial attitudes reflect more than racial prejudice toward blacks. Whites' opinions on various racial issues and policies are not reducible to a single factor or set of factors. As Sniderman and Piazza put it, white racial attitudes involve a "bundle of considerations" (1993, 29). Complexity also means that racial attitudes are not necessarily bundled neatly together (Sniderman, Tetlock, and Carmines 1993). Knowing how someone feels about interracial marriages does not necessarily tell you how he or she feels about busing. Different considerations may explain white attitudes about different types of racial policies (Kinder and Sanders 1990). For some whites, opposition to government programs that could enhance black employment opportunities may come in part from resistance to government intervention as a general matter, but for these same whites, opposition to open housing laws may reflect the desire to keep their communities racially exclusive.

A second conclusion might be drawn, however, one that applies to blacks as well as whites. Public opinion reflects the larger political process. The political elite can directly influence public attitudes. With its *Brown* ruling, made well before any majority support for racial integration or equal opportunity for blacks, the Supreme Court set into motion a chain of events that ultimately caused political attitudes to change. Congressional debate and presidential leadership, along with the dramatic events taking place in the civil rights movement, were also all important agents of change in public opinion on civil rights.

Presidents, especially, can profoundly shape and change public attitudes on civil rights. In his memoirs, retired Supreme Court Justice William O. Douglas strongly criticized President Eisenhower for not doing enough to promote the cause of racial equality, writing "if he had gone to the nation on television and radio telling people to obey the law and fall in line, the cause of desegregation would have been accelerated. Ike was a hero and he was worshipped. Some of his political capital spent on the racial cause would have brought the nation closer to the constitutional standards. Ike's ominous silence on our 1954 decision gave courage to the racists who decided to resist the decision" (quoted in Ashmore 1994, 103). Contrast Eisenhower's silence on civil rights to what Graham judged to be President Johnson's "courageous" and "consistent" championship of civil rights (1990, 272). On the debate over the 1968 open housing bill, Graham writes, "in explaining the surprising turnaround on the open housing bill that spring, Lyndon Johnson's consistent and courageous support is easily overlooked, since it was a background constant. The President had sprung his open housing surprise in January 1966, when it was widely judged as overreaching if not quixotic, and he had kept the pressure right up until the house accepted the Senate's amendments without a conference 27 months later" (1990, 272).

Then compare Johnson's position on civil rights to President Nixon's. Nixon had begun to retreat from the legacy of *Brown* as the furor over busing deepened and spread northward. In a speech to Congress in which he lamented the "evils of busing," Nixon stated, "all too often, the result has been a classic case of the remedy for one evil creating another evil. In this case, a remedy for the historic evil of racial discrimination has often created a new evil of disrupting communities and imposing hardship on children 'both black and white' who are themselves wholly innocent of the wrongs the plan seeks to set right" (quoted in Ashmore 1993, 229). Nixon's speech gave conservative legitimacy to principles of equal treatment and integration at the same time that it began a new Republican assault on government enforcement of such principles. Republicans, principally Barry Goldwater, had initially attacked civil rights enforcement as the unconstitutional expansion of the federal government, but Nixon now attacked it in moral terms as well. Government enforcement of civil rights became morally problematic. Although enforcement included federal fund cut-offs to schools that refused to desegregate and lawsuits initiated by the Justice Department, it also increasingly became linked to busing and affirmative action.

In a political climate in which presidents and politicians no longer distance themselves from racial policies but attack them, black opinion on racial policies has also changed. While most blacks still favor racial equalization policies, their support has slowly eroded, especially in the areas of school desegregation and targeted federal programs for blacks and minorities. The drop in black support is all the more noteworthy since it has occurred evenly across all demographic and political groups within the black community. Black opposition to minority aid, in other words, has increased not only among those who call themselves conservative or Republican, but for liberals, Democrats, the young, the old, and college graduates, the last group tending to be the most race-conscious (Tate 1994). Black opinion has probably been affected less by relentless moral attacks on racial programs than by criticism of their effectiveness. Urban and rural school districts remain highly segregated in spite of several decades of court-mandated busing. Republican administrations' weak records on civil rights enforcement may have also caused blacks to lose faith in the federal government's ability to improve their economic and social standing. This drop in black support for government-run racial programs also coincides with three decades of growing public cynicism about government.

Those who follow politics most closely are most susceptible to changes in attitude (Zaller 1992). Educated Americans, in particular, tend to be politically better informed than the noneducated. In his book *Public Opinion and American Democracy*, V. O. Key wrote that "formal education may serve to indoctrinate people into the more-or-less official political values of the culture" (1961, 340, quoted in Zaller 1992, 98). Today, no national leader, Republican or Democrat, is willing say that racial discrimination and segregation are morally acceptable. However, there is increasing agreement among political leaders that government efforts to improve opportunities for blacks in employment and education are morally wrong. It is thus all the more to be expected, as these new civil rights values are framed by the political elite, that those groups who were initially slow to accept racially egalitarian values now increasingly embrace them, and that those groups who initially favored aggressive government desegregation and racial equality now increasingly reject such goals. These developments flow logically from the larger debate over civil rights.

A Note on the Wording of Questions, Tables 9.2–9.6, 9.8

Whites have right to keep segregated neighborhoods (General Social Survey [GSS]): "Here are some opinions other people have expressed in connection with black-white relations. Which statement on the card comes closest to how you yourself feel? White people have a right to keep blacks out of their neighborhoods if they want to, and blacks should respect that right." [agree-disagree]

Open housing law (GSS): "Suppose there is a community-wide vote on the general housing issue. There are two possible laws to vote on. One law says that a homeowner can decide for himself who to sell his house to, even if he prefers not to sell to blacks. The second law says that a homeowner cannot refuse to sell to someone because of his race or color. Which law would you vote for? [1. Homeowner can decide. 2. No discrimination.]

Busing (GSS): "In general, do you favor or oppose the busing of black and white school children from one school district to another?"

Federal school intervention (American National Election Study [ANES]): "Some people say that the government in Washington should see to it that white and black children are allowed to go to the same schools. Others claim that this is not the government's business. Have you been concerned enough about this question to favor one side over the other? [If yes] do you think the government in Washington should see to it that white and black children go to the same schools, or stay out of this matter as it is not its business?"

Federal job intervention (ANES): "Some people feel that if black people are not getting fair treatment in jobs the government in Washington ought to see to it that they do. Others feel that this is not the federal government's business. Have you had enough interest in this question to favor one side over the other? [If yes] should the government in Washington see to it that black people get fair treatment in jobs or leave these matters to the states and local communities?"

Minority aid (ANES): "Some people feel that the government in Washington should make every effort to improve the social and economic position of blacks. Others feel that the government should not make any special effort to help blacks because they should help themselves. Where would you place yourself on this scale, or haven't you thought much about this?" [1. Government should help blacks. 2. Blacks should help themselves].

Note

1. President Johnson's speech to Howard University graduates in 1965, in which he claimed that America was now entering the "second" and "most profound stage of the battle for civil rights," where government needed not only to guarantee "equality as a right and a theory but equality [as] a fact and as a result," bolsters such views (see Graham 1990).

10

Civil Rights in a Multicultural Society

Luis Ricardo Fraga and Jorge Ruiz-de-Velasco

It has been observed that the Civil Rights Act of 1964 was not designed to deliver the "promised land." Certainly its reach was more modest, focused as it was on limiting the most egregious forms of discrimination affecting equal access to employment, public accommodations, and decent public schooling. Moreover, it is important to keep in mind that the act was understood by many of its early proponents as only a "first step" in efforts to help African Americans and others realize political equality. It was surely a necessary and critical step, but clearly only a beginning. Nonetheless, it cannot be denied that the act had its origins in the hopes and dreams of many disenfranchised individuals who sought to realize the American "promised land." More than mere political incorporation, this meant full and equal enjoyment of all the economic opportunities and social benefits of common citizenship. As we reassess the act thirty-five years later, it is no surprise that we are soon back to these original hopes and dreams. We once again assess the act in light of its historic ability to deliver on the promise of common citizenship dedicated to the inalienable individual rights to life, liberty, and the pursuit of happiness: "the American dream" in a multicultural society.

In this chapter, we argue that the failure of African Americans, Latina/os, and other ethnic and racial minority groups to make greater political, economic, and social gains is rooted, at least in part, in the inherent limitations of the formal legal rights that characterize the Civil Rights Act of 1964 and in an overreliance on a legal rights-based strategy as the principal means through which communities of color have pursued greater political incorporation and economic security.[1] This rights-based strategy is fundamentally limiting in a number of significant ways that currently prevent it from serving to further enhance the political and economic status of African Americans, Latina/os, and other communities of color.

First, the language and structure of the Civil Rights Act effectively obfuscate, and therefore fail to resolve, the question of whether or to what extent the rights and duties of American citizenship accrue to "individuals" or to "groups" within the polity. The act articulates individual rights but makes those rights contingent on an individual's affiliation with some racial, ethnic, gender, or religious group. Over time, individual protection and remedies for discrimination have been justified on a case-by-case basis by reference to individual discrimination, group discrimination, or both. Litigation pursuant to the Civil Rights Act necessarily requires the identification of a "rights holder," and this rights holder has often been an individual who stands as a proxy for a racial, ethnic, gender, or religious group. To be sure, this ambiguity about whether rights should properly be held by individuals or groups is not limited to litigation over formal legal rights but rather permeates political advocacy at all levels of government. Our point here is that the unresolved tension between the claims of individual rights on the one hand, and those of group justice on the other, continues to divide us and cannot be resolved by recourse to our civil rights laws alone.

Second, the rights-based form of legal and political advocacy too often lends itself to a logic of victimization as a form of legitimating relief for the "victimized" individual or group. By this logic, attention is drawn to a passive and powerless "victim" and to a morally corrupt (i.e., racist) and powerful "perpetrator" of discrimination (Bumiller 1988). A victim (or the victim class) is entitled, by this logic, to special government protection. Victims are entitled, by virtue of their powerlessness, to have their disputes taken out of the legislative political arena and to seek remedies protected in the form of adjudicated law. Certainly the Bill of Rights and our civil rights laws are dedicated to the proposition that we all have rights that cannot be stripped from us by powerful interests or majorities. But the victim logic associated with rights-based advocacy is limiting insofar as some of the most crucial problems faced by communities of color, such as educational, economic, and social inequalities, are not always about victims and perpetrators. These problems are about the way we organize our economy, our schools, and our cities, and they beg for collective action on a scale that cannot be democratically achieved merely by apportioning rights.

We have learned, moreover, how easily the logic of victimization lends itself to competing claims of victimization by whites, whose group interests have been increasingly recognized and protected by the courts.[2] Whether characterized as "reverse discrimination" or "white backlash," it is clear that the logic of victimization cannot provide a consistently principled way of deciding between the claims of a minority and the claims of a majority when they are in direct competition for economic, material, and social goods. Successful claims of white victimization have pushed communities of color to demand that their rights be protected even more affirmatively by the government. This consequential "ratcheting up" of the victim logic undercuts the credibility of all claims to special protection and limits the nation's ability to promote the enactment of public policy favorable to the long-term substantive needs and interests of communities of color.

Third, the protection of opportunity, that is, the right to equal access to public and economic resources, is understood largely in zero-sum terms within the logic of formal rights. The vindication of rights, by definition, focuses only on a redistribution of existing resources or access to opportunities. Greater rights for some are too often understood as fewer rights for others. This is particularly so when disputes arise over some limited or "scarce" economic or social good. Too little attention is paid within the rights framework to how the nation might pursue developmental policies that might expand the total stock of opportunities available to Americans regardless of race or class.

Fourth, this rights-based strategy does not require any group, whether a majority or minority, to justify its claim for special protection or redistribution of resources by reference to a larger, more universally shared public interest. This lack of focus on shared interests severely limits the possibilities for communities of color to build effective coalitions with a broader set of partners who might be persuaded to see their common interests. The white working class is one such potential partner, as are those concerned with economic growth, crime reduction, or the quality of public education.

Finally, the demands of our evolving multiculturalism have placed considerable new strains on rights-based logic. Continued high levels of immigration, particularly among Asians and Latina/os, have greatly increased the multiculturalism of the United States. Immigration continually replenishes groups who possess cultural and linguistic characteristics that are perceived as detriments to their advancement within American institutions of education, housing, and employment. Do recent immigrants have the same claims to special protection under a law such as the

Civil Rights Act when they do not have a history of discrimination in this country? How many years do they have to be in the United States before they can make such a rights-based claim under the act? Within our increasingly multicultural society, there is now also considerable class variation within racial and ethnic groups (Glazer 1983, 315–36; W. J. Wilson 1987, 1996). As members of protected groups enter the middle and upper classes, should they be eligible for the same protections as those in the working class? What guidance does the Civil Rights Act offer for resolving these new and often conflicting claims?

We do not mean to suggest that civil rights enforcement is unnecessary or irrelevant to contemporary social problems. To the contrary, vigilant enforcement of the Civil Rights Act in the service of formal equality must be maintained. We are also aware of the need for civil rights protection from more subtle institutional discrimination. Policies and practices of employment, law enforcement, financial lending, and university admission must be carefully scrutinized for systematic bias. But this type of formal legal protection does little to legitimize the benefits received by an alleged victim in a way consistent with majoritarian consensus building. We believe that the pursuit of a rights-based strategy as the primary means of advancing the interests of communities of color can achieve only limited success. Likewise, overreliance on the courts is unlikely to lead to substantial improvement in the material well-being of communities of color.

The Civil Rights Act was never intended to be the sole means of advancing the interests of communities of color in the United States. It is easy in retrospect to see how the architects of Lyndon Johnson's "War on Poverty" saw the battle to equalize opportunity and eradicate poverty as one that needed to be fought on two fronts. The Civil Rights Act of 1964 was only one of those fronts. It recognized that the state needed to be affirmatively involved in assuring the formal equality of individuals in the nation. But we have too easily forgotten that the Civil Right Act of 1964 was accompanied by the Economic Opportunity Act of 1964, and that both were quickly followed in 1965 by the Elementary and Secondary Education Act. These related pieces of legislation acknowledged that legal protections and social reforms would be meaningless—or at least of very limited impact—without corresponding reforms in the structure of economic opportunity. The Johnson administration's approach was to win support for such legislation by stressing its importance to all Americans as a matter of sound policy, regardless of the racial dimensions of the problem. In James Q. Wilson's words, Johnson's success could be largely attributed to his ability to "convert the demands of blacks into demands for social and economic progress . . . a basis of action common to all individuals" (J. Q. Wilson 1982, 416).

One observable consequence of this two-pronged approach was that child and family poverty rates declined dramatically for all racial and ethnic groups from the levels of the 1940s and '50s and continued to decline in the decade between 1969 and 1979. More significantly, the *relative* inequality of child and family poverty among racial and ethnic groups also declined during this period.[3] But all of this has changed with the decline of public investment and involvement in the economy that occurred in the 1980s.

In the eighties, we saw the elimination or reduction of federally funded job training programs, low-income housing subsidies, integrated low-income housing construction bonuses, reductions in Aid to Families with Dependent Children, reductions in the federal contribution to education programs, and the passage of a more regressive tax code (Reich 1992). In addition to the retrenchment of old programs, the eighties saw great political resistance to new collective action efforts in family leave policy, day care subsidies, and even child vaccination programs. All of this public retrenchment took place in the face of new pressures from a globalized economy that moved many jobs to foreign countries.[4]

Although aggressive civil rights enforcement must continue, the demands of an increasingly multicultural society require that a rights-based strategy be fully complemented by a policy-based strategy that attempts to build an *informed public interest.* A policy-based strategy is one that focuses overwhelmingly on the legislative branch. It does not depend on the judicial branch to provide its greatest successes. This strategy places the responsibility for developing public policy, both its original formulation and its legislative enactment, in the hands of those who were the earliest beneficiaries of the Civil Rights Act—African American, Latina/o, and other leaders of communities of color, as well as in the hands of influential legislative supporters. By this logic, leaders of communities of color accept the responsibility for their own self-determination. In our view, these leaders must pursue such a strategy if they wish to work toward the enactment of public policy that serves the long-term material interests of their constituents.

Moreover, this strategy requires that benefits be provided to segments of the population not on the basis of narrowly defined self-interest, as tends to occur under the rights-based strategy, but rather on the basis of a broader public interest. This strategy serves to build coalitions across diverse groups. In this way it respects majoritarian legitimacy, a fundamental principle of the American political process. When successful, the programs it enacts should have considerable permanence, being established by consensus building rather than by judicial force. In the end, only a policy-based strategy can meet the demands of a multicultural society by expanding the scope of collective action.[5] Such a strategy promotes an expansion of resources and public goods, rather than simply changing the current distribution of public goods. It promotes economic progress, not just economic rights. And it retrieves an element of the rights-based strategy that has been lost sight of: that common citizenship is based not just on a share of public goods but on commitments, responsibilities, and interests shared with other individuals and segments of the society. A politics dedicated to securing greater public commitment to collective action is what we mean by an informed public interest. This is the key to expanding opportunity, consistent with the original goals of the 1964 Civil Rights Act, in an increasingly multicultural society like that of the United States.[6]

It may be useful to examine the two conceptual frameworks that underlie the rights-based strategy: the melting pot and the mosaic. These frameworks represent competing solutions, or more accurately paradigmatic ideals, to the challenges of governance amid group diversity. Each of these frameworks has a rich history within the United States. The melting-pot metaphor is most often used to explain how the nation integrated large numbers of European immigrants within many of its institutions from the late nineteenth through much of the twentieth century. It is often invoked to suggest the unique character of U.S. citizenship as embracing all who live within the national borders, provided that individuals relinquish, to some degree, the linguistic and cultural traits of their countries of origin and adopt the cultural traditions of the American mainstream, including the English language and the values and principles of American democracy.[7]

The metaphor of the mosaic, although it also appeared at the turn of the century, became part of the discourse of mainstream American politics much more recently. It is most often associated with advocates for minority rights; among its strongest proponents have been leaders of ethnic and racial minority groups. The conceptual framework of the mosaic sees the strength of U.S. society in the presence and enhancement of racial and ethnic distinctiveness within the American mainstream. Although an extreme view of the mosaic ideal might call for racial and ethnic separatism, most proponents advocate that the maintenance of distinct cultural and linguistic practices should be guaranteed by the state. Each of these conceptual frameworks, the melting pot and the mosaic, must be understood as a response to the nation's historical experience of diversity, and each can claim to be rooted in time-honored American beliefs about the relationship of the individual to the state.

These two conceptual frameworks provide the lenses through which we can consider the relevance of a rights-based strategy of social inclusion, such as that embodied by the Civil Rights Act, in contemporary multicultural society. In assessing each of these ideals, we can begin to see the contours of an alternative strategy—one that integrates the best practices of each and holds more promise than either for responding to the demands of a multicultural society.

The Melting Pot

The logic of assimilation inherent in the conceptual framework of the melting pot embodies a view of history that teaches the perils of cultural tribalism. "For the Founders," writes Allan Bloom, "minorities are in general bad things, mostly identical to factions, selfish groups who have no concern as such for the common good" (Bloom 1987, 31). Through subsequent waves of Southern European, African, Latin American, and Asian immigration, assimilation—the central concept underlying the melting-pot framework—became the dominant mode of defusing the real and perceived challenges posed by human diversity to democratic government well into the 1950s. Both Alexis de Tocqueville in the late 1830s and Gunnar Myrdal a century later in the 1940s marveled at the American alchemy that seemed to forge peoples of disparate lands, cultures, and creeds into a new race. To many historians, including Arthur Schlesinger, the assimilationist aspiration to melt all comers into a "new race of man" was America's "brilliant solution for the inherent fragility of a multiethnic society" (Schlesinger 1992, 13). Theodore Roosevelt had expressed the same sentiment, writing in the mid-1920s that "The one absolutely certain way of bringing this nation to ruin . . . would be to permit it to become a tangle of squabbling nationalities, an intricate knot of German-Americans, Irish-Americans, English-Americans, French-Americans . . . each preserving its separate nationality" (Roosevelt 1926, 456). The recurrent debates of the 1980s and '90s over language policy and bilingualism in Florida and California offer stark contemporary examples of this assimilationist position. "At its most concise," writes Ronald Schmidt, "the argument is that the adoption of non-English ballots and bilingual education policies has charted the United States onto a new and dangerous course toward ethnolinguistic conflict and deep political division, and for which the declaration of English as the sole 'official' language is an important corrective measure" (Schmidt 1994). For adherents of the melting-pot theory, history seems to teach that too much diversity leads only to public discord and political instability.

To the melting-pot assimilationists, the cultural, racial, or ethnic identity of an individual is mutable and transitory. Within the assimilationist camp there is general agreement about the ultimate goal and value of cultural assimilation: the achievement of unifying values, ideology, language, and customs. But there has been disagreement about how best to achieve this unifying national culture. Social and cultural conservatives have argued that assimilation simply means that minorities can and should conform to the Anglo norms of the dominant culture (Dworkin and Dworkin 1982). For others, among them Milton Gordon, the melting pot symbolizes the biological and cultural transmutation "of the Anglo-Saxon peoples with other immigrant groups and a blending of their respective cultures into a new indigenous American type" (Gordon 1964, 85). This second, more egalitarian position may be identified as liberal assimilationism. It is clear that to the melting-pot assimilationist, cultural identity is not fixed. At its best, the melting-pot ideal teaches that to be an American is to transcend racial, ethnic, cultural, and religious lines—to be first and foremost an individual who is bound to other individuals by a common national identity. In the end, the notion of a common identity and the importance of national unity are central themes for adherents of the melting-pot framework.

The ideal of common citizenship is central to melting-pot adherents of both the conservative and liberal schools. To melting-pot assimilationists, equality also has a very distinct meaning and value for both the state and the individual. Within the melting-pot framework of free and equal citizenship, emphasis is on the politically recognized formal equality of individuals before the law. "Equality," writes Gordon, "is defined as equality of opportunity . . . but not in terms of results or condition, a matter which is left to the myriad workings of the competitive process. . . . Proponents of this model insist that it represents traditional American ideals and principles of the Enlightenment on which the American republic was founded" (Gordon 1985b, 527).[8] This, in fact, is the view of equality that James Q. Wilson claims informed passage of the Civil Rights Act in 1964.

The advocates of the Civil Rights Act of 1964 were quite clear that they were talking about rights in the traditional sense. . . . [Equal treatment meant] only that a federal government, which takes money from all taxpayers without discrimination, cannot spend money on taxpayers with discrimination. . . . The senators explicitly ruled out the possibility that the right to nondiscriminatory treatment could lead to any larger claims, such as a person's so-called right to a certain kind of education, or so-called right to have money spent to achieve certain objectives. (Wilson 1982, 416)

It follows from the notion of common citizenship that rights and duties in the melting-pot society accrue to individuals whose relationship to the state is unaffected by considerations of class, race, or religious affiliation. Groups of people do not, as such, receive formal recognition from legal or political institutions. Along these lines, Supreme Court Justice Clarence Thomas has written that "it is above all the protection of *individual* rights that America, in its best moments, has in its heart and mind." In assessing the Reagan years, Justice Thomas bemoans the administration's failure to make an effective case against the dangers of a civil rights policy "entrenched as an interest-group issue rather than as an issue of principle and universal significance for all individuals" (Thomas 1988, 392, emphasis in original).

Another cornerstone of common citizenship in the melting-pot framework is a policy of nondiscrimination in the service of a race-blind constitutional order. Of course government can and should "intervene legally through legislation or executive orders to prevent discrimination in such areas as employment, education, voting, public facilities, and public accommodations. But such prevention is focused on *specific acts which can be proven to be discriminatory* and not on the promotion of integration through direct governmental action" (Gordon 1985b, 526, emphasis in original). With respect to private housing and associations, the melting-pot logic counts on free market forces and individual choice to work their own solutions. But the implicit faith has always been that the moral force of formal equality, common values, and the standardizing forces of modernization would be enough to diffuse primordial ethnic animosities and lead to voluntary social integration in American.

The Mosaic

In the classic expression of the mosaic ideal, each racial and ethnic culture in a nation is viewed as a precious stone adding its own uniqueness to a united but differentiated whole. In contrast to melting-pot adherents, who believe that diversity is the root cause of civic disunity, adherents of the mosaic framework believe that civic disunity is a result of the brutal suppression of human diversity. The lesson drawn from the mosaic framework is that the biggest threat to democratic government is intolerance and the distrust and resentment it breeds among the less empowered groups in society.

Paradoxically, historians and social scientists trace the birth of the mosaic paradigm to the turn of the nineteenth century, when the melting-pot ideal held the greatest sway. According to Gordon, "The first manifestations of an ideological counterattack against draconian Americanization came not from the beleaguered newcomers . . . but from those idealistic members of the middle class" who felt that "debilitating psychological consequences, family disorganization, and juvenile delinquency" among immigrant minority groups that could be linked to forced assimilation (Gordon 1985a, 252–53).

More recently, the mosaic framework has been used to elucidate and validate the histories of ethnic and racial groups who tended to be excluded from traditional discussions of American history. Although slave narratives have been known and studied for many years, they rarely figured prominently in histories of the South. Similarly, historical accounts of the southwestern United States rarely included discussions of the importance of Mexican communities to the development of mining, trade, agriculture, and ranching that are still the backbone of many state economies in the southwestern states. Discussions of the role of Asians and Native Americans were similarly rare.[9]

In the mosaic framework, America is seen as a nation containing many nations. Thus, according to theorist Horace Kallen, we realize our greatness as a nation when we foster a republic that is in substance "a democracy of nationalities, cooperating voluntarily and autonomously through common institutions in the enterprise of self-realization through the perfection of man according to their kind" (Kallen 1924, 254). From this perspective there is no civic need for a unique, unifying concept of Americanness. Indeed, to be an American is to be multicultural—to value diversity for its own sake and to adopt tolerance as a preeminent civic virtue. Anyone can be "American" without giving up his or her own ethnic or racial identity. "In a multi-cultural polity," writes Schmidt,

individuals can have both "ethnic" and "national" (as well as "gender," "sexual preference," and other) identities, since a multi-layered identity is a fact of life for most already. Bilingual individuals [for example] are perceived, in this [view], as richer, more nuanced, more complex, more fully developed human beings than are those who are monolingual. Indeed, in this setting it is the monolinguals—whether in English or some other language—who are viewed as "culturally deprived." (Schmidt 1994, 28)

The cultural pluralism of the mosaic perspective implies the equal status of all ethnic and racial groups, each of which retains its group identity. Within the mosaic framework, free and equal citizenship requires more than mere neutrality on the part of legal and political institutions. Instead, adherents insist on a positive commitment by government to the equal worth of all individuals *and* constituent groups in a society. This conception of equality thus "insists that government must treat people as equals in the following sense. It must impose no sacrifice or constraint on any citizen in the service of a public goal that the citizen could not accept without abandoning his sense of his self-worth" (Dworkin 1983).

Dworkin argues that this belief contains two further implications. First, equality demands, as a matter of right, that no citizen or group receive less than an equal share of community resources. Second, the logic of the mosaic demands that economic policies supported by the government not fall more onerously on any one group than another. Thus for example, economic policies that tolerate a certain level of unemployment are unjust because they ask "some people [and minority group members disproportionately] to accept lives of great poverty and despair . . . just in order that the great bulk of the community may have a more ample measure of what they are forever denied" (Dworkin 1983). In such cases, equality demands that income transfers, welfare benefits, and other redistributive programs targeted to communities of color be instituted as a matter of right. President Clinton's advocacy, during his first year in office, of a public right to affordable health care is an example of the mosaic view that substantive equality is a matter of moral right.

If ours is a "democracy of nationalities," and if it is true that all of us belong to some ethnic or racial group, then it follows that "democracy for the individual must by extension also mean democracy for his group" (Gordon 1985a, 253). Thus we derive the group basis of rights. According to this view, government has an affirmative moral duty to recognize diversity and to assure equality in light of that diversity. These duties of the government arise from the moral requirements of equality within the mosaic framework. And this "right" to substantive equality, arising as it does from moral duty, cannot be compromised by any instrumental calculations of the state. The victims of past injustice hold the right to full restitution as a political trump card against all other claimants on the community's resources (Dworkin 1977).

Assessing the Melting Pot and the Mosaic

The core insight of the melting-pot ideal is that it draws attention to the importance of common citizenship and democratic governance. Common citizenship is based on a unifying vision of the common good and of the common duties necessary to achieve that end.[10] The common good entails, at a minimum, the adoption of a set of values, attitudes, and core beliefs that, within its own logic, serves the larger public interest. The term "Americanization," used at the turn of the century, captured these ideas very well. Of course the historical deficiency of this ideal was that it erroneously and unnecessarily located common citizenship within a largely Eurocentric, and sometimes exclusively Anglo-Saxon, cultural norm that ultimately alienated many ethnic and racial groups. To the extent that nonmainstream ethnic and racial groups wanted to become citizens, the price paid was often the loss of language and other traits from home countries or cultures. Indeed, turn-of-the-century notions of Americanization relegated some groups—African Americans, Mexican Americans, Asian Americans, and Native Americans—to a permanently hybridized state. They could never look like the Anglo-Saxon American ideal and, indeed, antimiscegenation laws were enacted, primarily, to ensure that this would never change. While these groups could integrate in some arenas, they could never fully assimilate. The definition of the common public interest was very narrow, and little debate or discussion about its content or character was allowed. This narrow vision of the public interest prompted a defensive reaction from groups that wanted to maintain their distinctiveness; it also prompted corresponding prejudices among their own members and similar intolerance for the views of other groups. Ironically, the prevailing narrow view of what it meant to be an American only served to undermine the central goal of common citizenship. Understandably, racial and ethnic solidarity became rallying cries among the excluded and the melting-pot theory was discredited as the protest movements of the 1960s and 1970s unfolded. But the melting-pot focus on common citizenship and on an overarching sense of public purpose in the service of democracy should still to be of central relevance to us today.

The mosaic ideal can be understood largely as a reaction to the melting-pot ideal. Its core insight was to give expression to the values of tolerance and respect for diversity as basic, inescapable facts of the human condition. It made the case that tolerance is a basic precondition of a stable, democratic, inclusive government with a diverse citizenry. It also recognized the poverty of the idea of formal equality in an ethnocentric and exclusive social and political environment. It recognized too that political equality is impossible without the foundations of economic security and education necessary for effective political participation.

The mosaic ideal, however, tends to allocate rights to groups rather than to individuals and encourages a balkanized politics of group interests that undermines the idea that there are civic privileges and duties that transcend race and ethnicity. Group identity is valued, but often for the wrong reason, namely its instrumental value in making demands on the collectivity. As a result, the political arena lacks a unifying concept of personal citizenship—separate and apart from ethnic and racial identities—that might help citizens see themselves as part of one nation with a common purpose and common duties.

It is easy to understand how a rights-based strategy developed to serve the interests of African Americans would embody a logic closer to that of the mosaic than to that of the melting-pot ideal. As a necessary first step in efforts to overcome rigid barriers of exclusion, such a strategy has tended to focus on the identification of victims, unjustly hurt by policies and practices under the law. Unfortunately, in a multicultural society, the logic of victimization leads to similar competing claims by many different groups, including whites who charge reverse discrimination. And there appears no consensus-based principle for distinguishing between these competing claims. Those not benefitting from such a strategy accuse its proponents of using disingenuous appeals to the common good for purely selfish gain. Retrenchment and backlash by substantial segments of the citizenry should therefore come as no surprise. Rights-based logic tends to see competition for the distribution of social and economic resources as a zero-sum game. Through legal protections, the previously excluded gain a competitive edge, but to the extent that they become winners, others now become losers.

Most significantly, identity group politics undermines the broader sense of public interest that should serve as the basis for public policy. Although particular groups may gain through collective action, there is no broader gain—but rather a loss—for the broader form of collective social action that can bring with it majoritarian legitimacy and greater community resources.

All of this suggests that we need to focus on how ethnic and racial identity become relevant in political terms—on how law and public policy might make racial and ethnic identity more or less instrumental to individual groups. Good work in this direction has already begun. Paul Sniderman and colleagues, for example, have shed light on how different policy approaches to redistributive efforts and affirmative action for African Americans affects the level of racial polarization among white Americans. They have found that the specific basis of appeals for minority incorporation are crucial to broad public support. Sniderman and his colleagues conclude that "When Americans react to contemporary issues [involving] race with consistency, it is as much because of politics as race" (Sniderman, Tetlock, Carmines, and Peterson 1993, 219).[11] How an issue is defined, then, offers rich opportunities for changing how Americans understand questions of civil rights (Baumgartner and Jones 1993). But issue definition can also affect behavior and attitudes in ways that allow individuals to see the advantage of identifying a policy with their own—or some other ethnic—group's narrow interests (Fraga 1992; Fraga and Anhalt 1993; Hollinger 1995).

Similarly, Edsall and Edsall have convincingly chronicled the way that democratically endorsed civil rights policies, coupled with declining federal investment in employment, training, and education programs, have pitted African Americans and other minority groups against lower-middle-income whites as they compete for jobs and status in a shrinking national economy. Working-class whites have come to see redistributive policies as racial issues, while minorities in distressed communities are also encouraged to correlate demands for resource redistribution in terms of their own racial and ethnic affiliations. In this divisive climate, the rights-based logic of redistribution has engendered resentment among white, working-class voters, turning them into a powerful force for a Republican Party that promises change in the civil rights agenda (Edsall and Edsall 1991, 12). It bears emphasizing that both the Edsalls and Sniderman and colleagues draw attention to the importance of issue, interest, and solution definition by political actors as well as to the images or perceptions of reality that they seek to create or perpetuate. This influence may have important implications for the mobilization of interest groups along racial and ethnic lines irrespective of any concrete facts about how government action will affect any given individual's or group's economic or social interests.

The relationship of race, class, and important transformations in the American economy have been studiously examined by William Julius Wilson (1987, 1996), Orfield and Ashkinaze (1991) and West (1993b). Throughout the last thirty-five years, the formal rights plank of the Great Society program has remained a constant in law and politics. But the economic and human capital investment plank has foundered and been largely destroyed. In the process, the emphasis of the Kennedy-Johnson era on making a case for public investment that transcended racial and ethnic politics has been lost. Lost as well has been the modest progress that was made against poverty in the 1960s and early '70s, which seemed to benefit ethnic and racial minorities.[12] There is mounting evidence in the inner cities that the laissez-faire policies we have pursued have made ethnic identification more instrumental to groups and individuals and ethnic competition for scarce resources more likely. Cornel West's critique of the "pitfalls of racial reasoning" sheds light on the ways that government policy can make race and ethnicity instrumental in the political process—making it more likely that people will mobilize for change on the basis of racial and ethnic appeals (West 1993b). Indeed, there are many minority activists and intellectuals who advocate various strategies of self-reliance, racial pride, and sometimes even xenophobic separatism. As community resources decline, racial and ethnic solidarity becomes instrumental in the competition for group advantage.

Again, we do not suggest that there is no longer any need for vigilant civil rights enforcement. Individual and institutional discrimination persists and must be prevented. We are under no illusions that the United States has now become a color-blind society. But it must be acknowledged that an exclusively rights-based strategy, such as that provided by the 1964 Civil Rights Act, is as limiting as it is constructive. It does not allow for the enactment of a broader public policy focused on material well-being that will serve the long-term interests of the individuals and groups it is designed to assist. This is especially the case in a multicultural society where ever-increasing diversity means ever-increasing competition among diverse groups for resources (Glazer 1983). Even when gains are made, they are vulnerable to criticism by those who perceive relative disadvantage.

Toward an Informed Public Interest

Our growing multicultural and multiethnic diversity requires a reconsideration of whether a rights-based logic is now the most effective way of resolving the inherent tension between diversity and the demands of common citizenship prerequisite to stable democracy. We draw now on the melting-pot and mosaic ideals to suggest the outlines of what an increasingly necessary complement to a rights-based strategy would entail. We refer to this policy-based strategy as an effort to realize an *informed public interest.*

The first precondition to the attainment of an informed public interest is a politics that fosters in each of us a sense of common citizenship and civic identity.

Common citizenship in the American context requires that each of us be invested in a core set of democratic ideals, institutions, and civic responsibilities that help us to see how we are bound together as a nation with common interests to protect. The ideals we share are those articulated in the Constitution, which have been succinctly summarized by Schlesinger: a recognition "of the essential dignity and equality of all human beings, [and] of inalienable rights to freedom, justice, and opportunity" (Schlesinger 1992, 27).[13] The institutions to which we must all commit ourselves are those of democratic process: a faith in the value of open public debate, free and universally accessible elections, the unencumbered right to petition the government, and the right to peaceful protest. The duties we must share are those of participation in the affairs of the state and the community, the duty to vote, and to contribute to democratically attained collective ends. These commitments imbue all of us with a sense of common purpose and future.

A second precondition to the attainment of an informed public interest is a continued commitment to rational deliberation in the public arena. It is clear that considerable debate should occur as to the nature of our common purposes and the evolving contours of our civic ideals. A commitment to democratic ideals does not, ipso facto, determine the policies or institutions necessary to their attainment. Rational deliberation, bounded though it may be by the constraints of time, resources, prejudices, and current paradigms of understanding, must occur. The deliberation must be based on articulated and reasoned evidence. Too often debate in the political arena has not been about real issues or interests. Instead, so called "wedge issues" are raised, e.g., inner-city crime, welfare cheating, illegal immigration—not because they necessarily are problems, but because these issues appeal to our lowest instincts and to racial stereotypes that can sway voters. We must eschew race baiting and racial, ethnic, gender, and homophobic biases in politics and focus instead on open deliberation.

A third and final precondition is that we must work to assure that previously excluded voices are heard in public debates over the design and implementation of public policy. For any citizen to be an effective and informed participant in the political arena he or she must have the education and the minimum economic security that form the foundation of meaningful participation. Opening our political system to all voices in the society is critical to the stability of democracy in a multicultural nation.

To argue that we must embrace a civic identity to foster a sense of common citizenship is not to say that we must surrender our identities as members of specific racial, ethnic, or other communities and cultures. The reality of the American experience, as Hollinger has written, is that we all "live in many circles simultaneously and that the actual living of any individual life entails a shifting division of labor between the several 'we's' of which the individual is a part" (Hollinger 1995, 106). This type of inclusive participation is what Cornel West refers to as a "cultural politics of difference" (West 1993a, 3–32). Differences in individual and group perspectives should not merely be tolerated, they should be encouraged in order to enhance the richness of the views that can be brought to bear on the pursuit of common purpose. As West states, "human particularities and social specificities [are affirmed] in order to construct new kinds of connections, affinities, and communities" (West 1993a, 29). Difference is not valued for its own sake. It is valued because it is what allows us to best appreciate what it is we have in common and how our destinies as citizens of a common nation are linked. In sum, the informed public interest can only be attained through an inclusive, deliberative consideration of the common purposes that unify us as a nation.

Leadership from various racial and ethnic groups is required to broaden our understanding of the public interest, to inform the discussion through perspectives that have traditionally been excluded. For example, African Americans, Latina/os, Asian Americans, and Native Americans are a minority in all state and federal legislative bodies and in most local legislative bodies. To the extent that these officials and their supporters advocate policy choices based exclusively on racial and ethnic self-interest, they are not likely to prevail in a largely majoritarian legislative process. Racial and ethnic group interest advocacy, especially when couched in the language of formal rights, is not likely to be endorsed by legislators who view themselves as representing the interests of whites.

To address this problem some analysts, following a rights-based approach, have advocated legislative decision-making schemes, including concurrent majority and super-majority proposals, which statutorily mandate that the interests of minority public officials be give substantial weight in the final stages of the legislative process (Guinier 1991a, 1991b). This incorporation by right rather than by consensus is likely to meet with fatal political resistance. By contrast, a consensus-based approach requires that representatives of communities of color promote legislative "policy images" that facilitate legislative coalition building (Baumgartner and Jones 1993). This goal can be accomplished through the couching of policy proposals in terms that appeal to communities of color as well as to whites and the larger community as a whole. The enhancement of education, housing, employment, and health care opportunities can be shown as beneficial to many different segments of society. The promotion of these benefits can appeal to universally held concerns, including cost savings, long-term economic growth, reduction in crime, and reduction in the cost of law enforcement and imprisonment.

This policy-based approach does not bank on the election of minority group members to legislative bodies, per se. It does, however, rely on enforcement of election laws, such as the Voting Rights Act, to assure that communities of color have a clear opportunity to elect representatives of their first choice who will have an incentive to advance these communities' interests. We are suggesting that these officials can serve as the catalysts in the formation of progressive coalitions with other legislative supporters.

Our policy-based strategy requires that all groups, but especially groups organized on the basis of race and ethnicity, engage directly in redefining the public interest. It is in the direct self-interest of ethnic and racial leaders to do so and success or failure is largely in the hands of these leaders and their legislative supporters (West 1993b). Success, of course, is not guaranteed, but we should realize that self-determination is within reach to the extent that leaders can articulate a public interest that is not zero-sum and focuses as much on resource development as it does on resource distribution in policy areas of direct material consequence such as public education, housing, and employment. An informed public interest that demonstrates how important needs of the poor and working classes, among whom ethnic and racial minority group members are disproportionately represented, can be met consistent with the self-identified needs of corporate interests, middle-class taxpayers, and overall economic growth, should serve to expand collective action in ways that will endure. At a minimum this strategy includes consensus-building based on shared interests and focused on universal material well-being, community-wide resource development, and consensus-based arguments for group achievement.

We do not naively expect that it will be easy to develop an informed public interest, nor do we expect it will always lead to success for those in greatest material need. But it is clear to us that the demands of the current global economy militate against a myopic focus on defining public policy solely in terms of individual or group rights. Formal rights promote formal equality. Formal equality without supportive, material public policy based on broad societal consensus leads to the types of limited upward mobility experienced by so many residents of central cities in the United States. In a multicultural society, we must work for a politics that builds a long-lasting majoritarian consensus for collective action in the public interest, not as a matter of right but as a matter of sound policy.

A multicultural society presents special challenges to the nation and its constituent communities that cannot be met fully within traditional understandings of rights such as those provided by the 1964 Civil Rights Act. The nation must foster a strong civic identity among citizens at the same time that there is a proliferation of individual and group identities. As well, it must attempt to develop a principled way of making decisions among competing group demands. For communities of color, the challenges are no less daunting. They must attempt to maintain self-determination within the requisites of majoritarian decision-making. They also must make sure that formal inclusion results in substantive opportunity and material gain. We believe that a civil rights logic alone cannot meet these challenges, principally because it will not, by itself, form the basis of public commitment to investment strategies that can improve the work security and standard of living of ethnic and racial groups in the United States. Greater public commitment to collective action in the service of social and economic progress for all Americans is more likely to lead to the attainment of the goals that originally inspired the 1964 Civil Rights Act.

Notes

1. The Civil Rights Restoration Act of 1991 substantially clarified the scope of the law but ultimately suffers from the same legal rights-based logic.

2. See, e.g., *Regents of the University of California v. Bakke*, 438 U.S. 265 (1978); *City of Richmond, VA v. J.A. Croson Co.*, 488 U.S. 469 (1989); *Hopwood v. State of Texas*, Nos. 94-50569; 94-50664 (5th Cir., 1996); *Shaw v. Hunt*, 94 U.S. 923 (1996); *Bush v. Vera*, 116 S. Ct. 1941 (1996). See also Richard Perez-Peña, "A Rights Movement that Emerges from the Right," *New York Times*, 30 December 1994, p. A13.

3. In 1959, for example, the incidence of child poverty for all groups was 26.1%. By 1969, that figure had dropped to 15.6%—a dramatic 40% reduction. Similarly, in 1969 the disparities between the incidence of poverty among whites as compared to African Americans and Latina/os was 30.7 and 22.9 percentage points respectively. By 1979, the disparity in child poverty rates between whites on the one hand and African Americans and Latina/os on the other had narrowed to 24.4 and 16.6 percentage points respectively. See "Recent Changes in Poverty Rate and Distribution of Income" (Hearing of the Subcommittee on Human Resources, Committee on Ways and Means, House of Representatives), 102 Cong., 10 September 1992, Serial 102–34, testimony of Sheldon Danziger, p. 114. See also Danziger and Gottschalk 1992.

4. For a careful exposition of this argument see Robert Reich 1992. Public education and job training serve as apt examples of this shift in public investment. Despite growing demands on public education, Reich argues that federal support for elementary and secondary education programs fell by about 33% in the 1980s from previous levels, creating further disparities among the states and local districts. In addition, federal funding to train workers dropped by more than 50% during the 1980s from the decade prior. See Reich 1992 and sources cited therein.

5. We are suggesting that leaders work, in Schattschneider's terms, to expand the "scope of conflict" and the "mobilization of bias" in the service of articulated long-term collective interests. See E. E. Schattschneider 1960, 1975, 1988; see also Baumgartner and Jones 1993.

6. We believe that the term "multicultural society" is useful insofar as it reminds us that interracial and interethnic tensions are just special cases of the more universal process of cleavage and integration found across a variety of social boundaries, including those based on gender, sexual orientation, class, religious affiliation, and physical or mental disability. Although we believe that the concepts we discuss below apply with equal force to many of these social cleavages, we will restrict our discussion to examples of interethnic and interracial conflict in order to be consistent with the original focus of the Civil Rights Act.

7. An extremely lucid recent discussion of the framework of the melting pot is provided by esteemed historian Arthur Schlesinger, Jr., 1992.

8. Gordon is talking here about the liberal tradition among the melting-pot assimilationists. His term for this strand of assimilationism is "liberal pluralism."

9. See, e.g., FitzGerald 1979.

10. As previously noted, the melting-pot ideal also encompassed very broad notions about the importance of common culture, language, and customs. We draw attention only to the more limited notion of the demands of common citizenship, following Schlesinger 1992.

11. See also Sniderman and Piazza 1993.

12. See note 4 above.

13. We are, of course, well aware that these ideals coexisted with slavery, sexism, and exclusion at the founding of the nation. It was, however, a national commitment to these ideals that over time has allowed the realization of more dignity, freedom, justice, and opportunity for many segments of the American population.

The Fife and Drum March to the Nineteenth Century

Thoughts on the Emerging Separate but Equal Doctrine

Barbara Phillips Sullivan

We have *all* been programmed to . . . handle [the difference between people] in one of three ways: ignore it, and if that is not possible, copy it if we think it is dominant, or destroy it if we think it is subordinate. But we have no patterns for relating across our human differences as equals. As a result, those differences have been misnamed and misused in the service of separation and confusion.

—Audre Lorde, *Sister Outsider*

The term "diversity" has played a significant role in federal court decisions concerning the issues of equality and discrimination that were the focus of the Civil Rights Act of 1964.[1] The term first gained currency in the 1970s because of the significance attached to Justice Powell's opinion in *Regents of the University of California v. Bakke*,[2] which recognized student population "diversity" as a compelling state interest that justified the use of racial classification in medical school admissions.[3] Though vague as to the principles it purported to embody, the term "diversity" seemed to conceptualize minority inclusion in the First Amendment project of academic freedom, apart from any need for redress of past or present racial discrimination.[4]

Professor Robert N. Davis argues persuasively that the idea of diversity later conceptualized by dissenting Justices Powell and Rehnquist in *Mississippi Universi-*

ty for Women v. Hogan (1982) departs from the earlier definition.[5] After *Hogan*, the troublesome nature of diversity became obvious, as the term moved from its lodging in dissent to shape judicial response in cases involving issues of sex- and race-segregated institutions. The *Hogan* incarnation of "diversity," anchored in notions of "tradition," carries "separate but equal" baggage in its justification of "traditional arrangements" in higher education. As Justice Powell wrote in his dissenting opinion, "A distinctive feature of America's tradition has been respect for diversity. This has been characteristic of the peoples from numerous lands who have built our country. It is the essence of our democratic system. At stake in this case as I see it is the preservation of a small aspect of this diversity. But that aspect is by no means insignificant, given our heritage of available choice between single-sex and coeducational institutions of higher learning."[6]

That "tradition," as Professor Davis pointedly notes, includes not only single-sex but also single-race public institutions.[7] Those single-race institutions of higher education are manifestations of the "tradition" of racial inferiority and segregation endorsed by *Plessy v. Ferguson*.[8] Unless there is some principle by which to distinguish these institutions from their nineteenth-century origins, then "tradition" is clearly incompatible with equality. Professor Wendy Brown-Scott has offered an alternative, principled "reconstructed meaning of equality" as part of the theoretical underpinning for the eradication of white supremacy in institutions of higher education, but her theory requires the hard work of recognizing and remedying the pervasive, enduring significance of the legacy of slavery—the hard work that is avoided by the catchphrase "diversity."[9]

The term "diversity" is troublesome for its chameleon-like quality alone. It has also been considered problematic because of its use in accentuating differences and divisiveness, its elevation of cultural over national identity, its contribution to a heightened sense of separateness rather than of community. It is also open to the charge that its judicial development proceeded "in an unprincipled fashion without explanation as to whether the articulated benefits allegedly derived were consistent with diversity as we had come to understand it."[10] Underlying these criticisms of diversity is one of the great myths utilized by the political majority to maintain its domination—that America as we know and love it is threatened by group identities. I do not agree that the theory of America as one people managed at some time in the past to keep American society "whole." To the extent that communities become increasingly conscious of group identity and interests and forge informed, intergroup coalitions, I think society in general will be all the better for it.

I join in criticizing the concept of "diversity" because I think it prevents the transformation of society that would result from recognizing the continuing and pervasive significance of race in our society and remedying the effects of present and past racial discrimination. This new diversity concept emerges at a time when popular opinion, legislatures, and the judiciary are signaling a hostility to equality claims by African Americans and turning away from the reality of racism and from necessary, effective remedies. As David Benjamin Oppenheimer concludes in his compelling account of the connection between events in Birmingham and the introduction and passage of the Civil Rights Act of 1964, our civil rights future is imperiled by a failure to appreciate fully the change in the law effected by the militant, nonviolent Birmingham direct action campaign:

> To most of our current students, and an increasing majority of the population, it [Birmingham] is nearly ancient history. As a result, our country is losing the sense of connection between the enforcement of the Civil Rights Act, and the utter deprivation of human rights that gave rise to the great struggle for freedom and dignity which led to its enactment. The "fatal attraction" of the term "diversity" is its potential to call us away from the project of eradicating the legacy of slavery, a project renewed by the national consensus that resulted in the Civil Rights Act of 1964.[11]

I oppose the use of the term "diversity" for two reasons: (1) because it incubates the separate but equal doctrine rejected in *Brown v. Board of Education*,[12] with implications for the complicity of federal courts in the failure of the Second Reconstruction (in the same way that *Plessy v. Ferguson*[13] was the judiciary's contribution to the failure of the First Reconstruction), and (2) because it displaces the need to recognize and remedy the effects of present and past discrimination. The emergence of the concept of diversity gives the lie to the profound hope that the civil rights movement would transform society. Merely to celebrate "diversity" is tacitly to endorse the failure to transform the social, political, and legal institutions that perpetuate race and gender subordination.[14]

"Diversity" as a New Form of "Separate but Equal"

The curious nature of the concept of diversity becomes apparent in equal protection decisions that followed *Bakke* and *Hogan*. In *United States v. Fordice*,[15] for example, the state of Mississippi contested charges that its failure to integrate its eight public universities was a violation of the equal protection clause and Title VI of the Civil Rights Act of 1964.[16] In remanding with an invitation to the state to provide educational justifications for maintaining these eight institutions, the Supreme Court "flag[ged] diversity as a noble goal without careful examination" and "left the door of the past ajar and some of the old ghosts are creeping into our modern jurisprudence."[17]

On remand, the district court heard 103 witnesses and produced an indexed opinion and remedial decree with appendixes in excess of two hundred pages.[18] The results are a revealing illustration of what can be expected from the current un-principled concept of diversity. The remedy crafted by the district court permitted, *inter alia*, all eight state-supported universities traceable to *de jure* segregation (three "historically black" and five "historically white") to continue in existence; the provision of specific additional funding to some of the institutions; uniform ad-missions standards among all the state institutions; further study by the State Board of Institutions of Higher Learning; and a monitoring committee to review and analyze submissions by defendants and to make recommendations to the court.[19]

A review of the district court's response to two of the plaintiffs' issues, employ-ment practices and "climate,"[20] illustrates why a reasonable person would not know that plaintiffs "won" this case and supports the perception that the new equal protection jurisprudence may revive *Plessy*. The *Ayers* plaintiffs contended that "defendants' employment . . . policies and practices perpetuat[ed] segregation by resulting in racially identifiable faculty and administrators."[21] The court found that for the system as a whole in fiscal year 1992, 94% of the full professors at the historically white institutions were white and 2% were black, and that 98% of the administrators at those institutions were white and 2% were black.[22] By institution, the percentage of faculty holding full professor status was as follows: (a) University of Southern Mississippi, 97% white and 1% black; (b) University of Mississippi, 96% white and 0.5% Black; (c) Mississippi University for Women, 100% white and 0% black; (d) Delta State University, 97% white and 1% black; (e) Mississippi State Uni-versity, 94% white and 2% black.[23] Nevertheless, defendants were not ordered to take any remedial action with respect to employment.[24]

The district court then turned to an aggregate issue it termed "climate" in re-sponse to the plaintiffs' claim that the racial climate at these historically white in-stitutions is hostile to black students.[25] Looking at the University Of Mississippi, where I taught, the district court noted that in 1983 the university had "disassociat-ed" itself from the use of the Confederate flag as a pep symbol at athletic events, and that although the school band still plays "Dixie," it does so less frequently than before and, moreover, that the views of those who oppose the song are accommodated by the band's playing of "The Battle Hymn of the Republic."[26] The court also noted that in 1988, when the first black fraternity house on campus was burned on the eve of its opening, white fraternities joined in contributing donations to replace the house.[27] The district court found it "ironic" that out of concern for the damage inflicted on black students by the racially hostile campus environment, some black faculty discouraged potential black students from attending the university.[28]

Unimpressed by the striking racial disparities in employment and by a campus climate so hostile to blacks that black faculty would discourage black students from applying, the court failed to note other obvious indexes of the legacy of white supremacy: the university's involvement with and support of racially segregated sororities and fraternities in a system firmly dominated by whites; the sports teams named "The Rebels" and their accompanying "school spirit" items emblazoned with this name and the image of "Colonel Rebel"; the continued homage paid to the Confederate cause by campus street names such as "Rebel Drive" and "Confederate Drive"; the school's continued use of the nickname "Ole Miss," adopted when this was a *de jure* segregated institution and also, reportedly, the "affectionate" form of address used by mythical slaves for the mythical plantation mistress (although in my experience, this same mythical creature is referred to in the black community as "Miss Ann," connoting not quite the "affection" imagined by whites); the school shop named "The Rebel Shop" with its profusion of "Rebel" items; the naming of the law school building to honor a man who believed fervently in the inferiority of black people and actively worked to maintain slavery, and so on. While "desegregated" in the sense that the institution may no longer enforce an explicit "whites only" admissions and hiring policy, the notion of "diversity" permits the institution to perpetuate as an integral part of its culture the legacy of its racially segregated, white supremacist tradition.

Nevertheless, the district court found that "African-Americans are becoming more and more comfortable"[29] and found anecdotal testimony critical of the racial climate less compelling than the "objective" measure showing that the historically white institutions have higher retention rates for black students than do the historically black institutions.[30]

This version of "diversity" recalls into equal protection jurisprudence the standard articulated by the Court in *Plessy v. Ferguson*.[31] In that case, the Court considered an equal protection challenge to a state statute providing for separate railway cars for whites and blacks and found the statute entirely consistent with the protections of both the Thirteenth and Fourteenth Amendments. *Plessy* and the plaintiffs' pyrrhic victory in *Ayers* depend on a certain formalism to compel suspension of disbelief in the face of claims that "equality" under the law was realized in these decisions. *Plessy* purports to support the view that "the object [of the Fourteenth Amendment] was undoubtedly to enforce the absolute equality of the two races before the law."[32] *Ayers* purports to do no less. In both instances, recognition of the subordination of blacks to the preferences of the majority is studiously avoided.

"Diversity" Is an Obstacle to Racial Equality

The concept of "diversity" embodies no meaningful response to the continuing need in our society to achieve the promise of the constitutional amendments for true equality. Without ties to some principle of justice, the concept is merely utilitarian in achieving other values—in *Bakke* the goal was a robust academic environment—little more in itself than a pleasant thought: "variety is the spice of life." Easier and more engaging than acknowledging the effects of past and present discrimination, "diversity" permits the continued enjoyment of racial privilege at the price of subordination of "others."[33] Far from being a healthy concept, "diversity" indulges in what popular culture refers to as "deep denial."[34]

Popular denial of the continuing significance of race in our society is rampant and well documented.[35] Whites consistently declare the workplace and other spheres of life to be fair and nondiscriminatory, while minorities continue to find themselves subjected to discrimination in virtually every aspect of life.[36] Asserting the existence of a level playing field and rhetorically invoking a "color-blind" Constitution to discredit the continuing effects of racial domination, whites can turn away from issues of justice to the concept of "diversity." The concept of "diversity" is the medium through which the status quo can be "neutrally" maintained and racial stereotypes persist.[37] Instead of contributing to the transformation of society, "diversity" provides a respectable cover for the status quo and its unstated assumptions, assumptions that need not be examined, assumptions that cause a judge to associate the sound of drums with men and the sound of flutes with women or to declare racial equality achieved when African Americans have the "freedom of choice" to walk among a faculty that remains 96% white while listening to the strains of "Dixie" along Rebel Drive on the way to L. Q. C. Lamar Hall.

The story of Professor Charles R. Lawrence illustrates the usefulness of "diversity" in perpetuating the racial subordination inherent in the status quo. In 1990 he taught a law school seminar in which students could enroll only with the consent of the instructor. Of the twenty-six students selected, only six were European-American while twenty were students of color. Some white students protested to the dean, claiming reverse discrimination. The institution's response was to resist Professor Lawrence's project of creating a seminar for the "primary and central purpose [of] further[ing] the interests of subordinated students and their communities."[38] This purpose was at odds with the purpose for which the institution hired Professor Lawrence and admitted the students of color: "diversity." As Professor Lawrence explains, "the law school had admitted students of color and it had hired me so that we could attend to its business, the business of perpetuating elites. We were there to add color, to share what we knew of those-who-would-be-ruled with the future rulers, and perhaps to be assimilated at the margins of the ruling elite. The liberation of colonized communities of color was not on the law school agenda. The law school's goals for diversity did not include the transformation of a white supremacist society."[39]

As this story makes clear, "diversity" cannot be transformative because it perpetuates the condition of white supremacy—the failure to make students of color and their communities central to the mission of the institution. The diversity concept makes it easy to turn away from the difficult task of fundamental change and institutional transformation required if the legacy of *Plessy* is to be dismantled.[40]

Equal protection jurisprudence must be grounded in concepts of racial justice to move in a direction capable of responding to the unfinished business of the constitutional amendments, the civil rights movement, and its resulting civil rights legislation as our multiracial, multicultural society enters the twenty-first century. The civil rights movement was not premised on any concept of diversity but on equality and empowerment.[41] Professor Guinier succinctly captures the essence of the movement when she explains that "the concept of participatory democracy was the heart of the civil rights 'mass movement'"[42] and that the movement's goals included *both* community autonomy and participatory democracy.[43] As Guinier notes, the values and goals were not those of "a self-limiting movement to assimilate blacks."[44] Rather, a social transformation was envisioned; Guinier cites the platform adopted in 1972 at the National Black Political Convention and endorsed by both Coretta King and Bobby Seale "articulat[ing] a revolution of values, a social transformation placing 'community' before individualism . . . justice before unjust order, and morality before expediency."[45]

Describing the Virginia Military Institute and the Citadel as "fraternal organizations whose initiates emerge as full-fledged members of an all-male aristocracy" and objecting to taxpayer funding of these institutions, fourth circuit Judge K. K. Hall observed, "As we prepare, together, to face the twenty-first century, we simply cannot afford to preserve a relic of the nineteenth."[46] Neither should we preserve an equal protection jurisprudence tied to nineteenth-century white supremacy that undermines efforts to create a just society and serves, instead, as the Trojan Horse for *Plessy*.

Notes

1. Pub.L.No.88-352, 78 Stat. 241. This legislation, *inter alia*, prohibits segregation or discrimination on the basis of race, color, religion, or national origin in places of public accommodation and prohibits discrimination in employment based on race, color sex, religion, or national origin.

2. *Regents of the University of California v. Bakke*, 438 U.S. 265 (1978).

3. *Bakke*, 438 U.S. at 314.

4. Davis 1994, 11, 11–30.

5. *Mississippi University for Women v. Hogan*, 458 U.S. 718 (1982).

6. *Mississippi University for Women v. Hogan*, at 745 (Powell, J., dissenting).

7. Davis 1994, 37–38.

8. *Plessy v. Ferguson*, 163 U.S. 537 (1896).

9. Brown-Scott 1994, 64–65.

10. See Davis 1994, note 3; Carrington 1992.

11. See Oppenheimer 1995, 678–79.

12. *Brown v. Board of Education*, 347 U.S. 483 (1954).

13. *Plessy v. Ferguson*, 163 U.S. 537 (1896).

14. As Cass Sunstein has noted, virtually any claim as to the purpose, goals, and values of the civil rights movement will arouse controversy (Sunstein 1995). Sunstein vigorously disputes the currently popular claim that the movement was committed to a norm of color blindness and opposed all racial classifications. He characterizes the movement as being fundamentally grounded in valuing freedom from desperate conditions and opposition to caste. Lani Guinier captures a vibrant sense of the transformative agenda of the movement in describing the voting rights arena: "voting rights activists sought also to expand the liberal vision toward a re-distributive agenda premised on equality of condition, and not just freedom from overt discrimination" (Guinier 1991b, 1086–87).

15. *United States v. Fordice*, U.S., 112 S. Ct. 2727 (1992).

16. *Fordice*, 505 U.S. 717 at 723.

17. See Davis 1994, 49–54.

18. *Ayers v. Fordice*, 879 F. Supp. 1419 (N.D. Miss. 1995).

19. *Ayers*, 879 F. Supp. at 1494–96.

20. Ayers at 1462–63, 1471–72.

21. Ayers at 1459.

22. Ayers at 1460.

23. Ayers at 1460 n. 196.

24. Ayers at 1462.

25. Ayers at 1466.

26. Ayers at 1467.

27. Ayers at 1467.

28. Ayers at 1467–68.

29. Ayers at 1471.

30. Ayers at 1472. The court contended that the higher retention rate was "evidence that the defendant HWIs [historically white institutions] . . . are doing something right."

31. *Plessy v. Ferguson*, 163 U.S. 537 (1896).

32. *Plessy*, 163 U.S. at 544.

33. Harris 1993, 1713. "Others" is a category constructed by the ideology of white supremacy which creates two categories: the first category is comprised of "whole, complete, entitled human beings (read white)" and the second category consists of "others." See Lawrence 1995, 835–36.

34. Tsuang 1989, 671–72. Professor Lawrence points out that the "color-blind" approach of making explicit racial categories unlawful does not make those categories and their consequences disappear. He identifies "denial" as a particular "cost" of the color-blind approach: "the narrow doctrinal view of what counts as racism helps spread the epidemic of denial. Now reactionary voices, the same voices that resisted integration, have seized upon the liberal rhetoric of colorblindness to call for an end to race-conscious remedies while, with a barely disguised conspiratorial chuckle, they disseminate the most malignant racially coded messages" (Lawrence 1995, 837).

35. Hacker 1992.

36. National Conference of Christians and Jews 1992.

37. The dissonance between whites' expressions of egalitarianism and what they actually do in their interactions with African Americans is explored through discussion of several empirical studies by Eleanor Marie Brown 1995, 513.

38. Lawrence 1995, 841–42.

39. Lawrence 1995, 844 (footnotes omitted).

40. The continuing and pervasive impact of racism on virtually all aspects of life in the United States is presented with both anecdotal and empirical evidence by T. Alexander Aleinikoff 1992.

41. Guinier 1991b, 1081. See also Peller 1990, 767 n. 15.

42. Guinier 1991b, 1085.

43. Guinier 1991b, 1081–86.

44. Guinier 1991b, 1086–87.

45. Guinier 1991b, 1087 n. 43

46. *Faulkner v. Jones*, 51 F.3d at 451.

12

Civil Rights, the Constitution, Common Decency, and Common Sense

Bernard Grofman

When judged in terms of the idealistic hopes of many of their supporters, the Civil Rights Act of 1964 and other early civil rights legislation must be regarded as great disappointments. The 1960s optimism that an end to legally sanctioned discrimination would lead to a society of equals, where persons were no longer viewed through the lens of skin color, proved misguided. The United States still has powerful remnants of a "caste" system in which the color of one's skin may be as important in affecting chances for success in life as the content of one's character.[1] While the black middle class has expanded considerably, on a variety of indices the gap between black America and white America has grown larger, not smaller, since 1964. The ratio of black employment to white employment is worse now than it was in 1964, and a far higher proportion of blacks than whites live in poverty or on welfare. While blacks and whites graduate high school in almost equal proportions, the reading and math skills of black high school graduates lag dramatically behind those of their white counterparts. Perhaps worst of all, black infant mortality rates are far higher than those of whites. There is what seems to be a permanent black underclass—geographically segregated, beset by limited education, broken families, and omnipresent violent crime (Farley and Allen 1987; Jaynes and Williams 1989; Massey and Denton 1993). In sum, we are still a very long way from achieving Martin Luther King's dream. The issue of race refuses to go away.

Yet, despite continuing stark inequalities and continuing discrimination against African Americans, contemporary debates about civil rights no longer address the question of how to end discrimination or achieve real equality between the races; instead they center on the supposed inequities of affirmative action. Civil rights issues are once again at center stage in American politics, but what are being protested are not the inequities caused by discrimination against blacks but the actions that have been taken to end that discrimination. Today the reforms brought about by the Civil Rights Act of 1964 in employment, housing, and education are under attack.[2] Virtually all forms of affirmative action are being labeled "reverse discrimination" against whites. Defenders of the civil rights legacy of the past are on the defensive, as seen in President's Clinton's less than ringing endorsement of affirmative action, "Mend it, don't end it," and in the 1996 passage of Proposition 209 in California calling for "color-blind" practices, which has been interpreted by its leading supporters as requiring an end to all (or virtually all) affirmative action practices.[3]

While the principal attack on current civil rights policies comes from the conservative camp, an increasing number of liberals have also come to reject many of the directions in which civil rights enforcement has gone since the passage of the 1964 Civil Rights Act. Even among those sympathetic to civil rights goals, affirmative action is sometimes seen as like Frankenstein's monster in the 1930s movie version of Mary Shelley's masterpiece: massive, lumbering, and lacking clear direction. Policies are not very well articulated—indeed, they are stitched together out of incompatible parts. Affirmative action in particular is apparently out of control and has taken on a life of its own.

The chief complaint about civil rights policy is, of course, that it has lost sight of its original and completely praiseworthy goal of ending discrimination and requiring race-neutral treatment and hared off instead after norms of proportionality in result. The real consequences of the past thirty-five years of government policies, it is claimed, have been very different from and very much less desirable than those that were intended. Just as economists and others have argued that welfare policies designed to provide a safety cushion for the "deserving" poor have reduced incentives to work and led to an increase in illegitimacy and welfare dependency, contemporary civil rights policies are alleged to create a variety of perverse incentives and highly undesirable unintended consequences. The litany of complaints is a long one. Civil rights policies, it is alleged,

(a) have replaced the idea of equality of opportunity with a system that requires race-based preferences so as to create what is little more than a racial and ethnic spoils system;

(b) implicitly assume that our primary identity is defined by the color of our skin or the language spoken by our ancestors rather than by our shared U.S. citizenship and the common commitments of a constitutional covenant;

(c) create race-norming of standards through affirmative action practices that implicitly reinforce the idea that differences in achievements across racial and ethnic lines are inevitable;[4]

(d) harm U.S. competitiveness in multiple ways, e.g., by removing personal incentives for investment in human capital (supposedly, minorities won't see the need to invest in skills since they will get hired/promoted anyway, while whites will see the benefits of such investment reduced by affirmative hiring and promotion policies); by creating a vast bureaucracy and a complex set of regulations to enforce affirmative action policies that greatly increase the cost of doing business in the United States; and by making it very difficult to hire on the basis of merit or fire on the basis of non-performance if race might be implicated;[5]

(e) have generally been a failure in terms of raising the living standards of blacks and other minorities, except possibly for minority groups (such as white women) who already had middle-class skills/values;

(f) are simply not cost-effective and/or have largely achieved their goals of ending discrimination by now, with remaining inequities the result of differences in human capital and motivation;[6]

(g) have, through affirmative action policies, fostered white resentment of minorities who have advanced in spite of lower seniority and lesser skills than whites or who have, on account of race, gotten jobs for which they are unqualified;

(h) have, through affirmative action policies, created a "culture of victimhood" in which minorities view differential treatment based on actual differences in behavior or performance as discriminatory; and

(i) have created a "rights-based" society in which an ever increasing number of groups claim an ever increasing number of rights[7] and entitlements to "special" protection.[8]

While I believe that many of these allegations are either mistaken or overstated,[9] I do not wish to defend current policies in this essay.

I aim instead to carve out a middle ground between those who think that race should never be taken into account in decisions about jobs or education and those who believe that proportional representation by race in universities and the workforce is tantamount to a constitutional commandment. I believe that civil rights policies for the United States can be constitutionally grounded and formulated on the basis of common decency and applied with common sense.[10]

My analysis has seven postulates: (1) discrimination against blacks still exists and requires legal remedy; (2) civil rights policies must be based on moral principles that command wide assent; (3) the crafting of race-conscious remedies is inevitable in the presence of race-conscious discriminatory practices; (4) the notion of hiring on the basis of "merit" must be rethought, in that "merit" cannot be judged solely by the results of paper-and-pencil tests; (5) the term "affirmative action" has outgrown its usefulness because it has come to mean everything from efforts to publicize job openings to rigid quota rules; (6) actions to remedy past discrimination have a stronger moral force and a far different constitutional authority than diversity preference, per se; and (7) as long as socioeconomic and educational disparities persist, antidiscrimination legislation and litigation can have only a limited impact in changing the fundamental racial inequalities in our society.

Race Still Matters

My first presupposition is that we are still very far from a world where race does not matter. Discrimination against African Americans continues to take place, even if in ways that are less overt than "colored only" water fountains. Controlled experiments demonstrate continuing elements of discrimination against black Americans in housing and employment (Bergmann 1996, chapter 5).[11] Similarly, *ceteris paribus,* blacks are more likely to be stopped by the police or followed by store detectives and less likely to be picked up by cruising taxicabs or given entrance to posh stores that require admittance by the buzzer. Lynchings may be largely a thing of the past, but skinheads and other white supremacist thugs are still killing African Americans solely because they are black. Perceptions that "blacks are different"—less intelligent, less hardworking, and more prone to criminal behavior than whites (or than other minorities such as Asian Americans)—persist, even though most white Americans are generally unwilling to acknowledge publicly that they hold such views.[12] In a revealing recent social-psychological experiment, for example, we learn that it would take vast sums of money to persuade a typical white American to change his skin color to black.

Widely Shared Moral Principles

My second presupposition is that civil rights legislation must rest on the bedrock of widely shared moral principles. Critical, in my view, to civil rights policies that can gain widespread public assent are the twin principles of *nondiscrimination* and *non-stigmatization*. Whatever else 1960s supporters of civil rights may have wanted, it is clear that they endorsed the "nondiscrimination principle" for state action, namely that discriminatory state action is constitutionally repugnant.[13] By discrimination I mean what that term has traditionally meant: invidious intentional discrimination against a disliked minority solely on the basis of race or some other suspect criterion. It is also clear that 1960s supporters of civil rights would have endorsed what I call the "non-stigmatization principle," namely that under most (if not all) circumstances, given the history of the United States, when it comes to race, "separate is not equal" even if the separate (public) facilities being compared are equal down to the thirteenth decimal place.[14] I think that today we could obtain wide (though not, of course, unanimous) agreement on these principles.[15] Unfortunately, however, such principles don't get us very far with respect to the "hard cases" that now command public attention,[16] but it is still useful to remember just how far we have come in thirty-five years to be able to say that those two principles would now command near-universal assent![17]

Race-Conscious Remedies Are Needed for Race-Conscious Discrimination

My third presupposition is that in some circumstances, because of the existence of discrimination tied to race, race-conscious remedies for that discrimination are simply unavoidable. My own approach to affirmative action is based on the notion of the realistic politics of a second-best world (Grofman and Davidson 1992). If race were not such a pervasive factor in social judgments, if the United States had no history of enslaving blacks, exterminating Native Americans, and discriminating against virtually everyone with darker skin tones (except of course surfers and sunbathers), color-blind government policies would not be just an ideal but a workable alternative. Justice Clarence Thomas's recent call to be totally "color-blind" is, unfortunately, "history-blind." If we were to accept his views, we would find ourselves unable to craft sensible policies that address both continuing discrimination and the lingering effects of past discrimination.[18]

Merit Is Not Identical to Skills Shown on Paper-and-Pencil Tests

My fourth presupposition, and one that I believe most Americans would find uncontroversial, is the notion that merit is not identical with skills shown on paper-and-pencil tests. In particular, elements of character and promise such as demonstrated willingness to work hard, previous job performance, or persistence in the face of adversity are also very much indicators of "merit."[19] Similarly, most Americans would accept the commonsense view that small differences in test scores may not mean very much. Thus, rather than race-norming scores to determine admissions or job selection, it would be more reasonable to establish *minimum* standards to screen out those who should not qualify and then use other criteria to make the final selection—or simply use a lottery to choose between those who fall above the threshold (Guinier 1996). If a lottery were used, or if the additional screening criteria were applied in an evenhanded fashion, this would be likely to increase the number of minorities without violating our basic notions of fairness. Thus, in my view, much of the debate over the supposed conflict between affirmative action and "merit-based" hiring is misguided, because it posits that the sole appropriate measures of merit are the results of paper-and-pencil tests.

"Affirmative Action" Has Outgrown Its Usefulness

The term "affirmative action" has come to cover a multitude of processes, some widely supported, others deeply unpopular. In my view, the term has ceased to be useful in policy debates because it now encompasses everything from outreach efforts to minority communities to rigid quotas even in settings where no discrimination has been legally demonstrated.[20]

When policies and statutes are couched in antidiscrimination terms, they can often command wide assent; when they are couched in terms of affirmative action, public support plummets. Yet most Americans would have no trouble agreeing that, say, special efforts should be made to publicize job openings so that all potential applicants have an equal chance to compete. Even the "token" job interview, perhaps all too often only a token, can still be defended on the grounds that what I will call expectational racism (i.e., stereotypes grounded in realistic expectations about the odds that a minority will in fact be qualified), can still be refuted by evidence about a particular individual—but only if there is an opportunity to present that evidence. Even more broadly, few Americans would object to special efforts to improve the quality of schools in neighborhoods where poor resources at home make it harder for kids to learn. There is likewise wide support for creating genuine equal opportunity, so long as this is not seen as a predetermined way to create special training programs available only to minorities. Opponents of current civil rights policies are disingenuous when they claim, for example, that affirmative action is "nothing but quotas," just as defenders of those same policies are disingenuous when they refuse to admit that some affirmative action policies (as they have been implemented) are, in fact, quotas.

Civil Rights vs. Diversity

Too much of the debate over civil rights has been marred by lumping together needed remedies for real discrimination and the goal of promoting "diversity." Debates about affirmative action today almost always confuse two very different situations: (1) those dealing with legally imposed remedies for past discriminatory practices, and (2) those dealing with voluntary attempts to promote diversity in schools or the workplace.[21] What is appropriate in the context of legally required remedies for past discrimination ("remedial action") and what is appropriate in terms of a general concern for diversity (what I would characterize as "diversity preference") are, in my view, quite different.[22]

For companies whose racially discriminatory practices have been demonstrated, I believe that most Americans would accept the need for an accelerated pace of minority entry-level hiring and accelerated promotions to qualified minorities to compensate for past exclusionary and unjust practices, even though they would still reject double standards (race norming) for retention and promotion.[23] I believe that remedies for past discrimination can legitimately include steps to force the employer to create, with all deliberate speed, the pattern of employment by race or gender that we can realistically expect would have occurred had there never been discrimination in the first place.[24] Even where previous discrimination has not been proved, I believe that many Americans would accept the need for race-conscious and gender-conscious programs to recruit minorities, even while they would reject different standards for retention and promotion for members of different races.

The preference for diversity per se, by contrast, is not mandated by the constitutional principle of equal protection, nor is it a principle that could command widespread assent in all contexts.[25] In many ways, moreover, the debate about diversity preferences is a sideshow, diverting us from the main event, which is how best to eliminate the continuing manifestations of actual discrimination against minorities.[26] However, claims for something like diversity preference seem to me to be especially strong in two domains, education and community service.

In higher education there is a long history of preference for diversity (e.g., a geographic mix of students, athletes, tuba players for the marching band), and the strong argument, at least in the humanities and the social sciences, that the classroom experience is enhanced when a wide range of perspectives are represented.[27] Thus, the *Bakke* compromise (race may be used as an admissions criterion as long as it is not weighted too highly), does make sense in the context of college admissions.[28] Of course we must be careful to set realistic thresholds for admittance. Setting people up to fail is no favor, especially if failure ends up discouraging someone from trying again in a context where he or she is more likely to succeed. College-level classes require a minimum level of verbal and mathematical skill, and the minimum requirements are greater still at the more elite universities.[29]

In the case of police, the argument is again not really about diversity but about job performance. In particular, given our legacy of past discrimination, it seems reasonable on commonsense grounds to believe that black police may be more effective than white police in winning trust and enforcing law and order in black neighborhoods.[30] Of course it also seems plausible, given our country's past history, to believe that a virtual absence of black police would have severe consequences for the perceived and actual fairness of the social order.

The Equal Protection Clause Is Not a Universal Panacea

My final presupposition is that the constitution's equal protection clause is not a universal panacea. There are many pernicious racial inequalities that lack a direct constitutional remedy because they do not fit into the framework of discrimination on the basis of race. Equality cannot always be commanded with a lawsuit.[31] As long as there is a legacy of past discrimination and continuing socioeconomic disparities, equal treatment alone will not afford equality of result. Realistically speaking, were completely neutral performance standards to be used for most high-level jobs (as well as for college and graduate school admissions), a much lower proportion of African Americans would be found with the necessary training and skills, for all kinds of historical reasons. Minorities suffer from the lingering effects of past and present discrimination and from continuing socioeconomic and cultural disparities (such as the presence or absence of books in the home), that cannot be wished away. These disparities will have consequences for language and skill acquisition, for work habits, and even—in terms of fetal nutrition and verbal stimulation during infancy—for intelligence, and they can result in differences that are immensely difficult to overcome.[32]

Education is increasingly the key to success in our society and it is there that much of the effort to change the unequal status of blacks must focus. Racial disparities will continue to be especially great in the best-paying and most prestigious jobs until we raise the level of black educational attainment. In addressing the situation of black America it is necessary to begin at the bottom if we are to have success at the top.[33]

Notes

1. Despite my recognition of our increasingly multiracial society (see Fraga and Ruiz-de-Velasco, chapter 10 of this volume) and the problem of gender-based discrimination, in this essay I deal primarily with civil rights issues as they apply to African Americans because I regard the problem of race, the need to cope with the legacy of slavery and Jim Crow, as a bone lodged in the throat of American society. Just as it has been for the previous two centuries, the problem of race will be the most important domestic issue of the twenty-first century.

2. Similarly, the changes brought about under the Voting Rights Act of 1965—race-conscious congressional and legislative districting—are also under attack (Grofman 1995; Reeves 1997; Grofman 1998), as is the legacy of the Immigration Reform Act of 1965. While the main focus of recent immigration reform efforts has been closing U.S. borders to illegal immigration and denying government services to those who are already here illegally, a backlash against legal immigration is also underway. This backlash is symbolized by the proposed denial of welfare benefits to legal immigrants who are not (yet) citizens, proposals to scale back total numbers of legal immigrants, and proposals to change the character of legal immigration by limiting its use in uniting families and by giving strong advantages to better-educated, more affluent would-be immigrants.

3. Public attitudes toward affirmative action are complex and depend on exactly how questions are framed (see, e.g., Kinder and Sanders 1996; Tate and Hampton, chapter 9 of this volume; and Sniderman, Tetlock, and Carmines 1993). For example, although Proposition 209, the language of which rejected preferential treatment, passed in California, a comparable initiative in Houston, which specifically called for an "end to the use of Affirmative Action for women and minorities," failed.

4. Similarly, contemporary civil rights policies are attacked on the ground that they cast doubt on the actual achievements of minority members, which become attributed by others (especially whites) not to the actual abilities and hard work of these minority members but to the supposed preferential treatment they received through affirmative action policies.

5. In particular, it is alleged that employers will settle discrimination claims out of court even when they are unfounded, merely because the costs of litigating such claims are so high, and that the anticipation of lawsuits discourages employers from applying the same performance standards to minorities and non-minorities, thus forcing them to use proportionality of results as their standard lest they be sued successfully. However, there is little empirical evidence to support this argument (see Leonard 1989; Burstein, chapter 7 of this volume). On the other hand, some economists argue that the threat of Civil Rights Act enforcement and related legal threats actually decrease minority hiring. Because em-

ployers know that once hired, minorities will be hard to fire, employers are reluctant to hire minorities in the first place (see, e.g., Bloch 1994, 104). To the extent that this argument can be proven, the claim that affirmative action policies harm whites must be unfounded.

6. Indeed, the even stronger claim has been made by one libertarian scholar that had it not been for artificial government support for discriminatory behavior, discrimination in the United States would have died out long ago though the natural operation of market forces. By the logic of the market, employers seek the best workforce for the least money; discriminating in favor of white workers would introduce unnecessary expense and therefore inefficiency into the labor market (Epstein 1992).

7. The claim is also frequently made that the term "discrimination" has been redefined in inappropriate ways so as to affect domains of social conduct that are far beyond the scope of what was, in 1964, thought of as discrimination—often in ways that substantially affect free speech interests, e.g., gender harassment suits based on *Playboy* photos in the locker room or job suspensions based on use of language that might be interpreted as implying racial prejudice.

8. Indeed, especially (but certainly not exclusively) among African Americans, there has been some concern that current civil rights policies no longer focus on efforts to redress the lingering effects of historical discrimination on African Americans but now erroneously emphasize generic claims to "victimhood." Even more specifically, it is claimed that some groups, including groups the majority of whose members are recent immigrants with no real claim to having suffered from the lingering effects of past discrimination in the United States, are often treated better by government policies than the former slaves to whose plight the Civil War amendments were primarily directed.

9. Attacks on so-called affirmative action are especially overblown when they wrongly lump together as targets those practices used as legally required remedies for proven discrimination and those whose principal justification is simply a claimed need for diversity (see below).

10. For an attempt to appeal to honesty, common sense, and common decency in the context of race and the criminal justice system, see Kennedy 1997.

11. Implicit or explicit racial appeals are also important in many political campaigns involving a black candidate, especially in the South (Reeves 1997, chapter 5).

12. As former federal judge A. Leon Higginbotham put it, "The precept of black inferiority is the hate that raged in the American soul through over 240 years of slavery and nearly 90 years of segregation. . . . The ashes of that hate have, over the course of so many generations, accumulated at the bottom of our memory. There they lie uneasily like a heavy secret that whites can never quite confess, and blacks can never quite forgive" (1997, 11).

13. In the 1960s as now, there was no consensus about how to deal with purely "private" discrimination or where to draw the line between the public and private spheres.

14. See chapter 11 of this volume by Barbara Phillips Sullivan.

15. For a discussion of standards of proof for discrimination, see appendix 1 by Kadane and Mitchell and appendix 2 by Lempert in this volume.

16. In the aftermath of the passage of the Civil Rights Act of 1964, it became apparent that colorblind law, like the idealistic vision of children of different races growing up in an atmosphere free of prejudice, was not adequate to deal with the complexities caused by the interaction of race and class, continuing racism in the private sphere, the lingering effects of past discrimination, and growing cultural diversity. As Hugh Graham argues in chapter 3 of this volume, the focus of civil rights policies in the 1970s and thereafter became far more complex than simple enforcement of the twin principles of nondiscrimination and non-stigmatization. Skrentny (1996) offers an intriguing discussion of the evolution of civil rights policies that suggest a combination of political manipulation (in which Richard Nixon helped create a "wedge issue" for the Republicans to use against their Democratic opponents), and an administrative preference for numerical—and thus manageable—standards.

17. On the other hand, I am skeptical of the attempts by liberal legal scholars and political philosophers to articulate a philosophical justification for the most extreme forms of preferential treatment, since many of these justifications are anchored in a cloud cuckoo-land. For Ronald Fiscus (1992, 13,

63–64), for example, concern for merit takes a back seat to the idea that fairness requires that all races be equally represented in all professions, since that is what supposedly would occur in an ideal world devoid of racism (Fiscus 1992, 91–92).

18. It is sometimes argued (most commonly by white defenders of color-blind practices) that race-conscious policies create uncertainties among minority members themselves as to their own abilities. I have never found this a compelling argument; those African Americans who succeed "against the odds" have many reasons to be proud. That they may have been given a helping hand does not demean their achievements. We all have, in one way or another, been given helping hands.

19. Of course, even when paper-and-pencil tests do not test items that are directly relevant to job performance, they may be used because their results are seen as a signal of a willingness to invest in human capital that bodes well for future job performance (Spence 1974).

20. For example, Rosenfeld deliberately uses the term affirmative action to include modes of preferential treatment (1991, 47). Certainly that is not how the term was first used.

21. Of course, some of these "voluntary" forms of affirmative action will come in situations where legal discrimination might have been proven but where settlement out of court was thought preferable, or where jurisdictions or companies chose to engage in affirmative action in part to ward off potential lawsuits.

22. I prefer the phrase *remedial action* to refer to plans put into place as a result of litigation or out-of-court settlements that have specifically been crafted as remedies for a pattern and practice of what is (or at least appears to be) actual discrimination. In contrast, I use the term *affirmative action* only to refer to action that is prospective, designed to assure future fairness of treatment in the absence of any specific legal finding of discriminatory practices whose consequences are to be remedied. I use *diversity preference* to refer to giving preference (at the margin) to members of a given racial or other minority over equally qualified others.

23. Policies designed to eliminate illegal discrimination unavoidably impose costs of compliance even on the innocent, but we must balance such costs against the evil of failing to remedy discrimination. Of course, attempts to eradicate discrimination down to the last decimal place are, as a practical matter, simply impossible because of the problem of enforcement costs and diminishing marginal payoffs to enforcement efforts.

24. Consider the following example, in which we posit that a southern state has failed to hire blacks on its state police force and that a federal district court has found a history of past discrimination and needs to craft a remedy. Assume that black candidates make up 20% of all those who are qualified to serve but that no blacks currently serve. Assume a steady force of 3,000 state troopers, with 100 hired yearly to replace the 100 who retire. If we hire 20 blacks per year out of 100 job openings, it will be thirty years before blacks make up 20% of the force. In fact, for the next fifteen years, blacks will remain less than 10% of the force, and for the first five years, blacks will be less than 4% of the force. Given the history of past discrimination and the slowness with which "natural replacement" will remedy it, for a court to order that more than 20 black troopers be hired per year does not seem unfair, on balance, despite its consequences for new white job applicants.

25. The school board of Piscataway High School (New Jersey) faced budget cuts in 1989 that led to staff cuts. There were two teachers at the school doing similar jobs, of equal seniority and, apparently, equal performance, one white, one black. The school board chose, for no announced reason other than a preference for diversity, to fire the white teacher (Gutmann 1996, 118). That teacher sued and, not surprisingly, won at the district and appellate levels. As James Turner, former assistant attorney general for civil rights in the U.S. Department of Justice, notes, "From the time Title VII was passed, no court had ever held that it was proper to fire incumbents to maintain or create diversity." Turner also observes that "A coalition of civil rights organizations recently paid off the white teacher to end the case to avoid an adverse Supreme Court ruling" (Turner 1997, 23). While eliminating racial stereotypes and providing role models for minority members are important, these goals do not rise to the level of constitutional commands, and their implementation raises difficult constitutional questions (Gutmann 1996, 131).

26. In most contexts, I would still advocate some diversity-oriented hiring at the entry level as long as there is not a subsequent double standard as to the criteria for success and as long as it clear that minimum criteria will still need to be satisfied for acceptance (see discussion of college admissions below). I do not think it necessary to promote diversity, per se, but I do believe in giving people a chance. Because tests are of limited value in predicting the future success rates of all applicants, a period of probation can be useful to separate those who can and will succeed from those who can't or won't. But realism dictates that the likely success rates of minorities and nonminorities during the probation period (and with respect to subsequent retention/promotions) are unlikely to be equal.

27. There is also a long history of de facto discrimination in higher education that benefits whites, e.g., "legacies" or preferences given to children of alumni and special treatment for friends of trustees and relatives of the rich (see, e.g., Frammolino, Gladstone, and Weinstein 1996).

28. The *Bakke* rationale for diversity preference does not, however, apply with the same relevance outside the classroom context.

29. At the college level, minority dropout rates tend to be high at prestigious institutions, except for those very elite schools (like Harvard) that can attract the best minority students. See Thernstrom and Thernstrom 1997, chapter 14.

30. Similarly, women police may be more effective than male officers in handling domestic disputes, in part because they appear less threatening because of their gender. Here, too, the argument for adding women to the force becomes one not about diversity but about recognizing domains of superior performance that may not be acknowledged in, say, height, weight, and strength standards for police officers.

31. For an elaboration of this point (although not one with whose views I always agree), see Halpern 1995.

32. As I hope is apparent, this comment should not be misinterpreted as support for genetic theories of racial differences in intelligence. To the contrary, such theories tend to deny or downplay the importance of social, nutritional, and environmental context on cognitive development.

33. As my colleague A Wuffle metaphorically phrases the point, "No amount of manipulating the toothpaste tube at the top end will produce much toothpaste if almost all of the toothpaste has been left down at the bottom."

Afterword: U.S. Civil Rights Policies
in Comparative Perspective

Robin M. Williams, Jr.

The reader who has persevered thus far will have found discussions of an extraordinary American panorama: where we have come from, how we got here, the consequences of the journey, and some possible futures stemming from the uneasy present. These chapters remind us, in scholarly detail, of the enormously complex, uneven, and protracted processes of social change and resistance to change that have shaped the current situation and will affect future developments.

Experienced observers have been known to subscribe to the old saw that in Washington, D.C., the dragon slain on Friday breathes fire again on Monday. As this book abundantly documents, no victory is final; the rules of the game are always being contested; civil rights once gained must forever be defended. All the more reason, therefore, for the perspectives generated by the present stocktaking and assessment.

In our appropriate and useful focus on civil rights in the United States, moreover, we need not forget that this examination leaves aside about 95% of the world's people. Among the more than 190 countries that now are members of the United Nations, there obviously is enormous diversity in policies and practices relating to the concept of "rights" in general and to civil rights in particular.

A worldwide perspective necessarily reveals the frequency and magnitude of violent collective conflicts within states that involve massive violations of human rights. Although such conflicts have complex causes and involve diverse social cleavages—regional, class, ideological, and others—most of the more severe conflicts occur either between states and their ethnic minorities or among different ethnic groups (or "ethnies") themselves. These ethnies are defined by markers of cultural distinction combined with notions of common origins or descent (D. L. Horowitz 1985; van den Berghe 1987). The ferocity and intractability of such ethnic conflicts are sharply exemplified in the recent cases of Biafra, the former Yugoslavia, Sudan, Sri Lanka, Iraq, Armenia-Azerbaijan, Georgia and other successor states and regions of the former Soviet Union, Cambodia, Thailand, Rwanda, and Burundi, among many others (Gurr 1993). Civil wars, communal violence, protracted guerrilla fighting, and state-sponsored attempts to suppress or destroy whole peoples have taken a worldwide toll of misery and destruction, entailing since World War II somewhere between 11 and 20 million deaths (Williams 1994, 50). Genocide and near genocide are not rare, and states are the greatest killers of their own people (Rummel 1994; I. L. Horowitz 1992; van den Berghe 1990).

We cite these phenomena to highlight the point that in much of today's world, the very concepts of civil rights or human rights are ignored, denied, or rejected. When dictatorial regimes of centralized states attempt to rule over multiethnic populations, the "rights" of suppressed minorities typically disappear. The long, well-known record of expulsions, denials of political voice, expropriations, political murders, and death squads is enough to show the magnitude of the problem. And the reluctance of the United Nations, until very recently, to intervene to forestall or check attempted genocide and "ethnic cleansing" shows the deep difficulty of effective amelioration (Kuper 1985).

Since World War II, there has been a striking record of inaction and hesitancy on the part of individual national states and the United Nations and other international agencies in responding to state-incited genocide, violent state suppression of ethnic minorities, and political murders and massacres. Calls to implement the 1948 Universal Declaration of Human Rights (including the twenty-one articles that primarily concern civil rights) have been met by claims that alleged violations are domestic affairs immune to external intervention. The doctrine of noninterference, in turn, invokes the principle of the absolute sovereignty of the national state. In effect, modern national states claim absolute authority over a territory and its population. Such sovereignty is conferred not by the consent of the subjects or citizens but by recognition from other national states. The fact that the heads of many states attained their positions through internal warfare and political murders may help to explain their reluctance to endorse international humanitarian and peace-keeping interventions. Thus, in practice, the primary source of human rights today still is conferral by the sovereign entity of the national state. It may not be too much to say that national sovereignty is the current equivalent of the divine right of kings.

Doctrines of rights, however, are rendered more complex and problematical by the salience since World War I of the principle of the "self-determination of peoples." This idea—so apparently liberating—can be invoked to justify endless claims to political autonomy and secessions on the part of ethnic and religious minorities. The explosive combination of absolute state sovereignty with self-determination is an invitation to ethnic conflict. It is also a recipe for genocide when "state" and "nation" are seen as coterminous, so that the absolute state must be ethnically homogeneous—*Ein Volk, Ein Staat.* Thus emerges the lethal mixture of state absolutism, popular sovereignty, and ethnic self-determination. These doctrines often are strongly invoked under basic structural conditions of great economic and social inequalities within societies with weak but centralized and militarized states (Gurr 1993). The results are hardly conducive to the preservation of human rights. Of course, the broad "principles" do not directly generate state policies and practices. But the practical implications, nevertheless, deserve close attention.

In comparison with much of the Third World, the industrialized democracies in the interstate "Peace Zone" stretching from Finland to Japan have managed in considerable measure to foster domestic social peace through diverse policies of ethnic integration, accommodation, compromise, and cooptation. The establishment of regimes of political and civil rights in most of these countries has been achieved over long periods of struggle and shifting political alignments (Tilly 1992). It is easy to conclude from this familiar story that power prevails—that in some real sense might makes rights. But deeper questions concern the sources of "power" and ask by what criteria are social demands and claims judged to be legitimate. Numerous efforts to formulate ethical principles (Rawls 1971, Novick 1975) and practical guidelines (Bronfenbrenner 1973) have produced long and confusing lists of criteria. But the most common politically relevant arguments—aside from sheer power or immediate political expediency—seem to center on four main criteria:

1. *Need:* humane considerations that are held to be applicable to members of a given moral community (fellow citizens, members of religious body, persons in distress anywhere);

2. *Social status:* rights attached primarily to kinship, age, gender, caste, ethnic group, occupation, political office, and citizenship;

3. Merit: valued abilities and achievements; past efforts or sacrifices on behalf of a collectivity (e.g., military service, pioneer settlement);

4. Compatibility with other values and goals, e.g., age-based rights *versus* tests of ability or performance.

Even from this brief survey of criteria, it is immediately apparent that great cross-cultural differences could exist, which is, of course, the case. A prominent current example is the case of rights of citizenship in three Western societies. Citizenship in the United States basically rests on the policy of *jus soli.* Immigrants may attain citizenship merely by a sufficient period of residence plus a routine examination. France applies a similar policy, with the added expectation that new citizens will become fully assimilated to French culture. In contrast, Germany uses the principle of *jus sanguinis:* the test is that of descent, of German ancestry. The result is that a recent immigrant from the former Soviet Union can quickly gain citizenship whereas a third-generation resident of Turkish origin can achieve citizenship only through a long and difficult process.

This comparison illustrates a major cross-societal difference: achieved versus ascribed status as the basis for certain rights. Further examination leads to the observation of worldwide tensions between policies that define rights as individual rather than collective (e.g., as belonging to states or communal groups). In the United States, the contrasting perspectives have figured strongly in recent political debates. Members of dominant social formations often challenge policies of categorical compensatory or remedial action by calling for individual-based criteria. Historically, of course, so-called "individualism" did not prevent massive group preferences that favored the dominant ethnies. To claim otherwise is to ignore the near genocide of Native Americans, slavery, racial, religious, and ethnic discrimination, veterans' preferences, admissions quotas in universities, and so on. Nevertheless, the individualistic ideology has had a powerful political appeal in opposition to humanitarian claims and to policies intended to compensate for disadvantages derived from past and current institutional discrimination. Abundant evidence shows that on average the American white population endorses the general notion of equality of opportunity but accepts existing inequalities and rejects redistributive policies aimed at substantial equality. Within this ideological world, opponents of affirmative action see it as unfairly giving certain groups preferential treatment, while its advocates define its purpose as remedial and ameliorative of past group discrimination.

It is important to recall that many of the most "effective" preferential systems around the world have been instituted and maintained by politically dominant elites to favor members of their own class, party, or ethny. Cases in point include whites in South Africa and in the United States, Malays in Malaysia, Russians in the Soviet Union, Jews in Israel, Northern Muslims in Sudan, Sinhalese in Sri Lanka, and many, many others across time and space. These impositions by politically dominant ethnies typically cause resentment, at least in modern times, and frequently lead to overt conflict (Gurr 1993).

Such dominance arrangements are not, of course, what is now meant by "affirmative action" in the United States, where the term is used to cover a wide range of policies and practices. Opponents of affirmative action use political rhetoric, often successfully, to conflate affirmative action with "quotas," but historical and comparative studies show that the most rigid quotas have favored the privileged or dominant social formations. Contemporary "affirmative actions" in the United States, as this volume documents, include the following possibilities (cf. Rothman 1977, Williams 1977):

1. Informational and educational programs;

2. Arranging for positive interethnic interactions;

3. Strict judicial and administrative enforcement of antidiscrimination laws and regulations;

4. Notification and publicity concerning opportunities for "minority" persons in education, employment, business, political access, public facilities, and civic affairs;

5. Direct solicitation and aggressive search, e.g., for university admissions, civil service jobs, business contracts;

6. Use of ethnic category as one factor in actual practice, including, for example, promotions and dismissals;

7. Remedial programs such as tutoring and on-the-job training;

8. Categorical preferences, based primarily but not exclusively on ethnic origins ("reverse discrimination");

9. Quotas: absolute preferences, tied to obligatory numbers or proportions;

10. Reparations, sometimes claimed but rarely accepted.

The actual complexity contradicts the stereotyping, but the Q-word slogans often prevail.

In short, a comparative perspective suggests that (1) categorical discrimination by dominant groups is a common source of conflict and political instability; (2) civil rights grow out of incessant struggles and are maintained, if at all, in the same way; (3) nondiscriminatory policies promote social integration but are insufficient to compensate for past and persisting institutional discrimination; (4) remedial policies constitute an important supplement to nondiscrimination and can be applied with flexibility and specificity to attain constructive outcomes.

Yet what are seen by disadvantaged groups as remedial policies easily become preferential policies or reverse discrimination in the eyes of those outside the designated categories. Thus, whatever the label, such differential treatment typically causes political controversy. And, indeed, comparative studies do show that preferential policies often are evaded and that when they are effective they tend to solidify into fixed claims supported by (newly) "vested" interests (cf. Horowitz 1985, chapter 16). The actual outcomes depend on contextual factors that vary greatly from one society to another—for example, relative size and political resources of contending groupings, the extent and kind of reciprocal concessions, and the timing and sequencing of actions (Williams 1994).

In the United States, salient criticism of civil rights policies, and especially of what is called affirmative action, often takes the form of the well-worn "slippery slope" argument. In this view, once you have set your feet on the slippery slope of any policy of remedial or compensatory action, you are destined to slide all the way to rigid numerical quotas devoid of any relation to merit or other redeeming social values. Typically the argument then presents a worst-case analysis, assuming that out of all conceivable outcomes the result will be the least desirable. As the preceding chapters show, this prognosis rests not on careful empirical analysis but primarily on anecdote and assertion. The last three decades of the American experience—in which even the mildest forms of affirmative action have been vigorously contested—do not bear out the slippery slope scenario.

To repeat a common observation, affirmative action policies can and do have radically different consequences in different sociopolitical and economic contexts. This apparently banal generalization shows its power when examined in specific cases. Compensatory economic policies are most likely to be implemented without serious backlash during periods of prosperity and when the target group is a small minority that has been severely disadvantaged by past discrimination. When two large ethnies vie for influence within the same polity, it may be possible to have acceptable trade-offs between political priority for the numerically dominant group and economic opportunity for an advantaged but politically weaker ethny. The classic case is Malaysia. Again, political concessions tend to be quick and obvious, whereas the effects of economic preferences tend to be slower and less immediately visible, so that costs become apparent before benefits are evident.

Visibility is important. Many programs that are not usually labeled as affirmative action do serve the same purposes. Thus, the elimination of tracking in the public schools has the effect of altering the status of pupils with low performance scores. Changes in curricula, teacher training, and the use of standardized tests may take the form of widening the criteria of achievement and providing for more racially inclusive measures of excellence (Thernstrom 1992, 131–43).

It is plausible to suppose that preferential or compensatory policies would be less likely to elicit strong backlash reactions when the target groups are small or in other respects do not constitute a highly visible threat to politically potent competitors. The likelihood of perceived threat will depend also on both the scope and the particular arena of a given policy. Very broad in scope are such programs as the Malaysian constitutional mandates for Malay preferences or India's provisions for scheduled castes and tribes. Such comprehensive arrangements contrast with more narrowly focused programs such as land ownership, bank credit, military service, university admissions and scholarships, remedial education, hirings, promotions, certain levels of civil service employment, and so on. Probable reactions may also depend greatly on whether programs are explicitly ethnic or are defined in terms of economic status, region, or residence requirements (see Horowitz 1985, 653–80).

Beyond the most obvious categories of the kinds just noted, there are numerous subtle variations in the degree of formality of ongoing practices: whole systems of preferences can grow up without explicit legislation or public acknowledgment. Impressive ingenuity is often used in the systematic evasion of formal requirements or regulations, as when ethnic individuals or firms are used as "fronts" that disguise the locus of effective control and corresponding benefits.

Every serious comparative examination reveals extreme variations in the extent to which either international agreements or domestic laws and statements of principles are actually implemented (cf. Vaxberg 1989). Readings of constitutions, state declarations, and laws may tell us very little about the extent to which these are effective resources for those whose nominal rights are violated. A crucial consideration is whether or not individual persons (rather than states or other corporate actors) have access to authorities that can redress their grievances.

Similarly, analyses of cross-national variations in affirmative action policies usually encounter related problems in law enforcement and human rights issues. Numerous scholars have commented on the putative cleavage between societies that emphasize individual rights, such as freedom of expression, and those that give priority to the collective goals of order, military "security," and safety net policies (cf. Shelley 1989, 42–55).

Law enforcement itself often becomes a source of hidden or open illegal violence. Violations of civil rights or of nominally universal human rights are prominent features of police behavior, especially but certainly not exclusively in authoritarian political regimes (Zafaroni 1989, 57–67). Still another essential dimension in cross-cultural variations in civil rights is the very definition of the actors to whom the rights apply. Is a particular right applicable to and valid for all persons residing in the state's claimed territory, for citizens only, for some but not all noncitizen residents? Must the valid holders of a right all belong to a designated category? Or only those who have experienced certain losses or deprivations (e.g., from direct discrimination)? Do rights adhere only to separate human individuals or may collectivities also have rights?

For the maintenance of order and social peace, in all questions of rights, differing legitimate social claims have to be balanced against one another. Absolute rights inevitably clash with other absolute rights, resulting in unresolvable contradictions. So every right is limited by other rights, and rules of reason, consideration, and accommodation must come into play if escalation into conflict—and subsequent suppression—are to be avoided. If there is no acceptance of such rules of "common sense," the claims of opposing rights can only be settled by force (see the argument of Van Dyke 1985, chapter 2). A basic argument for the validity of group rights rests on the premise that collectivities (corporations, ethnies) can and do have compelling interests that are not simply the additive interests of the constituent individual members; these interests may have sufficient consensual support and moral justification to confer on them the status of rights (Van Dyke 1985, 208).

All arrangements intended to reduce ethnic opposition and conflict will be subject to stress over time. Circumstances will change; population ratios may diverge; the economic status of regions and industries may shift; new ethnic rivals may appear as the result of immigration. Preferential policies that initially had the moral high ground of rectifying past injustices may come to be seen as unfair favoritism. Power sharing that at first satisfied rival claims may eventually breed contention and, ultimately, violence.

The moral is that all bargains and settlements are tied to time, place, and circumstance and require continual monitoring and renegotiation to remain viable—not an easy lesson and one that often is disregarded.

Appendixes

Legal Standards of Proof of Discrimination

Appendix 1

Statistics in Proof of Employment Discrimination Cases

Joseph B. Kadane and Caroline Mitchell

Title VII of the Civil Rights Act of 1964, 42 U.S. Code 2000(e), made it an unlawful employment practice for an employer to discriminate against employees or applicants because of an employee's race, sex, religion, or national origin. Later amendments to the civil rights laws added age and handicap to the list of protected categories. See, e.g., the "Age Discrimination in Employment Act," 29 U.S.C. 726, and the "Americans with Disabilities Act," 29 CFR Part 36 (26 January 1992).

Employment discrimination classically consisted of different and less favorable treatment to the victim, as compared with the treatment given to others at the workplace. Consider the employer who accepts applications for construction foremen jobs from men only. Women applicants are disadvantaged and treated less favorably and can therefore file a sex discrimination claim alleging a violation of Title VII. Similarly, a union or employer who refuses to accept applications for receptionist jobs from blind applicants may be charged with a violation of the Americans with Disabilities Act.

Theories for Proof of Discrimination

Disparate Treatment

Two different legal theories have been used to prove claims of unlawful employment discrimination. The disparate treatment methodology alleges that the defendant intentionally based the employment decision on a forbidden factor such as age, race, sex, national origin, religion, or handicap. Disparate treatment is intentional discrimination against the victim, by definition, because of his or her membership in a protected class. Disparate treatment claims can involve a series of incidents of intentional discrimination against a victim, such as racially derogatory or hostile remarks or sexually harassing conduct. The disparate treatment claim does not usually depend on proof of discrimination against others in the protected class or on allegations of a "pattern and practice of discrimination" that affects all of the employees in that class.

Disparate treatment cases often rely on "anecdotal evidence" of discrimination. Anecdotal evidence includes testimony by the plaintiff and other victims of discrimination of intentional discrimination directed at persons similarly situated at the workplace. Take the example of a woman professor who claims she was denied tenure on the basis of her sex because the professors on the tenure committee believe that women are not qualified to hold tenured positions. If the plaintiff can produce direct evidence of discriminatory remarks indicating the committee's bias against women, this direct anecdotal evidence may prove intentional discrimination. The classic burden of proof in a disparate treatment case is that set forth in the Supreme Court decision in *McDonnell-Douglas v. Green*, 411 U.S. 792, 800; 93 S. Ct. 1817, 1823 (1973). This ruling determined that in order to prove a case of disparate treatment, the plaintiff must prove (1) that he or she belongs to a protected group; (2) that he or she was qualified for the hire or promotion at issue; (3) that he or she was passed over for the promotion or hire; and (4) that the employer went on to secure the application of a person in a non-protected class who was then given the job. Examples of disparate treatment include the refusal to consider men for jobs as airline stewardesses, a refusal to hire women for work in coal mines because it is considered "bad luck," and the sexual harassment of a woman by the superintendent of her place of work.[1]

Under the *McDonnell-Douglas* model, after the plaintiff has proved a *prima facie* case, the burden shifts to the defendant to produce evidence of a nondiscriminatory legitimate business reason for rejecting the plaintiff. For example, the defendant may claim that a black plaintiff was not as well qualified for the job in question as was the successful white candidate. After the defendant produces this evidence, the plaintiff is given a last opportunity to show that the defendant's reasoning is false or is a "mere pretext" for discrimination (*McDonnell-Douglas v. Green*, 411 U.S. 792, 802–4 [1973]).

The most recent pronouncement of the Supreme Court on disparate treatment is a case of age discrimination, *Hazen Paper Co. v. Biggins*, 113 S. Ct. 1701, 1706 (1993). The Court in *Biggins* reiterated that in order to prove disparate treatment, the defendant's liability depends on whether the protected trait (in this case age) "actually" motivated the employer's decision. Thus the plaintiff has the ultimate burden in a disparate treatment case of proving that the forbidden factor was an actual motivating factor in the employer's treatment of the plaintiff.

Disparate Impact

"Disparate impact" is the second theory used by victims of discrimination. Disparate impact is an alternative theory of liability under Title VII of the Civil Rights Acts of 1964 and 1991, the Age Discrimination in Employment Act, and the Americans with Disabilities Act. The disparate impact theory of recovery claims that employment practices that are facially neutral in their treatment of different groups in fact fall more harshly on one protected group than on others. A particular business practice thus causes a "disparate impact" of less favorable treatment to members of a protected group. Because of the disparate impact, such a practice is discriminatory, provided it cannot be justified by business necessity (see *International Brotherhood of Teamsters v. U.S.*, 431 U.S. 324, 336; 97 S. Ct. 1843, 1855 52 L. Ed. 2d 396 [1977]).

Unlike the disparate treatment theory, disparate impact does not require the plaintiff to prove that there is intentional discrimination or a discriminatory motive. A disparate impact case claims that a neutral employment practice, adopted by the employer without any deliberately discriminatory motive, may in operation nevertheless result in discrimination. The Supreme Court has upheld the use of disparate impact analysis to show that subjective employment decision-making may be unlawful due to its adverse impact on minorities. (See *Watson v. Fort Worth Bank and Trust*, 487 U.S. 977, 991 [1988]).

In order to establish a *prima facie* case of disparate impact discrimination, the plaintiff must show that a specific employment practice or policy caused a significant disparate impact on a protected group (*Wards Cove Packing Co. v. Atonio*, 490 U.S. 642, 656 [1989]). Once the plaintiffs establish a *prima facie* case that some business practice results in different and less favorable treatment of minorities, the burden shifts to the employer to produce evidence demonstrating the business necessity for its challenged employment practice. Under *Wards Cove*, the burden of ultimate persuasion as to discrimination always remains with the plaintiff, just as it does in a disparate treatment case. If the employer presents evidence of a justifiable business necessity for a practice, plaintiffs may still prevail in their discrimination claim if they can persuade the court that other policies or practices can serve the employer's interest without having an adverse impact on the protected class.

An example of a neutral business practice that has a disparate impact is an employer's requirement of a high school diploma as a prerequisite for hire into a job in an area where fewer blacks than whites possess a high school degree. The employer may be unable to show that the high school degree is a valid objective criterion for predicting success on the job. Thus the neutral practice of requiring all garbage collectors to have high school degrees has a disparate impact on blacks, as it excludes more blacks than whites from consideration for the job. The employer may claim a business necessity for the degree. The plaintiff can rebut this argument by showing that a reading test might serve the employer's interest just as well.

Consider the employer who uses the "drag test" for firemen applicants, a test that requires that all applicants be able to drag a hundred-pound weight for fifty yards. This is an objective and neutral criterion that can be met by 90% of the male applicants but by only 30% of the female applicants. Such a practice excludes more women than men from the job. However, the city may defend the necessity of the "drag test" by showing it is a valid job performance requirement, since firemen must drag or carry heavy hoses or victims of fires in order to do their jobs. In such a case, plaintiffs may find it difficult to propose a replacement test that would allow the city to predict whether fire applicants can handle hoses or carry victims but has no "disparate impact."

Use of Statistics in Disparate Impact Cases

There are three categories of evidence that can be used by a plaintiff in an attempt to prove discrimination under either disparate treatment or disparate impact: (1) direct evidence of discrimination, such as discriminatory statements or admissions by the decision-maker that prove bias against certain protected groups; (2) circumstantial comparative evidence of "disparate treatment" showing that the plaintiff was treated less favorably than others who were similarly situated but were not members of the protected group; and (3) statistics showing that a neutral practice adversely impacts the plaintiff. In proving a disparate impact case, statistics can be the most important form of evidence.[2] There, the plaintiff generally claims unfavorable treatment to members of the victim class because of a neutral job rule. Consider a disparate impact case in which women seeking a bank vice president job must score well on a subjective interview with senior male executives. Discrimination can be inferred by appropriate statistical evidence showing fewer women in the job than one would expect if the promotion interviews were gender-neutral. This proof may be coupled with comparative evidence of disparate treatment such as anecdotal evidence by other women who were treated badly during promotion interviews, or direct statements by the president showing a discriminatory animus (e.g., "What would our customers think if we had a female vice president?").

One of the earliest instances of statistics being used to prove an employment discrimination case was the Supreme Court decision in *Hazelwood School District v. United States*, 433 U.S. 299 (1977). In that case, blacks alleged that the school district had failed to hire enough black teachers given the total number of teachers and the number of black teachers seeking jobs. Far fewer blacks were employed as teachers at Hazelwood than were employed as teachers in the surrounding community labor markets. The Supreme Court ruled that "where gross statistical disparities can be shown, they alone in a proper case constitute prima facie proof of a pattern or practice of discrimination." In *Hazelwood*, the Hazelwood School District was accused of a "pattern and practice" of race discrimination for not having hired a sufficient number of black teachers compared to other local districts. It was claimed that the subjective interview process had an adverse impact on blacks. Individual black teachers also complained of disparate treatment in that less qualified whites got the jobs in question. (The *Hazelwood* case is discussed in detail below.)

Statistics in Disparate Treatment Cases

Statistics have also been used to bolster a plaintiff's argument that a protected group is not being fairly treated in a given workplace. See, for example, *Furnco Construction Corp. v. Waters*, 438 U.S. 567 (1978), in which the court admitted into evidence the statistics concerning the racial makeup of the employer's workforce. The court noted that statistical evidence, although not wholly irrelevant on the issue of discriminatory intent, would have a limited value. Mere statistical evidence that the workforce is racially or sexually "unbalanced" or disproportionate does not necessarily prove intentional discrimination. The imbalance could result from other nondiscriminatory factors, such as mere chance or a scarcity of applications from qualified members of the protected class.

Statistics are often used in a class action suit to prove disparate treatment and "intentional discrimination" against an entire class. In a class action, the plaintiff generally claims that he and others in the same class were discriminated against because of a pattern and practice of discrimination directed towards members of the protected class. In *Hazelwood*, the plaintiffs claimed that they as black school teachers were not being hired by Hazelwood Schools because of an intentional racial bias against blacks.

Statistics in Adverse Impact Cases

Regression Analysis

Statistics can be used in cases to prove the "adverse impact" on the protected class by examining the adverse effects of a policy or practice on the protected class. In attempting to adduce statistical proof of discrimination, the plaintiff may introduce a variety of statistical data: pass/fail ratio analyses, "success rates" for members of the protected class compared to the success rate for others, labor pool and workforce comparisons, or regression analyses seeking to estimate the effect of particular variables such as age, race, education, job experience, or job performance in relation to a single dependent variable such as salary or promotion grade.

For example, consider the proposition that a certain university discriminates across the board against its women faculty by paying male professors more than it pays females. In *Wilkins v. University of Houston*, 654 F.2d 388 (5th Cir. 1981), the statistics used by the plaintiff included data on the pay to all faculty members of all ranks and both sexes hired after 1972. The plaintiff's proposition was that women professors were discriminated against because men were paid more and held higher positions than women even when their experience and length of service was equal.

In this case, however, the plaintiff's case failed because her statistics failed to take into account the "market effect." The particular colleges within the university at which these professors taught affected their salaries, with professors in the colleges of medicine and engineering (where male faculty predominated) earning more than professors in teaching and nursing (where female faculty predominated). Thus the plaintiff could not prove that a female associate professor of nursing who earned less than a male associate professor of medicine was the victim of sex discrimination rather than of free market economics. The court also found that the plaintiff's salary data were flawed and insufficient, since they did not distinguish between doctoral and lesser degrees held by various professors. The degree attained affected both the initial salary level and the rank that a given professor could ultimately achieve.

Pass/Fail Ratios in Adverse Impact Cases

Pass/fail statistics are generally used to compare the "success rate," defined as the percentage of the protected group who receive jobs or raises in comparison to the "majority." The pass/fail statistical analysis involves a comparison of the percentage of members in the minority protected class who receive the desired job or promotion, compared with the percentage of the "comparator" majority group, e.g., whites or males who have been hired or promoted. There is generally a comparison of these percentages (two factors, and thus a 2×2 table). For example, if one is comparing the pass/fail rates of women applying for firefighting jobs, the ultimate comparison would be the "pass rate" or "success rate." The pass rate for females is defined as the number of successful female applicants divided by the total number of female applicants. Similarly, the pass rate for males is defined as the number of successful male applicants divided by the total number of male applicants.

If for example, 10 females of 500 are successful, but 995 males out of 1,000 are successful, the "pass rate for females" (2%) is much less than the "pass rate for males" (99.5%). Such comparisons involving the pass rates of the protected group can be used for any type of facially neutral business rule.

The use of pass/fail comparisons was accepted by the Supreme Court in *Albemarle Paper Company v. Moody*, 422 U.S. 405 (1975), a case involving the applicability of a scored pre-employment test that was claimed to have an adverse impact on black applicants. In *Albemarle Paper*, substantially fewer black applicants who successfully passed the scored test received jobs. The pass/fail comparison between the black group and the white group was found to be statistically significant. Statistics were part of the proof required for a case of disparate impact employment discrimination.

The plaintiff class in *Albemarle Paper* consisted of current and former black employees at a paper mill in Roanoke Rapids, North Carolina. The paper company had required applicants for employment in skilled jobs to have a high school diploma and to pass two tests: "the revised beta" and the "Wonderlic" test. The revised beta was supposedly a measure of nonverbal intelligence, while Wonderlic purported to measure verbal facility. The company defended the case by claiming a business necessity for its use of both tests (even though its expert analysis to validate these tests was done only on the eve of the trial). The company claimed that the test scores of "successful" supervisory employees showed a statistically significant correlation with their application scores on both the beta and the Wonderlic tests. The trial court accepted this testimony and ruled for the defendant.

The court of appeals in *Albemarle Paper* rejected this purported business practice on the ground that neither the high school education requirement nor the personnel tests were validated as showing a statistically significant correlation with job performance. The court of appeals relied in part on the "EEOC Uniform Guidelines on Employee Selection Procedures," 29 C.F.R. Part 1607, in which EEOC discusses the necessity of validation of tests used as the basis for employment-related decisions. The appellate court reversed the trial court's finding for the defendant.

On appeal, the Supreme Court noted that *Albemarle*, in addition, allowed black workers to transfer to skilled jobs only if they could pass the beta and Wonderlic tests with a score of 18. Few blacks scored 18 or higher, in contrast to whites. The tests thus also caused adverse impact on those few blacks already employed at the company. The statistics in *Albemarle Paper* presented to the trial court included an analysis done on the eve of trial by the company's expert in industrial psychology to validate the job-relatedness of the testing. His study dealt with ten jobs that were highly skilled. One hundred and five employees in the plant participated in the study. These 105 employees were each given the beta and Wonderlic tests. Within each job group, the study compared the test scores of each employee with an independent ranking of the employee made by the employee's supervisor. The expert then computed the statistical correlation between the test scores and the supervisor's ranking. In keeping with the conventions of his field, the expert regarded as "statistically significant" any correlation that could have occurred "by chance" only five times or less in one hundred trials.

The Supreme Court in *Albemarle* decided that the paper company lacked sufficient business necessity to continue using tests that had an adverse impact on blacks at the plant. After being challenged by the plaintiffs, the defendants failed to "validate" their tests in accord with the EEOC guidelines on employee selection.

The general statistical methodology involved in the pass/fail cases is to compare the pass/fail rate of the protected class with the pass/fail rate of the majority group. Any differences are explained by (a) application of illegal, discriminatory and invalid selection criteria; (b) mere chance; (c) other factors not related to either discrimination or chance. A "statistically significant" difference in the observed pass rates means that under the hypothesis of equal pass rates, the probability of pass rates as more discrepant than observed is smaller than some arbitrary number, such as .05.

Labor Pool Analysis in Adverse Impact Cases

Population and workforce comparisons have been used to determine whether a hiring practice has an adverse impact on minority groups. Population and workforce comparisons involve statistical comparisons concerning some portion of the labor pool and some portion of the employer's workforce. The seminal case on population and workforce analysis is *Hazelwood Schools v. U.S.* The Hazelwood school district located in northern St. Louis County, Missouri, was accused by the U.S. Department of Justice of race discrimination against blacks, in that qualified blacks were not being hired as school teachers in the period 1970–1973. The hiring process at Hazelwood involved the submission of a written application to a central district office and the candidates' subjective interviews by officials at the school where the teaching vacancy existed. As of the 1968 school year, 17,550 students were enrolled in the district, of whom only 59 were black. By 1973, 576 blacks were enrolled out of 25,166 students. Black students constituted slightly over 2% of the student population. Plaintiffs claimed that there was intentional discrimination (a bias against hiring blacks and "disparate treatment" in that qualified blacks were not being hired, while less qualified whites were). Plaintiffs also claimed that the district used business practices (subjective interviews) that had an adverse impact on blacks.

There was a buyer's market for school teachers in St. Louis in the early '70s. In 1972, there were 234 teacher vacancies and 3,127 applications for those jobs; in 1973, 282 vacancies and 2,373 applications. As of 1973, only 22 teachers of 1,231 faculty were black. According to 1970 census figures, there were 19,000 teachers employed in the St. Louis area and 15.4% were black.[3]

The U.S. government sued Hazelwood Schools for a pattern and practice of discrimination against blacks. The government's proof consisted of (1) anecdotal evidence of racially discriminatory incidents (going to prove disparate treatment of blacks); (2) statistics proving disparity in hiring; (3) the adverse impact created by the "neutral" business practice of subjective interviews, which deprived blacks of a fair chance at being hired; and (4) separate individual disparate treatment cases, involving alleged acts of intentional discrimination against fifty-five black applicants who had been unsuccessful, although their credentials compared favorably to whites who were hired. The case was initially filed on both disparate treatment and disparate impact bases.

Both the plaintiffs and the defendants went to great lengths to define their own labor pools as a foundation for their statistical analysis. The possible labor pools included (1) a comparison of the number of black teachers with the number of black students (the court rejected this as an irrelevant number); (2) a comparison between the number of black teachers employed at Hazelwood School District and black teachers available for hire at Hazelwood in the relevant applicant labor pool market; and (3) the percentage of black teachers employed by Hazelwood compared to the percentage of blacks employed as teachers by other local schools.

On appeal, the Supreme Court was asked to determine whether the court of appeals had properly found race discrimination based on the "adverse impact" model and shown by statistical proof, and on the disparate treatment model and anecdotal evidence of black applicants in sixteen individual cases. The key statistic was that 15.4% of the teachers in the county were black, while Hazelwood had only 1.8% black faculty. Direct evidence of intentional discrimination against black applicants included proof that Hazelwood was responsible for newspaper advertisements for teacher hires that specified "whites only."

The Supreme Court first considered how to define the labor pool. The U.S. government had argued that the proper comparison was between the racial composition of Hazelwood's teaching staff and the racial composition of the qualified public school teacher population of the surrounding county. Qualified black teachers in the county (excluding the city) amounted to 5.7% of the total relevant teacher pool, whereas the proportion of blacks on Hazelwood's staff was 1.8%. The Supreme Court did its own calculation of statistical significance, using the "standard deviation" as its measure of predicted fluctuations from the expected value. It calculated that the number of blacks on the Hazelwood teaching staff should have been 63 in 1973 and 70 in 1974; the actual figures for those years were 16 and 22, respectively. The difference between the observed and the expected values was more than six standard deviations in 1973, and more than five standard deviations in 1974. The Court found that if the difference between the expected and observed values was greater than two or three standard deviations, then it was unlikely that teachers were hired without regard to race. The *Hazelwood* Court thus put its imprimatur on the "Two Standard Deviation Rule."

There was a great fight in the Supreme Court about whether the relevant labor pool should include the entire labor market area of St. Louis County, including the city of St. Louis itself, which was under a consent order for a 50% black hire rate for teachers. Excluding the city of St. Louis, the proportion of black teachers in the relevant labor market was 5.7%; including St. Louis raised that proportion to 10.5%. It made no difference in the result in this particular case, however, since even with the smaller number of 5.7%, the hiring rates of the school were more than five standard deviations than what would be expected if race had played no role. The Supreme Court's analysis in *Hazelwood* was just the beginning of a series of adverse impact cases in which the parties engaged in extensive debate about the nature of the labor pool.

The "Bottom Line" Defense

Defendants can defend certain business practices by showing that despite the use of alleged discrimination, the process viewed as a whole still has no adverse impact, for the "bottom line" is that minorities are treated equally. The key case on the "bottom line" defense is *Connecticut v. Teal,* 457 U.S. 440 (1982).

Under the "bottom line" theory of defense, when an employer is sued for a violation of the discrimination law, the employer nevertheless claims that the bottom line result of all business practices is an appropriate racial balance. In *Connecticut v. Teal,* black employees of the state of Connecticut claimed that blacks were not being promoted as supervisors in the welfare department because of a biased test on which blacks scored proportionately lower than whites. The test results showed that 48 blacks and 259 whites of 329 candidates took the test. The passing score was set at 65. Only 54.17% of the blacks passed, compared to 79.54% of the whites. The pass rate for blacks was thus only 68% of the pass rate for whites. (The data were slightly skewed because 15 of the 329 people were unidentified as to race, and this group had a 60% pass rate.)

The Connecticut Department of State had an affirmative action program to ensure a significant number of minority supervisors. The overall result of the selection process, including the affirmative action component, showed that of 259 white candidates, 13.5% were promoted; of 48 black candidates, 22.9% were promoted. Thus, the defendant argued that the "bottom line" result was more favorable to blacks than to whites and that it was therefore not guilty of employment discrimination. The Supreme Court found that the comparative lower pass rates for the examination were statistically significant and indicated a *prima facie* case of adverse impact upon minorities. However, the result of the entire hiring process reflected no such adverse impact. The question was whether the "bottom line" precluded a finding of a Title VII adverse impact violation against the employer.

In holding that the "bottom line" was no defense, the Court noted that the Civil Rights Act prohibits practices that would "deprive or *tend to deprive* any individual of employment opportunities." Thus, if a particular test has an adverse impact upon one segment of the population, it is discriminatory regardless of the bottom line.

Statistics in Discrimination in 1994

Let us now examine the conflicting statistical methods and conclusions utilized in virtually all of the well-tried class action cases. The same conflicts recognized by the Supreme Court more than twenty years ago in *Hazelwood* continue to permeate debates on present-day statistics for proof of employment discrimination. Adverse impact cases today provide a battleground for the debate between statisticians as to who presents more credible evidence. As the Supreme Court cautioned in *Bazemore v. Friday,* 478 U.S. 385; 106 S. Ct. 3000 (1986), "Whether in fact plaintiff's statistics will carry the plaintiff's ultimate burden will depend in a given case on the factual context of each case in light of all the evidence presented by both the plaintiff and the defendant." Commentators emphasize that "when otherwise relevant evidence is challenged on methodological grounds, the burden should normally be on the challenger (a) to present credible evidence that the statistical proof is defective and (b) to present a plausible explanation of how the asserted flaw is likely to bias the results against his or her position" (see Baldus and Cole 1986, vii).

Current Issues in Data Base Selection

One of the key issues for both statisticians and lawyers is the identification of the relevant labor market. Much of the current use of statistics in employment discrimination cases depends on the selection of the appropriate data base.

In *Equal Employment Opportunity Commission v. Olson's Dairy Queens, Inc.* (989 F.2d 165, 5th Cir. [1991]), the EEOC alleged that Dairy Queen discriminated against blacks. The evidence produced by the EEOC showed a pattern of intentional racial discrimination in not hiring blacks at fast-food locations. The EEOC's statistics consisted of an "external availability analysis" that compared the hiring history of Dairy Queen with the percentage of black food preparation and service workers in the relevant Standard Metropolitan Statistical Area (SMSA) labor market. The EEOC's data base was further refined by reflecting travel time to and from store locations. Use of this "commuting distance" factor accounts for the fact that in a tight job market, people may be willing to travel one to two hours each way for work. The EEOC's data base compared the travel time to and from Dairy Queen locations to the average travel times for black food preparation and service workers in the SMSA. Travel times were confirmed by census data. The job applications and hire data provided evidence that hundreds of job seekers did not reside in the immediate vicinity of their work locations and were willing to travel in order to work.

The plaintiff EEOC's statistics based on applicant flow data showed a significant disparity between the percentage of blacks applying for jobs and the percentage of blacks hired at Dairy Queens. The employer's study in rebuttal analyzed only one Dairy Queen location. The employer's defense was that most stores hired persons who lived close to the store. Since few blacks lived close to the stores, the stores did not hire many blacks. But the statistics presented by the EEOC showed that the actual hiring data at the stores produced a different ratio of blacks to non-blacks than would be expected if the hiring policy was neutral as to race. The foundation of the EEOC's statistical opinion was the labor market availability analysis, which showed that blacks comprised 19.8% of the labor pool for two particular stores and 8.1% of the labor pool for a third store. However, blacks comprised only 6.5% of the hires at these two stores, while they comprised 9.4% of the hires at the third location. The plaintiff's expert concluded that "there was less than one chance in 100,000 that the observed hiring patterns in the two Spring Branch stores could have resulted from race neutral hiring practices, and less than 3 chances in 10,000 (.026) that the hiring practices in the Belaire Stores resulted from race neutral hiring practices."

In a separate test, the expert's study compared the percentage of blacks among the applicants for Dairy Queen jobs to the percentage of blacks among those hired. Blacks constituted 29.6% of the 1,800 applicants whose race was known. At one of the stores, Spring Branch, 30.1% of the applicants were black; 39.5% of the applicants at Belaire were black, as were 27.6% at the Katie store. In comparison to the blacks in the applicant pool, only 13.2% blacks were hired by Spring Branch, 27.3% by Belaire, and 11.1% by Katie. Given the racial mixture of applicants at the stores, the study concluded that the likelihood that Olson Dairy Queens' actual hiring patterns were "race neutral" was less than 1 chance in 10,000 for Spring Branch, less than 7 chances in 1,000 for Belaire, and less than 2 chances in 1,000 for Katie.[4]

The district court found against the plaintiff EEOC on the grounds of the defendant's expert's statistical analysis. The defendant's statistical analysis looked at a snapshot of the Spring Branch store in April 1990. It examined the Spring Branch workforce, which consisted mainly of white teenagers living a short distance from the store. It then concluded that the labor pools for the other stores also consisted of people residing a short distance from the stores. The company submitted that blacks were not hired because they did not live close to the stores. The actual labor pool at Spring Branch in April 1990 consisted predominantly of white teenagers living close to the store.

The district court's finding that there had been no discrimination was overturned by the circuit court, which endorsed the applicant flow analysis propounded by the EEOC's expert.[5] The court emphasized that EEOC's expert analyzed actual applications and travel times to show that the labor pool for jobs at the Dairy Queen stores came from persons living within travel distance of the stores, not just those living within the immediate vicinity.

In *Jenson v. Eveleth Taconite Company* (D.C. Minn. No. 5-88-164), the plaintiff claimed disparate treatment of female applicants in hire and promotion for high-level mining positions. Applicant flow data was used to show disparate treatment in hiring female laborers for employment at a mine. However, the particular data in this case was based on 274 applications reviewed during the hiring process. The standard deviation of the disparity in female hiring was 1.12. Thus the statistics alone did not support the inference that women were not being hired for reasons other than their lack of representation in the available applicant pool.

This case is interesting because of anecdotal evidence of intentional discrimination by the company, including direct statements by hiring supervisors such as "women do not belong in the mines." It is possible that such sexist statements discouraged women from applying for jobs at this place of employment and that underrepresentation of women in the applicant labor pool was a result of the chilling effect created by these bigoted statements. Other sexist factors at the workplace included graffiti, photos, comments, and conduct constituting sexual harassment. Some foremen at the mines with supervisory and hiring power actually participated in creating sexual graffiti, photos, and comments that were hostile and offensive to reasonable females.

Such practices might influence whether any woman in her right mind would want to work at these mines. This case was a multipronged attack on a company's hiring and promotion practices and environmental treatment of women. The disparate treatment portion of the case claimed that women were intentionally not being hired as laborers because of their sex. From 1981 through 1990, women comprised from 3% to 5% of the hourly workforce at the Eveleth mine. In the early 1980s, the taconite industry experienced a downturn and Eveleth laid off a number of its hourly workers according to seniority. In 1986 and 1987, the mine began to recall the laid-off workers. In preparation for start-up of a closed down line, 46 individuals were hired in 1989 as laborers. Of these, 44 were men and 2 were women.

The plaintiff's statistical expert claimed that disparities in hiring women greater than two standard deviations would indicate that the hiring practice at the company was not "sex neutral," that is, that the disparity between men and women hired was caused by factors other than chance. The court accepted the "Two Standard Deviation Rule" as an appropriate rule. The plaintiff's hiring claim was based on Eveleth's hiring of 46 hourly laborers out of 274 applications, 25 of them from women and 249 from men.[6] Eveleth made offers to 3 women; 2 accepted. Forty-four men accepted laborer positions.

The plaintiff's statistical expert used an applicant flow analysis based on 274 applications in the pool. The experts claimed that women represented 17.2% of the laborer applications. The 17.2% availability of women in the labor pool resulted in an expectancy that 8.1 of the 47 laborers hired would be women.[7] The hiring of only 2 women thus created a disparity of 6.1% female hires. The expert concluded that the standard deviation of the disparity was 2.55, which exceeded the two standard deviation rule and proved discrimination on the basis of sex.

A workforce analysis of women's availability was also compiled from the 1980 census data. However, the relevant labor market used was individuals employed as laborers, excluding construction workers and the unemployed. The availability of this population was computed for three separate geographical areas in the neighborhood of the Eveleth mine. Based on her comparative workforce data, the expert for the plaintiff testified that the female availability rate in the labor markets was greater than the 17.2% figure resulting from applicant flow data. Accordingly, the expected number of female hires was higher for each of the labor markets than the applicant flow data at Eveleth. The comparative workforce data on the five-county surrounding area, as modified by adding figures from the 1990 census, allowed the plaintiff's expert to conclude that female availability in the relevant labor market in the five-county area was 30.98%. Using this availability of female workers, the standard deviation of disparity in hiring females was 3.75 standard deviations. The plaintiff's expert claimed that this was evidence of factors "other than chance" in the hiring of females.

Some of these "other factors" were revealed by the anecdotal evidence. Women testified that when they sought applications during the hiring period, they were falsely told that the mine was not hiring and that applications were not being taken. However, men got applications. One of the women received an application only after informing the person that her father also worked at the plant. In years past, the manager in charge of personnel had also been heard to state that "women do not belong in the mines" and the personnel manager himself and other employees told sexist jokes, made sexist statements, and created an atmosphere of sexual harassment for women.

The defense expert also analyzed the applicant flow data based on the 274 applications. The defense expert determined that 9.1% of the applicants were women; thus, the expected number of female hires was 4.19%.[8] The resulting disparity in the hiring of women was 2.19 and the standard deviation of the disparity was 1.12 standard deviations.

The court rejected the plaintiff's applicant flow data on the ground that the plaintiff had used the wrong pool for the applicant flow, counting only those applications where laborer or "anything" on the application was the applicant's first choice of jobs. The court struck the plaintiff's applicant flow data study and thus had only the plaintiff's comparative workforce data and Eveleth's applicant flow data. In this case, the court was presented with two statisticians' reports, one on each side of the "Two Standard Deviation" benchmark.

A serious flaw in the plaintiff's statistical study appeared to be that the expert based the standard deviation on her conclusion that 58 of the applications were filled out by females (17.2%). However, the actual data from the applications showed that only 35 women applied for laborer positions during the period. The court thus rejected the plaintiff's expert's designation of certain female applications as laborer jobs and found that some of the applications were not properly included in the plaintiff's expert's "pool" of 58 female applicants. After throwing out the plaintiff's applicant flow data analysis, the court accepted the data of the defendant's expert, who had used the same 274 applications to conclude that there was a standard deviation of the disparity in female hiring of 1.12. Thus, the court accepted as a matter of law that a disparity in female hires alone does not support the inference that women were not hired for reasons other than their representation in the pool.

Both statisticians in this case presented evidence of the claimed disparate impact. Under disparate impact theory, the plaintiff is responsible for isolating and identifying the specific employment practices that are allegedly responsible for any observed statistical disparities (see *Wards Cove Packing Co. v. Atonio,* 50 E.P.D. §39,021 [U.S. 1989]).[9] Under the disparate impact theory, the plaintiff claimed that word-of-mouth hiring, nepotism, and a sloppy system for accepting and retaining applications were facially neutral policies that discriminated against women. However, the court found that the plaintiff had failed to offer meaningful statistical proof showing a disparity in hiring women. The plaintiff was unable to show under a disparate treatment analysis that women should have been hired but were not hired although they were in the applicant pool. Under disparate impact analysis, the court rejected the plaintiff's claim that the low number of women in the mines was caused by business practices such as word-of-mouth hiring, nepotism, the defendant's "sloppy" system for applications, and intentional gender bias by the mine foremen. (The defendant proved that the objectionable statements that "women do not belong in the mines" were made by a supervisor not involved in the hiring of the laborers.)

The plaintiff also claimed sex discrimination in promotion, and the plaintiff's expert statistician devised a probability sampling analysis. The results of this analysis showed a disparity in promotions of women to the position of "foreman." The analysis looked at the number of women who were available for promotion to foreman. However, this analysis was based on the percentage of women in the hourly workforce. No woman had ever been promoted to foreman at the mines. The plaintiff's analysis calculated the number of weeks of foreman's work available (whether permanent or temporary) and the number of weeks that a female could be expected to work as a foreman. The standard deviation of the disparity between the number of weeks worked by women and the number of weeks worked as a foreman was 4.79.

The court noted that there was an inexorable "zero" for women who had worked as foremen: "The presence of a zero looms large and indicates that Eveleth Mines' promotion practices have at least a disparate impact on women." However, the court was troubled by the proof that was offered in support of the plaintiff's claim of class-wide discrimination. The plaintiff failed to offer proof of specific instances in which women were discriminated against in not being promoted to foreman. The court further noted that the plaintiff's expert premised her probability sampling analysis on the assumption that all women and all men employed as hourly employees were available for promotion to foreman. However, the company countered by claiming that the foremen were usually employees in higher levels of jobs and were almost always trained on all of the jobs that they would be supervising. In other words, the employees' job classification, knowledge, and work experience were relevant criteria for promotion to foreman. All female employees were not similarly situated. The court found that the plaintiff's statistical analysis ignored those relevant nondiscriminatory differences between female hourly employees and that the measure of female availability for promotion was not a proper measure of the number of females who could be expected to be appointed to foreman. The plaintiff's probability sampling analysis as a statistical proof was rejected by the court.

The court was left with one piece of the plaintiff's proof: what has been called "the inexorable zero." No women were ever promoted to foremen. In *Int'l. Brotherhood of Teamsters v. U.S.*, 431 U.S. 324, 336; 97 S. Ct. 1843, 1855 52 L.Ed.2d 396 (1977), the Supreme Court noted that "no amount of wrangling can change the numerical evidence of disparity which the inexorable zero illustrates." The defendant mine company sought to prove that its failure to promote women to the foreman position was not caused either by an employment policy with an adverse impact on women or by discriminatory intent. Women did give testimony of discriminatory animus: a woman who expressed an interest in being promoted to foreman was told, "you know, you got foreman potential. If there *ever were* to be a woman foreman I would make sure it would be you." The company offered as its explanation the fact that few women have the training or experience necessary to be considered for the job of foreman. The court found that these proffered explanations were insufficient to rebut the plaintiff's evidence of discrimination.

The defendant's subjective decisional criteria were examined under the disparate impact theory (see *Watson v. Fort Worth Bank and Trust*, 487 U.S. 977 [1988]). The plaintiff argued that the defendant's failure to promote even one woman to foreman justified an inference that the promotion policies have a disproportionate adverse impact on women. The defendant countered that job-related qualifications explain why women had not been promoted to foreman. However, the court found that the mine failed to show that its promotion policy was justified.

It found that management personnel make promotions to foreman by applying subjective criteria such as "attitude" and "interest." In light of the sexual harassment existing at Eveleth, a likely cause of the disparity in promoting women was the sexual stereotyping at the mine. Even an evaluation of an employee's experience and ability involves a degree of subjectivity. Eveleth foremen and management apparently actively identified male hourly laborers who had the "right stuff" to be foremen but never attempted to identify similar females. The court found that the mine had not presented a meaningful justification for the disparate impact worked by its subjective promotion practices.

The court further found that the mine knew that women were underrepresented in foremen positions. It concluded that the use of subjective and ambiguous criteria for making promotions constituted proof of discriminatory intent sufficient to support the conclusion that the plaintiff had proven discriminatory intent beyond a preponderance of the evidence. The court then found that the plaintiff had established disparate treatment in promotions to foreman for certain of the women. At a later hearing on liability to individual members of the class, the individual women plaintiffs were required to show that they satisfied basic criteria for serving as foremen but were nevertheless passed over (*Jenson v. Eveleth Mines*, U.S. Dist. Lexis 17617, [1996]).

In *Gomez v. AVCO*, 816 F. Supp. 131 (D.C. Conn. 1993), the plaintiffs, Portuguese machinists, claimed that AVCO Company employed a neutral practice with an adverse impact on Portuguese. That neutral practice was a rule requiring that an employee have eight years of practical experience to become eligible for promotion to a skilled trade position without serving an apprenticeship. In this case, the plaintiffs had a statistician who argued that the proportion of Portuguese in the qualified labor market was significantly greater than the number of Portuguese skilled machinists at AVCO. The plaintiffs concluded that 4% of the qualified labor market consisted of Portuguese machinists while only 0.6% of the machinists at AVCO were Portuguese. The plaintiffs' statistics were based on a comparison of the AVCO skilled machinist workforce with the machinist workforce of four large manufacturing employers in the area.

The plaintiffs' expert had great difficulty in determining the qualified labor pool in this case. Since the EEO-1 data that companies are required to keep does not break down data by national origin, it was difficult for the plaintiffs to determine the number of Portuguese machinists in the vicinity of Hartford, Connecticut. The defendant also argued that the plaintiffs' sample was too geographically limited to present the qualified labor pool in the area, since most of the workforce commuted from towns outside the immediate metropolitan area. The defendant argued that the qualified labor pool should extend to include all of those within commuting distance, claiming that the labor pool included 93,501 people, the number of those in the Fairfield–New Haven Counties who worked in precision crafts (e.g., machinists).

Statistics on the racial composition of the population can be based on scientific sampling techniques, and the court accepted the plaintiffs' methodology for determining the number of Portuguese machinists in the labor pool. The defendant next attacked the plaintiffs' statistical expert by claiming that the plaintiffs' use of data from only four of six comparative companies skewed the results. The plaintiffs contended that the two other companies had seniority practices that were equivalent to the eight-year rule and that including those two companies would give a diluted average number of Portuguese machinists, because those two companies were also discriminating by refusing to employ Portuguese machinists under the eight-year rule.

The court questioned the role of the plaintiffs' counsel in selecting the initial data for the expert and then found that this maneuver by plaintiffs' counsel had tainted the pool of statistics relied upon for the comparable company analysis. The court noted that "it would have been more prudent to leave to an expert the job of editing the data. Plaintiffs' counsel must inevitably have been involved in determining the analysis required by the law; however, definition of what jobs are at issue is not the function of the Plaintiffs' attorney, but rather the function of the experts." The court found that the plaintiffs' statistical analysis had three notable weaknesses. The sample of skilled machinists in the area was used for the actual qualified labor pool. However, two companies' workers were eliminated from this sample without justification, possibly skewing the results and making the sample less conclusive.[10] Finally, the plaintiffs had a problem in determining Portuguese national origin by basing their decision solely on surnames of employees, which could potentially result in either an under-inclusive or an over-inclusive sample.[11]

However, the court noted, "frailty in Plaintiffs' figures does not render them legally invalid." The court went on to note that the plaintiffs' statistical evidence did not prove that the eight-year rule caused the disparity. The plaintiffs conceded that no statistical expert could determine this conclusively and that their statistical expert could not definitively judge the precise cause of the disparity. The plaintiffs argued that the four companies who had adequate representations of Portuguese machinists did not have a similar eight-year rule; therefore it must be inferred for purposes of the plaintiffs' proof that the eight-year rule caused the disparity. The court found this evidence insufficient because it did not prove that the absence of the eight-year rule in the practices of the four companies was the only significant factor causing appropriate representation of Portuguese at those companies, as distinguished from the makeup of AVCO's workforce. There were many other differences between AVCO and the other four companies, any one or combination of which could have caused the statistical disparity between Portuguese and non-Portuguese at the other four companies as compared to AVCO. Accepting that reasoning, AVCO's use of the eight-year rule was not a sufficient cause of the disparity.

The court went on to find, however, that the testimony of a labor union leader proved that AVCO knew that the use of a ten-year seniority rule for skilled jobs had an adverse impact on minorities. By testimony of the former chairman of the Skilled Trades Council of Local 1010, the court found that AVCO in its 1970 labor agreement switched from a ten-year to an eight-year rule for the very purpose of increasing minority enrollment in the skilled trades. This suggests that seniority under the ten-year rule was a recognized factor in deterring minority participation in the workforce. It is not unreasonable to infer that if a ten-year rule diminished minority hiring in machinists' jobs, the eight-year rule would have the same effect. On that basis, a finder of fact could find for the plaintiff on the causation factor, as the court in this case did.

The above selected cases demonstrate that plaintiffs' statistical proof can be fraught with problems in the design of the database and in the analysis of the comparison groups. An even greater problem is the lack of any uniformity in the courts' treatment of what is necessary to prove discrimination by statistics.

Statistical Criteria in Recent Cases

There are three different kinds of criteria used to decide whether two properly chosen populations differ: the 80% rule (or 80% + 1 rule), standard deviations, and tests of significance. Before reviewing cases using each of these criteria, it will be useful to discuss how they relate to one another. In this discussion, the simplifying assumption is made that the data follow a normal (i.e., Gaussian, or bell-shaped) distribution. Since averages tend to this distribution as the number of independent items averaged gets large (a result known in the probability and statistical literature as the central limit theorem), this assumption is reasonable in the context of many of the cases being reviewed.

There are two fundamental sources of uncertainty in principle in each of these cases: uncertainty about the underlying policy of the employer (is it race-neutral?), and uncertainty due to sampling a finite number of instances (i.e., employees). As discussed below, the 80% rule ignores the second kind of uncertainty, while the standard deviation and test of significance rules, (which, under the assumption of normality, are equivalent), ignore the first kind.

The EEOC's Uniform Guidelines on Employee Selection Procedures, 29 C.F.R. 1607 proposed that adverse impact exists when members of a minority (race, sex, or ethnic group) are selected at a rate that is less than 80% of the rate for the group with the highest selection rate.

To take the 80% rule to its extreme, suppose that in the relevant time period, a company had only one qualified black applicant, whom it did not hire. Then the proportion of blacks hired would be zero. Zero, the selection rate for blacks, is less than whatever the rate of successful qualified white applicants is. These data would appear to fail the 80% rule, making the employer liable for discrimination. Because of the extreme nature of this outcome, the 80% rule has been modified, though the legal decisions do not make it clear who made the modification, or when. The new rule is an "80% + 1" rule, which would require, in this extreme case, a population of two unsuccessful qualified black applicants to make the employer liable.[12] Thus the 80% rule and the "80% + 1" rule both raise problems when the sample size is small. The essential difficulty with them is that they ignore sampling variability; an employer with a completely race-neutral hiring policy could fail the 80% or 80% + 1 rule by happenstance.

A demonstration of this difficulty is found in *Guinyard et al. v. City of New York, et al.,* 800 F. Supp. 1083 (E.D. N.Y. 1992). The candidates for police department promotions from lieutenant to captain took written and oral examinations. Out of a total of 104 people who took the examination, only 3 were Hispanic; out of 47 people who passed, only 2 were Hispanic; out of 60 people promoted, only 1 was Hispanic. The number of black candidates, while larger in each group, comprised barely 10% of the total taking the examination, 9% of those passing, and 6% of all those eventually promoted. The plaintiff's expert claimed that the selection rates for blacks and Hispanics were each less than 80% of the selection rate for whites. However, the small sample pool does not provide a basis for concluding that there is adverse impact, and this is what the court found. The court denied motions for summary judgment and remanded the case for discovery and trial.

In *Dicker v. Allstate Life Insurance Company,* No. 89C 4982, 61 E.P.D. 42, 211 (N.D. 11. 1993), the plaintiff's expert "identified a substantial disparity (77.6 percent) under the '80 percent rule' in the rates of employment between blacks and whites who entered a job classification after January 1, 1985. He acknowledged, however, that the disparity in promotions was not significant at the conventional levels of significance because of the small sample size (24 blacks)." Again, the court denied a motion for summary judgment.

The other two criteria—numbers of standard deviations and tests of significance— are closely related. Tests of significance ask whether, if the null hypothesis of no racial difference in hiring were true, the probability of data as extreme as or more extreme than that observed would be less than some arbitrary cutoff number. They have been used extensively in statistics since the early part of this century and were advocated especially by R. A. Fisher. Fisher used a .05 or .01 level of significance, for no particular theoretical reason. Even though the rhetoric of significance testing sounds impressive—"the hypothesis of race neutrality is rejected at the 5% level of significance"—the meaning of the statement makes it less useful than one might think. What it means is that if the same statistical procedure were used in an infinite stream of cases, in each of which the hypothesis of race neutrality were exactly true, in only 5% (or 1%) of the cases would the procedure reject the null hypothesis. It is thus less impressive than it sounds.

In particular, it has several weaknesses. First, it assumes an infinite stream of cases, in each of which the assumption of race neutrality is true. Thus the statement pertains to a hypothetical infinite stream of cases, and not to the particular case being adjudicated. There is no reason to think that a calculation done relative to a hypothetical infinite stream of cases need have relevance to a particular case.

Second, the level of significance (.05 or .01 or whatever) is an arbitrary constant in the procedure. There is no sound basis in statistics for one choice over another. Since the result, whether the null hypothesis is accepted or rejected, is critically dependent on the choice of this constant, this arbitrariness strikes at the heart of the use of the procedure in court.

Third, the procedure does not examine the probability of the data observed under other hypotheses, such as plausible amounts of race non-neutrality. Thus the procedure assumes the position of the defendant (i.e., race neutrality).

In addition, if significance is found, it does not permit one to say that the null hypothesis (here race neutrality) is incorrect. The only conclusion it allows is that either something unusual happened or the null hypothesis is false. One cannot conclude which of these is the case, nor can one give a probability on which of these two may have occurred in this instance. If significance is not found, it permits no conclusion to be drawn. Lack of significance does not mean that the null hypothesis, here race neutrality, is correct. Significance is easy to misinterpret, as if it were the probability of the null hypothesis (see, for example, *EEOC v. Olson Dairy Queens*). This is a Bayesian statement, unavailable in the paradigm of significance tests.

There are two kinds of tests of significance, one-tailed and two-tailed tests, depending on whether the phrase "as or more extreme" is interpreted to mean "too high" or "too high or too low." In discrimination cases, only one-tailed tests seem appropriate, because employers are not being charged with lack of race-neutrality in such a way as to favor the protected group.

For moderate to large samples, most test statistics used in employment cases have a distribution under the null hypothesis well approximated by a normal (also called Gaussian, or bell-shaped) distribution. Having chosen a one-tailed test and assumed a normal distribution of the test statistic under the null hypothesis, there is a one-to-one relationship between the level of the test (the arbitrary cutoff number mentioned above) and the number of standard deviations. Some values of this relationship are given in table 1.1.

It is an elementary mistake to interpret the level of a test as the probability of the null hypothesis. Rather, it is the probability of data as extreme as or more extreme than that observed were the null hypothesis true. Making statements about the probability of the null hypothesis, here the probability of no discrimination, is what courts would like to have and attorneys would like to discuss, but is unavailable using the methods courts have traditionally favored.

Some courts accept a 5% level of statistical significance (*Albemarle Paper Co. v. Moody*

Appendix Table 1.1 Equivalent Standard Deviations for One-Tailed Tests of Significance under Normality

Level of test	.05	.025	.01	.001	.0001
Number of standard deviations	.651	.962	.333	.10	3.65

422 U.S. 405, 430 [1975]). Others, using standard deviations, give 1.96 as the critical level (*Palmer v. Shultz*, 815 F.2d 84, 96 [D.D. Cir. 1987]). In *EEOC v. Jordan Graphics, Inc.* 769 F.Supp. 1357 (W.D.N.C. 1991), the court found 3.19 standard deviations insufficient, citing *Allen v. Prince George's County, Md.* (737 F.2d 1299, 1307 [4th Cir. 1984]) to the effect that "a standard deviation less than one full standard deviation over the threshold of three (3) set by *E.E.O.C. v. Federal Reserve Bank of Richmond*, 30 E.P.D. 33269, 698 F.2d 633, 639 (4th Cir. 1983) rev'd on other grounds sub nom., *Cooper v. Federal Reserve Bank of Richmond*, 467 U.S. 867; 104 S. Ct. 2794 (1984) was insignificant." Hence, courts vary from 1.65 to 4 in the number of standard deviations they require, or, equivalently, from 5% to well less than .001% of a percent in significance level.

The level of confusion about the use of significance testing raises the question of whether there is a useful alternative. Many statisticians believe that a different kind of statistics, called Bayesian statistics, offers just such an alternative. For a general view of Bayesian ideas, as applied specifically to legal evidence, see Robertson and Vignaux (1995). For a somewhat more methodologically oriented view, Finkelstein and Levin (1990, chapter 3) is quite helpful. Finally, for a full report on an age discrimination case done in the Bayesian way, see Kadane (1990). A useful general comparison of statistical methods and philosophies is given in Barnett (1982).

Courts might be well advised to make use of the provision in the federal code allowing them to appoint their own experts (in statistics or in anything else).[13] For example, the court in *Dicker v. Allstate* remarked that an expert "does not define the 'hazard estimation' method, which he characterizes 'as well known,' none of the sources on statistics consulted by this Court, however, mentions or defines this test." When courts are so baffled by the statistics that are offered, they should make use of the remedies provided in the law to obtain suitable assistance. It is likely, however, that use of this provision in the law is limited by the fact that it is unclear who pays for the court's expert. The parties are unlikely to want to pay and the courts generally lack the funds.

Conclusions

As we review the history of the use of statistics in employment discrimination cases, we find it striking how differently legal thinking and scientific thinking deal with their literatures. In law, precedent is very important, because it makes the law more predictable. "The life of the law has not been logic, it has been experience," wrote Justice Holmes (1881, 1963, 5). For this reason, courts are reluctant to overrule an existing precedent, even when convinced that the older thinking can be improved upon, is incorrect, or even is a serious mistake. Scientific thinking, by contrast, regards the most recent work as the most reliable guide, as it can take advantage of all of the past literature in arriving at conclusions. Scientific papers are published only if they are regarded as advancing beyond what was available before.

In this instance, the first attempts to use statistics in employment discrimination cases are not necessarily the best. But the improvement and new methods that statisticians as scientists welcome tend to be disregarded by a legal structure that sometimes seems determined to repeat its mistakes.

Notes

1. Sexual harassment constitutes disparate treatment because it results in a less favorable work environment where the victim must subject himself or herself to sexual propositions, vulgar jokes, or otherwise offensive and unwelcome conduct as a condition of the job. Coworkers may believe that harassment, sexual taunts, and sexist comments are inoffensive and funny, while the victim finds such conduct a barrier to equal employment opportunity.

2. This does not suggest that statistics are not useful in some disparate treatment cases. But disparate treatment requires not only less favorable treatment but also intent to discriminate. Statistics may prove that the minority group is not adequately represented in the category of bank vice presidents. The plaintiff must still show that she was not promoted to bank vice president because of her sex. Statistical demonstrations that males with fewer credentials were treated more favorably are uncommon in disparate treatment arguments because of the great expense and difficulty of a single plaintiff's funding such an analysis.

3. That percentage figure included the St. Louis city school district that was under an affirmative action plan to hire minority teachers. In the entire county, only 5.7% of the teachers were black if the city of St. Louis was excluded.

4. This conclusion is a misstatement of what can be obtained from a classical test of significance. Properly stated, it would be that were Spring Branch racially neutral, the probability of seeing data as more discrepant than observed is less than one in ten thousand. The statement here, which has intuitive appeal as a desirable way to express conclusions, requires a Bayesian analysis.

5. An extensive description of the two experts' reports is found in the district court's opinion, which can be found at p. 803 F. Supp. 1215 (1990).

6. The court decision specifies 259 men, but that figure is incompatible with the total of 274 applications, 25 of which are from women. Since the decision proceeds to cite the numbers 274 and 25 several times but does not mention 259 again, we conclude that 259 is an error.

7. Forty-six who were offered and accepted employment, plus one woman who was offered but declined employment.

8. If in fact the plaintiff's expert coded an application as female based solely on the name, this could introduce a significant error. Plaintiffs said that 17.2% of applicants were female; defendants claimed 9.1%.

9. Note that the burden of proof as stated in *Wards Cove Packing Co.* has been modified by the Civil Rights Act of 1991, which specifically overruled the *Wards Cove* model. Under the Civil Rights Act of 1991, if a specific employment practice is responsible for an observed statistical disparity, the defendant must prove the business necessity of this practice.

10. This conclusion by the court defies logic. If three companies (the defendant and two others) all use the discriminatory eight-year rule, it would be useful to know how AVCO's Portuguese hires compare to those of the two other discriminators, and also how the three discriminator companies compare to the ratio of Portuguese machinists at the four companies without the eight-year rule.

11. Note, however, that a decision to exclude a Portuguese from hire is based on the subjective per-

ception of the name as Portuguese, or hearsay community knowledge as to who is Portuguese, which may or may not be accurate. So these "methods" are also "under-inclusive or over-inclusive."

12. Under the "80 + 1 rule," one adds one more person to the actual number in the minority group to determine whether that new sum yields a number equal to 80% of the pass rate for whites. If so, then no adverse impact is presumed.

13. Coulam and Fienberg 1986 report the experiences of one such expert.

Befuddled Judges: Statistical Evidence in Title VII Cases

Richard Lempert

Statistics trouble courts. This is not news, nor is it surprising. One need only read the pages of social science journals to realize that even those in the business of statistical data analysis are often criticized by their peers for not getting things quite right. Surely one cannot expect judges or juries, who seldom possess statistical expertise, to navigate statistical thickets without occasionally, or more than occasionally, messing up. But herein lies the problem. When the law allows statistical evidence, indeed when it not only allows statistical evidence but places it at the center of lawsuits, as it often does in Title VII litigation, we expect the statistical evidence to resolve cases fairly and we expect courts to understand the evidence and to avoid egregious errors.

At least since *Hazelwood School District v. United States*, a case that is now more than twenty years old, statistics have been at the heart of Title VII employment discrimination lawsuits. This chapter is concerned with how well statistical evidence has been used in such suits and the kinds of problems that arise. To make these assessments, I canvassed a sample of Title VII cases with an eye to the quality of the statistical evidence given courts and the ability of courts to evaluate that evidence properly. My sample is not a random one, an irony I acknowledge in a paper on statistics. Rather, this project reflects its outgrown origins, an assignment to comment on Kadane and Mitchell's analysis of the use of statistics in Title VII cases. My sample consists of the seventeen Title VII cases involving statistical evidence that they cited in the original version of their work. Kadane and Mitchell did not, of course, cite cases at random. Instead, they focused on leading cases from the Supreme Court and federal courts of appeals as well as on cases with which they were especially familiar or which illustrated points they wanted to make.

Sampled Cases

I do not think that relying on the Kadane-Mitchell sample is a serious handicap given my goals. I am not trying to estimate population parameters, and since Kadane and Mitchell did not select cases with my concern for case quality in mind, the conclusion I draw from their chosen cases—that the statistical evidence in Title VII cases is often not handled well—is likely to characterize many cases they do not cite. This expectation is supported by the analyses of researchers who have looked at different cases than I do (Sugrue and Fairley 1983; Meier et al. 1984).

A potentially more serious sample bias problem stems from the fact that most of the cases Kadane and Mitchell cite—indeed a large proportion of the cases readily available for anyone's analysis—are appellate cases. Appellate cases are not a random sample of all Title VII cases filed or of all those in which statistical evidence is used. Rather these are cases in which statistical or other issues were sufficiently disputed that a trial was merited and in which even the trial did not end all argument. One would expect that if statistical analyses were done well and convincingly, many cases would settle without a trial, or that in the event of a trial, the loser would see no point in appealing. Thus what we see in available cases may not fairly represent the quality of the statistical evidence across the range of Title VII litigation, and problems with statistics in Title VII litigation may not be as important a concern as this chapter might seem to suggest. My best guess, however, is that even in this respect this chapter is not misleading. Many of the cases in the Kadane and Mitchell sample are important precedents that help set standards for the use of statistics in less well-known cases. Moreover, there is no reason to believe that the difficulties that statistical evidence poses for courts in job discrimination cases are fundamentally different from the difficulties courts face in dealing with statistical evidence in other contexts. The evidence indicates that across a range of cases, statistical evidence is often misevaluated or poses other problems for courts (Fienberg 1989), although it may be, as I have argued elsewhere, that appellate courts will have more difficulties than will trial courts in understanding unfamiliar statistical evidence (Lempert 1988).[1]

Simple Statistics

What first strikes me about the cases in the Kadane-Mitchell sample is that the statistical analyses that these cases report are often simple or "unsophisticated." I do not mean by this to make the point that Kadane and Mitchell do, namely, that the classical or frequentist approach that characterizes statistics in Title VII cases does not directly confront the key questions the courts must resolve, and that a Bayesian approach would be preferable. While I happen to agree, at least in principle, with Kadane and Mitchell on this point, I can forgive the courts this kind of "unsophistication" completely, for it reflects conventions that courts cannot be expected to challenge. Rather I am referring to statistical evidence that courts seemingly rely on, although judges must realize that the evidence cannot resolve the difficult issues they confront. For example, one encounters cases in which plaintiffs first show that some proportion of a labor force or applicant pool consists of some protected group (e.g., minorities, women) but a much smaller proportion of those hired come from that group. A statistician then testifies that the proportion of group members hired is several standard deviations smaller than what would be expected if the group in question was not systematically disadvantaged, and the conclusion urged is that therefore you have discrimination. Well, therefore you *don't* have discrimination; therefore you have a difference that should be explained.

One possible explanation *is* discrimination. Another possible explanation is that the hiring model implicit in the statistical test is untenable. Before concluding that the observed pattern reflects discrimination, more tenable models must be explored and the likelihood of nondiscriminatory hiring discarded. The hiring model implicitly tested in these simple "standard deviation" tests of the null hypothesis of no discrimination is a random binomial model that presupposes that workers in some labor force or applicant pool are hired or not hired or promoted or not promoted by chance, rather than on the basis of traits that predict job success.[2] If this is how hiring should occur—that is, if jobs are supposed to be offered to people selected randomly from an applicant pool—then percentage disparities (e.g., 50% of job applicants are female; 30% of those hired are female) expressed in standard deviation terms can indicate that it is extremely unlikely that a group characteristic such as sex did not affect job decisions. But no one claims that hiring, promotion, or other job-related decisions should be made at random, nor is it usually credible to contend that factors that may legitimately be considered in job decisions are uncorrelated with gender, race, age, or other factors that define protected groups. In these circumstances social scientists, in any context except the courthouse, would regard standard deviation disparities of the kinds courts sometimes cite and seemingly rely on as, in themselves, providing little evidence that anything improper was going on. To develop such evidence, more plausible job decision models should be tested, models, for example, which assume that job decisions reflect education, experience, supervisor ratings, employment history, drug test results, and the like. Only if members of a protected group fared more poorly than nonmembers after considering such factors would the hypothesis of discrimination seem likely.

Why then do court decisions often prominently feature random model statistics? There are several possible reasons. One is that some judges may not understand the statistics they receive. If a statistician testifies that a standard deviation statistic means that observed disparities between protected group status and job success would arise by chance fewer than one time in a thousand, a judge may mistakenly believe that this means there is less than one chance in a thousand that group status did not figure in the hiring decision (Thompson and Schumann 1987).[3] But I think this source of error is unlikely, for other cases suggest that judges have no difficulty grasping the weakness of the random model. I think two other reasons are more important, one of which is unconsidered respect for a somewhat confused precedent and the other of which respects the same precedent and is perfectly appropriate for a court.

First, *Hazelwood,* the key Title VII precedent on statistical evidence, was decided during the same term but after the Supreme Court decided *Castenada v. Partida*, a jury discrimination case. Adapting the *Castenada* precedent to the hiring context, the Supreme Court wrote of minority group hires, "'if the difference between the expected value and the observed number is greater than two or three standard deviations,' then the hypothesis that teachers were hired without regard to race would be suspect."[4] This language attaches a conclusion about discrimination in hiring to a standard, within the interior quotes, that was written with the proof of jury discrimination in mind. In doing so, it ignores a crucial difference between jury discrimination cases and Title VII cases. Except for the challenge stage, jurors are supposed to reflect a random cross section of the community or something close to it.[5] Hiring, however, is aimed at securing the most capable workforce, not a random selection from those available. Thus contrasting juror selection decisions with the expectations of a random model is appropriate, but comparing job decisions with such expectations is not.

There is, however, another, more legitimate justification for the *Hazelwood* standard. This stems from the fact that evidence and legal rules are not independent. Although people usually think that evidence leads to legal rulings, it is equally true that legal rules shape the evidence produced. A legal rule that shifts the burden of producing evidence from plaintiffs to defendants based on statistical conclusions rooted in random, and hence unrealistic, job decision models is not necessarily a poor choice. If the evidence needed to test richer models is more readily available to defendants than to plaintiffs, such a burden-shifting rule can be efficient or for other reasons make sense. The lead case here is *Griggs v. Duke Power Co.*, which held that if it can be shown that an employment test has an adverse impact on a protected group, the burden shifts to the employer to show the job-relatedness of the test. Thus showing a statistical disparity, expressed in standard deviation terms, is enough for a plaintiff to prevail even though nothing about that disparity negates the possibility that it is rooted in legitimate job-related reasons. A defendant, in order to prevail, must, by validating the test, show that those job-related reasons exist. Although the context is slightly different, it is not unreasonable for courts to allow similar burden shifting where the issue is whether minority hiring or promotion disparities are related to group membership.

If, however, courts shift burdens in this way, they should be clear, for there is a subtle issue here. The Title VII plaintiff must show on the basis of all the evidence that discrimination is more likely to have occurred than not. Two views are plausible. One might argue that statistics showing only disparities from random decision probabilities seldom are enough to suggest that job discrimination is more likely than not.[6] Alternatively one might argue that a defendant's inability to attribute a plaintiff's evidence of disparities to legitimate factors means that the plaintiff's claims are probably correct. *Hazelwood*, in apparently opting for the latter argument, provides defendants with incentives to produce evidence, which makes a defendant's failure to produce evidence still more probative of job discrimination. Thus, given the incentives *Hazelwood* has provided, the *Hazelwood* standard may make considerable sense.

Nevertheless, when courts emphasize statistics showing uncontrolled disparities, one gets the feeling that they are not very knowledgeable readers of statistics. This is because judges often write as if such statistics prove discrimination rather than simply establish a playing field in which a defendant's failure to respond has probative value. Indeed, in some cases where defendants respond with their own statistics, courts seemingly set the plaintiff's standard deviation analysis against the defendant's controlled rebuttal and compare the probative value of the two statistical approaches. But if the plaintiff's standard deviation disparities are properly used only for burden shifting, they should not be weighed against the defendant's efforts. Rather, the defendant's efforts should be examined in their own right for their adequacy in rebutting a presumption of discrimination. If they are inadequate, as when the defendant has used a clearly inappropriate model, the defendant should lose even if its model is no worse than the plaintiff's, for *Hazelwood* gives legal significance to an unrealistic plaintiff's model but extends no such special significance to a defendant's equally flawed efforts to rebut.

While the Supreme Court's ruling in *Hazelwood* is, as I hope I have shown, defensible, the opinion itself does little to give one confidence in the high Court's grasp of statistics. Not only does the two or three standard deviation test seem to rely more on the reflexive use of inapposite jury selection precedent than it does on an appreciation of the statistical issues involved, but the test itself gives one pause. Which is it, two or three deviations? There is a difference. If the random selection model provided the appropriate benchmark, a two standard deviation disparity between the percentage of minority group members in the workforce and the percentage hired would be an unlikely result, but not such an unlikely one as necessarily to be surprising. Among companies that hired at random or by criteria unrelated to race, we would expect to see minority representation as much as or more than one out of forty times.[7] If, for example, one examined the workforce composition of thirty companies that actually hired at random, it would be surprising if at least one company did not appear by the two standard deviation test to be discriminating. Three standard deviation disparities, on the other hand, occur fewer than two times in a thousand. When one encounters such a disparity, the hypothesis of random effects is far less credible. Yet judging from the Supreme Court's casual reference to a two or three standard deviation disparity, it appears that the extra standard deviation difference does not matter.[8]

Hazelwood also illustrates another feature common to judicial discussions of statistics in Title VII cases: the strength of the race-hiring relationship receives no formal attention. All the Court attends to are raw disparities (1.85% of Hazelwood's teachers were black, 5.7% of teachers in the county excluding St. Louis were black, and 15.4% of county teachers including St. Louis were black), and the significance levels associated with the disparities (beyond five standard deviations in 1974 when 5.7% black was used as the labor pool proportion). Significance levels do not, however, mean that a relationship is strong in the sense that one factor (e.g., race) largely determines another (e.g., who gets hired). If samples are large enough, almost any factor that one cares to specify will meet the Court's two standard deviation test.

Focusing on significance levels that do not speak directly to relationship strengths tends to obscure an intriguing legal question: what should courts do when a characteristic like race or gender affects hiring decisions, but only to a small degree? One answer, which is the answer suggested by significance tests, is that there are no degrees of discrimination; all discrimination is wrong, and if a disparity is not the result of pure chance, the complete panoply of judicial remedies is appropriate. Is this sensible? I don't think so. Suppose a woman sues for gender discrimination and can introduce data showing that 36% of female applicants were hired compared to 37% of similarly qualified male applicants. If sample sizes were large enough, this difference could exceed two, three, or even five standard deviations, and discrimination might be the only plausible explanation for it. But what are a female plaintiff's damages in this case? What are the damages of one thousand women? More importantly, what remedies are appropriate? If a disparity due to discrimination is only 1%, we are unlikely to be able to identify where the discrimination resides or to tweak the system to eliminate the discrimination against women without creating discrimination against men.

The EEOC has sought to deal with this problem with its so-called 80% rule.[9] As Kadane and Mitchell indicate, courts have adopted this test and appropriately modified it to deal with small samples. The 80% rule looks not just at the significance of disparities but also at their magnitude. Actionable discrimination is ordinarily presumed only if a disparity is both significant at the .05 level and protected group members are selected at a rate that is less than 80% of the rate for the group with the highest selection rate. So long as this "rule" is interpreted with the flexibility that its EEOC drafters intended, it may for legal purposes be a serviceable measure of relationship strength where the random model applies even if it is not a precise statistical measure and even if, as Meier and his coauthors point out, it is occasionally misinterpreted by courts, legal scholars, and the EEOC itself (Meier et al. 1984).

The Supreme Court is not the only court that gets confused by the statistical issues that arise in Title VII cases. Consider, for example, the case of *Wilkins v. University of Houston*. In *Wilkins*, a group of female faculty claimed that the University of Houston discriminated against women in promotions, salary, and other respects. *Wilkins* was an unusual case in that the plaintiff's statistical case rested largely on the defendant's analyses. The Fifth Circuit struggled mightily and in good faith with the evidence, but in the end it seemed quite confused.

In *Wilkins* the plaintiff's statistical evidence was regarded by the court, with good reason, as inadequate to show discrimination, but a plausible plaintiff's case could be based on the defendant's statistical evidence. The plaintiff's evidence on the salary issue, which is the issue I shall focus on, consisted largely of gross statistical disparities that compared such measures as the overall mean salaries of women with the mean salaries of men and mean salaries controlling for single variables such as race, age, and length of service. For three of seven such comparisons, differences were significant beyond the .02 level. It is not clear whether other differences were significant or whether tests were simply not done. The court did not focus on the significance of these disparities, for it demanded an analysis that took into account the simultaneous influence of variables the plaintiffs had controlled individually or not at all. The court's demand was justified because salaries reflect various factors, and effects associated with gender might exist because women are less well-situated than men with respect to variables that legitimately affect salary levels. For example, in the early to mid-1970s, the period that figures in *Wilkins*, women, who had only recently begun to enter the academy in large numbers, were more likely than men to have been in junior ranks, to have had short times in rank, and to have been in poorly paid departments and colleges.

Given the inadequacy of their statistical data, the women plaintiffs might have been out of court except that the defendant university had done a regression analysis of its salary structure controlling for the kinds of factors the plaintiffs had neglected. In the defendant's model there was a statistically significant negative coefficient on the gender variable, indicating that, controlling for other factors, women were paid less than men. The point estimate of the cost of being female rather than male was $1,388 per year.[10] Confidence intervals around this estimate were not presented (as is true of all cases in the Kadane-Mitchell sample), although a court might well want to know whether it was plausible, within the context of the model, to suppose that despite the significance of the point estimate, the cost of being female might be close to zero.

The defendant's regressions were, however, also not good enough for the court, at least when offered as plaintiff's evidence. They were not good enough because the court transformed its correct understanding that statistical significance does not necessarily signify substantive importance into a too quick dismissal of the evidence. The judges did this by focusing, apparently at the defense expert's urging, on the fact that when the gender variable was entered after all the other variables in the defendant's model, incremental explained variance increased by only 0.8% from 52.4% to 53.2%. In focusing on the incremental explained variance, they ignored the substantial salary decrement associated with being female and assumed that all salary variance that might be explained either by gender or by some "legitimate" variable was explained by the legitimate variable.[11] In justification, the court wrote, "Plaintiffs introduced no evidence that sex was not, in a statistical sense, independent of the other independent variables in the model (e.g., department, rank, experience, and degree)."

What this confusing sentence apparently means is that the plaintiffs had not shown that sex was correlated with the other variables in the model. If sex was actually uncorrelated with those variables, its maximum contribution to the variance in individual salaries was only 0.8%, too small to concern a court or to provide substantial evidence of gender discrimination, or so the court assumed. The court's analysis dismisses the possibility that the model's other independent variables might be proxying for sex and so explaining variance[12] that was in fact due to discrimination.[13]

There are problems with this conclusion. First, the court ignored an apparently real gender effect as indicated by the statistical significance of the gender variable.[14] Second, the court dismissed any gender effect as *de minimis* based on the limited ability of gender uniquely to explain variance. In doing so, it ignored the fact that the model's best estimate of gender's impact was that being female cost a woman $1,388 after controlling for variables that might be expected to legitimately affect salary. There is nothing *de minimis* about this estimate. Third, the court closed its eyes to the fact that gender was certainly correlated with other variables (e.g., rank) in the model. Had it asked for data showing correlations, the information would almost certainly have been available.[15] Finally, the court did not realize that if it was right and gender was uncorrelated with other variables that might legitimately affect salaries, it was wrong to dismiss the statistics that plaintiffs originally provided on the ground that they did not control for legitimate variables. On the court's independence assumption, controlling for other variables would not have changed the association between being female and faring poorly. Thus the court, or defense, had it both ways. The plaintiff's statistics failed to prove discrimination because gender is almost certainly correlated with factors that legitimately affect salaries. The defendant's regression analysis did not prove discrimination because it was not shown that gender is correlated with those legitimate factors.

An important reason why the court made the mistake it did is that it failed to appreciate the connections between statistical models and legal standards. Plaintiffs in Title VII cases must show that it is *more likely than not* that they were disadvantaged by gender, race, or some other protected characteristic. They are not required to show that the *only possible explanation* for a disadvantage associated with their group status is membership in the protected group. If the latter were the standard, the court's focus in *Wilkins* on the variance uniquely explained by gender would have been what the law demands, but the law's standard is not nearly so high. Thus the court in *Wilkins* mirrored the mistake of the Court in *Hazelwood* in that neither court attended to the implications of legal standards for statistical models. If the *Hazelwood* Court intended its two or three standard deviation test to do anything more than shift the burden of producing evidence, it erected too low a standard, for nothing in Title VII suggests that job decisions must be random with respect to all factors that are correlated with race. *Wilkins* on the other hand set too high a standard, for nothing in Title VII indicates that disparities between groups are permissible unless group membership is the only possible explanation for them. A standard like this would be more extreme than the "beyond a reasonable doubt" standard of criminal cases, and Title VII cases need only meet the civil standard of a preponderance of the evidence.

Although I have criticized the court in *Wilkins*, I have considerable sympathy for the judges who decided the case. They were trying to get things right. They realized that they should demand more than a demonstration of uncontrolled relationships between gender and job rewards to make out a case of discrimination, and they sensed that the strength as well as the existence of such a relationship should concern them. Moreover, and this is fundamental to its problems, the court was ill-served by both sides in the case. The university's expert seems to have presented its data in ways that put a misleading, pro-defense spin on the regression results, and not only does it appear that the plaintiffs did not do the kind of statistical work they should have done, but it also seems from the court's opinion that the plaintiffs did not even offer a statistical expert to contest the defense expert's interpretation. This is astonishing in a case arising in the academy, where one would assume that experts could be found in abundance.

My sympathy for the court is, however, somewhat dissipated by the conclusion to its discussion of the faculty salary issue. Here it tried to cement its critique by pointing to the failure of either side to show that certain random disturbance assumptions that underlie ordinary least squares analysis were met, and it also suggested that the university's model may have been weak because of unanswered questions about whether variables were erroneously included or excluded, whether the linear model was appropriate, and whether the fact that the model explained only 52% of the variance in salaries meant the model was unreliable. The court cited in connection with these criticisms an important article on regression analysis in legal proceedings that Franklin Fisher wrote in the *Columbia Law Review*, but it used this article not to understand the regression analysis it confronted but rather as a further excuse to dismiss the regression results. The court's desire to poke as many holes as possible in the statistics suggesting discrimination, rather than to understand the issues involved, was most evident in the judges' concern that the Houston model may have been unreliable because it explained only 52% of the variance. To explain this much variance with a relatively parsimonious model is to do well by conventional standards.

The court's cookbook-like list of potential flaws in the model is particularly disquieting because it suggests that its treatment of statistical evidence may have been more a formal justification of its decision than the reason for it. Courts, including the Supreme Court, too often seem to selectively cite or misinterpret evidence to support the decisions they reach. When this occurs, one suspects that the grounds given for the decision are not those that motivated the court, and one fears that the true grounds reflect such impermissible considerations as political preferences or improper bias. Since mistaken statistical arguments are often obvious to trained readers, courts face a particularly high risk to the legitimacy of their decisions when they make errors or throw out in shotgun form possible objections to models or demand tests that are either inappropriate or unlikely to matter much.

There is another, broader issue that the *Wilkins* court's model specification questions raise. I call this the "whose model" issue. In *Wilkins* this question should have been easy, for the plaintiff was relying on the defendant's model. If the defendant chose to specify a linear model with particular variables, it is in a poor position to complain that the model is mis-specified, and it is not the court's task in a civil case to make objections that a party's behavior waives. But for argument's sake, suppose the regression models had been prepared by the plaintiff and the defendant had expressed the court's concerns. Should the court have endorsed the defendant's position and dismissed the plaintiff's evidence because it had not shown that the assumptions its model incorporated were valid?

The question returns us to the fundamental question of what Title VII should require of statistical evidence. I have suggested that it should require more than simply showing an uncontrolled relationship between a protected status and disadvantaging decisions. This does not mean that it should require, as the *Wilkins* court seems to intimate, that all factors that might legitimately affect job decisions be controlled or that all possible functional forms of relationships be explored. The former requirement is impossible to meet, for not all legitimate factors may be measured in a way that allows them to be included in regressions. The latter misunderstands the functional form issue because, as with other examples I have given, it disassociates statistics from models. If, for example, a linear model fits the data and suggests discrimination, the fact that discrimination is not indicated by a nonlinear model does nothing to help the defendant unless it can plausibly argue that for normative or behavioral reasons, factors affecting job decisions should not or do not combine in a linear fashion, or that the linear form unduly weights certain cases and so misleadingly estimates important effects. Such arguments are, however, part of the defendant's case and not the plaintiff's. There is no reason why the plaintiff should have to refute them in advance.[16] The situation would be different if the plaintiff were using a highly unconventional specification, since one could be reasonably confident that more conventional specifications had been explored first. Plaintiffs in these circumstances should be required to reveal what their exploration showed and, assuming that more conventionally specified models did not indicate discrimination, explain why their preferred specification is more adequate than more conventional ones. Otherwise plaintiffs could, without theoretical or empirical justification, fit models to desired results.

The more general point, which can involve a difficult line to draw, is that in the typical Title VII case both plaintiff and defendant have access to relevant data and statistical experts, with the defendant often having better access and more money for experts. In these circumstances, except where there are serious problems with the plaintiff's statistics, such as the unexplained use of an unconventional model or a failure to include a number of obviously relevant, available explanatory variables, the burden should be on the defendant to show that a possible weakness in model construction in fact affects crucial results. For example, suppose that the model in *Wilkins* showed that women were paid less than men after considering field, age, rank, time in rank, and publications. The defendant might criticize the plaintiff's model for omitting teaching evaluation scores or a measure of grants acquired. These criticisms may be fair, but a court should not dismiss the plaintiff's case or find her evidence unpersuasive because of them. The defendant should first be required to show that these factors are important, legitimate considerations in setting salaries and then, in the ordinary case, demonstrate through its own regression analyses that the suggestion of discrimination in the plaintiff's model disappears when such factors are considered.

Only if a defendant can show *a priori* that an omitted factor is crucial in salary setting—as might be the case in a small college that prized teaching and used student evaluations to assess it—should the court disregard a plaintiff's statistical results when a defendant who could have refuted the results statistically simply suggests that the results are, in principle, refutable. To put this another way, in presenting the *Wilkins* model I hypothesized, the plaintiffs are in effect saying, "We think that what really and legitimately counts in salary setting around here are field, age, rank, time in rank, and publications. Other things may count but even taken together they are not likely to matter a great deal." The defendant is responding, "We think that student evaluations and the ability to get grants matter a great deal." Only if such claims by a defendant are obviously correct and a good bet to explain an apparent gender or race effect should a court reject a plaintiff's regression results for specification inadequacy. Otherwise, so long as the defendant is as well situated as the plaintiff to do additional statistical analysis, a judge's response to a defendant should be, "That's an interesting speculation. It's not implausible, but *show me.*"

I have devoted considerable time to the *Wilkins* opinion because the court's effort to deal seriously with the statistical evidence illustrates so many of the mistakes courts can make. The *Wilkins* case is not, however, the only case other than *Hazelwood* in the Kadane-Mitchell sample where courts are confused by statistical evidence.

I will give two further examples that illustrate different problems. Consider first *Equal Employment Opportunity Commission v. Olson's Dairy Queens, Inc.*, another Fifth Circuit case. *Dairy Queens* involved statistical evidence exploring whether Dairy Queens' hiring patterns at several stores were race-neutral. The case analysis included a statistical comparison between the proportion of blacks hired by Dairy Queen and the proportion of blacks in its applicant pool. Three aspects of the statistics in this case merit comment. The first is that the defendant's argument, which prevailed in the district court, looked closely at one store's workforce, which consisted mostly of white teenagers who lived within a short distance of the store, and concluded from this that the labor pools for the stores consisted mainly of those residing in the immediate locale. The district court went wrong here; when the issue is whether those hired owe their jobs to a racially discriminatory process, one cannot look at those hired, find that they share some characteristic other than race, and assume that that is why they were hired.

The appellate court, which reversed the trial court, caught this error, for it credited the EEOC's expert analysis. The EEOC looked at the applicant pool and analyzed travel times to show that the labor pool for Dairy Queens included more than those living within the immediate vicinity and then went on to show an implausibly large discrepancy on any hypothesis other than discrimination between the proportion of blacks in the labor pool and the proportion of blacks hired by the Dairy Queens.

Given my questioning of statistics that simply show the implausibility of discrepancies between the proportion of people hired from a protected group and the proportion of the labor pool belonging to that group, one may wonder whether the EEOC offered evidence sufficient to prove discrimination. I believe it did. In *Dairy Queens*, unlike many other Title VII cases, the defendant's explanation for the gross discrepancy was not that black and white job applicants differed on a host of other job-relevant characteristics (it would have been difficult to make this case for unskilled Dairy Queen positions), but rather that the labor pool for Dairy Queen jobs was restricted to near neighborhoods. When the EEOC showed that this was not the case, Dairy Queen had no benign hypotheses left to explain racial discrepancies in its workforce apart from the possibility that they arose by chance, and this hypothesis was disproved by the EEOC's simple statistics.

The more general point here is that statistical analyses in Title VII cases should be aimed at rejecting hypotheses other than discrimination that might plausibly explain the lesser success of protected group members. When, as in *Dairy Queens*, there are no plausible hypotheses except chance, the plaintiff should bear only the burden of rejecting the chance hypothesis. When the defendant offers a specific hypothesis to explain the discrepancy, an analysis which excludes both the defendant's specific hypothesis and the possibility of a random effect should be all the plaintiff need offer. If a defendant does not suggest that a matter is in issue, the plaintiff should not have to deal with it, even if it is a possibility.

Finally, while I have no problem with the Fifth Circuit's decision in *Dairy Queens*, there is one glaring statistical misunderstanding. The court quotes with approval an expert's statement that, "there was less than a one in 100,000 (.00001) chance that Olson's observed hiring practices . . . could have resulted from race-neutral hiring patterns."[17] Maybe the expert said this, but if he did, both he and the court that cited his statement with approval were mistaken. The expert's analysis does not tell us the chance that Dairy Queens' hiring patterns could have resulted from race-neutral hiring patterns. Rather it tells us that had Dairy Queens hired people at random from its labor pool (as identified by the EEOC and accepted by the appellate court) with respect to race and all criteria correlated with race, the disparity between the proportion of blacks hired by Olson and the proportion in its labor pool would occur less than one time in 100,000. This figure does not, however, say anything about the likelihood that hiring without regard to race (which I assume is what is meant by "race-neutral"), would have led to the discrepancy observed. There are potentially many criteria, race-neutral on their faces, which might have led to the observed discrepancy. To give just one example, if each Dairy Queen store preferentially hired teenagers who were regular customers, the statistics for stores in white neighborhoods might have been as extreme as those the plaintiff's expert analyzed, yet race would not have entered into the hiring decision.[18] The court's misunderstanding of the import of the statistic it was given appears not to have mattered in *Dairy Queens*, for the decision appears correct; but in another case it might matter.

The last case I shall focus on is *Jenson v. Eveleth Taconite Company*, a district court case and hence richer in its discussion of the evidence than most circuit court cases are. In this case the trial court first had to resolve a dispute between the plaintiff and the defendant over the proper definition of the applicant pool, and then, having resolved this issue in the defendant's favor, it had to decide if the defendant had discriminated against women. There was substantial evidence indicating that two women who sought job applications were falsely told that the mine was not hiring and were refused applications at a time when men were given them; that the mine's personnel manager (but apparently not the person who made hiring decisions in the relevant time period) had been heard to say that "women do not belong in the mines"; and that the mine manager in charge of hiring had been inconsistent in his testimony about hiring criteria.[19] In addressing another issue, moreover, the judge found that there was hostile environment sexual harassment because male workers told sexist jokes, referred to women in sexually derogatory terms, and displayed lewd photos, and management did little to prevent such behavior. Moreover, even accepting the defendant's definition of the applicant pool, the statistical evidence was consistent with discrimination; only two women had been hired by the mine although the expected number of female hires was 4.19.

The court, however, saw the statistical data as favoring the defendant rather than the plaintiff since only 1.2 standard deviations separated the expected from the actual number of women hired. Indeed the judge not only found that this disparity was insufficient to prove discrimination, but he also saw it as supporting his view that the anecdotal evidence suggesting discrimination was weak.

The judge in this case appears to have taken *Hazelwood*'s suggestion that a two or three standard deviation disparity is potentially strong proof of discrimination to mean that a disparity of less than two standard deviations lends little support to an inference of discrimination and may suggest its opposite. In interpreting the significance level this way, the court failed to consider the "power" of statistical tests and did not realize that when only a few members of a protected group apply for a job, even strong relationships may not be statistically significant. He thus saw the failure to find a statistically significant effect as supporting his view that the anecdotal evidence was not strong enough to prove discrimination. Actually the statistical evidence was consistent with and should have been seen as reinforcing the suggestion of discrimination that the anecdotal evidence provided.

The opinion in *Eveleth* is not, however, a result-oriented one reflecting a judge's hostility to women or a bias against women or civil rights actions. Not only did the judge find for the women plaintiffs in this case on their sexual harassment claims, but he ignored statistical likelihoods in evaluating the claim that women had been discriminated against in promotions to foreman. The judge treated as persuasive proof of intentional discrimination the fact that no woman had ever been promoted to a temporary or actual foreman position—a statistic he called the "inexorable zero." Yet only three promotions to temporary foreman and none to regular foreman occurred during the period beginning in 1982 that the court focused on. Even if promotions were made by lot, it would not be surprising if no woman were promoted. And taking into account not only the mine's small proportion of women workers, but also job skills, seniority, and other factors that properly influence promotion decisions, zero promotions for women would probably have been the expected number. The court thus went from overvaluing the meaning of significance tests to dismissing statistical inference entirely. At the root of each mistake seems to be the judge's failure to appreciate the implications of the fact that few women were potentially subject to discrimination. Yet it would be a mistake to be too critical of this judge. He took great care in analyzing facts and data in parts of this case I do not discuss, and he showed no biases for or against either party in his decision.

Even though there were fewer than twenty cases in the Kadane-Mitchell sample, I could have drawn from it different examples for this critique.[20] Fortunately, in a number of the seemingly most result-oriented decisions, appellate courts reverse, but appellate courts don't catch all errors below, and they make their own mistakes. Judges, as I said at the outset, too often have trouble with statistics. The challenge lies not in finding cases to criticize; rather it lies in finding ways to improve the situation. Since I probably cannot improve much on the suggestions contained in a report prepared by the National Research Council's Panel on Statistical Assessments as Evidence in the Courts, on which I served (Fienberg 1989), I shall give this difficult task shorter shrift than it deserves. I do, however, have some conclusions to share from my reading of Title VII cases.

First, many judges realize the difficulties that statistical evidence poses. This is poignantly illustrated by the reflections of the Fifth Circuit panel on the task they confronted in the *Wilkins* case:

> We are no more statisticians than we are physicians, and counsel who expect of us informed and consistent treatment of such proofs are well advised to proceed as do those who advance knotty medical problems for resolution. Our innate capacity in such matters extends to "the inexorable zero" and perhaps, unevenly, somewhat beyond; but the day is long past,—past at least since the Supreme Court's sophisticated analysis in *Castenada v. Partida*, when we proceed with any confidence toward broad conclusions from crude and incomplete statistics. That everyone who has eaten bread has died may tell us something about bread, but not very much. (410)
>
> One cannot read this conclusion without feeling sympathy for all judges who try to do their jobs well but confront evidence that is beyond them.

Judges clearly need help in dealing with statistical evidence, but helping them is no easy task. This is not because judges are dumb—most are smart people even if many have had a minimal mathematical education or have forgotten the mathematics they once knew. Rather it is because the nature of judicial work provides few ways of helping judges cope with statistical problems.

The two obvious modes of helping judges—education and the appointment of neutral experts—both have their pitfalls. While it might seem that statistics courses for judges are a good idea—and they may be—they must be carefully designed or they risk doing more harm than good. Too often students take away from elementary statistics courses cookbook formulas and rules of thumb, like the rule that treats a relationship as meaningful only if it is significant beyond the .05 level. As we have seen, judges can get in trouble when they apply statistical rules of thumb. This is not surprising, because even rules that are good guides to statistics users in most instances may not be good guides in most cases reaching trial. These cases are the result of a lengthy filtering process. If settlements are particularly likely where rules of thumb are a good guide to decisions, the settlement process will disproportionately eliminate such cases. In addition, the rules of thumb available to courts were, with the exception of the 80% rule, developed with the concerns of academic disciplines and not with those of the legal system in mind. Thus if judges are to be taught statistics, the effort should not be to teach them the statistics they would learn in an introductory course, but rather should focus on the underlying logic of statistical tests and concepts, the meaning of models and their relationships to legal standards, and the uncertainty and flexibility of statistical analysis. Even so, we must recognize that for some judges a little learning will be a dangerous rather than a helpful thing, and it is unlikely that most judges can be exposed to more than a little learning through continuing education.

Judges therefore must be educated during trials as well as in advance. Yet if education is the goal, it would be hard to design a less effective system than one in which two teachers, one labeled "plaintiff's expert" and the other "defendant's expert," are paid to disagree about most consequential matters. Clearly there is room for the more widespread and wiser use of neutral experts in cases involving statistical evidence. There are, however, serious difficulties in using neutral experts, including added expense, the biases of so-called neutrals, and the difficulties of employing experts when no party is responsible for informing them. Since problems like these are treated in the literature on expert testimony (see, e.g., Gross 1991), I shall not discuss them further, nor shall I seek to elaborate on others' discussions of how neutral experts might be used in cases involving statistics (Fienberg 1989) except to make one point. If the goal of using neutral experts is to allow the judge (and a jury in jury cases) to better understand the statistical evidence, often the expert need not analyze the data or present results as "the truth" to the court. Instead the court's expert might meet with the parties' experts before trial to promote agreement on data sources and models, provide written critiques of the opposing expert's reports, suggest additional data that should be collected or tests to be done, and appear in open court to answer questions from the judge and the opposing lawyers.

Judges need help not only in understanding statistical evidence but also in thinking through issues at the intersection of law and statistics. Here the academy can play a major role, for the issues that arise are the stuff of scholarly articles. The cases I read suggest that the following are among the questions that should be addressed. First, what does it mean to prove a matter through statistics by the preponderance of the evidence? What, if any, generalities can we arrive at about the relative weight to be accorded statistical and anecdotal evidence? When should statistically insignificant disparities associated with race or gender be treated as evidence of nondiscrimination and when should they be taken to suggest discrimination even if, standing alone, they are not adequate proof? How does one evaluate admittedly flawed models that suggest discrimination or nondiscrimination? When should statistical results be dismissed because of model flaws and when are potentially flawed models sufficiently robust that in the context of a specific case they can be taken as strong or even dispositive evidence?

A second focus suggested by my case reading should be on the models that law implies. Courts need help in thinking through these issues, for they often seem unaware of their existence. In particular, it is important for judges to understand the implications of legal standards for how job decisions or other behavior should be modeled and for the quality that can be demanded of models. What, for example, are the circumstances in which the random binomial model is properly used to prove job discrimination or to shift production burdens if not risks of non-persuasion? Reversing the focus, can we say something not about the statistics the law calls for but about the legal norms implied by various statistical analyses? How may courts be helped to perceive this connection?

Closely related to these issues is what I have called the "whose model" issue. We have an adversary system which presupposes two sides to an issue. While the plaintiff has an obligation to present a *prima facie* case, in many trials the ultimate test is not whether the plaintiff has told a story that touches all the legal bases needed to prevail but rather whether it is the plaintiff or the defendant who has told the more convincing story. What does this aspect of the adversary system imply when it comes to statistical stories? How adequate need a plaintiff's model be to make out a *prima facie* case? At what point is it the responsibility of a defendant to show that arguable improvements on the plaintiff's model in fact matter? If the plaintiff and defendant each present plausible models, the one suggesting discrimination and the other finding none, should the defendant prevail or, as with most competing trial narratives, is the fact finder free to choose? If the fact finder is free to chose, what considerations should guide the choice? And how should statistical stories be combined with nonstatistical ones? Logically, there can be situations where statistical evidence that is alone insufficient to prove a case may in combination with similarly insufficient anecdotal evidence constitute the preponderance of the evidence. What can we say about these situations, and how can they be distinguished from situations where statistical evidence lends little to the anecdotal evidence or even calls it into question and vice versa? Questions are also raised if one side's evidence is largely statistical and the other side's anecdotal. Does one kind of evidence necessarily trump the other? How does the relative weight to be accorded statistical and anecdotal evidence turn on law and precedent?

Finally, we saw from the cases that courts sometimes go wrong by treating statistical precedents the way they treat other precedents. Thus, the two or three standard deviation test of *Hazelwood* becomes hardened and applied in statistically inappropriate ways in later cases, and the influence of the "inexorable zero" in the *Eveleth* case seems to reflect the Supreme Court's approving use of the term in *Brotherhood of Teamsters* (342 at n.23) rather than the facts in *Eveleth.*

When a court is confused about competing statistical claims, the lure of apparently on-point precedent is attractive. But statistics are almost always case-specific, and what may make sense in the context of one case's statistics may not make sense in another statistical context. For example, in *Brotherhood of Teamsters,* hundreds of line drivers were hired during a three-and a-half-year period and none was black. In *Eveleth* three people were promoted to temporary foreman and none was a woman. The zero statistic does not imply discrimination in *Eveleth* in the way it does in *Teamsters,* yet out of respect for precedent, the judge in *Eveleth* gives it much the same force. If precedents were not statistical, courts would be well equipped—it is their stock in trade—to see how cases might be distinguished. But statistically untrained judges are poorly equipped to make distinctions regarding statistical precedent. Commentators need to help courts understand what statistical tests and conclusions mean in precedential cases and what this implies for the respect accorded such precedent in different future actions.

Finally, the cases suggest that courts often bear considerable responsibility for their own statistical failings. Title VII litigation is often inescapably political, and judges' value preferences can easily get bound up with their evaluation of evidence. One reads opinions from the Supreme Court on down in which evidence is reviewed or interpreted in ways that seem aimed at defending the court's conclusions rather than disclosing what motivated them. Sometimes the selective misinterpretation or ignoring of evidence almost compels the conclusion that the court's reasons for decision bore little relation to the reasons it presented. In the ordinary case, judges often can get away with misinterpretations of evidence, for only those well acquainted with the record are aware that the court is distorting the facts. With statistical evidence, escaping criticism for bad-faith opinions or even good-faith misinterpretations of the evidence is more difficult. Statistical evidence is often central in Title VII cases and must be mentioned; if it has been misassessed, the court's opinion often reveals that. Result-oriented judging is thus a major threat not only to the proper use of statistical evidence both in its rarest form of preference-driven verdicts and in its more common form, which is a tendency to perceive ambiguous evidence as consistent with preestablished preferences, but it also threatens the legitimacy of the decisions courts reach. Courts in Title VII cases should therefore be aware both of the possibility that their preferences or intuitions may influence how they wish to perceive hard-to-understand evidence, and of the limits of their ability to understand statistics. They should not accept statistical arguments they do not fully understand simply because the arguments are consistent with a result that seems justified on other grounds. While judges must come to grips with any statistical evidence offered, they need not resolve all conflicts in the evidence to reach their decisions, and when they cannot resolve statistical conflicts, they risk the legitimacy of their decisions to pretend they have. If resolving a statistical conflict is so central to the decision that it also risks legitimacy to leave the issue unresolved, the court should reopen the hearing to seek further clarification of the issues by the parties or, in appropriate cases, it should seek help from a neutral expert. Hiring law clerks with strong statistical backgrounds is also not unwise, although relying on clerks who know more statistics than the judge but whose backgrounds do not extend beyond a course or two may exacerbate rather than alleviate problems.

I have laid out a full agenda for courts, academics, and others concerned with Title VII litigation. Since I do not specialize in Title VII litigation, I am not the appropriate person to write on these issues. As with my criticism of judges who have done their best to resolve difficult cases, raising questions is easy. As with the actual business of judging, answering the questions I pose is difficult. The law of Title VII is not always clear, and even when it appears clear its statistical implications may be hazy. Moreover, we are likely to make little progress if we expect statistical evidence to answer precisely the questions Title VII suits raise. But all the law requires in a Title VII cases is a probabilistic answer, a determination whether illegal discrimination is more likely than not. Probabilities are of course the province of statistics. While statistical evidence will not necessarily provide unequivocal answers, if handled well it is often the best available evidence that bears on the likelihood of discrimination. Courts hearing Title VII cases cannot avoid statistical evidence, and if they could they would not want to, for discrimination often leaves statistical tracks. To do justice, judges must perceive these tracks when they are there and realize when they are absent. Sometimes this is difficult, even for professional statisticians. So it is no wonder that in some cases statistics seem to obscure more than they illuminate, or that in reading Title VII cases, it is easy to find judges who appear befuddled. Many of the cases I read are, however, unlike the cases I discuss, in that judges seem to handle the statistical evidence well. Thus I do not despair of judges confronted with statistical evidence. More often than not, they get things right. The challenge to judges and the purpose of this paper is to increase the probability that this will happen.

Notes

1. One reason is that trial judges may pose questions to the parties' statistical experts, and they can appoint their own "neutral" experts if they wish.

2. I shall refer to the random binomial model simply as the "random model" in the discussion that follows.

3. In the criminal context, Thompson and Schumann call this the prosecutor's fallacy.

4. *Hazelwood* 309, note 14.

5. In *Castenada* the Court was dealing with a "key man" system of jury selection, and it did not hold that such systems were *prima facie* unconstitutional. Even in the key man system, however, the Court's normative model of jury selection is still one that yields a representative cross section of the community or something close to it.

6. In some circumstances they probably would be, for disparities may be so great given what we know about the distribution of skills that it is implausible to believe that such large disparities could exist absent discrimination. In these circumstances, however, even simple statistical analyses such as standard deviation disparities would probably not be needed to make out the plaintiff's case. See, e.g., *International Brotherhood of Teamsters v. United States*, 431 U.S. 324 (1977).

7. The justice who wrote *Hazelwood* would probably have expected a figure of one in twenty rather than one in forty, for it seems that the Court set a two standard deviation threshold because it associated this with the .05 probability level which is a conventional (if sometimes poorly used) marker of statistical significance in the social sciences. But the association between disparities of two standard deviations and a .05 significance level exists only when two-tailed tests of significance are appropriate. Because in Title VII cases we are typically concerned only with the underrepresentation of protected group members, a one-tailed test, which implies a standard deviation disparity of 1.65, is arguably often appropriate. Courts, however, sometimes reject one-tailed tests as if they suspected statistical experts of rigging data. If one-tailed tests are accepted, as they sometimes should be, and the probabilities associated with two-tailed disparities of two or three standard deviations maintained, the probabilities of chance giving rise to crucial disparities should be doubled. The point made in the text remains, however, the same, namely, that there is a meaningful difference between the two standards that the Court tosses off as if the difference between what they entail were inconsequential.

8. Often it will not, for when there is serious systematic discrimination and even moderately large samples, deviations from random selection models are likely to exceed even three standard deviations.

9. C.F.R. 1607.4(d) 1982.

10. The coefficient on the gender variable indicated that other factors being equal female faculty earned $694 less than the overall mean, while male faculty earned $694 more.

11. The defendants helped foster this illusion by presenting just two models, one with only legitimate variables and another with the legitimate variables plus gender, and comparing the variance explained by the two models. The court's impressions might have been different had the defense presented a single forward step-wise regression, which might have suggested that gender was a more important predictor of salary than were a number of the legitimate variables.

12. As Lincoln Moses, commenting on an earlier version of this chapter observed, the focus on explained variance amounts to assessing whether the two groups have different means even after taking (linear) account of experience, education, age, etc. It is really not about variance.

13. The sentence quoted in the text continues, "thus, there has been no showing that the incremen-

tal contribution of sex to the variation explained by the University's models is understated because part of its influence has been erroneously attributed to the other independent variables."

14. The court seems confused here. It writes, "plaintiffs did not introduce evidence that the value of the coefficient of the sex variable is significant notwithstanding the fact that only .8% more of the total variation was explained when sex was added into the model." Yet earlier the court had written, " a t statistic test demonstrates that the coefficient for the sex variable is significant." What the court probably means by the language quoted first is that the plaintiff did not explicitly show that adding sex to the other variables in the defense model yielded a statistically significant increase in explained variance, but the fact that gender makes a real contribution within the context of the model is implicit in the statistical significance of its coefficient.

15. Since this was an appellate court, it could not ask for new evidence. It may be that a correlation matrix for the equation's variables was somewhere in the statistical record below, but the full record might not have been transmitted to the court, or the court might not have appreciated what it had.

16. I am not saying that plaintiffs should avoid testing their models for sensitivity to specification bias.

17. Since the legal burden on employers is to hire without regard to race, "hiring without regard to race" is what the term "race-neutral" should mean. Otherwise the statistic is not addressing the issue the court must resolve. There is a danger that experts and courts will understand language differently, which requires care to avoid.

18. Because of the correlation between neighborhood hiring preferences and employee race, such preferences might not be allowed under the Civil Rights Act since they could be a subterfuge to avoid the act. This would not, however, make a good-faith application of a neighborhood residence preference race-regarding.

19. One of these women received an application after saying that her father was a salaried employee of the mine.

20. See, e.g., *Allen v. Prince George's County, Maryland*, 737 F.2d 1299 (1984), which approves the lower court's rejection of regression results showing that in 1980 blacks were paid on average $1,500 less than similarly qualified white employees. In justification, *Allen* cites two possible flaws that almost certainly would not have undermined the implications of discrimination and the fact that regression analyses are "extremely complicated". *E.E.O.C. v. Jordan Graphics, Inc.*, 769 F. Supp. 1357 (W.D.N.C. 1991) concludes that a disparity of 3.19 standard deviations between the "number" of blacks hired and the "number" available for hiring (I assume the court is really speaking of proportions), was insufficient to establish a *prima facie* showing of discrimination because (citing precedent), "a standard deviation less than one full standard deviation over the threshold of three (3) set by *Federal Reserve Bank of Richmond* was insignificant." *E.E.O.C. v. Federal Reserve Bank of Richmond* 698 F.2d 633 (1983) shows considerable confusion over the justifications for one-tailed tests and wrongly rejects one-tailed test statistics. *Bank of Richmond* may be contrasted with *Palmer v. Schultz*, 815 F.2d 84 (D.C. Cir. 1987), which has a good discussion of the difference between one-tailed and two-tailed tests and correctly rejects a one-tailed test due to subtle characteristics of the claim advanced. However, *Palmer* goes on, incorrectly in my view, to reject one-tailed tests generally in Title VII litigation.

Bibliography

Publications

Aleinikoff, T. Alexander. 1992. "The Constitution in Context: The Continuing Significance of Racism." *University of Colorado Law Review* 63: 325–73.

Amaker, Norman. 1988. *Civil Rights and the Reagan Administration*. Washington, DC: Urban Institute Press.

Anderson, J. W. 1964. *Eisenhower, Brownell and the Congress: The Tangled Origins of the Civil Rights Bill of 1956–1957*. Tuscaloosa: Univ. of Alabama Press.

Appiah, K. Anthony, and Amy Gutmann. 1996. *Color Conscious: The Political Morality of Race*. Princeton: Princeton Univ. Press.

Arias, M. Beatriz, and Ursula Cassanova, eds. 1993. *Bilingual Education: Politics, Practice, and Research*. Chicago: Univ. of Chicago Press.

Ashenfelter, Orley, and Ronald Oaxaca. 1987. "The Economics of Discrimination: Economists Enter the Courtroom." *American Economic Review* 77: 321–25.

Ashmore, Harry S. 1994. *Civil Rights and Wrongs: A Memoir of Race and Politics, 1944–1994*. New York: Pantheon.

Baldus, D., and J. Cole. 1986 Supplement. *Statistical Proof of Discrimination*. Colorado Springs: Shepard's/McGraw-Hill.

Barnett, V. 1982. *Comparative Statistical Inference*. 2d ed. Chichester, NY: John Wiley & Sons.

Baron, James N. 1992. "Organizational Evidence of Ascription in Labor Markets." In *New Approaches to Economic and Social Analyses of Discrimination*, ed. Richard Cornwall and P. W. Wunnava, 113–43. Westport, CT: Praeger.

Bass, Jack. 1981. *Unlikely Heroes: The Dramatic Story of the Southern Judges Who Translated the Supreme Court's Brown Decision into a Revolution for Equality*. New York: Touchstone.

Baumgartner, Frank, and Bryan Jones. 1993. *Agendas and Instability in American Politics*. Chicago: Univ. of Chicago Press.

Beckley, Gloria T., and Paul Burstein. 1991. "Religious Pluralism, Equal Opportunity, and the State." *Western Political Quarterly* 44: 185–208.

Belton, Robert. 1990. "The Dismantling of the Griggs Disparate Impact Theory and the Future of Title VII." *Yale Law and Policy Review* 8: 223–56.

———. 1993. "The Unfinished Agenda of the Civil Rights Act of 1991." *Rutgers Law Review* 45: 921–64.

Belz, Herman. 1991. *Equality Transformed: A Quarter-Century of Affirmative Action*. New Brunswick, NJ: Transaction Publishers.

Bergmann, Barbara R. 1986. *The Economic Emergence of Women.* New York: Basic Books.

———. 1996. *In Defense of Affirmative Action.* New York: Basic Books.

Berkowitz, Edward D. 1987. *Disabled Policy: America's Programs for the Handicapped.* New York: Cambridge Univ. Press.

———. 1994. "A Historical Preface to the Americans with Disabilities Act." *Journal of Policy History* 6: 96–119.

Black, Earl, and Merle Black. 1992. *The Vital South: How Presidents Are Elected.* Cambridge: Harvard Univ. Press.

Bloch, Farrell. 1994. *Anti-Discrimination Law and Minority Employment: Recruitment Practices and Regulatory Constraints.* Chicago: Univ. of Chicago Press.

Bloom, Allan. 1987. *The Closing of the American Mind.* New York: Simon and Schuster.

Blumrosen, Alfred W. 1972. "Strangers in Paradise: *Griggs v. Duke Power Co.* and the Concept of Employment Discrimination." *Michigan Law Review* 71: 59–110.

———. 1984. "The Law Transmission System and the Southern Jurisprudence of Employment Discrimination." *Industrial Relations Law Journal* 6: 313–52.

———. 1993. *Modern Law: The Law Transmission System and Equal Employment Opportunity.* Madison: Univ. of Wisconsin Press.

Bobo, Lawrence. 1983. "Whites' Opposition to Busing: Symbolic Racism or Realistic Group Conflict?" *Journal of Personality and Social Psychology* 45 (6): 1196–210.

———. 1986. "Group Conflict, Prejudice, and the Paradox of Contemporary Racial Attitudes." In *Eliminating Racism: Means and Controversies,* ed. P. A. Katz and D. A. Taylor. New York: Plenum Press.

Bound, John, and Richard Freeman. 1989. "Black Economic Progress: Erosion of the Post-1960s Gains in the 1980s?" In *The Question of Discrimination,* ed. S. Shulman and W. Darity, Jr. Middletown, CT: Wesleyan Univ. Press.

Brauer, Carl M. 1983. "Women Activists, Southern Conservatives, and the Prohibition of Sex Discrimination in Title VIII of the 1964 Civil Rights Act." *Journal of Southern History* 49: 37–56.

Bronfenbrenner, Martin. 1973. "Equality and Equity." *The Annals, AAPSS* 409 (September): 9–23.

Brooke, Edward W. 1966. *The Challenge of Change: Crisis in Our Two Party System.* Boston: Little, Brown.

Brown, Colin, and Pat Gay. 1985. *Racial Discrimination: Seventeen Years After the Act.* London: Policy Studies Institute.

Brown, Eleanor Marie. 1995. "The Tower of Babel: Bridging the Divide between Critical Race Theory and 'Mainstream' Civil Rights Scholarship." *Yale Law Journal* 105: 513–47.

Brown, Peter A. 1991. "Ms. Quota." *New Republic* 15 April, 18–19.

Brownell, Herbert, with John P. Burke. 1993. *Advising Ike: The Memoirs of Attorney General Herbert Brownell.* Lawrence, KS: Univ. of Kansas Press.

Brown-Scott, Wendy. 1994. "Race Consciousness in Higher Education: Does 'Sound Educational Policy' Support the Continued Existence of Historically Black Colleges?" *Emory Law Journal* 43: 1–81.

Bumiller, Kristin. 1988. *The Civil Rights Society: The Social Construction of Victims.* Baltimore: Johns Hopkins Univ. Press.

Bureau of National Affairs. 1964. *The Civil Rights Act of 1964.* Washington, DC: Bureau of National Affairs.

Burstein, Paul. 1985. *Discrimination, Jobs, and Politics: The Struggle for Equal Employment Opportunity in the United States since the New Deal.* Chicago: Univ. of Chicago Press.

———. 1990. "Intergroup Conflict, Law, and the Concept of Labor Market Discrimination." *Sociological Forum* 5: 459–76.

———. 1991a. "Legal Mobilization as a Social Movement Tactic: The Struggle for Equal Employment Opportunity." *American Journal of Sociology* 96: 1201–25.

———. 1991b. "'Reverse Discrimination' Cases in the Federal Courts." *Sociological Quarterly* 32: 511–28.

———. 1992. "Affirmative Action, Jobs, and American Democracy." *Law and Society Review* 26: 901–22.

———. 1993. "Affirmative Action and the Rhetoric of Reaction." *The American Prospect* 14 (summer): 138–47.

———, ed. 1994. *Equal Employment Opportunity.* New York: Aldine de Gruyter.

Burstein, Paul, and Mark Evan Edwards. 1994. "The Impact of Employment Discrimination Litigation on Racial Disparity in Earnings." *Law and Society Review* 28: 79–111.

Burstein, Paul, Marie Bricher, and Rachel Einwohner. 1995. "Political Alternatives and Policy Change." *American Sociological Review* 60: 67–83.

Button, James W. 1989. 2d ed. *Blacks and Social Change: Impact of the Civil Rights Movement in Southern Communities.* Princeton: Princeton Univ. Press.

Cain, Glen G. 1986. "The Economic Analysis of Labor Market Discrimination: A Survey." In *The Handbook of Labor Economics,* vol. 1, ed. Orley Ashenfelter and R. Layard, 694–785. New York: Elsevier.

Card, David, and Alan B. Krueger. 1993. "Trends in Relative Black-White Earnings Revisited." *American Economic Review* 83: 85–91.

Carlson, Susan M. 1992. "Trends in Race/Sex Occupational Inequality: Conceptual and Measurement Issues." *Social Problems* 39: 268–85.

Carmines, Edward G., and James A. Stimson. 1989. *Issue Evolution.* Princeton: Princeton Univ. Press.

Carmines, Edward G., and W. Richard Merriman, Jr. 1993. "The Changing American Dilemma: Liberal Values and Racial Policies." In *Prejudice, Politics, and the American Dilemma,* ed. P. M. Sniderman, P. E. Tetlock, and E. G. Carmines, 237–55. Stanford: Stanford Univ. Press.

Carrigington, Paul D. 1992. "Diversity!" *Utah Law Review,* 191–209.

Carter, Stephen L. 1993. "The Black Table, the Empty Seat, and the Tie." In *Lure and Loathing,* ed. Gerald Early, 55–79. New York: Penguin.

Casper, Jonathan D. 1972. *Lawyers before the Warren Court: Civil Liberties and Civil Rights, 1957–66.* Urbana: Univ. of Illinois Press.

Cathcart, David A. 1991. *The Civil Rights Act of 1991.* Philadelphia: American Law Institute–American Bar Association.

Chafe, William H. 1981. *Civilities and Civil Rights: Greensboro, North Carolina and the Black Struggle for Freedom.* New York: Oxford Univ. Press.

Citizens Commission on Civil Rights. 1982. *"There Is No Liberty . . .": Congressional Efforts to Curb the Federal Courts and to Undermine the Brown Decision.*

Cobb, Roger W., and Charles D. Elder. 1972. *Participation in American Politics: The Dynamics of Agenda Bulding.* Boston: Allyn and Bacon.

Cobb, Roger W., Jennie-Keith Ross, and Marc Howard Ross. 1976. "Agenda Building as a

Comparative Political Process." *American Political Science Review* 70: 126–38.

Cohen, Susan, and Mary Fainsod Katzenstein. 1988. "The War over the Family Is Not over the Family." In *Feminism, Children, and the New Families,* ed. Sanford M. Dornbusch and Myra H. Strober. New York: Guilford Press.

Combs, Michael. 1984. "The Federal Judiciary and Northern School Desegregation: Law, Politics, and Judicial Management." Paper presented to American Political Science Association.

Congressional Quarterly. 1965. *Congress and the Nation, 1945–1964.* Washington, DC: Congressional Quarterly Press.

Converse, Phillip E., Warren E. Miller, Jerrold C. Rusk, and Arthur C. Wolfe. 1969. "Continuity and Change in American Politics: Parties and Issues in the 1968 Election." *American Political Science Review* 63: 1085–1105.

Cortner, Richard D. 1968. "Strategies and Tactics of Litigants in Constitutional Cases." *Journal of Public Law* 17: 287–307.

Costain, Anne N., and W. Douglas Costain. 1985. "Congressional Response to Women's Movement Issues, 1900–1982." *Congress and the Presidency* 12: 21–42.

Coulam, R. F., and S. E. Fienberg. 1986. "The Use of Court Appointed Statistical Experts: A Case Study in Statistics and the Law." In *Statistics and the Law,* ed. M. H. DeGroot, S. E. Fienberg, and J. B. Kadane. New York: J. Wiley and Sons.

Cover, Robert. 1975. *Justice Accused: Anti-Slavery and the Judicial Process.* New Haven: Yale Univ. Press.

Danielson, Michael. 1976. *The Politics of Exclusion.* New York: Columbia Univ. Press.

Danziger, Sheldon, and Peter Gottschalk, eds. 1992. *Uneven Tides: Rising Inequality in America.* New York: Russell Sage Foundation.

Davidson, Chandler. 1994. "The Recent Evolution of Voting Rights Law Affecting Racial and Language Minorities." In *Quiet Revolution in the South: The Impact of the Voting Rights Act, 1965–1990,* ed. C. Davidson and B. Grofman, 21–37. Princeton: Princeton Univ. Press.

Davidson, Chandler, and Bernard Grofman. 1994. *Quiet Revolution in the South: The Impact of the Voting Rights Act, 1965–1990.* Princeton: Princeton Univ. Press.

Davis, Robert N. 1994. "Diversity: The Emerging Modern Separate but Equal Doctrine." *William and Mary Journal of Women and the Law* 1: 11–30.

Dent, Harry. 1978. *The Prodigal South Returns to Power.* New York: J. Wiley and Sons.

Dentler, Robert A., D. Catherine Baltzell, and Daniel J. Sullivan. 1983. *University on Trial: The Case of the University of North Carolina.* Cambridge, MA: Apt Books.

Derthick, Martha, and Paul J. Quirk. 1985. *The Politics of Deregulation.* Washington, DC: Brookings Institution.

Detlefsen, Robert R. 1991. *Civil Rights under Reagan.* San Francisco: Institute for Contemporary Studies.

———. 1993. "Affirmative Action and Business Deregulation: On the Reagan Administration's Failure to Revise Executive Order No. 11246." *Policy Studies Journal* 21: 556–64.

Dionne, E. J., Jr. 1991. *Why Americans Hate Politics.* New York: Simon and Schuster.

Dobbin, Frank, John R. Sutton, John W. Meyer, and W. Richard Scott. 1993. "Equal Opportunity Law and the Construction of Internal Labor Markets." *American Journal of Sociology* 99: 396–427.

Donohue, John J., III, and James Heckman. 1991. "Continuous versus Episodic Change: The Impact of Civil Rights Policy on the Economic Status of Blacks." *Journal of Economic Literature* 29: 1603–43.

Donovan, Robert J. 1964. *The Future of the Republican Party.* New York: New American Library.

Dowden, Sue, and John P. Robinson. 1993. "Age and Cohort Differences in American Racial Attitudes: The Generational Replacement Hypothesis Revisited." In *Prejudice, Politics, and the American Dilemma,* ed. P. M. Sniderman, P. E. Tetlock, and E. G. Carmines, 86–103. Stanford: Stanford Univ. Press.

Dworkin, Anthony, and Rosalind Dworkin. 1982. *The Minority Report: An Introduction to Racial, Ethnic, and Gender Relations.* 2d ed. New York: Holt, Rinehart and Winston.

Dworkin, Ronald. 1977. *Taking Rights Seriously.* Cambridge: Harvard Univ. Press.

———. 1983. "Why Liberals Should Believe in Equality." *New York Review of Books,* 3 February.

Edelman, Lauren B. 1992. "Legal Ambiguity and Symbolic Structures: Organizational Mediation of Civil Rights Law." *American Journal of Sociology* 97: 1531–76.

Edsall, Thomas Byrne, with Mary Edsall. 1991. *Chain Reaction: The Impact of Race, Rights, and Taxes on American Politics.* New York: Norton.

Ehrenberg, Ronald, and Robert Smith. 1991. *Modern Labor Economics.* 4th ed. New York: Harper Collins.

Eisenberg, Theodore. 1991. *Civil Rights Legislation: Cases and Materials.* 3d ed. Charlottesville, VA: Michie Co.

Eisner, Marc Allen. 1993. *Regulatory Politics in Transition.* Baltimore: Johns Hopkins Univ. Press.

Epstein, Cynthia Fuchs. 1988. *Deceptive Distinctions.* New Haven: Yale Univ. Press.

Epstein, Lee. 1985. *Conservatives in Court.* Knoxville: Univ. of Tennessee Press.

Epstein, Richard. 1992. *Forbidden Grounds: The Case against Employment Discrimination Laws.* Cambridge: Harvard Univ. Press.

Eskridge, William N., Jr. 1991. "Overriding Supreme Court Statutory Interpretation Decisions." *Yale Law Review* 101 (November): 331–455.

Fairfax, Jean. 1978. "Current Status of the Adams Case: Implications for Blacks and Other Minorities." In *Beyond Desegregation: Urgent Issues in the Education of Minorities,* 36–46. Papers from the series of seminars on critical problems and issues in education of minorities. New York: The College Entrance Examination Board.

Farkas, George, Paula England, Keven Vicknair, and Barbara Stanek Kilbourne. 1994. "Skill, Skill Demands of Jobs, and Earnings Among Euro-American, African-American, and Mexican-American Workers." Unpublished paper, University of Texas at Dallas (earlier version presented at the 1992 annual meeting of the American Sociological Association).

Farley, Reynolds, and Walter R. Allen. 1987. *The Color Line and the Quality of Life in America.* New York: Russell Sage Foundation.

Feagin, Joe, and Melvin P. Sikes. 1994. *Living with Racism: The Black Middle-Class Experience.* Boston: Beacon.

Featherman, David, and Robert Hauser. 1978. *Opportunity and Change.* New York: Academic Press.

Federal Bureau of Investigation. 1994. *Hate Crime Statistics 1992.* Washington, DC: U.S. Department of Justice.

Ferguson, Ronald F. 1995. "Shifting Challenges: Fifty Years of Economic Change toward Black-White Earnings Equality." *Daedalus* 124: 37–76.

Fienberg, Stephen E., ed. 1989. *The Evolving Role of Statistical Assessments as Evidence in the Courts.* Committee on National Statistics and Committee on Research on Law Enforcement and the Administration of Justice; National Research Council. New York: Springer-Verlag.

Finkelstein, Michael O., and Bruce Levin. 1990. *Statistics for Lawyers.* New York: Springer-Verlag.

Fiscus, Ronald J. 1992. *The Constitutional Logic of Affirmative Action,* ed. Stephen L. Wasby. Durham: Duke Univ. Press.

Fishel, Jeff. 1973. *Party and Opposition.* New York: David McKay.

Fisher, Anne B. 1985. "Businessmen Like to Hire by the Numbers." *Fortune* 16 September.

Fisher, Franklin M. 1980. "Multiple Regression in Legal Proceedings." *Columbia Law Review* 80: 702–36.

FitzGerald, Frances. 1979. *America Revised.* Boston: Little, Brown.

Fleming, Jeanne J. 1988. "Public Opinion on Change in Women's Rights and Roles." In *Feminism, Children, and the New Families,* ed. Sanford Dornbusch and Myra Strober, 47–66. New York: Guilford Press.

Foner, Eric. 1988. *Reconstruction: America's Unfinished Revolution, 1863–1877.* New York: Harper.

Fossett, Mark A., and K. Jill Kiecolt. 1989. "The Relative Size of Minority Populations and White Racial Attitudes." *Social Science Quarterly* 70 (4): 820–35.

Fraga, Luis Ricardo. 1992. "Self-Determination, Cultural Pluralism, and Politics." *National Political Science Review* 3: 132–36.

Fraga, Luis Ricardo, and Bari Elizabeth Anhalt. 1993. "Ethnic Politics, Public Policy, and the Public Interest." Paper presented at the annual meeting of the American Political Science Association, Washington, DC, 2–5 Sept.

Frammolino, Ralph, Mark Gladstone, and Henry Weinstein. 1996. "Admission Rules at UCLA Eased for Rich." *Los Angeles Times* 21 March.

Freeman, Jo. 1975. *The Politics of Women's Liberation.* New York: Longman.

Fried, Charles. 1991. *Order and the Law: Arguing the Reagan Revolution.* New York: Simon and Shuster.

Fuchs, Lawrence H. 1990. *American Kaleidoscope: Race, Ethnicity, and the Civil Culture.* Middletown, CT: Wesleyan Univ. Press.

Gamson, William A., and A. Modigliani. 1987. "The Changing Culture of Affirmative Action." In *Research in Political Sociology,* vol. 3, ed. R. D. Braungart, 137–77. Greenwich, CT: Jai Press.

Giles, Micheal W. 1975. "HEW versus the Federal Courts: A Comparison of Southern Desegregation Enforcement." *American Politics Quarterly* 3 (January): 81–87.

———. 1977. "Percent Black and Racial Hostility: An Old Assumption Reexamined." *Social Science Quarterly* 58: 412–17.

Giles, Micheal W., and Arthur Evans. 1986. "The Power Approach to Intergroup Hostility." *Journal of Conflict Resolution* 30: 469–85.

Giles, Micheal W., and Kaenan Hertz. 1994. "Racial Threat and Partisan Identification." *American Political Science Review* 88 (2): 317–26.

Giles, Micheal W., and Melanie Buckner. 1993. "David Duke and Black Threat: An Old Hypothesis Revisited." *Journal of Politics* 55: 702–13.

Gillette, William. 1979. *Retreat from Reconstruction, 1869–1879.* Baton Rouge: Louisiana State Univ. Press.

Gitlin, Todd. 1995. *The Twilight of Common Dreams: Why America Is Wracked by Culture Wars.* New York: Holt.

Glaser, James M. 1994. "Back to the Black Belt: Racial Environment and White Racial Attitudes in the South." *Journal of Politics* 56 (1): 21–41.

Glazer, Nathan. 1978. *Affirmative Discrimination.* New York: Basic Books.

———. 1983. "The Politics of a Multiethnic Society." In *Ethnic Dilemmas 1964–82,* ed. N. Glazer. Cambridge: Harvard Univ. Press.

———. 1995. "Race, Not Class." *Wall Street Journal* 5 April.

Glennon, Robert Jerome. 1991. "The Role of Law in the Civil Rights Movement: The Montgomery Bus Boycott, 1955–1957." *Law and History Review* 9 (spring): 59–112.

Gold, Michael Evan. 1985. "Griggs' Folly: An Essay on the Theory, Problems, and Origins of the Adverse Impact Definition of Employment Discrimination, and a Recommendation for Reform." *Industrial Relations Labor Journal* 7: 429–598.

Goldin, Claudia. 1990. *Understanding the Gender Gap.* New York: Oxford Univ. Press.

Goldstein, Leslie Friedman. 1989. *The Constitutional Rights of Women.* Madison: Univ. of Wisconsin Press.

Gordon, Milton. 1964. *Assimilation in American Life.* New York: Oxford Univ. Press.

———. 1985a. "Assimilation in America: Theory and Reality." In *Majority and Minority: The Dynamics of Race and Ethnicity in American Life,* 4th ed., ed. Norman Yetman. Boston: Allyn and Bacon.

———. 1985b. "Models of Pluralism: The New American Dilemma." In *Majority and Minority: The Dynamics of Race and Ethnicity in American Life,* 4th ed., ed. Norman Yetman. Boston: Allyn and Bacon.

Graham, Hugh Davis. 1990. *The Civil Rights Era: Origins and Development of National Policy 1960–1972.* New York: Oxford Univ. Press.

———. 1992. *Civil Rights and the Presidency.* New York: Oxford Univ. Press.

———. 1993. "Voting Rights and the American Regulatory State." In Bernard Grofman and Chandler Davidson, eds., *Controversies in Minority Voting: The Voting Rights Act in Perspective.* Washington, DC: Brookings Institution.

———. 1998. "The Storm over Grove City College." History of Education Quarterly 38: 407–29.

Greenberg, Jack. 1968. "The Supreme Court, Civil Rights and Civil Dissonance." *Yale Law Journal* 77: 1520–44.

———. 1994. *Crusaders in the Courts.* New York: Harper Collins.

Grofman, Bernard. 1995. "*Shaw v. Reno* and the Future of Voting Rights." PS 28: 27–36.

———, ed. 1998. *Race and Redistricting in the 1990s.* New York: Agathon Press.

Grofman, Bernard, and Chandler Davidson, eds. 1992. *Controversies in Minority Voting: The Voting Rights Act in Perspective.* Washington, DC: Brookings Institution.

Grofman, Bernard, and Lisa Handley. 1998. "Estimating the Impact of Voting-Rights-Related Districting on Democratic Strength in the U.S. House of Representatives." In *Race and Redistricting in the 1990s,* ed. Bernard Grofman. New York: Agathon Press.

Gross, Samuel R. 1991. "Expert Evidence." *Wisconsin Law Review* 6: 1113–232.

Grossman, Joel B., and Stephen L. Wasby. 1971. "Haynsworth and Parker: History Does Live Again." *South Carolina Law Review* 23 (April): 345–59.

Guinier, Lani. 1991a. "No Two Seats: The Elusive Quest for Political Equality." *Virginia Law Review* 77: 1413–514.

———. 1991b. "The Triumph of Tokenism: The Voting Rights Act and the Theory of Black Electoral Success." *University of Michigan Law Review* 89: 1077–154.

———. 1996. "The Need for a National Conversation on Race." Remarks at the "E Pluribus Unum" Conference, Program in Chicano Studies, Stanford University, 10–12 Feb.

Gunderson, Morley. 1989. "Male-Female Wage Differentials and Policy Responses," *Journal of Economic Literature* 27: 46–72.

Gurr, Ted Robert. 1993. *Minorities at Risk: A Global View of Ethnopolitical Conflicts.* Washington, DC: United States Institute of Peace.

Gutmann, Amy. 1996. "Responding to Racial Injustice." In *Color Conscious: The Political Morality of Race,* ed. K. Anthony Appiah and Amy Gutmann, 106–78. Princeton: Princeton Univ. Press.

Hacker, Andrew. 1992. *Two Nations: Black and White, Separate, Hostile, Unequal.* New York: Scribner's.

Haldeman, H. R. 1994. *The Haldeman Diaries: Inside the Nixon White House.* New York: G.P. Putnam's Sons.

Halpern, Stephen C. 1980. "Title VI and Racial Discrimination in Educational Institutions." Paper presented to the American Political Science Association.

———. 1995. *On the Limits of the Law: The Ironic Legacy of Title VI of the 1964 Civil Rights Act.* Baltimore: Johns Hopkins Univ. Press.

Handler, Joel F. 1978. *Social Movements and the Legal System: A Theory of Law Reform and Social Change.* New York: Academic Press.

Harris, Cheryl I. 1993. "Whiteness as Property." *Harvard Law Review* 106 (8): 1709–91.

Harrison, Cynthia. 1988. *On Account of Sex: the Politics of Women's Issues 1945–1968.* Berkeley: Univ. of California Press.

Hatch, Orrin. 1980. "Loading the Economy." *Policy Review* 12: 23–37.

Hawkins, Chuck. 1993. "Denny's: The Stain That Isn't Coming Out: Can a Pact with the NAACP Help It Overcome Charges of Bias?" *Business Week,* 28 June, 98–99.

Haynes, Leonard L., III. 1981. "The Adams Mandate: A Format for Achieving Equal Educational Opportunity and Attainment." In *Black Students in Higher Education,* ed. Gail E. Thomas, 329–35. Westport, CT: Greenwood Press.

Heatherington, Marc. J. 1998. "The Political Relevance of Political Trust." *American Political Science Review* 92: 791–808.

Heckman, James, and Brook S. Payner. 1989. "Determining the Impact of Federal Anti-discrimination Policy on the Economic Status of Blacks: A Study of South Carolina." *American Economic Review* 79: 138–77.

Heinz, John P., Edward O. Laumann, Robert L. Nelson, and Robert H. Salisbury. 1993. *The Hollow Core: Private Interests in National Policy Making.* Cambridge: Harvard Univ. Press.

Hersch, Joni. 1991. "Equal Employment Opportunity Law and Firm Profitability." *Journal of Human Resources* 26: 139–53.

Higginbotham, A. Leon, Jr. 1997. "Foreword." In *Voting: Hopes or Fears?,* ed. Keith Reeves, xiii–xv. New York and London: Oxford Univ. Press.

Hochschild, Jennifer L. 1995. *Facing Up to the American Dream: Race, Class, and the Soul of the Nation.* Princeton: Princeton Univ. Press.

Hollinger, David A. 1995. *Postethnic America.* New York: Basic Books.

Holmes, O. W., Jr. 1881, 1963. *The Common Law.* Cambridge: Harvard Univ. Press.

Holmes, Steven A. 1991. "Affirmative Action Plans Are Part of Business Life." *New York Times,* 22 November.

Horowitz, Donald L. 1985. *Ethnic Groups in Conflict.* Berkeley: Univ. of California Press.

Horowitz, Irving Louis. 1992. *Taking Lives: Genocide and State Power.* New Brunswick, NJ: Transaction Books.

Huckfeldt, Robert, and Carol Weitzel Kohfeld. 1989. *Race and the Decline of Class in American Politics.* Urbana and Chicago: Univ. of Illinois Press.

Humphrey, Hubert H. 1976. *The Education of a Public Man.* Garden City, NY: Doubleday.

Jackman, Mary, and Michael J. Muha. 1984. "Education and Inter-group Attitudes: Moral Enlightenment, Superficial Democratic Commitment, or Ideological Refinement." *American Sociological Review* 49: 93–102.

Jacobson, Cardell K. 1985. "Resistance to Affirmative Action: Self-Interest or Racism?" *Journal of Conflict Resolution* 29: 306–29.

Jaynes, Gerald D., and Robin M. Williams, Jr., eds. 1989. *A Common Destiny: Blacks and American Society.* Washington, DC: Committee on the Status of Black Americans, Commission on Behavioral and Social Sciences, National Academy Press.

Jeffrey, Julie Roy. 1978. *Education for Children of the Poor: A Study of the Origins and Implementation of the Elementary and Secondary Education Act of 1965.* Columbus, OH: Ohio State Univ. Press.

Jencks, Christopher. 1985. "Affirmative Action for Blacks: Past, Present, and Future." *American Behavioral Scientist* 28: 731–60.

Jencks, Christopher, et al. 1979. *Who Gets Ahead?* New York: Basic Books.

Johnson, Lyndon B. 1971. *The Vantage Point.* New York: Popular Library.

Jones, Augustus J. 1982. *Law Bureaucracy and Politics: The Implementation of Title VI of the Civil Rights Act of 1964.* Lanham, MD: Univ. Press of America.

Kadane, Joseph B. 1990. "A Statistical Analysis of Adverse Impact of Employer Decisions." *Journal of the American Statistical Association* 85: 607–14.

Kagan, Robert. 1994. "Do Lawyers Cause Adversarial Legalism? A Preliminary Inquiry." *Law and Social Inquiry* 19 (winter): 1–62.

Kahlenberg, Richard D. 1996. *The Remedy: Class, Race, and Affirmative Action.* New York: Basic Books.

Kallen, Horace M. 1924. *Culture and Democracy in the United States.* New York: Boni and Liveright.

Kalven, Harry. 1965. *The Negro and the First Amendment.* Columbus, OH: Ohio State Univ. Press.

Kay, Susan Ann. 1980. "Sex Differences in the Attitudes of a Future Elite." *Women and Politics* 1: 35–48.

Kennedy, Randall. 1997. *Race, Crime, and the Law.* New York: Random House.

Kessell, John H. 1968. *The Goldwater Coalition: Republican Strategies in 1964.* Indianapolis: Bobbs-Merrill.

Kinder, Donald R. 1986. "The Continuing American Dilemma: White Resistance to Racial Change Forty Years after Myrdal." *Journal of Social Issues* 42 (2): 151–71.

Kinder, Donald R., and David O. Sears. 1981. "Mimicking Political Debate with Survey Questions: The Case of White Opinion on Affirmative Action for Blacks." *Social Cognition* 8: 73–103.

Kinder, Donald R., and Lynn M. Sanders. 1987. "Pluralistic Foundations of American Opinion on Race." Paper presented at the annual meeting of the American Political Science Association, Chicago.

———. 1990. "Mimicking Political Debate with Survey Questions: The Case of White Opinion on Affirmative Action for Blacks." *Social Cognition* 8: 73–103.

———. 1996. *Divided by Color: Racial Politics and Democratic Ideals*. Chicago: Univ. of Chicago Press.

King, Martin Luther, Jr. 1964. *Why We Can't Wait*. New York: Signet Books.

Kinoy, Arthur. 1983. *Rights on Trial: The Odyssey of a People's Lawyer*. Cambridge: Harvard Univ. Press.

Kirp, David. 1978. "Multitudes in the Valley of Indecision: The Desegregation of San Francisco's Schools." In *Limits of Justice*, ed. Howard Kalodner and James Fishman, 411–92. Cambridge, MA: Ballinger Publishers.

———. 1982. *Just Schools: The Ideas of Racial Equality in American Education*. Berkeley: Univ. of California Press.

Kluegel, James R., and Eliot R. Smith. 1983. "Affirmative Action Attitudes: Effects of Self-Interest, Racial Affect, and Stratification Beliefs on Whites' Views." *Social Forces* 61 (3): 797–825.

———. 1986. *Beliefs about Inequality*. New York: Aldine de Gruyter.

Kluegel, James R., and Lawrence Bobo. 1993. "Dimensions of Whites' Beliefs about the Black-White Socioeconomic Gap." In *Prejudice, Politics, and the American Dilemma*, ed. P. M. Sniderman, P. E. Tetlock, and E. G. Carmines, 127–47. Stanford: Stanford Univ. Press.

———. 1993. "Opposition to Race-Targeting." *American Sociological Review* 58: 443–64.

Kousser, J. Morgan. 1986. *Dead End: The Development of Nineteenth-Century Litigation on Racial Discrimination in Schools*. Oxford: Clarendon.

———. 1988. "The Supremacy of Equal Rights: The Struggle against Racial Discrimination in Antebellum Massachusetts and the Foundations of the Fourteenth Amendment." *Northwestern University Law Review* 82: 941–1010.

———. 1991. "Before *Plessy*, before *Brown*: The Development of the Law of Racial Integration in Louisiana and Kansas." In *Toward a Usable Past: Liberty under State Constitutions*, ed. Paul Finkelman and Stephen E. Gottlieb. Athens: Univ. of Georgia Press.

———. 1992. "The Voting Rights Act and the Two Reconstructions." In *Controversies in Minority Voting*, ed. Bernard Grofman and Chandler Davidson. Washington, DC: Brookings Institution.

Kuklinski, James H., and T. Wayne Parent. 1981. "Race and Big Government: Contamination in Measuring Racial Attitudes." *Political Methodology* 7: 131–59.

Kuper, Leo. 1985. *The Prevention of Genocide*. New Haven: Yale Univ. Press.

Kurland, Phillip, and Gerhard Casper, eds. 1975. *Sixty Landmark Briefs and Arguments of the Supreme Court of the United States: Constitutional Law*. Bethesda, MD: Washington Univ. Publications of America.

LaNoue, George R., and John C. Sullivan. 1994. "Presumptions for Preferences: The Small Business Administration's Decisions on Groups Entitled to Affirmative Action." *Journal of Policy History* 6: 439–67.

Lawrence, Charles R. 1995. "Forward: Race, Multiculturalism, and the Jurisprudence of Transformation." *Stanford Law Review* 47: 819–47.

Lawrence, Charles R., and Mari J. Matsuda, eds. 1997. *We Won't Go Back: Making the Case for Affirmative Action*. New York: Houghton Mifflin.

Lawyers Committee for Civil Rights under Law. 1965, 1978. *Annual Report*.

Lempert, Richard. 1988. "'Between Cup and Lip': Social Sciences Influences on Law and Policy." *Law and Policy* 10: 167–200.

Leonard, Jonathan. 1984. "Anti-discrimination or Reverse Discrimination: The Impact of

Changing Demographics, Title VII, and Affirmative Action on Productivity." *Journal of Human Resources* 19: 145–74.

———. 1989. "Women and Affirmative Action." *Journal of Economic Perspectives* 3: 61–75.

———. 1990. "The Impact of Affirmative Action Regulation and Equal Employment Law on Black Employment." *Journal of Economic Perspectives* 4: 47–63.

Lerman, Lisa G. 1978. "Discrimination in Access to Public Places: A Survey of State and Federal Public Accommodations Laws." *New York University Review of Law and Social Change* 7 (2): 215–311.

Lesher, Stephen. 1994. *George Wallace, American Populist.* Reading, MA: Addison Wesley.

Lieberson, Stanley. 1980. *A Piece of the Pie.* Berkeley: Univ. of California Press.

Lind, Michael. 1995. *The Next American Nation: The New Nationalism and the Fourth American Revolution.* New York: Free Press.

Lindblom, Charles E. 1977. *Politics and Markets.* New York: Basic Books.

Lipset, Seymour Martin. 1992. "Affirmative Action and the American Creed." *Wilson Quarterly* 16 (winter): 52–62.

———. 1992. "Equal Chances versus Equal Results." *Annals of the American Academy of Political and Social Science* 523: 63–74.

Lipset, Seymour Martin, and William Schneider. 1978. "The Bakke Case: How Would It Be Decided at the Bar of Public Opinion?" *Public Opinion* (March/April): 38–44.

Loevy, Robert D. 1990. *To End All Segregation.* Lanham, MD: Univ. Press of America.

Lorde, Audre. 1984. *Sister Outsider: Essays and Speeches.* Trumansburg N.Y.: Crossing Press.

Luker, Kristin. 1984. *Abortion and the Politics of Motherhood.* Berkeley: Univ. of California Press.

MacKinnon, Catherine. 1979. *Sexual Harassment of Working Women.* New Haven: Yale Univ. Press.

Mann, Robert. 1996. *The Walls of Jericho.* New York: Harcourt Brace.

Margolis, Michael, and Khondaker Hague. 1981. "Applied Tolerance or Fear of Government? An Alternative Interpretation of Jackman's Finding." *American Journal of Political Science* 25: 241–55.

Marshall, Thurgood. 1965. "The Protest Movement and the Law." *Virginia Law Review* 5: 785–803.

Massey, Douglas S., and Nancy A. Denton. 1993. *American Apartheid: Segregation and the Making of the Underclass.* Cambridge: Harvard Univ. Press.

McCann, Michael W. 1994. *Rights at Work: Pay Equity Reform and the Politics of Legal Mobilization.* Chicago: Univ. of Chicago Press.

McConahay, John B. 1986. "Modern Racism, Ambivalence, and the Modern Racism Scale." In *Prejudice, Discrimination, and Racism,* ed. J. F. Dovidio and S. L. Gaertner. Orlando, FL: Academic Press.

McConahay, John B., and J. C. Hough. 1976. "Symbolic Racism." *Journal of Social Issues* 32: 23–45.

McDowell, Gary L. 1989. "Affirmative Inaction: The Brock-Meese Standoff in Federal Racial Quotas." *Policy Review* 48: 32–37.

Meier, August, Elliott Rudwick, and Francis L. Broderick, eds. 1971. *Black Protest Thought in the Twentieth Century.* 2d ed. Indianapolis: Bobbs-Merrill.

Meier, Kenneth J., and Joseph Stewart, Jr. 1991. *The Politics of Hispanic Power: Un passo pa'lante y dos pa'tras.* Albany: SUNY Press.

Meier, Kenneth J., Joseph Stewart, Jr., and Robert E. England. 1989. *Race, Class, and Education: The Politics of Second-Generation Discrimination.* Madison: Univ. of Wisconsin Press.

Meier, Paul, Jerome Sacks, and Sandy L. Zabell. 1984. "What Happened in Hazelwood: Statistics, Employment Discrimination, and the 80% Rule." *American Bar Foundation Research Journal* 1984: 139–86.

Meltsner, Michael. 1973. *Cruel and Unusual: The Supreme Court and Capital Punishment.* New York: Random House.

Merida, Kevin. 1995. "Reverse Bias against White Men Not Big Problem, Study Reports." *Washington Post* 1 April, p. A3.

Metz, David H., and Katherine Tate. 1995. "The Color of Urban Campaigns." In *Classifying by Race,* ed. P. Peterson, 262–77. Princeton: Princeton Univ. Press.

Milner, Neal. 1992. "The Intrigues of Rights, Resistance and Accommodation." *Law and Social Inquiry* 17 (spring): 313–34.

Mingle, James R. 1981. "The Opening of White Colleges and Universities to Black Students." In *Black Students in Higher Education,* ed. Gail Thomas, 18–29. Westport, CT: Greenwood Press.

Munafo, Rachel Rossoni. 1979. "National Origin Discrimination against Americans of Southern and Eastern European Ancestry." *Catholic Lawyer* 25: 50–72.

Murphy, Reg, and Hal Gulliver. 1971. *The Southern Strategy.* New York: Scribner's.

Nakanishi, Donald. 1994. Comments at Conference on the Civil Rights Act of 1964: A Thirty Year Perspective. Washington, DC.

National Commission on Excellence in Education. 1983. *A Nation at Risk: The Imperative for Educational Reform.* Washington, DC: National Commission on Excellence in Education.

National Conference of Christians and Jews. 1992. *Taking America's Pulse: The National Conference Survey on Inter-Group Relationships.* Washington, DC: National Conference of Christians and Jews.

Neidert, Lisa, and Reynolds Farley. 1985. "Assimilation in the United States." *American Sociological Review* 50: 840–50.

Neier, Aryeh. 1982. *Only Judgment: The Limits of Litigation in Social Change.* Middletown, CT: Wesleyan Univ. Press.

Nieli, Russell, ed. 1991. *Racial Preference and Racial Justice.* Washington, DC: Ethics and Public Policy Center.

Nisbett, Richard, and Lee Ross. 1980. *Human Inference: Strategies and Shortcomings of Social Judgment.* Englewood Cliffs, NJ: Prentice-Hall.

Nixon, Richard M. 1968. *Nixon on the Issues.* New York: Nixon-Agnew Campaign Committee.

———. 1970. "Statement about Desegregation of Elementary and Secondary Schools." White House Press Release, 24 March.

Novick, Robert. 1975. *Anarchy, State, and Utopia.* New York: Basic Books.

Olson, Susan. 1990. "Interest-Group Litigation in Federal District Court: Beyond the Disadvantage Theory." *Journal of Politics* 52 (August): 854–82.

O'Neill, Dave M., and June O'Neill. 1992. "Affirmative Action in the Labor Market." *Annals of the American Academy of Political and Social Science* 523: 88–103.

O'Neill, June. 1990. "The Role of Human Capital in Earnings Differences between Black and White Men." *Journal of Economic Perspectives* 4: 25–45.

Oppenheimer, David. 1995. "Kennedy, King, Shuttlesworth, and Walker: The Events Leading to the Introduction of the Civil Rights Act of 1964." *University of San Francisco Law Review* 29: 645–79.

Orfield, Gary. 1969. *The Reconstruction of Southern Education: The Schools and the 1964 Civil Rights Act.* New York: Wiley-Interscience.

———. 1975. "Congress, the President, and 1966–1974." *Journal of Law and Education* 4 (January): 81–139.

———. 1978. *Must We Bus? Segregated Schools and National Policy.* Washington, DC: Brookings Institution.

———. 1983. *Public School Desegregation in the United States, 1968–1980.* Washington, DC: Joint Center for Political Studies.

———. 1986. "Hispanic Education: Challenges, Research and Policies." *American Journal of Education* 95 (1) (November): 1–25.

———. 1988. "Race and the Liberal Agenda: The Loss of the Integrationist Dream, 1965–1974." In *The Future of Social Policy in the United States,* ed. Margaret Weir, Ann Shola Orloff, and Theda Skocpol, 313–55. Princeton: Princeton Univ. Press.

———. 1995. "Congress and Civil Rights: From Obstacle to Protector." In *African-Americans and the Living Constitution,* ed. John Hope Franklin and Genna Rae McNeil, chapter 9. Washington, DC: Smithsonian Institution.

Orfield, Gary, and Carole Ashkinaze. 1991. *The Closing Door: Conservative Policy and Black Opportunity.* Chicago: Univ. of Chicago Press.

Orfield, Gary, and Susan Eaton. 1996. *Dismantling Desegregation: The Quiet Repeal of Brown v. Board of Education.* New York: New Press.

Page, Benjamin I., and Robert Y. Shapiro. 1992. *The Rational Public.* Chicago: Univ. of Chicago Press.

Panetta, Leon, and Peter Gall. 1971. *Bring Us Together.* New York: Lippincott.

Paulsen, Monrad G. 1964. "The Sit-in Cases of 1964: 'But Answer Came There None.'" *Supreme Court Review* 37–170.

Parmet, Herbert S. 1984. *JFK: The Presidency of John F. Kennedy.* New York: Penguin.

Peller, Gary. 1990. "Race Consciousness." *Duke Law Journal* 4: 758–847.

Perritt, Henry H. 1992. *Civil Rights Act of 1991: Special Report.* New York: J. Wiley and Sons.

Phillips, Kevin P. 1969. *The Emerging Republican Majority.* Garden City, NJ: Anchor Books.

Pildes, Richard H., and Richard G. Niemi. 1993. "Expressive Harms, 'Bizarre Districts,' and Voting Rights: Evaluating Election District Appearances after *Shaw v. Reno.*" *Michigan Law Review* 92: 483–587.

Pollitt, Daniel 1960. "Dime Store Demonstrations: Events and Legal Problems of the First Sixty Days." *Duke Law Journal* 3: 315–65.

Polsby, Nelson. 1966. "Strategic Considerations." In *The National Elections of 1964,* ed. Milton Cummings, Jr. Washington, DC: Brookings Institution.

Posner, Richard A. 1987. "The Efficiency and Efficacy of Title VII." *University of Pennsylvania Law Review* 136: 512–21.

Pottinger, J. Stanley. 1970. "Memorandum to School Districts with More than Five Percent National Origin Children." 25 May. Washington, DC: HEW Office for Civil Rights.

Rabkin, Jeremy. 1986. "The Reagan Revolution Meets the Regulatory Labyrinth." In *Do Elections Matter?,* ed. Benjamin Ginsberg and Alan Stone. Armonk, NY: M. E. Sharpe.

Radin, Beryl. 1977. *Implementation, Change, and the Federal Bureaucracy: School Desegregation Policy in HEW, 1964–1968.* New York: Columbia Teachers College Press.

Ralph, James R., Jr. 1993. *Northern Protest.* Cambridge: Harvard Univ. Press.

Ralston, Charles S. 1990. "Court vs. Congress: Judicial Interpretation of the Civil Rights Acts and Congressional Response." *Yale Law and Policy Review* 8: 205–22.

Rathjen, Gregory. 1976. "Lawyers and the Appellate Choice: An Analysis of Factors Affecting the Decision to Appeal." *American Politics Quarterly* 6 (October): 387–405.

Rawls, John. 1971. *A Theory of Justice.* Cambridge: Harvard Univ. Press.

Reagan, Michael D. 1985. "Federal-State Relations during the 1960s: Unplanned Change." In *Changing Patterns in American Federal-State Relations during the 1950s, the 1960s, and the 1970s,* ed. Lawrence E. Gelfand and Robert J. Neymeyer. Iowa City: Univ. of Iowa Press.

———. 1987. *Regulation: The Politics of Policy.* Boston: Little, Brown.

Rebell, Michael A., and Arthur R. Block. 1982. *Educational Policy Making and the Courts: An Empirical Study of Judicial Activism.* Chicago: Univ. of Chicago Press.

———. 1989. *Equality and Education: Federal Civil Rights Enforcement in the New York City School System.* Princeton: Princeton Univ. Press.

Reeves, Keith. 1997. *Voting: Hopes or Fears?* New York: Oxford Univ. Press.

Reeves, Richard. 1993. *President Kennedy.* New York: Simon and Schuster.

Reich, Robert. 1992. *The Work of Nations.* New York: Knopf.

Reider, Jonathan. 1985. *Canarsie: The Jews and Italians of Brooklyn against Liberalism.* Cambridge: Harvard Univ. Press.

"Rethinking Weber: The Business Response to Affirmative Action." 1989. *Harvard Law Review* 102: 658–71.

Riker, William. 1982. *Liberalism vs. Populism.* Prospect Heights, IL: Waveland Press.

Robertson, B., and G. A. Vignaux. 1995. *Interpreting Evidence: Evaluating Forensic Science in the Courtroom.* New York: J. Wiley and Sons.

Robyn, Dorothy. 1987. *Braking the Special Interests: Trucking Deregulation and the Politics of Policy Reform.* Chicago: Univ. of Chicago Press.

Rodgers, Harrell R., Jr., and Charles S. Bullock III. 1972. *Law and Social Change: Civil Rights Laws and Their Consequences.* New York: McGraw Hill.

———. 1976. *Coercion to Compliance.* Lexington, MA: Lexington Books.

Roosevelt, Theodore. 1923–26. *Works.* New York: Memorial.

Rosenfeld, Michel. 1991. *Affirmative Action and Justice: A Philosophical and Constitutional Inquiry.* New Haven: Yale Univ. Press.

Rosenfeld, Rachel A., and Kathryn B. Ward. 1991. "The Contemporary U.S. Women's Movement: An Empirical Example of Competition Theory." *Sociological Forum* 6: 471–500.

Rothbart, Myron, and Oliver P. John. 1993. "Intergroup Relations and Stereotype Change: A Social-Cognitive Analysis and Some Longitudinal Findings." In *Prejudice, Politics, and the American Dilemma,* ed. P. M. Sniderman, P. E. Tetlock, and E. G. Carmines, 32–59. Stanford: Stanford Univ. Press.

Rothman, Jack. 1977. *Issues in Race and Ethnic Relations.* Itasca, IL: F. E. Peacock.

Rummel, R. J. 1994. *Death by Government: Genocide and Mass Murder since 1900.* New Brunswick, NJ: Transaction Books.

Rupp, Lelia J., and Verta Taylor. 1987. *Survival in the Doldrums.* New York: Oxford Univ. Press.

Sarratt, Reed. 1966. *The Ordeal of Desegregation: The First Decade.* New York: Harper and Row.

Schattschneider, E. E. 1960, 1975, 1988. *The Semi-sovereign People: A Realist's View of Democracy in America.* New York: Harcourt, Brace, Jovanovich.

Scheingold, Stuart. 1974. *The Politics of Rights: Lawyers, Public Policy, and Political Change.* New Haven: Yale Univ. Press.

Schlei, Barbara Lindemann, and Paul Grossman. 1983. *Employment Discrimination Law.* 2d ed. Washington, DC: American Bar Association, Section of Labor and Employment Law: BNA Books.

Schlesinger, Arthur. 1992. *The Disuniting of America: Reflections on a Multicultural Society.* New York: Norton.

Schmidt, Ronald J. 1994. "Politics and Cultural Identity: What's at Stake?" Paper delivered at the Annual Meeting of the American Political Science Association at California State University, Long Beach, 1–4 Sept.

Schultz, Vicki. 1990. "Telling Stories about Women and Work: Judicial Interpretations of Sex Segregation in the Workplace in Title VII Cases Raising the Lack of Interest Argument." *Harvard Law Review* 103: 1749–843.

Schuman, Howard, Charlotte Steeh, and Lawrence Bobo. 1985. *Racial Attitudes in America: Trends and Interpretations.* Cambridge: Harvard Univ. Press.

Sears, David O. 1988. "Symbolic Racism." In *Eliminating Racism: Profiles in Controversies,* ed. P. A. Katz and D. A. Taylor. New York: Plenum Press.

Sears, David O., and Donald R. Kinder. 1985. "Whites' Opposition to Busing: On Conceptualizing and Operationalizing Conflict." *Journal of Personality and Social Psychology* 48: 1141–47.

Seligman, Daniel. 1982. "Affirmative Action Is Here to Stay." *Fortune* 19 April.

———. 1985. "It Was Forseeable." *Fortune* 22 July.

Shapiro, Robert Y., and Harpreet Mahajan. 1986. "Gender Differences in Policy Preferences: A Summary of Trends from the 1960s to the 1980s." *Public Opinion Quarterly* 50: 42–61.

Shaw, Theodore M. 1992. "*Missouri v. Jenkins*—Are We Really A Desegregated Society?" *Fordham Law Review* 61 (1) (October): 57–61.

Shelley, Louise I. 1989. "Human Rights as an International Issue." *The Annals, AAPSS* 506 (November): 42–55.

Sidanius, Jim, and Felicia Pratto. 1993. "The Inevitability of Oppression and the Dynamics of Social Dominance." In *Prejudice, Politics, and the American Dilemma,* ed. P. M. Sniderman, P. E. Tetlock, and E. G. Carmines, 173–211. Stanford: Stanford Univ. Press.

Sigelman, Lee, and Susan Welch. 1991. *Blacks' Views of Racial Inequality: The Dream Deferred.* New York: Cambridge Univ. Press.

Singer, Joseph. 1996. "No Right to Exclude: Public Accommodations and Private Property." *Northwestern University Law Review* 90: 1283–497.

Skrentny, John David. 1996. *The Ironies of Affirmative Action: Politics, Culture, and Justice in America.* Chicago: Univ. of Chicago Press.

Sleeper, Jim. 1990. *The Closest of Strangers: Liberalism and the Politics of Race in New York.* New York: Norton.

Smith, James P. 1993. "Affirmative Action and the Racial Wage Gap." *American Economic Review* 83: 79–84.

Smith, James P., and Finis Welch. 1989. "Black Economic Progress after Myrdal." *Journal of Economic Literature* 27: 519–64.

Sniderman, Paul M., and Thomas Piazza. 1993. *The Scar of Race.* Berkeley: Univ. of California Press.

Sniderman, Paul M., and Michael G. Hagen. 1985. *Race and Inequality: A Study in American Values.* Chatham, NJ: Chatham House.

Sniderman, Paul M., and Philip E. Tetlock. 1986. "Symbolic Racism: Problems of Motive Attribution in Political Analysis." *Journal of Social Issues* 42 (2): 129–50.

Sniderman, Paul M., Philip E. Tetlock, and Edward G. Carmines. 1993. "Prejudice and Politics: An Introduction." In *Prejudice, Politics, and the American Dilemma,* ed. P. M. Sniderman, P. E. Tetlock, and E. G. Carmines, 1–31. Stanford: Stanford Univ. Press.

Sniderman, Paul M., Richard A. Brody, and James H. Kuklinski. 1984. "Policy Reasoning and Political Values: The Problem of Racial Equality." *American Journal of Political Science* 28 (1): 75–94.

Sniderman, Paul M., Thomas Piazza, Philip E. Tetlock, and Ann Kendrick. 1991. "The New Racism." *American Journal of Political Science* 35 (2): 423–47.

Sniderman, Paul M., Philip E. Tetlock, and Edward G. Carmines, eds. 1993. *Prejudice, Politics, and the American Dilemma,* Stanford: Stanford Univ. Press.

Sniderman, Paul M., Philip E. Tetlock, Edward G. Carmines, and Randall Peterson. 1993. "The Politics of the American Dilemma: Issue Pluralism." In *Prejudice, Politics, and the American Dilemma,* ed. P. M. Sniderman, P. E. Tetlock, and E. G. Carmines. Stanford: Stanford Univ. Press.

Sowell, Thomas. 1976. "'Affirmative Action' Reconsidered." *Public Interest* 42 (winter): 47–65.

Spence, A. Michael. 1974. *Market Signaling: Informational Transfer in Hiring and Related Screening Processes.* Cambridge: Harvard Univ. Press.

Stampp, Kenneth M. 1965. *The Era of Reconstruction, 1865–1877.* New York: Knopf.

Steeh, Charlotte, and Howard Schuman. 1992. "Young White Adults: Did Racial Attitudes Change in the 1980s?" *American Journal of Sociology* 98 (2) (September): 340–67.

Stein, Colman Brez, Jr. 1986. *Sink or Swim: The Politics of Bilingual Education.* New York: Praeger.

Stewart, John G. 1991. "Roundtable of Participants in the Passage of the Civil Rights Act of 1964." In *This Constitution: The Bicentennial of the Bill of Rights,* ed. Raymond E. Wolfinger (fall issue).

Stewart, Joseph, Jr., and James F. Sheffield, Jr. 1983. "Correlates of Civil Rights Interest Groups' Litigation Activities." Paper presented to Southern Political Science Association.

Stimson, James A., Michael B. MacKuen, and Robert S. Erikson. 1995. "Dynamic Representation." *American Political Science Review* 89: 543–65.

Strauss, David A. 1991. "The Law and Economics of Racial Discrimination in Employment: The Case for Numerical Standards." *Georgetown Law Journal* 79: 1619–623.

Sugrue, Thomas J., and William B. Fairley. 1983. "A Case of Unexamined Assumptions: The Use and Misuse of the Statistical Analysis of Castenada/Hazelwood in Discrimination Litigation." *Boston College Law Review* 24: 925–60.

Sundquist, James L. 1969. *Making Federalism Work.* Washington, DC: Brookings Institution.

Sunstein, Cass. R. 1991. "Three Civil Rights Fallacies." *California Law Review* 79: 751–65.

———. 1995. "What the Civil Rights Movement Was and Wasn't (with Notes on Martin Luther King, Jr. and Malcolm X)." *University of Illinois Law Review,* 191–209.

Takaki, Ronald. 1993. *A Different Mirror: A History of Multicultural America.* Boston: Little, Brown.

Tate, Katherine. 1994. "Playing the Race Card." Paper presented at the annual meeting of the Midwest Political Science Association, Chicago.

———. 1994. *From Protest to Politics: The New Black Voters in American Elections.* Enl. Cambridge and New York: Harvard Univ. Press and Russell Sage Foundation.

Thernstrom, Abigail. 1992. "The Drive for Racially Inclusive Schools." *The Annals, AAPSS* 523 (September): 131–43.

Thernstrom, Stephan, and Abigail Thernstrom. 1997. *America in Black and White: One Nation, Indivisible.* New York: Simon and Schuster.

Thomas, Clarence. 1988. "Civil Rights as a Principle versus Civil Rights as an Interest." In *Assessing the Reagan Years,* ed. David Boaz. Washington, DC: Cato Institute.

Thomas, Gail E., James M. McPartland, and Denise C. Gottfredson. 1981. "Desegregation and Black Student Higher Educational Access." In *Black Students in Higher Education*, ed. Gail E. Thomas, 336–56. Westport, CT: Greenwood Press.

Thompson, William C., and Edward L. Schumann. 1987. "Interpretation of Statistical Evidence in Criminal Trials." *Law and Human Behavior* 11: 167–87.

Tilly, Charles, 1992. *Coercion, Capital, and European States, AD 990–1992*. Rev. ed. Cambridge and Oxford: Basil Blackwell.

Trent, William T. 1984. "Equity Considerations in Higher Education: Race and Sex Differences in Degree Attainment and Major Field from 1976 through 1981." *American Journal of Education* 92 (May): 280–305.

Tsuang, Grace W. 1989. "Assuring Equal Access of Asian Americans to Highly Selective Universities." *Yale Law Journal* 98: 659–78.

Turner, James P. 1997. "The Cost of a Tug of War: Why the Nation Suffers from the Political Struggle over the Civil Rights Division and Bill Lann Lee." *Washington Post National Weekly Edition* (22–29 December): 22–23.

Turner, Margery, Michael Fix, and Raymond J. Struyk. 1991. "Opportunities Denied, Opportunities Diminished: Discrimination in Hiring." Washington, DC: Urban Institute.

Tushnet, Mark. 1987. *The NAACP's Legal Strategy against Segregated Education, 1925–1950*. Chapel Hill: Univ. of North Carolina Press.

U.S. Commission on Civil Rights. 1963. *Civil Rights '63*.

U.S. Commission on Civil Rights. 1964. *Civil Rights '64*.

U.S. Commission on Civil Rights. 1967. *Southern School Desegregation, 1966–67*.

U.S. Commission on Civil Rights. 1968. *Racial Isolation in the Public Schools*.

U.S. Commission on Civil Rights. 1982. *The Federal Civil Rights Enforcement Budget: Fiscal Year 1983*. Washington, DC: U.S. Government Printing Office.

U.S. Advisory Commission on Intergovernmental Relations (USACIR). 1978. *Categorical Grants: Their Role and Design*. Washington, DC: U.S. Government Printing Office.

U.S. Advisory Commission on Intergovernmental Relations. 1984. *Regulatory Federalism: Policy, Process, Impact, and Reform*. Washington, DC: ACIR.

U.S. Advisory Commission on Intergovernmental Relations. 1993. *Federal Regulation of State and Local Governments: The Mixed Record of the 1980s*. Washington, DC: ACIR.

U.S. Department of Justice. Office of Legal Policy. 1987. "Redefining Discrimination: 'Disparate Impact' and the Institutionalization of Affirmative Action." Washington, DC.

U.S. Senate, Select Committee on Equal Educational Opportunity. 1972. *Toward Equal Educational Opportunity*, 92d Congress, 2d Session.

van den Berghe, Pierre L. 1987. *The Ethnic Phenomenon*. New York and Oxford: Elsevier.

———, ed. 1990. *State Violence and Ethnicity*. Boulder: Univ. Press of Colorado.

Van Dyke, Vernon. 1985. *Human Rights, Ethnicity, and Discrimination*. Westport, CT: Greenwood Press.

Vaxberg, Arkady I. 1989. "Civil Rights in the Soviet Union." *The Annals, AAPSS* 506 (November): 109–14.

Vogel, David. 1981. "The 'New' Social Regulation in Historical and Comparative Perspective." In *Regulation in Perspective*, ed. Thomas K. McCraw. Cambridge: Harvard Univ. Press.

Walton, Hanes, Jr. 1988. *When the Marching Stopped: The Politics of Civil Rights Regulatory Agencies*. Albany: SUNY Press.

Wasby, Stephen L. 1993. "The Transformed Triangle: Court, Congress, and Presidency in Civil Rights." *Policy Studies Journal* 21 (autumn): 565–74.

————. 1995. *Race Relations Litigation in an Age of Complexity.* Charlottesville, VA: Univ. Press of Virginia.

Watson, Denton L. 1990. *Lion in the Lobby: Clarence Mitchell, Jr.'s Struggle for the Passage of Civil Rights Laws.* New York: William Morrow.

Watson, Sidney Dean. 1994. "Minority Access and Health Reform: A Civil Right to Health Care." *Journal of Law, Medicine and Ethics* 22 (summer): 127–37.

Weinberg, Meyer. 1977. *A Chance to Learn: A History of Race and Education in the United States.* New York: Cambridge Univ. Press.

West, Cornel. 1993a. *Keeping Faith: Philosophy and Race in America.* New York: Routledge.

————. 1993b. *Race Matters.* New York: Vintage Books.

Whalen, Charles, and Barbara Whalen. 1985. *The Longest Debate.* Cabin John, MD: Seven Locks Press.

Williams, Robin M., Jr. 1977. *Mutual Accommodation: Ethnic Conflict and Cooperation.* Minneapolis: Univ. of Minnesota Press.

————. 1994. "The Sociology of Ethnic Conflicts: Comparative International Perspectives." *Annual Review of Sociology, 1994* 20: 49–79.

Wilson, James Q. 1982. "Responses." *Harvard Educational Review* 52: 415.

————. 1989. Bureaucracy. New York: Basic Books.

Wilson, William Julius. 1987. *The Truly Disadvantaged: The Inner City, the Underclass, and Public Policy.* Chicago: Univ. of Chicago Press.

————. 1996. *When Work Disappears: The World of the New Urban Poor.* New York: Knopf.

Wolff, Miles. 1990. *Lunch at the 5 and 10.* Chicago: I. R. Dee.

Wood, B. Dan. 1990. "Does Politics Make a Difference at the EEOC?" *American Journal of Political Science* 34: 503–30.

Young, Andrew. 1991. "Roundtable of Participants in the Passage of the Civil Rights Act of 1964." In *This Constitution: The Bicentennial of the Bill of Rights,* ed. Raymond E. Wolfinger (fall issue).

Zabalza, Antonio, and Z. Tzannatos. *Women and Equal Pay: The Effects of Legislation on Female Employment and Wages in Britain.* New York: Cambridge Univ. Press.

Zafaroni, Eugenio Raul. 1989. "The Right to Life and Latin American Penal Systems." *The Annals, AAPSS* 506 (November): 57–67.

Zaller, John R. 1992. *The Nature and Origins of Mass Opinion.* New York: Cambridge Univ. Press.

Zangrando, Robert. 1980. *The NAACP's Crusade against Lynching, 1909–1950.* Philadelphia: Temple Univ. Press.

Zinn, Howard. 1964. *SNCC: The New Abolitionists.* Boston: Beacon.

Court Cases

Abbott v. Burke, 153 N.J. 480, A.2d 450 (1988).

Adams v. Richardson, 356 F. Supp. 92, 480 F.2d 1159, D.C. Cir. (1973).

Adarand Constructors, Inc. v. Pena, 513 U.S. 1008, 115 S.Ct. (1995).

Albemarle Paper Company v. Moody, 442 U.S. 405 (1975).

Alexander v. Holmes, 369 U.S. 19 (1969).

Alexander v. Holmes County Board of Education, 396 U.S. 1218 (Justice Black, as Circuit Judge), 396 U.S. 19 (1969) (Per Curiam).

Allen v. Prince George's County, Maryland, 737 F.2d 1299 (1984).

Alyeska Pipeline Co. v. Wilderness Society, 421 U.S. 240 (1975).

Atonio v. Wards Cove Packing Co., 768 F.2d 1120, 1125–30 (9th Cir. 1985), reh en banc 767 F.2d
   462 (9th Cir. 1985), rev'd 490 U.S. 642, 104 L.Ed. 2d 733, 109 S.Ct. 2115 (1989), on remand
   54 E.P.D. (D. Wash. 1991).

American Tobacco Co. v. Patterson, 456 U.S. 63 (1982).

Ayers v. Fordice, 879 F. Supp. 1419 (N.D. Miss. 1995).

Bazemore v. Friday, 478 U.S. 385 (1986).

Bell v. Maryland, 378 U.S. 226 (1963).

Bob Jones University v. United States, 461 U.S. 574 (1983).

Bolling v. Sharpe, 347 U.S. 497 (1954).

Boynton v. Virginia, 363 U.S. 454 (1960).

Brown v. Board of Education, 347 U.S. 483 (1954).

Bush v. Vera, 116 S.Ct. 1941 (1996).

Carolene Products v. United States, 304 U.S. 144 (1938).

Castenada v. Partida, 30 U.S. 482 (1977).

City of Mobile v. Bolden, 447 U.S. 55 (1980).

City of Richmond v. J.A. Croson Co., 488 U.S. 469 (1989).

Columbus Board of Education v. Penick, 443 U.S. 449 (1979).

Connecticut v. Teal, 457 U.S. 440 (1982).

Contractors Association of Eastern Pennsylvania V. Hodgson, 440 U.S. 854 (1971).

Cooper v. Federal Reserve Bank of Richmond, 467 U.S. 867, 104 S.Ct. 2794 (1984).

Cornelius v. Benevolent Protective Order of the Elks, 382 F. Supp. 1182 (D. CT. 1974).

Cornelius v. NAACP Legal Defense Fund, 473 U.S. 788 (1985).

Dandridge v. Williams, 397 U.S. 471 (1970).

Dayton Board of Education v. Brinkman, 443 U.S. 526 (1979).

Dicker v. Allstate Life Insurance Company, No. 89C 4982, 61 E.P.D. 42, N.D. 11 (1993).

E.E.O.C. v. Federal Reserve Bank of Richmond, 698 F.2d 633 (1983).

E.E.O.C. v. Jordan Graphics, Inc., 769 F. Supp. 1357, W.D.N.C. (1991).

Equal Employment Opportunity Commission v. Olson's Dairy Queens, Inc., 989 F.2d 165, 5th Cir.
   (1991).

Faulkner v. Jones, 516 U.S. 910 (1995).

Fullilove v. Klutznick, 448 U.S. 448 (1980).

Furnco Construction Corp v. Waters, 438 U.S. 567 (1978).

Gardner v. Louisiana, 368 U.S. 715 (1961).

Gayle v. Browder, 352 U.S. 903 (1956).

General Electric v. Gilbert, 429 U.S. 125 (1976).

Golden v. Biscayne Bay Yacht Club, 530 F.2d 16 (CA 5), cert denied, 429 U.S. 872 (1976).

Gomez v. AVCO, 816 F. Supp. 131 D.C. Conn. (1993).

Green v. New Kent Co., 391 U.S. 430 (1968).

Griggs v. Duke Power Co., 401 U.S. 424 (1971).

Grove City College v. Bell, 465 U.S. 555 (1984).

Guinyard et al. v. City of New York, 800 F. Supp. 1083 (E.D. N. Y. 1992).

Hawkins v. Town of Shaw, 461 F.2d 1171 5th Cir. (1972).

Hazelwood School District v. United States, 433 U.S. 299 (1977).

Hazen Paper Company v. Biggins, 113 S.Ct. 1701 (1993).

Heart of Atlanta Motel, Inc. v. U.S., 379 U.S. 241 (1964).

Hopwood v. State of Texas, Nos., 94-50569, 94-50664 5th Cir. (1996).

International Brotherhood of Teamsters v. United States, 431 U.S. 324, 97 S.Ct. 1843 (1977).

Jenson v. Eveleth Taconite Company, 130 F.3d 1287 (8th Cir. 1997), 139 F.R.D. 657,660 D. Minn. (1991).

Jenson v. Eveleth Taconite Company, 824 F. Supp. 847, D. Minn. (1993).

Jenson v. Eveleth Mines, U.S. Dist. Lexis 17617 (1996).

Katzenbach v. McClung, 379 U.S. 294 (1964).

Laird v. Tatum, 408 U.S. 1 (1972).

Lau v. Nichols, 414 U.S. 563 (1974).

Marek v. Chesny, 473 U.S. 1 (1985).

McClesky v. Kemp, 481 U.S. 279 (1987).

McDonnell-Douglas v. Green, 411 U.S. 792, 93 S.Ct. 1817 (1973).

Milliken v. Bradley, 418 U.S. 717 (1974).

Mississippi University for Women v. Hogan, 458 U.S. 718 (1982).

Palmer v. Schultz, 815 F.2d 84, D.C. Cir. (1987).

Planned Parenthood v. Casey, 112 S.Ct. 2791 (1992).

Plessy v. Ferguson, 163 U.S. 537 (1896).

Railroad Company v. Brown, 84 U.S. 675 (1873).

Regents of the University of California v. Bakke, 438 U.S. 265 (1978).

Roberts v. Boston, 59 Mass., 5 Cush. 198 (1849).

Rogers v. Lodge, 458 U.S. 613 (1982).

San Antonio Independent School District v. Rodriguez, 411 U.S. 1 (1973).

Shaw v. Hunt, 94 U.S. 923 (1996).

Shelley v. Kraemer, 334 U.S. 1 (1948).

Smith v. Allwright, 321 U.S. 649 (1944).

Swann v. Charlotte-Mecklenburg Board of Education, 402 U.S. 811 (1971).

The Civil Rights Cases, 109 U.S. 3 (1883).

United States v. Fordice, 505 U.S. 717, U.S. 112 S.Ct. 2727 (1992).

United States v. Jefferson Co., 380 F.2d 385 (1967).

Walsh v. Boy Scouts of America, 993 F.2d 1267 (CA 7 1993).

Wards Cove v. Atonio, 490 U.S. 642 (1989).

Wards Cove Packing Co. v. Atonio, 487 U.S. 1232 (1988).

Washington v. Davis, 426 U.S. 229 (1976).

Watson v. Fort Worth Bank and Trust, 487 U.S. 977 (1988).

Webster v. Reproductive Health Services, 492 U.S. 490 (1989).

Wilkins v. University of Houston 654 F.2d 388, 5th Cir. (1981).

Contributors

The Editor

Bernard Grofman is Professor of Political Science and Social Psychology at the University of California, Irvine. His major fields of interest are American politics, comparative election systems, social choice theory, and the theory of representation. He has edited or coedited a dozen books, including *Electoral Laws and Their Political Consequences; Controversies in Minority Voting: The Voting Rights Act in Perspective; Quiet Revolution: The Impact of the Voting Rights Act in the South, 1965–1990;* and *Race and Redistricting in the 1990s.*

The Contributors

Paul Burstein is Professor of Sociology and Adjunct Professor of Political Science at the University of Washington. His primary interest is policy change in democratic countries, and his recent work focuses on how policy is affected by public opinion, interest groups, social movement organizations, and political parties.

David B. Filvaroff is Professor of Law at the State University of New York at Buffalo. After serving as law clerk to Supreme Court Justices Frankfurter and Goldberg, he became a special assistant in the Department of Justice, where he helped write the Civil Rights Act of 1964. He has been a member of the law faculties at the University of Pennsylvania and the University of Texas.

Luis Ricardo Fraga is Associate Professor of Political Science at Stanford University. From 1993 to 1996 he was director of the Stanford Center for Chicano Research. He has published in journals such as the *Journal of Politics, Urban Affairs Review, Political Research Quarterly,* and *West European Politics,* and is coeditor of *Ethnic and Racial Minorities in Advanced Industrial Democracies* (1992).

Hugh Davis Graham is Holland N. McTyeire Professor of American History and Professor of Political Science at Vanderbilt University. His recent books include *Civil Rights Era: Origins of National Policy 1960–1972* (1990) and *The Rise of American Research Universities: Elites and Challengers in the Postwar Era* (coauthored, 1997).

Jack Greenberg has been Professor of Law at Columbia University since 1984. From 1949 to 1984 he was with the NAACP Legal Defense and Educational Fund, from 1961 as director-counsel. He has argued forty civil rights cases before the Supreme Court, including *Brown v. Board of Education,* and is the author of *Crusaders in the Courts: How a Dedicated Band of Lawyers Fought for the Civil Rights Revolution* (1994) and winner of the Silver Gavel Award of the American Bar Association.

Gloria J. Hampton is a Ph.D. candidate in political science at Ohio State University. Her research interests include the study of elections and the politics of race.

Joseph B. Kadane is Leonard J. Savage Professor of Statistics and Social Sciences at Carnegie Mellon University. His most recent books are *Bayesian Statistics and Ethics in a Clinical Trial Design* and *A Probabalistic Analysis of the Sacco and Vanzetti Evidence* (with D. Schum), both published in 1996. His research interests include both theoretical and applied statistics.

Randall Kennedy is a professor at Harvard Law School, where he teaches courses on contracts, freedom of expression, and the regulation of race relations. He served as law clerk for Supreme Court Justice Thurgood Marshall and has written numerous articles for scholarly journals and magazines for the general public. He is the author of *Race, Crime, and the Law.*

J. Morgan Kousser is Professor of History and Social Science at the California Institute of Technology and author of *The Shaping of Southern Politics: Suffrage Restriction and the Establishment of the One-Party South, 1880–1910* (1974) and *Color-Blind Injustice: Race, Election Law, and the Undoing of the Second Reconstruction* (1998), as well as one hundred articles and book reviews on legal and political aspects of race relations in America.

Richard Lempert is the Francis A. Allen Collegiate Professor of Law at the University of Michigan Law School and Professor of Sociology and current chair of the department of sociology at the University of Michigan. He is the coauthor of *An Invitation to Law and Social Science* and *A Modern Approach to Evidence* and coeditor of *Under the Influence? Drugs and the American Work Force.*

Paula D. McClain is Professor of Government in the Woodrow Wilson Department of Government and Foreign Affairs at the University of Virginia. Her primary research interest is in racial minority group politics and she has published articles in the *Journal of Politics, American Political Science Review,* and *American Politics Quarterly.* She is the coauthor of *"Can We All Get Along?": Racial and Ethnic Minorities in American Politics.*

Caroline Mitchell practices law in Pittsburgh, specializing in employment discrimination, civil rights, wrongful discharge, and person injury cases. From 1973 to 1993 she taught at Carnegie Mellon University in the Department of Engineering and Public Policy. She has served as assistant general counsel for the Pennsylvania Human Relations Commission and has been a cooperating lawyer for the NAACP Legal Defense Fund since 1986.

Gary Orfield is Professor of Education and Social Policy at Harvard University's Graduate School of Education and Kennedy School of Government. His books include *Dismantling Desegregation: The Quiet Repeal of Brown v. Board of Education* (coauthored 1996) and *The Closing Door: Conservative Policies and Black Opportunity* (coauthored 1991) and he has published scores of articles.

Jorge Ruiz-de-Velasco is a research associate at the Urban Institute, Education Policy Center, and a doctoral student in political science at Stanford University. He received his A.B. in government from Harvard University, J.D. from the Boalt Hall School of Law at the University of California at Berkeley, and M.A. from the Stanford School of Education.

Barbara Phillips Sullivan was Associate Professor of Law at the University of Mississippi School of Law, where she taught jurisprudence, civil procedure, constitutional law, and voting rights law and policy. She is now program officer, Human Rights and International Cooperation, Peace and Social Justice program of the Ford Foundation. She has published on democracy and racial minority political participation and on social justice issues related to affirmative action and diversity.

Katherine Tate is Associate Professor of Political Science at the University of California, Irvine. Her research specializes in public opinion and voting, race, and urban politics. She is the author of *From Protest to Politics: The New Black Voters in American Elections,* coauthor of *African Americans and the Political System,* and the principal investigator of the 1996 National Black Election Study.

Stephen L. Wasby is Professor of Political Science at SUNY Albany. He writes primarily about the U.S. Supreme Court and other federal courts. His work on civil rights litigation resulted in *Race Relations Litigation in an Age of Complexity* (1995). He served as Bissell-Fulbright Chair in Canadian-American Relations at the University of Toronto in 1997–1998.

Robin M. Williams, Jr., is Henry Scarborough Professor of Social Science, Emeritus, at Cornell University and Visiting Professor at the University of California, Irvine. He is the author of several books, including *Mutual Accomodation* (1977) and *A Common Destiny: Blacks and American Society* (1989). His current work deals with comparative analyses of ethnic conflicts, civil warfare, and conflict resolution.

Raymond E. Wolfinger is Heller Professor of Political Science at the University of California at Berkeley. His most recent book, coauthored with five others, is *The Myth of the Independent Voter.* He has written extensively in leading political science journals on voter choice, turnout, and party registration.

Index

Abbott v. Burke (N.J., 1988), 85

abortion: as political issue, 152; strategies of litigation and lobbying, 81; tax-funded services, 54

ADA (Americans with Disabilities Act of 1990), 58–59, 78, 241, 242

Adams v. Richardson (1973), 79, 119, 122, 127

Adarand Constructors, Inc. v. Pena, (1995), 5, 62

adverse impact doctrine: in Griggs decision, 136, 154 n. 6, 266; labor pool analysis in Hazelwood Schools, 247–49; statistical proof of employment discrimination, 245–49

affirmative action: and cost of doing business, 221, 227 n. 5; current debate on, 1, 86, 220; current usefulness of, 224–25; definitions and requirements for, 137–38; framing of issue by political elites, 183; possibilities for, 235–36; Reagan era attempts to revise Johnson's executive orders, 57; surveys of white attitudes, 168

Affirmative Action Baby (Carter), 185

African Americans

discrimination and educational remedies, 219–27

education: college-level courses, 6 n. 6; litigation patterns in segregation cases, 79–80, 115; reading and math skills, 4, 219; students in southern white schools following 1964 Civil Rights Act, 100–103, 116. See also Brown v. Board of Education; busing, school; Hazelwood School District

employment discrimination: and EEOC v. Olson's Dairy Queens, 250–51, 261 n. 4, 273–74; studies centered on male workers, 130–31; use of pre-employment tests to screen applicants, 246–47

equal but separate treatment doctrine, 37, 83–84; Plessy v. Ferguson decision, xi, 40 n. 4, 83, 211

male workers' earnings, 143

racial attitudes toward civil rights' provisions, 178–81

as voters: effect of civil rights era on party loyalty, 6 n. 4, 10–11, 94, 96–97; Republicans' courting middle-class, 57

white and black views of black stereotypes, 184

age, and disparate employment treatment, 242

age, of blacks, attitudes toward federal aid, 180 table

age, of whites: as factor in segregated neighborhood survey attitudes, 172 table; opinions on aid to blacks and minorities, 177 table; opinions on busing, 174 table; opinions on government intervention in jobs, 176 table; opinions on government intervention in schools, 175 table; opinions on open housing, 173 table

Age Discrimination Act of 1975, 51, 241, 242

agenda-setting stage, of public policy process, x–xi

aid, federal: black attitudes toward, 179 table, 180–81, 187; to state and local governments for assistance programs, 46–47, 64 n. 4; white attitudes toward minority programs, 171, 177 table, 189

Aid to Families with Dependent Children, 194

Albemarle Paper Company v. Moody (1975), 246–47

Alexander v. Holmes County Board of Education (1969), 84–85, 111

Allen, Walter R., 145

Allen v. Prince George's County, Md. (1984), 260, 281 n. 20

Alyeska Pipeline Co. v. Wilderness Society (1975), 75

Amaker, Norman, 56

amendments, legislative: extended voting rights enacted by 1982 Congress, 56; proposed to derail Civil Rights Act, 22, 25–26

American Association of Retired Persons, 51

Americans with Disabilities Act (ADA) of 1990, 58–59, 78, 241, 242

American Tobacco Co. v. Patterson (1982), 81

amicus curiae activity, in judicial cases, 66–67

anecdotal evidence, admission of in disparate employment treatment cases, 242, 253, 274–75